IMMORTAL DAN

Daniel O'Connell in Irish Folk Tradition

Ríonach uí Ógáin

Published in Ireland by
Geography Publications,
Templeogue, Dublin 6W

ISBN 0 906602 40 8

Ríonach uí Ógáin is an archivist/collector with the Department of Irish Folklore, University College Dublin. She has published numerous articles on traditional song and music and has lectured widely on the subject. Among her publications is a compact disc/audio-cassette entitled *Beauty an Oileáin: Music and Song of the Blasket Islands* (Ceirníní Cladaigh), an article entitled 'Music Learned from the Fairies' *(Béaloideas vol. 60)* and the book *Clár Ambrán Bhaile na hInse* (Clóchomhar), consisting of an index of traditional songs collected in the west Galway area.

Front cover illustration:
Nineteenth century figure group, Daniel O'Connell surrounded by a group of six country people. The Department of Irish Folklore, University College Dublin.

Back cover illustration:
Daniel O'Connell and Biddy Moriarty, from a colour postcard (probably one of a series) in the Department of Irish Folklore, University College Dublin.

Cover design by Christy Nolan
Typesetting by Phototype-Set Ltd., Dublin
Printed by Colour Books

Contents

To Déaglán, Tuala, MacDara and Conall

Preface

An Rí gan Choróin: Dónall Ó Conaill sa Bhéaloideas was published by An Clóchomhar Teoranta, Dublin, in 1984. *Immortal Dan: Daniel O'Connell in Irish Folk Tradition* is based on that publication.

I would like to thank everyone who encouraged and helped me to prepare this publication including the following:

Those who gave so generously of their songs, stories and lore about Daniel O'Connell; the collectors of folklore in Ireland, who over the years have recorded our oral traditions; my friends and colleagues who have given me great encouragement and assistance. I would like to thank especially the Academic Publications Committee of University College Dublin, Anna Bale, Dr James Bennett, Maura Corcoran, Prof. John Coolahan, Dr Marian Deasy, Pádraig de Buis, Máire de Grás, Brian Donnelly, Dr Patricia Lysaght, Éamon McGivney, Sheila McMorrow, Adam McNaughton, Prof. John Moloney, Patrick Melvin, Dr Paula Murphy, An tOll. Séamas Ó Catháin, An tOll. Cormac Ó Gráda, An Dr Pádraig Ó Héalaí, Dr Thérèse Smith.

A special word of thanks is due to Micheál Ó Curraoin who was particularly helpful with translations.

The following people devoted a great deal of their time to reading the text, or parts of it, at various stages and made many helpful and constructive suggestions for which I am especially grateful: Prof. Bo Almqvist, Críostóir Mac Cárthaigh, Tom Munnelly, Dr William Nolan, Pat O'Connell, Dr Anne O'Connor, and An Dr Dáithí Ó hÓgáin. Finally, I would like to express my sincere thanks to Bairbre Ní Fhloinn for immeasurable encouragement and assistance.

Illustrations

Unless otherwise stated, photographs are published courtesy of the Department of Irish Folklore.

Abbreviations

AT	Antti Aarne and Stith Thompson, *The Types of the Folktale,* Helsinki 1973, first published 1961
BB	Broadsheet Ballad
CS	*An Claidheamh Soluis*
FMS	Folk Music Section, The Department of Irish Folklore, University College Dublin
IFC	Irish Folklore Collection, The Department of Irish Folklore, University College Dublin, the Main Manuscripts Collection (IFC) and the Schools' Manuscripts Collection (IFC S)
IG	*Irisleabhar na Gaedhilge*
IO	*Ireland's Own*
MI	Stith Thompson, *Motif-Index of Folk-Literature* (6 vols), Copenhagen 1955-1958
MN	St. Patrick's College, Maynooth
NL	The National Library of Ireland
NLW	The National Library of Wales, Aberystwyth
OB	*Our Boys*
RIA	The Royal Irish Academy
SMcC	Seán McCann Tape Collection, FMS
TIF	Seán Ó Súilleabháin and Reidar Th. Christiansen, *The Types of the Irish Folktale,* Helsinki 1967
TM	Tom Munnelly Tape Collection, FMS
UCC	University College Cork
UCD	University College Dublin

Chronological summary of events in the life of O'Connell selected because of their special significance for folklore

1775	Born at Carhen, Cahersiveen, county Kerry. Fostered out until four years of age. Studied with a local tutor.
1791	Started his education abroad in St. Omer, Douai and London.
1793	Witnessed the French Revolution.
1812	Sir Robert Peel, member of the Conservative party and political adversary of O'Connell, appointed Chief-Secretary to Ireland.
1815	Duel in county Kildare with John Norcot D'Esterre, member of the Trinity Guild of the common council. D'Esterre died as a result of the duel.
1823	Founding of the Catholic Association.
1828	Elected a Member of Parliament for county Clare.
1829	Catholic Emancipation granted.
1840	Founding of the National Association of Ireland for the repeal of the Act of Union.
1841	Elected Lord Mayor of Dublin.
1843	'Monster Meeting' at Tara as a result of which he was arrested and sentenced to a year's imprisonment.
1847	Died in Genoa, Italy.

Chapter 1

Folklore, history and O'Connell

Oral tradition contains a great deal of material about famous historical characters. One such person is Daniel O'Connell whose life has been well-documented in numerous historical works. There is a wealth and variety of folklore about O'Connell which is not to be found about any other historical personality in Irish folklore. No other character has generated the same amount of material.

Daniel O'Connell is an example, arguably an archetype, of someone who has an image in oral tradition which differs from the image presented in historical documentation. This raises the question of the relationship between folklore and history. It is not the intention here, however, to examine in detail the oral and the historical sources to prove their veracity or reliability. Nonetheless, history has a very important role to play in relation to oral tradition. Tales are told and songs are sung about important happenings in Irish history; wars, landlordism and the famine all feature in oral tradition. Fortunately, more and more historians are availing of the insights afforded to them by ordinary people who experience great historical events and who express this experience in lore, songs, tales and anecdotes.[1] As far as the greater part of Daniel O'Connell's life and character is concerned, the historical evidence presents recorded facts. Oral tradition consists of accounts, opinions, songs, stories and beliefs about O'Connell. The lore, stories and songs express the attitudes of those whom O'Connell influenced the most, and on whom he depended for support.

There are others who have featured strongly in oral tradition, people like Wolfe Tone, Robert Emmett, Thomas Davis, Charles S. Parnell and Éamon de Valera. Anecdotes are told about them. They are recalled and celebrated in song and story. But the amount of available folklore associated with them is minimal by comparison with that associated with O'Connell.

Obviously, not every historical character is reflected in a favourable light in folklore. Cromwell is an example of the villain in Irish folklore, and the songs and stories portray this image of him. In the oral accounts of hero and villain, of event and of opinion, historical context is an essential feature, as history and folklore are interwoven.

O'Connell is a person of monumental importance in Irish history. He is conventionally seen as the champion of the Catholic cause in the nineteenth century. He spearheaded mass organisation of the Irish Catholic population at the time. It was O'Connell who gave status to Roman Catholics and he was of primary importance in bringing about equal rights for them. Catholic Emancipation meant that legal discrimination against Catholics was removed and that they had a right to sit in Parliament, from which they had previously been banned unless they took an oath which renounced certain fundamental Catholic beliefs. In addition to the achievement of Catholic Emancipation itself, his significance lies in the fact that through his political activity, he made Irish popular opinion into a powerful force which could not be ignored.

This book presents an opportunity to enrich and develop that view of O'Connell, by illustrating that there was another vital dimension and a reaction to him, which was widespread, immediate, creative and imaginative. This reaction was rooted in centuries of a vibrant storytelling and singing tradition and is an example of the nineteenth and twentieth century expression of the folklore of heroes – in this case, of the hero, Daniel O'Connell. All of this oral material is an interpretation of events, and this could also be said of official records:

> A testimony is no more than a mirage of the reality it describes. The initial informant in an oral tradition gives, either consciously or unconsciously, a distorted account of what has really happened because he sees only some aspect of it and places his own interpretation on what he has seen.[2]

Although oral evidence may be an arrangement or distortion of the truth by the speaker, whether consciously or subconsciously presented, the individual speaker is part of a community and it is through the interaction and expression of individuals that an observer can come to know a community. Oral material has an important role to play in relation to many aspects of the community. It plays a part in the life of the storyteller and of the listener, and it has a reality and a context of its own. Nonetheless, it is of its nature a part of the community. As the folklorist J. Vansina has written:

> It cannot be sufficiently stressed that, in a last analysis, every tradition exists as such only in virtue of the fact that it serves the interests of the society in which it is preserved, whether it does so directly or indirectly, by serving the interests of the informant.[3]

Each discipline, folklore and history, has its own methodology and approach. Scholars in each of these areas use the same sources to a certain extent, although sources and source priorities differ a great deal in most cases. History is a secondary source to the folklore scholar, just as folklore is a secondary source to the history scholar.[4] History relies on written or documentary evidence whereas folklore concentrates on the phenomenon of the tradition itself, but it is probably impossible to make definitive distinctions between history and folklore.

At the time of folklore collection, traditions are, or were, immediately relevant. The folklorist Bengt Holbek has said that the bearers of tradition are 'ordinary human beings who use their cultural heritage to express their own needs and thoughts'.[5] This is the key to an understanding of the folk hero O'Connell, and historical analysis is peripheral to the nature and function of the folklore.

Genre Analysis and Sources

There are many ways in which the folklore about O'Connell can be presented and analysed. In this context, the statement that '"Pure" genres exist only as ideal types',[6] is pertinent. Each aspect of oral tradition is also part of yet another aspect or aspects. Various approaches have been suggested – for example, that the function of the oral material should be analysed or that emphasis should be placed on the tradition itself and on history.[7] Each of the methods recommended is important and relevant. Until further research and analysis take place both at a general and a specific level, a broader method might best be chosen, or methods could be brought together as might be appropriate for the material in question. In relation to Daniel O'Connell, the method selected here is based on the nature and emphasis of the material or its relevance. Lore, song, tale and anecdote are relatively easy to recognise, define and classify, and are clear genres in themselves. In instances where there is an overlap, and lore and tale are combined in a single narration, the message or point of the communication is used as a guideline in analysis. This particular approach suits the material about O'Connell, as the genres are in most instances clearly identifiable.

The archives of the Department of Irish Folklore, University College Dublin, are the principal source for this book. The greater part of the recorded folklore of O'Connell was collected between 1930 and 1993, and most of it between 1930 and 1950. When the Irish Folklore Commission was established in 1935, for the purposes of collecting, preserving and disseminating the folklore of Ireland, it was directed from headquarters in Dublin. During its lifespan, it employed a number of full-time and part-time collectors throughout Ireland. As it was felt to be one of the aspects of folklore most under threat at the time, emphasis was placed on the collecting and documenting of longer tales in Irish. In 1942, with the publication of *A Handbook of Irish Folklore,* a guidebook for field collectors in folklore was available, and under the section concerning historical lore a list was presented of several suggested headings and questions to elicit traditions of O'Connell, for example:

> Daniel O'Connell: popular belief that he was vulnerable only in his heel; birth-mark on O'Connell's back; his fame as a counsellor and lawyer (cases won by him, stories of his clever ruses, saviour of prisoners from death; O'Connell claims as damages tobacco sufficient to reach from client's foot to ear-top, previously cut off; O'Connell fails to get his fee from a client whom he had counselled to feign madness; O'Connell as counsel for defendant who had damaged an eye of the plaintiff in saving him from drowning); O'Connell as member for Ireland in the House of Commons (secures by a ruse permission to wear his hat in parliament;) . . . . .[8]

The questions were merely suggestions and a great deal of additional folklore was gathered, possibly because of a particular collector's inquisitive mind or special interest in O'Connell, or perhaps because of an informant's store of tales or songs about O'Connell. Without a doubt, the single most important full-time collector, in relation to documenting O'Connell traditions and as regards O'Connell's background and native district, was Tadhg Ó Murchú who worked as a full-time collector for the Commission from 1935 until 1958 and spent these years working for the most part in south-west Kerry. However, a number of other collectors made valuable and substantial contributions to the archive in this regard. Among these were the following full-time collectors, who were responsible for amassing a great deal of folklore about O'Connell:[9] Liam Mac Coisdeala, Conamara, Erris and south Mayo, 1935 to 1939; Seán Ó hEochaidh, counties Donegal and Sligo, 1935 to 1983; Proinnsias de Búrca, Conamara and Mayo, 1935 to 1944, 1965 to 1975 (also a special collector 1953 to 1964); Liam Mac Meanman, county Donegal, 1935 to 1937; Nioclás Breathnach, county Waterford, 1935 to 1937; Brian Mac Lochlainn, county Galway and some of the islands of Galway and Mayo, 1936 to 1939; Seosamh Ó Dálaigh, the Dingle peninsula, north Kerry, west Limerick, west Tipperary, west Cork and the Déise of Waterford, 1936 to 1951; Proinsias Ó Ceallaigh Múscraí, county Cork in 1936; Seán Ó Flannagáin, counties Galway, Mayo and Clare, 1937 to 1940; Seán Ó Cróinín, county Cork, 1938 to 1944, and 1959 to 1965; Caoimhín Ó Danachair, west Limerick in 1940; Tomás a Búrca, north Mayo 1940 to 1944; Calum Mac Gille Eathain, Conamara in 1946; Michael J. Murphy, counties

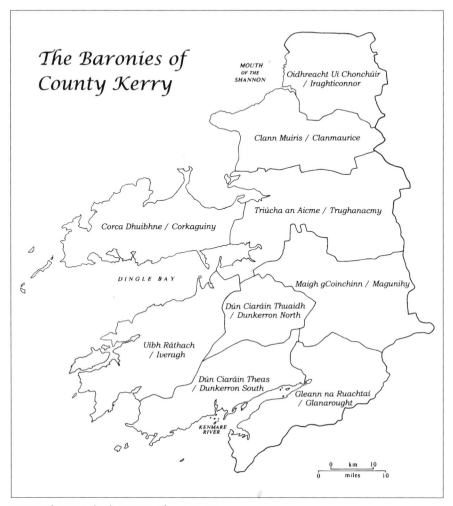

The Baronies of
County Kerry

MOUTH
OF THE
SHANNON

Oidhreacht Uí Chonchúir
/ Iraghticonnor

Clann Muiris / Clanmaurice

Triúcha an Aicme / Trughanacmy

Corca Dhuibhne / Corkaguiny

DINGLE BAY

Maigh gCoinchinn / Magunihy

Dún Ciaráin Thuaidh
/ Dunkerron North

Uíbh Ráthach
/ Iveragh

Dún Ciaráin Theas
/ Dunkerron South

Gleann na Ruachtaí
/ Glanarought

KENMARE
RIVER

Map indicating the baronies of county Kerry.

Antrim, Down, Armagh, Tyrone, Fermanagh, Derry, Louth, Sligo and Cavan, 1949 to 1983; Ciarán Bairéad, counties Galway, Mayo and Clare, 1951 to 1976; Micheál Ó Sírín Erris, county Mayo, 1951 to 1954; James G. Delaney, counties Kildare, Laois, Longford, Leitrim, Offaly, Roscommon, Westmeath and Wexford, 1954 to 1987. These names, dates and districts indicate that intensive, full-time collecting took place in many parts of Ireland between 1935 and the 1980s. In addition to the full-time collectors there were a number of special collectors and part-time collectors appointed for various periods of time, in various places, who recorded a great deal of O'Connell lore.

As well as the Department of Irish Folklore's Main Manuscripts Collection, which contains the work of the full-time, part-time, special

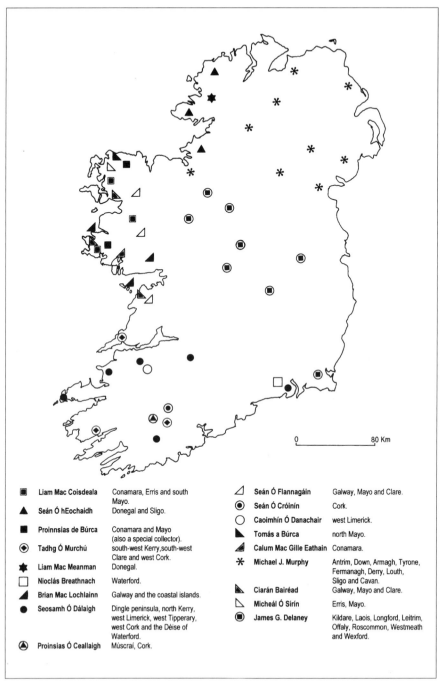

Symbol	Name	Area
▣	Liam Mac Coisdeala	Conamara, Erris and south Mayo.
▲	Seán Ó hEochaidh	Donegal and Sligo.
■	Proinnsias de Búrca	Conamara and Mayo (also a special collector).
◉	Tadhg Ó Murchú	south-west Kerry,south-west Clare and west Cork.
★	Liam Mac Meanman	Donegal.
□	Nioclás Breathnach	Waterford.
◢	Brian Mac Lochlainn	Galway and the coastal islands.
●	Seosamh Ó Dálaigh	Dingle peninsula, north Kerry, west Limerick, west Tipperary, west Cork and the Déise of Waterford.
▲	Proinsias Ó Ceallaigh	Múscraí, Cork.
◿	Seán Ó Flannagáin	Galway, Mayo and Clare.
◉	Seán Ó Cróinín	Cork.
○	Caoimhín Ó Danachair	west Limerick.
◣	Tomás a Búrca	north Mayo.
◢	Calum Mac Gille Eathain	Conamara.
✳	Michael J. Murphy	Antrim, Down, Armagh, Tyrone, Fermanagh, Derry, Louth, Sligo and Cavan.
◥	Ciarán Bairéad	Galway, Mayo and Clare.
◺	Micheál Ó Sírín	Erris, Mayo.
◉	James G. Delaney	Kildare, Laois, Longford, Leitrim, Offaly, Roscommon, Westmeath and Wexford.

Map indicating the areas in which full-time collectors worked for the Irish Folklore Commission between 1935 and 1971.

and other collectors, the Department's Schools' Manuscripts Collection also resulted in a number of accounts and tales of O'Connell. This latter collection is the result of a scheme organised between 1936 and 1938 with the assistance of the Department of Education and the teachers and senior pupils in the National Schools in the Republic of Ireland.[10] Although O'Connell is not named in the associated booklet 'Irish Folklore and Tradition',[11] tales and songs about O'Connell were included in the collection under the headings of 'Local Heroes', 'Local Poets', 'A Song', and 'Historical Tradition'. Since the establishment of the Department of Irish Folklore in University College Dublin in 1971, as successor to the Irish Folklore Commission, the work of collecting has continued, although now there is only one full-time collector employed in the Department of Irish Folklore, as well as a small number of part-time collectors. O'Connell folklore can still be collected, but the tales, songs and lore available nowadays are comparatively rare in contrast to the rich harvest gathered by the collectors who faced the field in the 1930s and 1940s.

In the Main Manuscripts Collections, insofar as they relate to Daniel O'Connell, the average age of the informants was seventy years, so that a number of the storytellers or singers were within a generation or two of O'Connell's time, and would certainly have experienced important events such as the centenary of Emancipation in 1929. Despite the fact that some small number of the informants were contemporaries or near contemporaries of O'Connell, only a few stated that they were acquainted with O'Connell. Some were tenants of the O'Connell family and may have met him occasionally. Those who spent some time with O'Connell, on occasions like the hunting expeditions in Derrynane, were apparently not involved in any way in O'Connell's political life. None of the storytellers said that they spent a great deal of time in O'Connell's company, in contrast for example, to the historian O'Neill Daunt.[12] On the subject of the occupation of the informants, the folklore collectors noted 'small farmer', 'farm labourer', '*spailpín*' (seasonal worker), 'fisherman', or 'stone mason' in most cases.

Only a small amount of lore was collected from women. This, of course, requires further examination in relation to the history of folklore collecting in general, especially as all of the full-time collectors with the Irish Folklore Commission were men. Another factor as regards O'Connell may be that, at the time when most of the collecting work was under way, O'Connell was still fresh in people's minds and a part of the political world, which was primarily a man's world. Most of the O'Connell folklore is in Irish and is from the counties on the western seaboard and this reflects the overall pattern of collecting. There were no full-time collectors of folklore in Dublin for example, where O'Connell's political activities had been so much a part of urban life and were doubtless still under discussion when the documenting of oral tradition was established. Uíbh Ráthach in county Kerry is the area in which most folklore about O'Connell was collected. This is especially true of the historical lore.[13] County Clare proved a rich source, most likely due to O'Connell's victory in a Clare election. Counties Galway, Mayo and Donegal were also fruitful as regards the folklore of O'Connell.

The position of the Irish language is relevant here. At the beginning of the nineteenth century it is estimated that there were at least two million Irish speakers. At least half of the Catholic population at the time spoke Irish only and many were bilingual.[14] Less than one hundred and fifty years later, when much of the folklore of O'Connell was documented, the Irish language was spoken by over eighty per cent of that part of the population which was to be found, for the most part, in certain districts in the far west of Ireland. In other areas the figure was ten per cent or lower. The history of literacy in Ireland is also important in this context. The educational system at the time when the folklore of O'Connell was being created taught the nation to read English, not Irish.[15] Chapbooks, which were very small cheap, printed books, were widely read. It was stated that fifty-two per cent of the population could read English between 1781 and 1790, but this figure is probably inflated.[16] The Catholic population, who comprised the vast bulk of the population in most of those areas where intensive collecting work was carried out, were the tradition bearers for the most part, and had a higher proportion of illiteracy than the other religious groups.[17] Therefore a substantial amount of the folklore of O'Connell was written down for the first time when the collectors went to work.

In the folklore manuscript collections which have been indexed to date, there are at least a thousand references to Daniel O'Connell, and in this book there is clearly room for only some representative examples. A certain amount of published and printed documentation has also been consulted as source reference. Although it is impossible to establish to what degree published material affected oral tradition, much of the published material contains folklore also found in oral accounts and it is of direct relevance therefore to the folklore about O'Connell. Many of these publications were available and extremely popular during O'Connell's lifetime, particularly chapbooks and penny books. Publications, in Irish and in English, must have influenced oral tradition to some degree.

Most of the people who contributed folklore on O'Connell went to primary school only, and many of them never attended school on a regular basis, if at all. Attendance at schools rarely rose above the level of fifty per cent until the 1920s. As a school subject, Irish history was first introduced as part of the curriculum in 1908. Some history books were critical of O'Connell because of his unsympathetic attitudes to the Irish language and to violence. Other books were banned by the British authorities because they were thought to have been a cause of the 1916 rising and teachers were also censured for their part in teaching history in a way that would incite an uprising. The history book most commonly used in schools throughout Ireland in the first decades of this century was by P.W. Joyce. It was first published in 1909 and was scholarly and objective in its presentation of the period from the seventeenth to the nineteenth centuries.[18] In the newly independent state, the officially sponsored version of history for schools was contained in the Department of Education notes for teachers in 1933, and these were in force from 1930 until 1962. It was only in the 1950s and 1960s that O'Connell began to be rehabilitated in Irish history. The folklore of O'Connell has therefore not been shaped or influenced to any substantial degree by the educational system in Ireland or by the teaching of history. Folklore is of its nature informal and the image of O'Connell documented by the folklore collectors was inherited by the storytellers and singers from their home life.

The Life of O'Connell

It is very difficult to date precisely the creation and development of folklore about O'Connell. By the time O'Connell was in political and physical decline, the folklore character was well-established. In most instances in the documented oral material, there is a date of recording given and frequently the material can be traced back some fifty years earlier or more. For example, an informant recorded in 1935 may say that he heard the story from his father in 1900, and that his father was then aged 80. He may also add that his father told him that he in turn had heard it fifty years previously. These facts, however, refer to only one particular narration or version of a narration. Folklore is, of its nature, fluid and flexible and in a constant state of change. Some of the tales which have been 'O'Connellised' pre-date the O'Connell era. The sense of timelessness and placelessness in oral tradition is an important factor here and it underlines the mingling in oral tradition of imagination and interpretation in relation to historically-recorded events.

Oral tradition is of primary significance in this study, but it is important to have a brief look at O'Connell as he is presented in documented history. There are some character traits and events which are part of the historical record and it would appear that oral tradition has selected and developed some of these traits and events.

Daniel O'Connell was born in 1775 in Carhen, Cahersiveen, county Kerry. In his youth, he was intimately involved with the Gaelic tradition and the Irish language. In accordance with the custom for middle-class families at the time, for the first four years of his life O'Connell was fostered with a local farming family. Their language was naturally Irish.[19] O'Connell was witness at firsthand to the lifestyle, customs and traditions of an Irish family in eighteenth-century Kerry and this was to form the basis of his keen understanding of the rural public in later life. O'Connell was brought back to Carhen to live, and later went to Derrynane to 'Hunting Cap', an uncle, who looked after his welfare and saw to it that O'Connell was educated abroad and that he studied law in London. And so, the young O'Connell had experienced the life of a country family and also the middle-class settings of Carhen and his uncle's house. Much of this experience took place at a time during the late eighteenth century which saw the emergence of a Catholic middle-class in Ireland. O'Connell was able to compare lifestyles, language and culture. Irish at that time was the vernacular of the poor, and was gradually being replaced by the middle classes in favour of English, in particular in matters of business and politics.

As a young man, O'Connell had witnessed some of the bloodshed of the French Revolution. In 1793, he and his brother were travelling from Calais to England. Louis XVI had been guillotined the day before they left and the brothers were treated as 'clericalist and reactionary' in an atmosphere which was rife with anti-aristocratic feeling.[20] O'Connell opposed the use of violence and bloodshed to achieve his two main political goals: freedom for Catholics to practise their religion in Ireland, and the repeal of the 1801 Act of Union.

In 1802, O'Connell married Mary O'Connell from Tralee and the correspondence between them indicates that they had a happy marriage.[21] O'Connell was very close to his wife and to his children although it was rumoured that he was something of a womaniser.[22] His appearance was attractive and handsome. He was dark and charming, and very personable. Having completed his legal studies, he was very successful as a confident, competent and highly ambitious lawyer. He was extremely self-confident. As he wrote to his wife on one occasion:

> Every case I have been concerned in one way or the other serves to increase my confidence in myself.
> ... Perhaps my vanity misguides me but the effect of my success is apparent.[23]

His 'courtroom qualities' ensured success in his career. Of these qualities, the most important aspects as reflected in oral tradition were his 'speed of response and his ability to read the minds of ordinary

Irish people'.[24] O'Connell worked extremely hard and was a public and financial success in the late 1790s and early 1800s. His name became a familiar one, due in part to his travels on the Munster circuit. His successes in the courtroom ensured further publicity and fame. His adversaries were many and some interpreted his courtroom manner as rough and insulting.[25] One in particular, Sir Robert Peel, who was appointed Chief-Secretary to Ireland by the Lord Lieutenant in 1812, appears regularly in folklore accounts. A significant event in folklore is O'Connell's duel with John Norcot D'Esterre who was a provision merchant and a naval contractor and also a member of the Common Council of Dublin Corporation. Shortly before the duel, O'Connell called the Dublin Corporation 'a beggarly Corporation'. D'Esterre, a Dublin Protestant who was in favour of Emancipation, challenged him to a duel which took place on 1 February 1815 and D'Esterre died as a result of the wound inflicted by O'Connell. This was an episode in his life which O'Connell later wished to forget, as it was in direct conflict with his opinions on bloodshed. However, because of its sensational appeal, the event captured public interest and bonfires were lit when the news spread that D'Esterre had been shot.

O'Connell was working on behalf of the Catholics in Ireland. He became the chief agitator in the Catholic movement. His task was a difficult one, as the poorer sectors of the Catholic population in Ireland were more interested in the immediate problems of paying the rent and taxes than in equal rights for Catholics and Protestants. In 1817, a famine in Ireland left death and disease in its wake and the potato crop, which had almost entirely failed, was the primary concern for most people. However, by means of the Catholic Association which had been established to raise support and finances for the Catholic movement, there was communication between the political leaders and the public. O'Connell, along with Richard Lalor Sheil and Thomas Wyse, had founded the Association which established a nationwide movement in support of political and religious reform. O'Connell travelled the length and breadth of the country encouraging people to join the Association. The contribution was a penny a month. The Roman Catholic clergy throughout Ireland supported O'Connell and the Association and this in turn helped to increase popular support of the movement. The Association had a strong chain of command and communication, and hundreds of thousands were under the direct influence of the committees.[26] In 1828 O'Connell was elected Member of Parliament for county Clare. Some of those who voted for him were evicted as a result, and bitter enmity ensued between the Catholic tenants and their Protestant landlords. O'Connell was not permitted to take his seat in the British Parliament because of his refusal to take the

Oath of Allegiance. The force of the Catholic movement was strong and united and Catholic Emancipation was granted in 1829. O'Connell had achieved his fame as the 'Liberator', as he was called, and also as a lawyer, and his popularity with the Catholic population was immense. He worked extremely hard and his sixteen-to-seventeen hour day bore financial and political fruit.[27]

In the 1830s, he directed his attention to the repeal of the Act of Union. He said that this agitation should be peaceful, legitimate and open. Although on the whole, pacifist behaviour was advocated by O'Connell, he was capable of using threatening language when he saw fit and also of using intimidating means of ensuring his, or his candidate's, success, as happened in the Kerry election of 1835.[28] In 1840, the National Association of Ireland was founded to further the cause of Repeal, and it had a large following. However, O'Connell became dispirited when he could see no results from his efforts. He began to travel around Ireland, addressing meetings and rallying support.

In 1841, he was elected Lord Mayor of Dublin and it could be seen from the crowds which followed him that he had massive support. The Repeal movement organised 'monster meetings', which were so called because of the size of the attendance, and O'Connell delivered powerful speeches at these meetings. A map illustrating the places where Repeal meetings were held in 1843, indicated his far-reaching influence.[29] Near contemporary opinion underlines O'Connell's powers of oratory:

> His best mood was close vigorous logic and scathing indignation. He sometimes uttered short fierce sentences of concentrated passion, which fell on the popular ear like tocsin.
>
> C. Gavan Duffy 1880[30]

O'Connell continued with the peaceful agitation and with the monster meetings at which upwards of 100,000 people were often present. In 1843, he was arrested on a charge of trying to undermine the Constitution and sentenced to a year's imprisonment as a result of his agitation, as part of the Government's campaign against Repeal. On his release, there was great public rejoicing but O'Connell had aged and had become disheartened. By the year 1846, however, a younger generation of political leaders had begun to emerge. These were the 'Young Irelanders' who saw that O'Connell's methods had failed. Although O'Connell's orations made frequent reference to bloodshed and war, the precise meaning and application of these terms were not clarified. The 'Young Irelanders' gave detailed descriptions of the types of warfare they now saw as necessary for Ireland to achieve independence. O'Connell was seen to advocate a strategy of what was called 'success by the threat of force rather than force itself'.[31] The ultimate political aims of the Liberator and of the 'Young Irelanders' were the same, but their attitudes to secular nationalism were different in that Davis had stronger views against sectarianism than O'Connell. O'Connell himself was physically and mentally weaker. His energies were greatly reduced and he died in 1847 in Genoa having failed to achieve Repeal. In accordance with his wishes, his heart was given to Rome and his body brought back to Ireland for burial.

In each of the different genres of folklore O'Connell is portrayed as a hero. While much of this folklore is quite removed from historical reality, it was history itself which led to the creation of this great folk hero. Heroes and villains are always fascinating and yet not every historical character becomes a hero or a villain. Heroes and villains depict a world of black and white, of good and evil. Had O'Connell been an ordinary person, he would probably not have become a folk hero. There must have been circumstances and events which led to the creation of O'Connell as a folk hero. One reason was that his political goals concurred with popular aspirations, particularly Catholic Emancipation and Repeal. His rural, Irish-speaking background meant that he could communicate with the rural population and that he understood them. O'Connell as landlord was physically and socially removed from his tenantry. He was not a landlord who brought great economic pressure to bear on his tenants and he did not choose friends or relatives as his agents.[32] He came to power at a time when the Catholic population of Ireland needed a leader. Previous leaders and movements had failed and there was no other forceful character to take charge. His election in Clare indicated his strength and gave cause for great celebration. It meant that he had status and power, and he was then firmly established as someone of great importance. So O'Connell's background, his character, his ability, the political climate and his popularity all helped to provide the necessary ingredients for the creation of the folk hero.

References
1. See in recent years for example M. Elliott 1989; O. MacDonagh 1988, 1989; C. Ó Gráda 1988; G. Ó Tuathaigh 1974-75.
2. Vansina 1965 76. See also *Nordic Institute of Folklore Papers No. 2* Dan Ben-Amos 'Do We Need Ideal Types (in Folklore)?' Turku 1992, in which the author explores 'the diversity of terms, their cultural instability and historical changeability; their predication upon class, region, and dialect', especially pages 21-26.
3. Vansina 1965 78.

4. Pentikäinen 1968 102.
5. *Nordic Institute of Folklore Papers No. 3* Holbek 'On the Comparative Method in Folklore Research' Turku 1991 14.
6. Honko 1968 61.
7. Pentikäinen 1968 118-127.
8. S. Ó Súilleabháin 1942 521-522.
9. The Irish Folklore Commission, Coimisiún Béaloideasa Éireann was disbanded in 1971 and its staff and holdings transferred to the newly established Department of Irish Folklore (Roinn Bhéaloideas Éireann), University College Dublin.
10. For a detailed history and analysis of the scheme see Ó Catháin 'Súil Siar ar *Scéim na Scol'* 1937-1938 *Sinsear* Dublin 1988 19-30.
11. An Roinn Oideachais Dublin 1937.
12. Daunt 1848.
13. See Chapter 2.
14. de Fréine 1965 128.
15. Akenson 1970 378.
16. Ó hÓgáin 1990 7.
17. *ibid.* 377-378.
18. Joyce 1909; see Mag Shamhráin 1991 231.
19. O. MacDonagh 1988 7-8.
20. O. MacDonagh 1988 26.
21. M. O'Connell ed. 1972 vol. 1 *passim.*
22. Edwards 1975 19; O. MacDonagh 1989 78-79. Although O'Connell's reputation was scarcely affected by Ellen Courtenay's accusation against him of raping her and being the father of her son who was allegedly born in 1818, the incident may have affected folk belief about O'Connell's promiscuous behaviour. For example: 'There was something that he was supposed to be a bit of a rake.' IFC 1803:153. Collected in 1972 by Michael J. Murphy from Frank 'Wings' Campbell, aged seventy-seven, townland and parish of Forkill, barony of Orior Upper, county Armagh.
23. M. O'Connell 1972 vol. 1 159.
24. O. MacDonagh 1988 67.
25. Gwynn 1947 74-75.
26. O. MacDonagh 1988 213.
27. *ibid.* 187.
28. Lyne 'Daniel O'Connell, Intimidation and the Kerry Election of 1835' *The Journal of the Kerry Archaelogical and Historical Society no. 5* 1972 74 -97.
29. O. MacDonagh 1989 225.
30. Duffy 1880 34.
31. R. Davis 1987 252.
32. O. MacDonagh 1988 189.

Chapter 2

The historical lore

In analysing the historical lore, the thrust or point of emphasis of the narrative is judged to be of primary importance. The individual narrative can be described as a personal account about O'Connell usually transmitted orally. It may also find its way into print and may then go on to become part of oral tradition. The historical lore includes material the purpose of which appears to be to retain a particular personal memory or to express an opinion about O'Connell. This genre does not seem to have any other point and it consists for the most part of opinions about O'Connell which are stated directly.[1] In contrast to the historical lore discussed in this chapter, the legends, tales and anecdotes about O'Connell, describe events and specific occasions, for the most part. They consist of narratives, which have beginnings, centre points and solutions to problems or endings to adventures. The historical lore does not contain these elements, in most instances.

Insofar as the historical lore relates to O'Connell, it consists of popular oral accounts, statements and opinions about events and character traits which are relevant to O'Connell and which are supported by documented historical evidence, or have at least some historical connection. On the whole, the historical lore is more personal and intimate than the other genres. It includes memories about O'Connell and statements or descriptions narrated either at first-hand or at a further remove, which are direct and comparatively precise. These include, for example, descriptions of monster meetings or of the Clare election. Certain accounts of court cases and other events in O'Connell's life are given in anecdotal style but are included here as part of the historical lore as they have a historical basis and seem, on the whole, to correspond quite closely to the presumed recorded reality.

The narrator's attitudes and beliefs, although not necessarily expressed, must be considered in assessing these accounts of historical lore. Although historical facts are presented frequently, there are many influences at work on these facts. The storyteller's background and life experience are important. Recognition must be made of the cultural

environment of the storyteller. As people listen to historical information, they will remember the aspects of the material which they
themselves believe are especially interesting or important. This is true
for each member of an audience so that no two oral accounts are
identical, thus bearing witness to the creative and flexible nature of
folklore. Thus, the storyteller speaks from a historical basis only insofar
as history coincides with his or her own information or outlook. The
informant selects the emphasis of the narrative itself and so indicates
the type or nature of the material.

The response of the audience and the physical setting of the
narration will change on each telling. The informant will vary the
telling to a greater or lesser degree. Depending, for example, on
memory, mood or time factors, the duration, presentation or communication will change, to name but a few variables.

The folklore about O'Connell contains accounts of numerous court
cases where he was involved as lawyer or as advisor to the defendant.
In these cases, O'Connell invariably emerges as the victor. Here, it is
difficult to make a clear distinction between historical lore and other
forms of folk narrative. In the folklore documentation which is
included here as part of the historical lore, there are instances where
named people also appear in the published historical material about
O'Connell.[2] Such accounts are included here with the historical lore,
rather than with the anecdotal material, when informants say that their
contemporaries, or their own informants' contemporaries remembered
the court case in question. Another criterion used in classifying the lore
is based on whether or not the court case has to do with land
ownership or tithes, or with a similar event which is historically
documented. If such historical documentation does exist, the account is
included with historical lore.

Most of the extant folklore about O'Connell was collected in the first
half of this century from informants who were often only a generation
or two removed from O'Connell's time. The personal style of the
storyteller brings the listener, or reader in this case, into immediate
touch with O'Connell. Tadhg Ó Murchú collected a great deal of
material from people whose relatives or neighbours remembered
O'Connell. For example, Seán Ó Sé (also known as 'G.Ó'), a farmer
from Cúil Thoir, Dairbhre, in the barony of Uíbh Ráthach, was aged
seventy in 1943 when recorded by Tadhg Ó Murchú, and Seán said
that a man by the name of Ceallachán Mac Cárthaigh, also from
Dairbhre, remembered O'Connell:

Ceallachán Mac Cárthaigh – ar na Teinnimh Íochtarach a bhí sé. Ba
chuimhin leis an Liberator *– bhíodh sé ag fiach lena chois.*[3]

(Ceallachán Mac Cárthaigh – he was living in na Teinnimh Íochtarach.
He remembered the Liberator – he used to hunt with him).

One of O'Connell's favourite pastimes was hunting, and in Kerry the local people, his friends from Dublin and his foreign acquaintances accompanied him on the hunt.

O'Connell is called both 'The Counsellor' and 'The Liberator' in the oral material but the latter is the term most frequently used. As a rule, he is called 'The Counsellor' in accounts which refer to a time or an event before Emancipation, and 'The Liberator' thereafter. The word Liberator is used in the English language. In the material in the Irish language, the words *'An Saoirseoir'* or *'An Fuascailteoir'* (Liberator or Emancipator) are rarely used, except in the songs. The words *'An Cunsailéir'* or *'An Seana-Chunsailéir'* are used frequently in the Irish language material and also the English word 'Liberator,' where O'Connell is referred to as *'An* Liberator' (The Liberator).[4]

Some informants said that their parents remembered seeing Daniel O'Connell. Liam Ó hAinifín, a seventy-five year old farmer, told Tadhg Ó Murchú in 1948 that his mother remembered Daniel O'Connell. Liam was from Laharan, Kiltallagh, which is about a mile and a half north-west of Castlemaine on the Tralee road in county Kerry:

> My mother remembered it *(i.e. the famine)*,[5] and she remembered Daniel O'Connell. She was eighty-six or seven, when she died,and she is dead twenty-seven years. She remembered to see *(sic)* him passing through Castlemaine and the people cheering for him – through Milltown and on to Castlemaine.[6]

In the following account the storyteller said that his father saw O'Connell:

> Of course Daniel O'Connell was the most noted counsel that was ever in the south of Ireland, and his name will live forever. The old people used to regard him like the Pope. Of course he was their only prop in a time of great suffering. There is no end to all the tales I heard about him from the old people. My father and Charlie Houlihan and Pats Danaher went to Tralee to hear him defend cases there.[7]

In this case, the storyteller was a farm labourer, Richard Denihan, who was born in 1865, in the Athea district of county Limerick, so that his parents were contemporaries of O'Connell. The narrator was eighty-five years of age in 1950 when this account was collected from him. On the whole, the manuscript collections indicate, as might be expected, that folk memory about O'Connell was most widespread in the barony of Uíbh Ráthach, O'Connell's native area, but the history of folklore collecting is also a relevant factor here.[8]

In 1954 Tadhg Ó Murchú was told by eighty-nine year old Séamus Liath Ó Súilleabháin, a farmer and a fisherman, from An Rinnín Bán, in the parish of Cathair Dónall, county Kerry that his mother worked for the O'Connell family:

Nuair a bhí an áit sin thall, i dtaobh thall d'abhainn (Abha an Bhailín – An Lóthar) fé phortaithe ag muintir (Chonaill) Dhoire Fhionáin, réal sa ló a bhí do chailíní ag cuir na móna suas ar an seana-bhóthar, i mbun tí Charey.

Bhíodh haincisiúir mar mhuiciris ar an gcliabhán acu, mar ghearrfadh an mhuiciris chrua na slinneáin acu. Is mó cliabh a chuir mo mháthair suas ann – Mairéad Deas (Ní Cheallaigh) – agus máthair Pheaidí Thaidhg – Máire Gheancach (Ní Shúilleabháin) agus iad ina gcailíní óga ann.[9]

(When the O'Connells of Doire Fhionáin (Derrynane) owned the bogs on the far side of the river *(The Bailín River – An Lóthar)*, the girls who carried the turf up to the old road just by Carey's house were paid sixpence a day.

They used to have a handkerchief as a slat (i.e. fastening) on the basket, because the hard slats cut their shoulders. My mother – Mairéad Dheas *(Ní Cheallaigh)* carried many a basket up there – as did Peaidí Thaidhg's mother – Máire Gheancach *(Ní Shúilleabháin)* – when they were young girls.)

In an account collected in Leathfhearann, in the parish of Cathair Dónall, in 1947, it was said that O'Connell was born in the house of his grand-aunt.[10] In accordance with the custom at that time, he was fostered by the Ó Síocháin family, where his nurse was Tadhg Ó Síocháin's wife. His fosterparents were able to feed him well with meat, a luxury which very few families in the area could afford at the time.[11]

As a young child, O'Connell had a very quick mind, a trait which people held in high esteem. According to the historian, Luby,[12] it took O'Connell only an hour to master the alphabet. O'Connell told the following account to O'Neill Daunt: 'I learned the alphabet in an hour. I was in childhood remarkably quick and persevering.'[13] The following oral account says:

Ghaibh seana-mháistir scoile an tslí agus thóg sé ar a bhachlainn é – an Cunsailéir – agus é ina leanbh, agus ar an uair sin bheireadh na seandaoine cír ina bpóca leo.

Thóg sé an leanbh ar a ghlúin agus thairrig sé chuige a chír agus thosaigh sé ar a bheith ag cíoradh a chinn agus an fhaid a bhí sé ag cíoradh a chinn, bhí an t-alphabet foghlamtha ag an ngarsún (uaidh). Dúirt an máistir leis an athair, féachaint amach don gharsún go raibh ana-inchinn aige – é a choimeád leis an scoil, agus go gcloisfí uaidh fós, agus féach gur chualathas, gurb é thug an chéad fhuascailt do mhuintir na hÉireann.[14]

(An old schoolmaster was passing by and he took him on his lap – the Counsellor – when he was a child, and at that time the old people used to carry a comb in their pocket.

He took the child on his knee and took out his comb and began to comb his hair and while he was combing his hair, the boy had learned the alphabet from him. And the master told the father to look after the boy, that he was very bright – to keep him at school, and that he would be famous yet, and that's what happened, he was first to emancipate the people of Ireland.)

Folklore shapes historical truth to conform to its own experience and outlook. In this case, O'Connell's cleverness is exaggerated by creating a more detailed, unusual and important occasion than that which is recorded in history. A particular trait is emphasised to create a concrete narrative and illustrate a particular type of O'Connell – a person who shows extraordinary cleverness, particularly in childhood. Probably the image of the schoolmaster and the combing of the hair were introduced in oral tradition to create a more dramatic narrative.

O'Connell's great future was not predicted by everyone however:

> *Nuair a bhí Dónall Ó Conaill ag éirí suas bhíodh mná uaisle Chiarraí ag magadh fá n-a phlucaibh agus faoi féin. Is é an t-ainm a thugaidís air 'Amadán Mhurchadha'. Tamall ina dhiaidh sin do bhí na mná céanna ag éisteacht leis ag plé cúise ag Seiseon Chiarraí agus is é adúradar nuair thángadar abhaile: 'Cia atá ina Chunsailéir uafásach acht 'Amadán Mhurchadha!'*.[15]

> (When Daniel O'Connell was growing up, the noble women of Kerry used to laugh at his fat cheeks and at himself. They used to call him 'Murchadh's Fool'. Some time after that, the women were listening to him defending a court case at the Kerry Assizes and when they came home they said: 'Who is the great Counsellor but Murchadha's Fool!')

This particular account is a published one for which no source is given. It is possibly from Kerry, as O'Connell's Kerry background plays an important role in it. The image of the fool is not in keeping with O'Connell as he is portrayed generally in folklore, although it is a common occurrence in folk legends that the fool performs extraordinary deeds.[16] In fact, the version quoted here is the only account of this attitude which has come to light. This isolated text may reflect an exceptional view of O'Connell, or it may be a unique documentation of something which was well-known in a particular area, but which was overshadowed by a reluctance to depict O'Connell in a negative light when he was held in such high esteem by most.

As was the custom, O'Connell went abroad to school as soon as he was old enough to do so:

...bhí an Liberator, *bhí sé ina gharsún – cuireadh in aos ocht mbliana go dtí Tír Ó mBaoill é chun aer na gcnoc a bheith aige – chun é a dhéanamh folláin is cruaidh.*

'Bhímis ag imirt bháire is football,' *a dúirt sé (athair an scéalaí), 'agus níor bhuail aon gharsún riamh liom' a dúirt sé 'b'aicteála ná é agus nuair a bhí sé i dtimpeall chúig mbliana déag,' dúirt sé 'aoise, do thóg a athair is a mháthair ... é. Chuireadar go* Belgium *é. Ansan a foghlaimíodh é, i gcoláiste i m*Belgium.'[17]

(... the Liberator, he was a boy – he was sent at the age of eight, to Tír Ó mBaoill to get the mountain air – to make him healthy and hardy. 'We used to play hurling and football,' he (*the storyteller's father*) said, 'and I never met a boy' he said, 'who was more active than he and when he was about fifteen years of age' he said, 'his father and his mother . . they sent him to Belgium. That's where he was educated, in a college in Belgium.')

This account was collected by Tadhg Ó Murchú in 1939 from Micheál Ó Síocháin, Tuar Sáilín, in the parish of An Dromaid, barony of Uíbh Ráthach, county Kerry. Micheál, a farmer, was then aged seventy-two. The narrative supports the folk image of O'Connell, that he was to be noticed in any company. The historical evidence can be expanded and built upon by including personal memory as in this instance of secondhand recall. Physical strength and endurance in O'Connell as a young man are traits which are preserved in oral tradition. These are suited to the image of the young, virile hero.

O'Connell spent some time studying in Louvain, St. Omer and Douai.[18] He was sixteen in 1791 when he started his education on the Continent. This was cut short after seventeen months because of the political crisis in France. It was the custom at that time for better-off Catholics to send their family to college abroad, if they could afford to do so:

> The Catholic gentry and merchants who had most to suffer from the State laws against education avoided the worst of them by sending their sons to the Irish colleges in France, Spain, Italy and the low countries.[19]

While at college, O'Connell, according to oral tradition, had a healthy appetite:

Céad is fiche punt sa mbliain a bhí dá dhíol as agus ní fhaighdís ach dhá bhéile bídh sa choláiste an uair sin. Ach scríobh sé abhaile chun an uncail ...

Dúirt sé gur thaithin an áit go maith leis ach go raibh putóga caola aige, go mbíodh ocras air ann, agus an bhféadfadh sé a thuilleadh a dhíol as. Dúrthas leis go bhfaigheadh sé a thuilleadh bídh dá ndíolfaí

20

a thuilleadh as. Ach n'fheadar conas a chuaigh do. Is baolach nár díoladh a thuilleadh as.[20]

(A hundred and twenty pounds a year was paid for him and they only got two full meals in the college at that time. But he wrote home to his uncle . . . He said he liked the place well enough but that his appetite was not satisfied, that he was hungry, and could he pay more for him. He was told he would get more food if more money were paid for him. But I don't know what happened to him. I'm afraid that no more was paid for him.)

O'Connell's education was supervised by his uncle and the relevant correspondence indicated that O'Connell sent to his uncle a long account of his living expenses and estimated future expenses and regretted that his uncle reprimanded him for his lack of economy. However, his uncle was consistently generous in forwarding money to O'Connell.[21]

Education and its accompanying literacy was held in high esteem by Irish people. Literacy in Irish was rare at the time and O'Connell's ability in this regard and in scholarship in general was noteworthy. In a booklet entitled *What Ireland Needs: The Gospel in the Native Tongue* by Rev. W. Fitzpatrick and other Protestant clergymen (London n.d.; preface dated 1880), the authors refer to a comment by one Rev. Thomas Dowling, a Kerryman, who stated following a tour to county Kerry, that among those able to read in Irish were five Roman Catholic priests and the celebrated Daniel O'Connell, who he often declared was the best Irish scholar he had ever met with.[22]

O'Connell Returns Home to Kerry: O'Connell the Landlord

To continue with Daniel O'Connell's life as it relates to Irish folklore, O'Connell eventually finished his studies and qualified as a lawyer. There are accounts describing the occasions when he came home to Doire Fhionáin (Derrynane) from London or from Dublin. Many accounts describe people going to meet him as he came home in his coach, so it appears that this became a custom. Local people, his tenants, would help carry the carriage up the slope of the hill, at Lóthar in Uíbh Ráthach, because this work was too heavy for the horses. Folk memory says that tenants of the O'Connell family were required to honour Daniel O'Connell, as illustrated in the following account:

Ná séideadh sé an biúigil (Dónall Ó Conaill) agus é ag casadh an tséipéil (S. an Lóthair)? Do shéideadh sé an adharc – agus do chaitheadh nach aon fhear bocht a bheith ag rith chuige ansan chun sá suas léi fé Bhun na nEasc – carráiste dhá chapall – buggy mór, dúnta – agus mara mbeifí chuige – dá bhfanfainnse sa bhaile,

21

bheadh rabhadh fachta amárach agam glanadh amach as mo chuid talaimh.[23]

(He (*Daniel O'Connell*) used to blow the bugle at the turn at the church (*An Lóthar*). He used to blow the horn – and every poor man had to run towards him and carry him up to Bun na nEasc – a two-horse carriage – a big closed buggy – and if they did not go to meet him – if you were to stay at home, you would have a warning got the following day to clear out of your land.)

Although this account does not describe a voluntary welcome home by the tenants, there is still a sense of adventure and drama in the account which is in keeping with parallel traits which are found in the folk legends about O'Connell, especially the emphasis on his importance and power. This image of O'Connell is in keeping with the portrayal of the powerful leader, where his homecoming is a great public occasion when he returns from court, from Dublin or, later on in his career, from Parliament. Other informants give similar accounts of the local people going to Com an Chiste to meet O'Connell's carriage on his return home.[24] According to one account the tenants in Kerry found that their work was not in vain, however, as the Counsellor gave a small keg of whiskey to those who pulled his carriage with ropes over Com an Chiste.[25] As a very important public figure, O'Connell attracted attention wherever he went and people used go to meet him elsewhere also and they drew his carriage behind them, as happened when he was met at Bunratty and his carriage was drawn as far as Ennis.[26]

Apart from accounts of O'Connell, the landlord, coming home to Doire Fhionáin and of his tenants going to meet him, documented oral tradition records very little about O'Connell as landlord, or indeed about the O'Connell family as landlords.

Although there is a tradition in folklore about O'Connell's sexual prowess, which is in keeping with a part of the folk hero's image, the *ius primae noctis* tradition does not appear in the extant material in relation to O'Connell.[27] In some instances, however, the informant says quite bluntly that O'Connell was said to have been fond of women. O'Connell used to pass a house west of Killorglin in county Kerry on his way to Killarney, and he:

used always stop and go in there for a drink of sour milk! (*Peatsaí Begley (the narrator) told this with a twinkle in his eye. After some persuasion he said: 'Of course, there was a good-looking woman in the house.'*)[28]

Occasionally, he was regarded in tradition as a promiscuous philanderer. It was said in Uíbh Ráthach in 1948 about the O'Connells:

'*bhí an diabhal orthu chun na mban*' ('they were mad for women') and that it was unsafe for any woman to walk near Com an Chiste for fear of them.[29] In one instance, it was said that O'Connell left sixteen illegitimate children behind him following a visit to west Clare although it was added that this was probably a rumour spread by English propaganda.[30] In referring to O'Connell's alleged promiscuity, however, informants tended to include this as an introduction to a tale, legend or anecdote, especially the anecdote which tells of O'Connell recognising that the child is his own, because of the child's cleverness.[31] It is said frequently in present day folklore that if a stone were thrown over the wall of an orphanage during Daniel O'Connell's time that it would surely hit one of his chidren, but this comment has not come to light in the documented folklore in the Department of Irish Folklore.[32] O'Connell's sexual prowess is treated in a lighthearted fashion and is regarded in most narrative accounts in an amusing light.

Court Cases

O'Connell was closely involved with his own tenants and other landlords' tenants in their court cases. Once, there was some agitation about a place called White Mountain which is between counties Carlow and Wexford:

> On the Western side of the Blackstairs Mountains stands the White Mountain. Here many a fierce encounter took place between the Wexford men and the Carlow men over its grazing rights. About eighty years ago Mac Murrough Kavanagh of Borris, descendant of Dermot Mac Murrough laid claim to the mountain and spent thousands of pounds in constructing roads, building houses and fences, and laying out farms for Carlow settlers. He also erected a barrack and had about twenty policemen to protect them but the 'Whitefeet' *(as the people who lived at the 'White Mountain' were called)* made short work of the barrack which was a wooden structure.
>
> They rolled down huge stones from the rocks overhead on it, and swept it clean away. The police escaped in their night attire. The fight ended in 1845 in a great lawsuit. The Wexford men were represented by Daniel O'Connell. Wexford won the case, and the Carlow men got only twenty-four hours to demolish their buildings and clear out of the county.[33]

Because of the nature of the event, it is easy to imagine how a story could be developed to emphasise O'Connell's power and his victory in legal cases, particularly in those having to do with ownership of land. The storyteller, Walter Furlong, of Grange, in the parish of Killann, barony of Bantry, in county Wexford, was a farmer of about sixty-eight years of age in 1938 when the above account was collected from him, and he got his information from his father who died aged eighty in about 1898.

The names of some famous people survive in living memory, in relation to O'Connell's court cases. There is an account about an occasion when he embarassed a certain barrister-at-law by the name of Thomas Goold.[34] Goold was so confused by O'Connell's teasing in court that everyone in court was highly amused.[35]

According to the historical documentation,[36] O'Connell was very friendly with Thomas Goold who was Master-in-Chancery in 1832.

O'Connell was renowned for his oratory, debate and quick tongue. The folk imagination was drawn to this talent and developed the trait in the creation of O'Connell's character in oral tradition.

O'Connell was often victorious in cases which were of great importance. In 1949, Seán Sigerson, aged seventy-seven, a stonemason, a fisherman and a farmer, of An Rinnín Dubh, parish of Cathair Dónall, barony of Dún Ciaráin Theas, told Tadhg Ó Murchú that O'Connell was said to have saved a man from the gallows:

> Saolaíodh Maitéas sa phríosún (i bpríosún Thrá Lí). Ar Meall na mBreac a bhí Mícheál (athair Mhaitéis). Cuireadh as san go Cumhair an Mhainichín é, agus do bhain accidence (sic) do – do mhairbh sé fear de Mhuintir an Doirín. An Seana-Chunsailéir (Dónall Ó Conaill) a bhí ag plé dho – do chrochfaí é mara mbeadh an Seana-Chunsailéir – do thug sé amach ar trí bliana príosúin é. Do dheaghaidh a bhean isteach sa phríosún in éineacht leis agus thug sí bliain ina theannta. Bhí Maitéas ar iompar aici (nuair a chuaigh sí isteach) – istigh sa phríosún a saolaíodh Maitéas. 'Maitéas an Phríosúin' a thugaidís air.[37]

(Maitéas was born in prison. Mícheál (Maitéas' father) was living in Meall na mBreac. He was sent from there to Cumhar an Mhainichín, and an accident befell him – he killed a man from Doirín. The Old Counsellor was acting on his behalf – he would have hanged if it hadn't been for the Old Counsellor – he got him off with only three years imprisonment. His wife went in to prison with him and she spent a year with him. She was expecting Maitéas (when she went in). Maitéas was born inside in the prison. They used to call him 'Prison Maitéas'.)

This kind of comment added to O'Connell's fame as a powerful lawyer and increased public confidence in him. In this instance, the storyteller, Seán Sigerson, was born in 1863 and so his people would have remembered O'Connell.

O'Connell did not win every court case, according to folklore. There are several oral accounts of a very famous case when he was acting on behalf of the defendant in the murder case of the 'Colleen Bawn'.[38] The man accused of the murder was hanged, O'Connell having failed to reduce his sentence. This was a historic case[39] which had great dramatic and sensational appeal and was the basis for Gerald Griffin's novel *The Collegians*, and later for a play by Boucicault entitled *The Colleen Bawn*.

According to folk tradition, O'Connell was not involved to any great extent in the Whiteboys movement,[40] although a large proportion of the rural population at the time supported secret societies. On one occasion, however, O'Connell is said to have hoodwinked them:

Charlie[41] told me that he went to Abbeyfeale to see Daniel O'Connell passing by in the mail-coach. When I was a *garsún (lad)*, I often heard tales of the coach being attacked by Whiteboys, and 'twas writs of eviction they used to be looking for.

I heard a tale long ago about Daniel O'Connell and an adventure he had in a mail-coach. He was travelling in a coach one day and he had a big bag of money with him and thousands of pounds in it. There was another man in the coach and he was all the time telling the passengers that he had a hundred pounds in his purse, and he hoped he wouldn't be robbed of it. *Mo léan*, they weren't gone only a few miles when a number of Whiteboys jumped out to them and held up the coach. They ordered the passengers out till they'd search them.

'*Ochón*', says Daniel O'Connell, 'I haven't anything worthwhile, but that man there has a hundred pounds.' The Whiteboys caught their man and they weren't long finding the hundred pounds and away with them.

They thought they had a good enough haul made. The man who was robbed turned to O'Connell to abuse him over telling the robbers about his money. O'Connell put his hand in his bag and took out a hundred pound and gave it to him. 'Here is your hundred pounds,' said he, 'if I hadn't done that they'd have searched myself and made off with several thousand pounds.'[42]

Several oral accounts exist about the famous Doneraile[43] conspiracy, where O'Connell succeeded in reversing the judgment:

A Protestant plan was hatched here for to wipe out the whole countryside of good land and transplant it with Protestants. A number was prosecuted for conspiracy and three were sentenced to be hanged on Saturday. Cork citizens were shocked, and said there was only one man in Ireland to free them, Dan O'Connell. They got ready Burke, and a very good horse, and off he goes for Doire Fhionáin. He landed at day-break. The Liberator was up, perhaps to go hunting with his famous hounds. Burke told his mission. O'Connell ordered breakfast and two horses to be fed. He got a light gig and drove on to Millstreet, changed horses there, and got two fresh ones. On he goes, and landed at the Imperial, Patrick Street. The horses fell dead from driving all night. The court was sitting, he couldn't wait for breakfast. He ordered lunch up to the Court. On his approach, there was a cheer from the watchers outside, that rose the hearts of the prisoners and followers inside. In the Liberator goes proudly and defiantly, puts on his wig, starts eating. O'Doherty was Crown Prosecutor. He had a nasal impediment, and O'Connell imitated it from time to time, as he was a great mimic. He meant to ruffle O'Doherty at the delight of the Court. At last, O'Doherty burst out, 'I have known false men and false facts.' 'How could facts be false?' said O'Connell. He bottled up O'Doherty and cleared all witnesses out but one. He examined him, and then another, but no two agreed. They were up at Dublin Castle and told what to swear. The result was he burst up the whole thing and those sentenced on Saturday were let off lightly.[44]

References to this particular court case are found in the historical lore from Kerry and from Cork.[45] There are also a number of published accounts of it in popular journals, such as *Ireland's Own*, and it is described in Canon Sheehan's *Glenanaar*.[46] It is a good example of a historically recorded event which became a part of folk tradition. The importance of this case has been emphasised elsewhere from the historical perspective.[47] The recorded oral accounts about the Doneraile conspiracy are in English and it would appear that no oral account was collected in Irish. This may indicate a tendency for oral accounts of O'Connell's historically documented court appearances to enter into the English language oral tradition, as English was the language of the courts and of administration.

Duels

O'Connell's duel with D'Esterre took place on the first of February in the year 1815 at dusk, in Bishopscourt in the parish of Oughterard, barony of South Salt, about thirteen miles from Dublin, just inside the Kildare border. D'Esterre, who was a renowned marksman, was shot by O'Connell in the hip and in the stomach and died two days later on the third of February from his wounds.[48] There are at least twenty-five accounts from several counties, recorded in Irish and in English, about O'Connell's duel with D'Esterre. Reference to the background to the duel is rare. Oral tradition prefers the concrete description of the event rather than explanations of the cause. Accounts describe the duel and O'Connell's victory:

Is mó cúinse agus is mó iarracht a thug na Sasanaigh chun Dónall Ó Conaill a bhaint dá luadracha. Sa tsaol úd ba mhinic a chaitheadh beirt challenge *combraic ar a chéile chun dul ag combrac le dhá phiostal. Bhí a lán babhtaí ag Dónall le daoine a bhreabtaí chun dul ag combrac leis, ach do dheineadh sé an bheart orthu i gcónaí. Cuirtí*

26

ar crainn cé chaitheadh an chéad piléar, agus níor thit an chéad urchar riamh go dtí Dónall.

Bhí sé féin agus Sasanach lá le chéile. Thit an chéad urchar go dtí an Sasanach, agus scaoil sé fé, agus do bhris sé fiacal ann, ach más ea do choinnibh Dónall a bhéal dúnta, agus níor labhair focal, mar dá gcaitheadh sé amach an fhuil bhí an lá fachta air. Thug Dónall fén Sasanach ansan, agus do leag, ach n'fheadarsa ar éirigh sé aríst. Tar éis é bheith leagaithe aige Dónall is ea chaith sé amach an fhiacal agus bolgam fola. Bhí fulang ann!

Ach do bhí sé (D'Esterre) insna hIndiacha ansan,[49] *agus do bhí sé déanta amach gurbh é a b'fhearr sa domhan chun piléar a chaitheamh. Cuireadh scéala chuige agus do tairgeadh mórán Éireann airgid do ach teacht agus* challenge *a chaitheamh air le súil is go leagfadh sé é. B'fhearr leo ná milliún punt go mbeadh sé sínte. Do tháinig, agus do chuir sé* challenge *ar Dhónall. Bhí Dónall sásta leis; níor chuir sé suas riamh do. An lá a bhíodar chun a bheith le chéilig, chuir Dónall cúig nó sé chasóga mhóra air fhéin, agus nuair a chonaic an D'Esterre chuige é, tháinig oiread bó chroí dho ná beadh aon mhoill air. Sara dtosnaíodar do chaith Dónall casóg do. Bhí sé á gcaitheamh do gur chaith sé sé cinn do chasóga dho. Bhí sé caol go maith ansan. Nuair a chonaic an D'Esterre an méid sin do chrith sé. Thug Dónall fé ndeara go maith an crithéán ag teacht air. Cuireadh ar crainn ansan cé chaithfeadh an chéad urchar. Thit an chéad urchar go dtí an D'Esterre. Ní bhídís féin ag féachaint ar a chéile in aon chor. Is iad na* second*aí a phointeáladh an láimh agus an piostal. Thit an chéad urchar go dtí an D'Esterre, agus do theip air. Dúirt Dónall lena* second *féinig an gunna dhíriú ar chnaipe a bhí i nglúin a bhríste.*

Do phointeáil an second *ar an gcnaipe.*

'Tairrig anois!' ar sé le Dónall.

Do thairrig Dónall. Is é an áit a fuair sé an piléar i mbun a bhoilg. Bhí muintir Shasana ar fad ag féachaint orthu an lá san le súil is go mbeadh Dónall treascartha. An nóimint a chaith Dónall, chuir sé dho, agus lena linn sin do liúigh an second *go raibh Ó Conaill marbh, mar do bhí a fhios aige go dianmhaith ar an ampladh a bhí ar Shasanaigh an lá san go mbeadh Dónall sínte; go ndéanfaidís cirteacha dho, gurb amhlaidh a d'íosaidís ina bheathaigh é, bhí an oiread san goimh orthu ach nuair a chonaiceathars cé bhí sínte ansan ba bhrónach an lá aige Sasanaigh é.*

Bhí an D'Esterre sínte, agus gan aon dul ar éirí aige. Bhí a phutóga ina gcriathar poll.

'Ba mhór an amadán duine mise,' ar seisean, 'nár fhan mar a rabhas faid is ná raibh aon easnamh orm. B'fhearra dhom é ná teacht anso ag déanamh saothair do mhadraí craosach. Níl éinne fé dheireadh leis ach amháin mo bhean is mo chlann. Ní har mhaithe liomsa ná le mo bhean ná le mo chlainn chuireadarsan fios orm.'[50]

(The English made several attempts to get rid of Daniel O'Connell. At that time two people often challenged each other to a duel with two pistols. Daniel had a lot of meetings with people who were bribed to meet him in a duel, but he always got the better of them. Lots were drawn to see who would have the first shot, and Daniel never got the first shot. He and an Englishman were together one day. The first shot fell to the Englishman, and he fired and he broke his tooth, but Daniel kept his mouth shut and didn't say a word, because if he spat out the blood he would lose the day. Daniel attacked the Englishman then, and laid him low but I don't know if he got up again. When Daniel had brought him to the ground he spat out his tooth and some blood. He was in pain. But D'Esterre – he was in the Indies at the time, and it was said that he was the best shot in the world. He was sent for, and offered a great deal of money if he would come and challenge him in the hope that he would kill him. They would give any money to see him dead. He came, and he challenged Daniel. Daniel was happy with it; he never refused a challenge. The day they were to meet, Daniel put five or six big coats on and when D'Esterre saw him coming he took heart and thought it wouldn't take long. Before they began, Daniel took off a coat. He kept taking them off until he had taken off six coats. He was quite thin then. On seeing this, D'Esterre started to shake. Daniel noticed how he started to shake. Lots were drawn then to see who would have the first shot. The first shot fell to D'Esterre. They did not look at each other at all. The seconds would point the hand and the pistol. D'Esterre had the first shot and he missed. Daniel told his own second to direct the gun at a button in the knee of his trousers.

The second pointed to the button.

'Fire now,' he said to Daniel.

Daniel fired. The bullet landed at the base of his stomach.

The English people were all looking at them that day, hoping that Daniel would be beaten. As soon as Daniel had fired, he fell, and the second shouted out that Daniel was dead, because he knew well how eager the English people were that day to see Daniel dead, so they could tear him apart, they would eat him alive, they were so angry; but when they saw who had been laid low it was a sad day for the English. D'Esterre was stretched out and wasn't able to get up. His insides were in a very bad way.

'I was a big fool,' he said, 'that I didn't stay as I was while I was comfortable. I would have been better off, rather than coming here to work for greedy dogs. No-one has suffered because of it, except my wife and family. It wasn't for my sake nor for the sake of my wife and family that they sent for me.')

This account was collected in Kerry in 1933. The duel between D'Esterre and O'Connell is immensely popular in oral tradition, and it is an important event in historical terms as well because it supports the popular view of O'Connell as conqueror, both of his personal enemy D'Esterre, who is ready to shoot O'Connell, and of the public enemy, D'Esterre, who represents England and the oppression of Irish Catholics.

An account from county Roscommon tells how D'Esterre's pistol locked:

> D'Esterre . . . . challenged Dan O'Connell for this duel and, of course, the people were wanting Dan to give in. D'Esterre was a noted man with the gun. And the people were saying that Dan wouldn't have a chance against him. But when the order was given for to fire, D'Esterre's pistol locked and Dan blew his brains out. And the people said that it was just God's will.[51]

No oral account has come to light from people who say that they or their contemporaries were present at the duel. In one instance we are told that the duel was fought with swords. Perhaps the situation in this instance is made more dramatic by the introduction of swords; it could possibly add to the nobility of the fight or there may be local traditions of sword fighting in south Armagh where the account was collected.[52] The following is the account in question:

> Do you know there was a fellow the name of D'Esterre with a sword, a duel: he *(Daniel O'Connell)* had a duel with a man the name of D'Esterre and either the young fellow or the mother asked him *(Dan)* where he was going.
>
> 'Aw, I'm going out,' says he, 'to get D'Esterre for your breakfast.' But he killed him . . . Aye . . Why . . straight thrust *(moves as in sword play)*: a straight thrust parry; high parry, low parry, left parry, withdraw; and thrust in sword business; that was sparring *(fencing)* . . . He had to kill him; if he wouldn't, he would be killed himself.
>
> Ah, Dan was a good man.[53]

Swords also appear in a Kerry version where an external force is introduced into the narrative. In this account, it is said that the reflection of light from the sword of O'Connell's second blinds D'Esterre between the eyes and that O'Connell succeeds in shooting D'Esterre as a result.[54] This emphasises O'Connell's heroic method of defeating the enemy and underlines his cleverness and ability to seize opportunities rather than his superior physical force in outwitting his opponent. In other versions from Kerry, a bow and arrow are said to have been used in the duel. Three of these versions are from the barony of Corca Dhuibhne, in west Kerry, and were recorded from the same speaker, Peats Dhónaill Ó Cíobháin, who was aged eighty-one in 1942, and lived in the parish of Cill Maolchéadair.[55] Peats Dhónaill said that a man by the name of MacNamara[56] helped O'Connell to kill the

Englishman, D'Esterre. In the fourth oral version where bow and arrow are used, a servant girl tells MacNamara that O'Connell's steersman or director is dishonest.[57] She tells this to MacNamara in Irish so that the rest of the company will not understand what she is saying. MacNamara immediately goes to O'Connell's assistance. He directs O'Connell's hand in the fight and the Englishman is killed. In some accounts it is said that O'Connell's second was called 'Fireball' MacNamara.[58]

A Galway version of the story tells how O'Connell won the duel because of his understanding of Irish. D'Esterre is not named but we are told that O'Connell's opponent was a gentleman. O'Connell's servant was a young fellow, who was aware that D'Esterre was wearing a coat of mail inside his waistcoat. He wanted to convey this information to O'Connell so that no-one else would know what he meant. He asked O'Connell in Irish: *'Cá maraítear na caoirigh in Éirinn?'* (Where do people kill sheep in Ireland?). O'Connell understood this question and knew that he would have to 'stick him in the neck where the butcher sticks the sheep in Ireland'. He therefore stuck his sword into his opponent's neck and so won the duel.[59] This motif of saving O'Connell, the hero, by use of the Irish language, which is not understood by the enemy, occurs again in the well-known account of O'Connell's salvation by a servant girl who warns him in Irish that he is being poisoned.[60]

A recurring motif in the accounts of the duel with D'Esterre is that O'Connell succeeds in escaping from the scene of the duel by spreading the news that D'Esterre has won the day and that O'Connell himself is dead; however in all of the oral accounts, as in history, O'Connell emerges the victor. Most of the accounts describe D'Esterre as an unparalleled marksman. In a few versions, we are told that D'Esterre is so skilled that, to frighten O'Connell, he was shooting the birds in the air as they were flying around just before the duel. As a result, O'Connell's victory is even more impressive.[61] Praising the skill of the vanquished increases the merit of the victory. The spot where the duel took place was kept enclosed by a fence for years after the event. At one time the mark of D'Esterre's heel could be seen where he had fallen, but in the 1930s all that could be seen was a stone marking the spot where the duel took place.[62]

The story of the duel with D'Esterre is the most prevalent of the accounts in historical lore. It has certain legendary traits which add to its popularity. O'Connell is placed in an era of swords and bows and arrows and becomes a kind of Robin Hood figure. His talent as a marksman is thereby romanticised and the image of the hero is magnified.

In both folklore and in the historical record, the moral consequences of the duel for O'Connell are a recurring feature. O'Connell was against bloodshed and violence for the achievement of political aims, due in part to his impressions of the bloodshed of the French Revolution. In folk tradition, it is said that after the duel he made the sign of the cross every time he passed by D'Esterre's house.[63] He is said to have provided financial support for D'Esterre's widow. Tradition also says that for years after the duel, he used to wear a black glove on the hand in which he held the pistol which shot D'Esterre.[64]

The frequency of this adventure in historical lore indicates the extent to which it caught the popular imagination.[65] It lends itself to easy recall because of the concrete nature of the events. The duel is prominent also in the song and verse tradition.[66]

O'Connell was involved in other duels apart from that with D'Esterre. One account states that O'Connell fought a duel with a man called Blennerhasset, but did not kill him.[67] In an account of another duel, O'Connell's opponent was on a big horse and O'Connell arrived on an old nag which had tin cans tied to its tail and around its neck.[68] The nag frightened the other horse which ran off. O'Connell went after it saying: 'Come back, you coward.' At a duel in England, O'Connell was asked to grant one wish to his opponent which O'Connell granted but the result of which was that O'Connell was not able to see his opponent to shoot him. O'Connell's one request then was to go and stand behind the other milestone. This was allowed but then O'Connell too could not be seen. That put an end to the duel and no shooting took place.[69] These minor duels which are told of in folklore underline the importance of O'Connell as a duellist and challenger.[70] They also emphasise the concept of O'Connell as a Cú Chulainn-type champion figure.[71]

The Clare Election and Catholic Emancipation

O'Connell's election to Parliament as Member for county Clare was a major symbolic victory for the Catholic population, and as such is celebrated in folklore and folk-song.[72] Following the success of a Protestant pro-Emancipation candidate in Waterford, Irish popular opinion became a force in British politics for the first time. O'Connell's election in Clare indicated once again the power of the Catholic Association. The election itself was an ordered, sober event and Vesey Fitzgerald, the sitting MP for Clare (1818-1828), was badly beaten. Folk memory recalls the bonfires, feasts and celebration and the way the great news was spread:

> When Daniel O'Connell was elected in the Clare election, the news of his election was signalled from the Clare hills with large bonfires, and the news was quickly spread in this way.[73]

31

In Kerry, news of O'Connell's election reached Cahersiveen within two hours of the announcement of the election results. The news was spread by people shouting it to each other:

..and there was no telegrams that time, but there was an account in Cahersiveen in two hours of his election being won. You'd screech here, and as far as your voice went, the next man screeched, and in two hours they had an account behind of him.[74]

Another contemporary description of the celebration tells how every window in the town of Callan in county Kilkenny was alight with candles in honour of Daniel O'Connell who had been elected in Clare.[75] Folk memory in the Ennis district recalls that about two thousand people gathered around the courthouse in Ennis to hear the result of the election.[76]

The landlords did not support O'Connell in the election and some of them threatened revenge on their tenants if they voted for him.

This was to be a great test for the Catholic cause. Some of the Landlords had threatened their tenants with eviction if they went to vote for O'Connell. Arthur forbade his tenants to leave their homes for to vote or out they would go. Father Bourke of Broadford went to each one of them and they refused. However, three promised to go. He said unless they felt they were needed he wouldn't send for them as they were poor men with large families, and they would surely be evicted. The long car came for them the last day of the election, and Paud Moroney, Springmount, Michael Hayes, The Wood and Tom Dinneen, Ballyda, were the three faithful stalwarts of all Arthur's tenants that recorded their votes for the great Dan in Ennis. Tom Dinneen was working in the bog when the car came and he went just as he was in his flannel waistcoat and no stockings and he didn't spare the horses. One of the horses fell in Spancelhill and they made the journey with the other two. It was a huge victory and there was no evictions. Arthur gave a great feast to all his tenants that didn't go to vote and they got a roasted ham to eat. They were always called the 'Ham Eaters' after and everywhere they showed their faces at Land League meetings etc. it was always thrown at them.[77]

The account quoted above was collected from Malachy Dinneen in 1938, when Malachy was seventy-nine years of age. He was from O'Briens Bridge in county Clare. The informant said that he heard the account from 'local discussion in his youth'.

We are told in the following account that those who were in power were against O'Connell:

I dtoghadh mór an Chláir bhí formhór na n-uaisle in aghaidh Dhónaill Uí Chonaill. Bhí beagán ar nós An O'Gorman-Mahon ina

*fhabhar, ach ba é cumhacht na sagart ba mhó ba bhun le bua mór
an Chonallaigh. Bhí sé ráite ná raibh fear i gcontae an Chláir ba mhó
olc agus fuath dho ná Seán Bindon Scott,*[78] *a chónaigh i gCathair Con,
ná fear gur lú air an creideamh Caitliceach.*

*Ní raibh dearmad ná gur dhein sé a mhíle dícheall in aghaidh an
Chonallaigh sa toghadh san, agus gur agair sé ar a thionóntaí a
n-easumhlaíocht nuair a thugadar a nguth dá ainneoin don
Chonallach.*[79]

(In the Great Clare Election, most of the gentry were against Daniel
O'Connell. There were a few, like The O'Gorman-Mahon who were
in his favour, but the power of the priests was the primary reason for
O'Connell's great victory. It was said that there wasn't a man in Clare
who hated and despised him more than Seán Bindon Scott who was
living in Cathair Con, a man who hated the Catholic faith. The truth is
that he tried his damnedest against O'Connell in the election and that
he threatened his tenants with their disobedience when they voted for
O'Connell in spite of him.)

Some people were victimised because of their support for O'Connell
in the election and left their homes in Clare to start a new life in west
Kerry:

In the time of O'Connell they were drummed away from Clare, a
family of the Lynches and a family of the Hartneys and two families of
the Prendergasts, they were driven away by their landlords because
they voted for O'Connell.

They came in canoes here, each family had a canoe and the canoe
was covered with the skin of a horse instead of canvas and they put
up under the canoes until they built some kind of houses.[80]

The documented historical evidence agrees that it was because of
the support of the clergy by means of the Catholic Association that
O'Connell was elected in Clare.[81] Certainly there was a great deal of
tension between the landlords and their tenants as regards voting for a
Catholic and especially for O'Connell.[82]

Little is found in the recorded folklore about O'Connell's
parliamentary career. No mention is made of O'Connell's participation
in parliamentary debates or of his oratory there, and the time he spent
in the British Parliament does not appear to be significant in folk
memory. The Parliament may have had little to do with the people or
may have been seen to have little to do with them. Physically,
parliamentary life was quite far removed from the life of the rural
population in Ireland, and this fact is reflected in the anecdotes and
tales about O'Connell. There was a difference between official politics
involving matters such as the Colleges Bill or the Regency Bill, and
popular politics involving matters such as Repeal, tithes and rebellion,

which were part of the fabric of everyday life and of its oral lore. There is a rare account in the historical lore which tells of a man, Micheál Mór Ó Foghlú, from Killorglin in Kerry, who went to hear O'Connell speaking in Parliament. O'Connell asked him for his opinion about the members of Parliament, to which Micheál replied:

> B'fhearr liom ná mo mhaoin shaolta go mbeidís uile bailithe le chéile agam ar Dhroichead na Leamhna, áit nár ghearr an mhoill orm féin agus mo chairde an galar casachtaí úd a leigheas agus a chur d'fhiachaibh orthu port eile a sheinnt in éagmais na feadaíle.[83]

(I would dearly love to gather them all together at Droichead na Leamhna, where I and my friends would cure their coughing very quickly and would force them to play another tune instead of whistling.)

This short account provides an example of the tendency in the historical lore to mention names, places and occasions which are an integral part of the storyteller's life, or to relate them to the storyteller's experience.

Another anecdotal account tells of O'Connell's refusal to give allegiance to the King of England when he was in Parliament:

> Nuair a chuaigh Ó Conaill ina measc, d'fhág sé a hata ar a cheann agus d'fhiafraíodar de dé chúis ná bainfeadh sé a hata dhe don Rí. Dúirt sé sin gur cheap sé ná raibh aon Rí ann ach an Rí a bhí acu féin in Éire.[84]

(When O'Connell went in their midst he left his hat on his head and they asked him why he wouldn't take it off in deference to the King. He said he thought there was no King but the King they had themselves in Ireland.)

Here, O'Connell, Ireland's representative, is portrayed as being prepared to take a stance against the King, a symbol of British power, and to represent the popular view of Irish people. However, on another occasion, he is said to have made a bargain with the Queen, Victoria, that if he got the crown for her, no Catholic would hang in Ireland on religious grounds from that time on. When the Queen came into Parliament everyone rose to their feet except O'Connell. He said he didn't realise she was a queen because she wasn't wearing a crown. O'Connell was said to be the person who was responsible for placing a crown on the Queen of England and she was so grateful that she granted Catholic Emancipation.[85]

O'Connell's fame, in purely historical terms, is due primarily to his achieving Catholic Emancipation, but in the historical lore his victory over D'Esterre appears to have been his most important single achievement, although reference is made on occasion to 'the time of Emancipation' as a base measurement of time in the same way as 'The Great Hunger', 'The Big Flood' and 'The Big Wind' became some of the great reference points of the nineteenth century. In Menlough, county Galway, Emancipation was referred to as the time of O'Connell's victory, and bonfires were lit to celebrate O'Connell's success in attaining it.[86] According to one account, however, there was little regard for it: 'O'Connell's Emancipation was just another bit of paper around the Bailieborough district.'[87] In the recorded oral material, no reference is made in the historical lore to the political or historical significance of Emancipation or to its effect on the Catholic population of Ireland. However, a few anecdotes have been collected which demonstrate the tendency in oral narrative to use concrete description to illustrate a point. In this case, the importance of Emancipation is underlined as follows:

> O'Connell was put down in Parliament you know: he was put down and they wouldn't listen to him: no matter what he said they wouldn't listen to him. But he went out to Russia, to the Czar of Russia; and he told the wrongs of Ireland and what was a-doing in it: he told the truth. And the queer fellow – the Czar:
> 'That's very bad,' says he, 'very bad work. Now,' he says, 'I'm giving you a note,' he says, 'to take back to the English Parliament.'
> And he pulled out a large sheet of paper and he wrote his name on the inside of it. And he told England to give the Emancipation Bill: either that or receive his sword *(in war)*.
> So Russia wasn't always bad: they mightn't be as bad as they're supposed to be.[88]

This account appears to be an illustration of Russian generosity to Ireland and of O'Connell's fame, rather than to document the Emancipation movement, however.

In another account, one man found it impossible to believe that O'Connell had achieved Emancipation:

> *(Narrator said the incident occurred)* 'the time Dan O'Connell won Catholic Emancipation.'
> I heard it told many a time in Carrickastickan. He was (by) the name of Peter Lennon as far as I'd know, and he was from Mullaghbawn. And, of course, going to Dundalk he'd have to go up Carrickastickan and Long Archie Murdock was in full go *(powerful influence)* at the time. Peter Lennon had a new crock in the cart coming home and Long Archie was working up the field. He stopped on the road and called him down.
> 'What do you want?' says Long Archie.
> 'It's passed,' says Lennon, 'Dan O'Connell has won Emancipation.'

'You're a liar,' says Murdock.

And begod he ups and breaks the new crock on Murdock's head and headed off like hell for home. When he got home he told the wife.

'Well,' says she, 'we were a long time struggling to get the price of that crock: but no matter, it was worth it.'[89]

Tithes

The tithes were of immediate concern to farmers in the early nineteenth century, and affected them in a more direct way than Catholic Emancipation. They were the cause of severe and violent unrest in Ireland, especially in the 1830s. They were a form of tax payable by all inhabitants based on a tenth of their income, irrespective of the size of their holdings or their religious affiliation, and levied for the upkeep of the local Protestant rector. O'Connell agitated against the tithe system and thereby increased his stature as leader. A story is told about him writing the word 'tithes' on the back of a cow which was for sale:

> Daniel O'Connell rose a fierce agitation and succeeded in abolishing the tithes. The cattle of a poor widow with fourteen children were seized by the sheriff for tithes in Ossory. O'Connell got the word 'Tithes' fixed and printed on the back of each animal. A big crowd collected, and the parson was in great glee. The cattle were offered for £70, £60, £50, £20, fourteen pence but no bidder. Back home went the cattle to Norry and her fourteen children.[90]

In two published versions of the same event, it is said that this was a story which Daniel O'Connell enjoyed relating, and that the person who stamped the word 'tithes' on the cattle was called 'Paddy'. Folklore has given O'Connell a more active and heroic role in the above version by involving him in the action of the tale. The storyteller's father in another account remembered having to pay a large percentage of the price of his crops to the Protestant minister, until O'Connell put an end to the practice. It is said in this account that the tithes were thrown out and the Protestant community were thenceforth expected to support their ministers, and the Catholics their priests.[91] Many instances of intercommunal violence occurred during the tithe wars and, in certain areas in Kilkenny and Waterford, Protestant rectors were killed. In a famous case in south Kilkenny in 1832 eleven policemen were killed and the well-known court case of Carrickshock ensued. O'Connell acted for the defence.[92] He frequently defended those charged with tithe-related offences. When he had put an end to the tithes system, he used to 'bury' them in the ground, as occurred in a symbolic drama in Waterford.

Tháinig Dónall Ó Conaill agus is é a chuir amach an deachú. Is é an áit a cuireadh an deachú ná amuigh aige Cnocán na mBuachaillí. Cuireadh síos sa talamh é.[93]

(Daniel O'Connell came and he got rid of the tithes. The tithes were buried over at Cnocán na mBuachaillí. They were buried in the ground.)

He also buried the tithes in Tipperary:

At the time of Daniel O'Connell, there was a rent imposed on the Catholic people for the upkeep of the Protestant clergy, called the tithes. Daniel O'Connell was in opposition to this and all the people followed him as they were delighted to have a leader. Daniel O'Connell buried the tithes on the Devil's Bit, which is marked by a little round hill on the Borrisnoe side of the Bit.[94]

This story was collected in county Tipperary and it is quite possible that the informant's parents remembered such an occasion. The narrator includes a comment that 'all the people followed him as they were delighted to have a leader'. This is obviously the informant's personal opinion, but is probably also the opinion of more than one individual and expresses a popular understanding of why O'Connell was so readily accepted as leader.

Samuel Lover describes 'the Burial of the Tithe' which took place sometime before 1834.[95] According to Lover's account, this was a great social occasion in which the entire community took part. A coffin was carried from the corpse-house and keeners followed the funeral as far as the burial ground of the tithes at the Devil's Bit, the same place where O'Connell buried the tithes. Oral tradition has introduced O'Connell as the person who did the burying and this, of course, ties in very well with his image as leader and popular supporter of the people against unjust laws. His handling of the tithe issue also provides an indication of O'Connell's ability to exploit a situation, with the creation of the tithe burial drama for political reasons.

Public Meetings
There are many references in folklore to meetings held by O'Connell in every part of Ireland, and to people gathering to listen to him. Sometimes no specific reason is given for O'Connell's address, and reference is seldom made to the political message therein. Usually, the informant describes the huge crowds at these meetings. Only on a rare occasion is reference made to the date of the meeting, and there is seldom any indication as to whether it was held to advance support for Catholic Emancipation through the Catholic Association in the latter half of the 1820s, or for Repeal in the 1840s. A few of the 'monster

meetings' took place at selected sites which had historical associations and were situated on a hilltop – for example, Tara and Mullaghmast – but the vast majority of these meetings were in strategically located country towns.[96]

An account from county Galway describes the huge crowd at a meeting held in Loughrea:

> In the year 1828, Daniel O'Connell held a big meeting in Loughrea. It was just before Catholic Emancipation and there was never seen such a crowd in Loughrea. The meeting was held in the fair green, it was packed with people and there was some of them up to their knees standing in the water of the lake. They came from all over the county Galway, and Catholics from county Clare were present at the meeting.
>
> All day long, the roads were thronged with people and horse carts, ass carts. The main road from Gort to Loughrea was thronged all night and early morning with horse creels and they packed with men coming all the way from Clare. There were horse loads from Ennis, Ennistymon, Corofin and from all over Clare, O'Connell's native county. *(sic)*
>
> There was a big dinner given to Daniel O'Connell in the Town Hall after the meeting. It was one of the biggest functions ever held in the town.[97]

The following is an account from a man whose grandfather attended one of these meetings and travelled about thirty miles to it from Blacklion in county Cavan to Sligo town:

> There was no market for our butter nearer than Sligo; there was no market in Enniskillen, at his time *(narrator's grandfather)* in his period; and he went to Sligo to the market, but he had to go there to meet O'Connell in it. He was on what you call the Repeal Association; he *(grandfather)* used to lift the money *(locally)* and he had to meet him and he hit on the day, the market day. And he brought two firkins *(of butter)*. I don't know was he married, he was not; my Daddy you know wasn't born this time; this far back; it was called 'The Catholic Rent', a penny *(per person in contribution)* and they used to lift it at the chapels. He had to go anyway and he attended the market anyway and he knew O'Connell was coming to it; and he believed there was a couple of hundred thousand at the meeting, often I heard my Daddy, God be good to their souls saying, my grandfather . . but there was no main roads he had to plough *(travel)* a lot of it *(journey)* through the country; and she was a mare *(which he was driving with the firkins)* which had a young foal. Down here in Barr-ann (?) but we'll leave that aside, but he met with O'Connell; there was a horrid *(huge)* gathering in it – I think he said there was odds of two hundred thousand, and he talked first – it was out of the coach he talked to them and it was all in Irish; and he *(grandfather)*

38

didn't think that there was fifty or fifty-five with him that understood the English language at the time: my grandfather had both. After giving a speech in their own language he translated it, but didn't finish it the same as in the Irish. He laid out, I mind to him saying, that there was hardship for them and telling them – his health was failing at the time – he said he was a tremendous big man. The coach was let down. The word of it was he said he was a bit late getting in anyway but he got his money dispatched to him anyway. It was impossible to get convenient *(to O'Connell)* with the gathering of people *(that)* was in it, and that's that. I doubt it was about the year of '30 or '32. The Emancipation was going through at the time; he was after getting that through at the time. He told them about that.

The meeting was in Sligo. In Sligo town.[98]

The account is representative of the popularity of this type of material in areas which didn't have any particular connection with O'Connell. Patrick Curnyn, the informant, was born at the end of the last century and his grandfather may well have been a contemporary of O'Connell.

There was another big meeting in Ennis, and again, there was a large crowd present and they were pushing their way forward to see O'Connell. We encounter the recurring motif of O'Connell's ability to dramatise a situation in a clever way:

> *Nuair a bhí an mórchruinniú acu in Inis, d'ordaigh an Conallach go ndéanfaí an chulaith éadaigh seo in aghaidh í thabhairt don fhear a rachadh faoi i dtosach agus a d'iompródh ar a ghualainneacha é.*
>
> *Ní raibh aon fhear maith ar an* meeting *ná raibh ag brú isteach i gcónaí mar shúil is go mbainfeadh sé tosach dhon chuid eile, agus go n-ardódh sé an Conallach ar a ghualainneacha leis.*
>
> *Bhí an búistéara beag seo a mba ainm dó Maguidhir, bhí sé ag brú isteach i gcónaí faoi chosa na bhfear mór, agus nuair a bhí an* meeting *i ndáil le bheith thart cá mbeadh mo dhuine ach ina sheasamh faoi chosa an Chonallaigh. Sháigh sé a chloigeann aniar faoi chosa an Chonallaigh, agus bhí an Conallach ina shuí ar a dhá ghualainn. Nuair a chonaic an slua mór an gníomh breá a bhí déanta ag an mbúistéara beag, thug gach uile dhuine cúnamh ansin dó, agus ligeadar liú astu a dhúiseodh na mairbh. Iompraíodh síos agus aníos é trí shráideanna Inse agus ní fhaca tú aon obair ariamh mar bhí acu ann. Tugadh teideal ansin don bhúistéara bhocht, chomh maith leis an gculaith éadaigh.*[99]

(When they had the big meeting in Ennis, O'Connell ordered a suit of clothes to be made for the man who would go underneath him first and would carry him on his shoulders. There wasn't a man at the meeting who wasn't pushing forward all the time, hoping to get before all the others, and to carry O'Connell on his shoulders. There was a little butcher called Maguire, he was pushing in under the big men's legs, and when the meeting was nearly over where was he but standing under O'Connell's legs.

He stuck his head under O'Connell's legs and O'Connell was sitting on his two shoulders. When the crowd saw the great deed the little butcher had achieved everyone helped him then and they gave a cheer which would raise the dead. He was carried up and down through the streets of Ennis and you never saw such work. The poor butcher was given a title then, as well as the suit of clothes.)

This account is an example of the type of concrete narrative which is so much a part of the historical lore. The informant, Séamus Ó Riagáin, heard this account in 1887, which places it very close to O'Connell's time, although no year was mentioned for the meeting.

From county Tipperary we are told that two workmen were threatened that they would be 'let go' if they went to O'Connell's meeting in Cashel. One of these workmen was the storyteller's father. The landlord told them they needn't come back if they went to the meeting. When they came back from the meeting the food for the day had been eaten and they were hungry, but they weren't let go.[100]

In county Monaghan, we are told that there were a million people present in a field known as Muiris' field when O'Connell spoke there.[101] There was such a large crowd present at the meeting at Tara in 1843 that less than one fiftieth of the people who were there could hear what was going on, according to one man who was at the meeting.[102] The Tara meeting is one of the most famous meetings of all and according to one report three-quarters of a million people gathered at it, although something over half a million is probably a more accurate estimate. It was estimated that 10,000 mounted police were present. Masses were said at altars around the site and a vast platform and dining pavilion were arranged. It was an indication of O'Connell's power and of the strength of political feeling at the time.[103] The pageantry staged by O'Connell and his chief supporters at this meeting involved a harper playing 'The Harp that once through Tara's halls' and symbolic and dramatic use of a green velvet cap which was edged with gold.[104] Apparently, he always wore a cap with a yellow band on it:

Ó, fear breá. Caipín a bhíodh air i gcónaí agus banda buí (ar an gcaipín).[105]

(Oh, a fine man. He always wore a cap with a yellow band on it (on the cap).)

At a meeting in Drogheda, O'Connell was presented with a linen tablecloth on which his own image was woven.[106] In another account we are told that the informant's grandfather used to go to O'Connell's meetings in Waterford, and the jacket the grandfather wore at three such meetings was preserved in the family.[107] A certain Tipperary couple were not to forget one of O'Connell's meetings according to another account. The informant's parents were at the meeting in Cabragh, county Tipperary, on 14 August 1845, and when they got home from the meeting, their potatoes were black.[108] This indicated the start of the potato blight for the couple.

Speeches and Language

O'Connell was a powerful speaker and some of his speeches were quite well-known. Newspaper reports were read eagerly by those who were able to read, but sometimes the assistance of a reader was required:

> There was an old man named William Kelly, who lived about a mile from Athboy on the road going into Kells and he used to get the paper regularly. Every evening, the neighbours would come in to hear him read the news and especially the speeches of Daniel O'Connell. Now, there would be many a big word in the speech when the old fellow would have to take a little time in order to spell it to himself first and it is then he used to say and often in the middle of a sentence too: 'Here O'Connell stops again.'[109]

O'Connell is said to have been a very effective speaker. His style was dramatic and appealed to his audiences despite his descent to 'vapid and vulgar personalities or jogtrot, over-laden cadences'.[110] His 'coarse eloquence' was characteristic of his speeches. One informant said that when O'Connell delivered his first speech in Ennis his voice and delivery were such that he managed to make everyone who was there change their point of view.[111] He had a strong voice, which helped him in his political life:

> I must mention, that he has received from nature an invaluable gift for a party leader; a magnificent voice, united to good lungs and a strong constitution. His understanding is sharp and quick, and his acquirements out of his profession not inconsiderable.[112]

Some of O'Connell's speeches indicate that he was something of a romantic. At a meeting in Clifden he said:

> I love the wild and majestic scenes through which I have this day passed in coming to your meeting. I love the music of the running waters, the silvery echoes of the mountain rill, and the sound of the torrent rushing over the brow of the precipice.[113]

Pragmatically, O'Connell praised the rural population and called them 'the finest peasantry on earth'. This tactic was probably designed for, and possibly also contributed to, the creation of a confident, loyal and disciplined following. Frequently, however, when it was politically convenient, O'Connell was ready to make unreasonable promises to the rural population about issues such as the abolishment of tithes.[114] Lecky says about O'Connell's oratory: 'Other orators studied rhetoric – O'Connell studied man.'[115] He seemed to be aware of what his audience wanted to hear. He used phrases such as 'Agitate, agitate, agitate!' in his speeches which helped to emphasise his image as leader.[116]

English was at the time the language of politics, and was seen in this light by people in Irish- and English-speaking areas alike. English was the language associated with official political and parliamentary life, with judges and with court cases. O'Connell spoke both in Irish and in English at his meetings. Arguably, his most emotionally moving speech was delivered in Irish in 1835 when he reduced the audience to tears, while addressing the meeting on the subject of the Rathcormack massacre of 1834, a bloody point in the tithe war which took place in county Cork.[117] In many areas, of course, only a small minority of those present understood him when he spoke in English and they translated his speech for the others. Local people in Clare, for example, used to go to his meetings and when they came home they went in search of the *fear teangan',* – someone who was established in the locality as a translator who translated from Irish to English in court cases. That person, who was presumably present at the meetings, translated O'Connell's speech into Irish for them.[118] O'Connell was censured for his use of English in his speeches and for thus helping to perpetuate British rule in Ireland.[119] An account from Cork says that he was not enthusiastic about Irish:

> They used to say that he wasn't in favour of Irish, although he had plenty Irish himself. It was easy to fool the man that was depending on Irish, when he had no English. A lot of people hadn't a word of English that time, or for years after.[120]

History tells us that, although O'Connell was an excellent Irish speaker, he did not speak it very often and did not see that it served any useful purpose. He was asked if he was aware that the rural population was speaking less Irish than formerly and he said :

> 'Yes,' he answered, 'and I am sufficiently utilitarian not to regret its gradual abandonment.'[121]

Despite his own expressed view, there were those to whom O'Connell spoke Irish only, as we are told:

> Ó, níor labhair sé aon fhocal riamh leo ach Gaelainn (leis na seandaoine).[122]

(Oh, he never spoke a word to them (*the old people)* that wasn't in Irish.)

This probably represents a pragmatic use of Irish in private by O'Connell. The ultimate irony in the folkore material about O'Connell is that most of it was recorded in Irish from native Irish speakers. So O'Connell is portrayed as a hero in a language the disappearance of which he did not regret and the decline of which he probably hastened; and in folklore it is the use of this very language which saves him on some occasions.[123]

O'Connell's Personality and Appearance
In addition to the historical lore which is directly related to, or has as its main theme, a specific event or occasion in which O'Connell participated, there are accounts which describe O'Connell's behaviour, personality or character. In most cases he is praised. Sometimes the nature of the narrative itself and the very fact that it became part of oral tradition is an indication of support for O'Connell and for his activities.

One story tells of his visit to Roscommon during the 1845-48 famine when local people were looking for assistance from him in getting work. Within a week, there was a notice posted looking for people to work at Lough Key to build quays. People went there but they were too weak to work. A container was set up and meal was provided for the men who were working on the quays. The men earned one shilling and threepence per week and all of this was said to be due to O'Connell's intervention.[124]

Another story describes O'Connell's intervention in a domestic matter. Seán Ó Súilleabháin, a workman, married a well-off farmer's daughter and the farm was promised to him. When there was no sign of the farm materialising, Seán went to O'Connell for help. O'Connell started a rumour that he was related to Seán and he came to Seán's house along with two gentlemen, and it was settled in O'Connell's presence that Seán would get the land. After that, Seán collected votes for O'Connell.[125]

O'Connell's generosity is mentioned in other accounts.[126] This kindness to the poor and the sometimes extravagantly generous deeds have biblical connotations and are reminiscent of the miracles of the multiplication of the loaves and fishes and of the wine at the wedding feast of Cana. For example, O'Connell is said to have given grass to a workman for his cow when he saw the fine fence the workman had built around a field.[127] O'Connell was at the races on another occasion and noticed that a woman who had a stall had not sold any drink. The Counsellor bought most of the drink from her and told one of the men who were standing around to get a jug and to divide the drink among the old people.[128] At the well one day, O'Connell asked a girl for a drink of water. She gave it to him in a wooden mug and when he handed the mug back to her there was a shilling in it.[129] A man once came to pay rent to O'Connell. He had the rent in his hat because his pockets were all torn. O'Connell called his wife and she gave the man a piece of linen to make new pockets.[130] These instances are examples of O'Connell's behaviour in the historical lore which seems to imply that he usually behaved in a manner which attracted favourable attention to himself. Generosity is a trait always admired in rural Ireland, and perhaps these many anecdotes of O'Connell's generosity are told so that O'Connell will conform in folklore to this desirable trait. In Gaelic Ireland, the leaders of old Gaelic families were part of what was known as the 'Big House' tradition, and were generous to the local population. O'Connell's generosity thus strengthened the image of the popular leader. A relevant comment in the preface to O'Connell's correspondence is as follows:

> ...the Gaelic culture from which he sprang had always expected the chieftain to give generously to all in need.[131]

As a well-known politician, O'Connell had a great deal of power so he was approached frequently by people who were looking for favours from him. On one occasion, a man wanted O'Connell to locate his grandfather's property in Dublin, to sell it, and to forward the money to him in England.[132] Apparently O'Connell did not relish these requests because of their frequency. He once said that he was tired of the 'one word from you' attitude which could answer any favour.[133] But seemingly he was happy to do favours for some people:

> *Bhí tine chnámh ar an gCoireán acu nuair a tháinig sé (Dónall Ó Conaill) amach as príosún, agus chuaigh duine dá chailíní (de chailíní aimsire an Bhuitléaraigh) chuaigh sí go dtí an tine chnámh. Ach dhíbir sé (an Buitléireach) í go háirithe, bhris sé an cailín mar gheall ar dhul go dtí an tine chnámh, má b'fhíor é. Ach chuaigh sí go dtí an Cunsailéir agus dhein sé rud éigineach di mar gheall air.*[134]

> (They had a bonfire in An Coireán when he *(Daniel)* came out of prison and one of the girls *(Butler's girls)* went to the bonfire. But he *(Butler)* sent her away anyway, he sacked her for going to the bonfire, if it is true. But she went to the Counsellor and he did something about it.)

O'Connell's reputation in folklore is that he was honest with his clients. A man came to him once asking for his help in a court case and offered him money, but although the farmer made every attempt to give the Counsellor money, O'Connell wouldn't accept it when he couldn't take on the case.[135]

O'Connell's favourite pastime seems to have been hunting and frequent mention is made of this sport in the historical lore. Indeed, history and historical lore agree about the importance of hunting in O'Connell's life.[136] For exmaple, a visitor to Ireland at the time said about O'Connell:

> When at Derrynane, hunting is his favourite exercise.[137]

When he came home from parliament he used to go hunting.[138] Folk memory recalls occasions when different people used to accompany him on the hunt, as in the following account for example:

> *Do bhíodh an Cunsailéir (Dónall Ó Conaill) ag fiach anso agus bhí sé (Diarmuid Ó Sé) ag féachaint air sin lá agus é in éineacht leis – athair máthar Pheaidí Conaill seo thíos – Diarmuid Ó Sé – bhíodh sé ag fiach in éineacht leis ..*
>
> *Ach bhí fiach acu a dúirt sé, mada rua a bhí á fhiach aige an gCunsailéir, lá agus aige daoine uaisle. Do bhí an mada rua traochta amach aiges na gadhair agus é istigh sa pháirc agus na daoine uaisle ina suí. Ach bhí an mada rua tabhartha, agus cad a dhein sé ach imeacht go dtí an Cunsailéir agus chaith sé é féin anuas ar a ghlúin. Dúirt sé (Diarmuid Ó Sé) go raibh sé ag féachaint air sin. 'Ó, mhuise, gheobhair do phas inniu,' a dúirt sé, 'ach ní bhfaighir go brách arís, má thagann tú thar n-ais.'*
>
> *Lá eile, a dúirt sé gur thánga sé agus do dhein sé an rud céanna. 'Do gheallas duit,' a dúirt sé (An Cunsailéir), 'dá dtagfá thar n-ais ná bhfaighfeá an tarna seans'. Scaoil sé na gadhair ina dhiaidh agus maraíodh é an tarna hiarracht.[139]*

(The Counsellor *(Daniel O'Connell)* used to hunt here and Diarmuid Ó Sé used to watch him. One day, when Diarmaid was with him – Peaidí Conall who lives down here, it was his grandfather – Diarmuid Ó Sé – used to hunt with him. ...But they had a hunt, he said, the Counsellor was hunting a fox, one day, he and some of the gentry. The hounds had exhausted the fox and he was inside in a field and the gentry were sitting down. But the fox was exhausted and what did he do only go to the Counsellor and threw himself on his knee. He *(Diarmuid Ó Sé)* said he was looking at that. 'Well, you'll be let go today,' he said, 'but you won't be let go ever again if you come back.' Another day, he said he came and he did the same thing. 'I promised you,' he *(the Counsellor)* said, 'if you came back that you wouldn't get a second chance.' He let the hounds after him and he was killed the second time.)

O'Connell liked to have the best hounds possible for the hunt:

> *Nuair a bhíodh aon fhiach fónta le bheith ann, bhí gadhar anseo mar*

thigh agus gadhar eile sa tigh seo thuas aige an mbeirt deartháir – na Cárthaigh- agus nuair a bhíodh aon fhiach fónta acu do chuireadh sé fios ar an dá ghadhar i gcónaí, Dónall Ó Conaill (an Liberator).[140]

(Whenever there was any kind of a good hunt planned, the two brothers – the McCarthys – had a hound here in one house and another hound in a house up here and when they had any sort of a good hunt, he, Daniel O'Connell *(the Liberator)* always sent for the two hounds.)

O'Connell kept a pack of beagles, perhaps the best in Ireland. He was very fond of hunting and used to kill four hares before breakfast. He read his letters and ate his breakfast on the side of the mountain after the hunt.[141]

O'Connell had numerous hounds for hunting.[142] There is a reference in one account to the informant's father who was a hunting companion of Counsellor O'Connell,[143] and another account names Peaidí (Riocaird) Ó Conaill as the Liberator's huntsman.[144] O'Connell used to pay those who helped him on the hunt:

Bhíodh fear ag gabháil (timpeall) anso, Tadhg an Ghadhairín, a thugaidís air, bhíodh gadhairín beag aige agus slabhra air agus do cheangaladh sé dhon raca é. Ach bhíodh an Cunsailéir (Dónall Ó Conaill) ag fiach an uair sin agus gadhair fhiaigh aige. By gor, do loirigeadh an Cunsailéir air an raghadh sé ag fiach.
'By gor, raghad,' a deireadh sé, 'tá sé ráite riamh go mb'fhearra dul ag fiach ná ag iarraidh déirce.' By gor, nuair a stadadar, tráthnóna, do chuir an Cunsailéir lámh ina phóca agus thug sé leathchróinn do. 'By gor, an rud a bhí ráite,' ar seisean, 'féach go mb'fhearra dom dul ag fiach ná ag iarraidh déirce.'[145]

(There was a man who used to go *(around)* here, Tadhg an Ghadhairín *(Tadhg of the small dog)* they used to call him – he used to have a small hound on a chain and he'd tie it to a rock. But the Counsellor *(Daniel O'Connell)* used to hunt at that time and he had hounds for hunting. By gor, the Counsellor asked him if he would go hunting. 'By gor, I will,' he said, 'it has always been said that it's better to go hunting than to go begging.' By gor, when they stopped in the evening, the Counsellor put his hand in his pocket and gave him a half a crown. 'By gor, that's what was said,' he said, 'it shows that it was better for me to go hunting than to go begging.')

Another source of pleasure in O'Connell's life, according to folk belief, was food. There were certain items of food which he favoured and among these were *sleabhcán,* which is laver or sloke, a type of edible seaweed, and the term refers also to the syrup which is made from it. *Sleabhcán* is mentioned in a few accounts. Tadhg Ó Murchú's father remembered the women of Doire Fhionáin (Derrynane) gathering and boiling *sleabhcán* and *tropáin*[146] for O'Connell during Lent. O'Connell ate a good deal of it and found no fault with it.[147] A chapbook account tells that O'Connell had an excellent appetite; he was never inclined to hold a conversation when he was eating and he didn't mind about the sequence of courses during a meal. He would start to eat meat again when he had finished eating two entire courses.

There are a number of accounts which describe O'Connell's physical appearance. For example:

> *Bhí sé ard, lúfar nuair a bhí sé óg – an Cunsailéir. Fear mór téagartha ab ea é, timpeall sé troithe.*[148]

(He was tall – agile when he was young – the Counsellor. A big strong man, about six foot.)

An oral account from Uíbh Ráthach says that O'Connell had a handsome appearance:

> *Chuala m'athair á rá go bhfaca sé dhá uair Seana-Dhónall (Ó Conaill). Fear breá dathúil ab ea é, a dúirt sé.*[149]

(I heard my father say that he saw old Daniel *(O'Connell)* on two occasions. He said he was a fine handsome man.)

The informant in this instance was born in 1870 so that his parents were certainly alive towards the end of O'Connell's lifetime and may well have seen O'Connell. A contemporary of O'Connell, a visitor to Ireland, gave a favourable account of him:

> His exterior is attractive; and the expression of intelligent good nature, united with determination and prudence which marks his countenance, is extremely winning. He has, perhaps, more of persuasiveness than of genuine large and lofty eloquence; and one frequently perceives too much design and manner in his words. Nevertheless, it is impossible not to follow his powerful arguments with interest, to view the martial dignity of his carriage without pleasure, or to refrain from laughing at his wit.[150]

The account quoted above is one of the few accounts which exist where the writer actually saw O'Connell. An almost contemporary account is lavish in praise:

> His frame is tall, expanded, and muscular; precisely such as befits a man of the people – for the physical classes ever look with double confidence and affection upon a leader who represents in his own person the qualities upon which they rely. In his face he has been equally fortunate; it is extremely comely. The features are at once soft and manly; the florid glow of health and a sanguine temperament are

diffused over the whole countenance, which is national in the outline, and beaming with national emotion. The expression is open and confiding, and inviting confidence; there is not a trace of malignity or wile – if there were, the bright and sweet blue eyes, the most kindly and honest-looking that can be conceived, would repel the imputation.[151]

But not everyone praised O'Connell's appearance. Another visitor from Germany, Johannes Kohl, had this to say about O'Connell's appearance on one occasion at a meeting of the Emerald Legion:

I must own he looked more ludicrous than dignified in his official costume as Lord Mayor.[152]

It was part of O'Connell's personality, and also part of the attraction of the Repeal movement and of his role as Lord Mayor, that he dressed in an ostentatious style so that he stood out on the political stage. This is Kohl's opinion and would appear to concur with historical accounts as well.[153] Because of O'Connell's flamboyant way of dressing, especially on particular occasions, and because he was apparently a good-looking man, his appearance was unforgettable. His gestures were also noteworthy and obviously effective. Kohl comments on some of these:

'Dan' himself rose next and adjusted his wig. This is a favourite trick with him, and occurs frequently in the course of an animated speech. ..In addition to this little manoeuvre of the wig he has various little tricks or habits. For instance, he frequently moves about on his heels, and turns now to the right, now to the left. He also makes great use of his hands when speaking; ... O'Connell's delivery is clear and firm.[154]

Popularity and Power

O'Connell's fame as a lawyer was widespread and he was seen as an able counsel for the defence. Sometimes, people were reluctant to become involved in any form of confrontation with him. We are told that there was a barrister who withdrew from a case because he became afraid when he heard that his opponent was to be Daniel O'Connell.[155] Another man sought a duel with O'Connell and then took fright and withdrew from the duel.[156]

O'Connell is praised for his achievements and his character. His cleverness is emhpasised: 'Dan O'Connell was one of the smartest men.'[157] It was a mark of great respect for someone to be as well-thought-of as Daniel O'Connell:

...do bhí a ainm in airde chomh mór agus do bhí ainm an Chunsailéara (Dónall Ó Conaill) aon lá riamh le feabhas.[158]

(...his name was held in the same high regard as that of the Counsellor *(Daniel O'Connell).)*

It was a sign of social standing that a person could be compared to Daniel O'Connell, who was placed on a level higher than that of the ordinary person. In the historical lore, O'Connell is compared in several accounts to other well-known historical characters. He was said to have been greater than Parnell,[159] and again it was said: 'Parnell was no bad man but Daniel O'Conell's name went up higher in praises.'[160] O'Connell's fame is underlined in other ways. It was suggested by Tom Steele, a strong O'Connellite, that the long ridge of mountains running through county Clare, a distance of twenty-five miles, should be called 'the O'Connell mountains', in commemoration of O'Connell's victory in the Clare election, and that a large lake on Mr Steele's estate, known as 'Cullane Lake' become 'Lough O'Connell'. Few people used the new names, however, apart from Mr Steele.[161] Oral tradition explains the derivation of certain names in some instances, relating them to O'Connell. It was said, for example, that 'The Star' strand near Miltown Malbay in county Clare was so called because D'Esterre, pronounced 'De Star' by the informant, used visit it regularly.[162]

The following account emphasises admiration for O'Connell:

In aigne na sean-Ghaeilgeoirí atá anois beagnach imithe uainn ba mhór le rá ainm agus cuimhne Dhónaill Mór Ó Conaill. Bhí bá chomh mór sin acu le Dónall gur fhéach sé ina súile mar a bheadh sórt Dia beag. Fiú i measc an dream is aineolaí dár mhair insan dúthaigh seo agus go dtí an líne seo bhí fios ar céad rud i dtaobh an 'Saoirseoir' agus nuair a thagaidís le chéile cois na tine insan oíche fhada gheimhridh ní hannamh a bheadh scéalta mar gheall ar ar dhéan sé agus ar bhuaigh sé d'Éire bhocht, agus ar an mbua agus treise fuair sé ar dearg-namhaid na hÉireann . . . d'airíomar scéalta do chuir drochthréithe ina leith ach ní bhacfad leo sin mar ní bhíonn saoi gan locht.[163]

(The old Irish speakers,who have nearly all gone now, had a lot of time for the name and memory of the Great Daniel O'Connell. They had such respect for Daniel that he was like a small God to them. Even amongst the most ignorant people who ever lived in this district and to the present day, they knew a hundred things about the Liberator and when they gathered around the fire in the long winter evenings they would often tell stories about all he had done and achieved for poor Ireland, and how he had conquered and overcome Ireland's bitter enemies . . . we heard stories accusing him of bad things but I won't bother with those because the wisest person is not without fault.)

This concealed criticism appears also in another account although priority is again given to the glowing praise:

Ní haon mhaith bheith á cháineadh mar nár dhein seo mar seo agus siúd mar siúd de réir dream na tromaíochta air. Ní raibh a mhacsamhail in Éirinn riamh gur mó go raibh meas agus cion na ndaoine eile ar fud na tíre ná ba mhó go raibh urraim do ná é, agus ní bheidh arís mar ná beidh a leithéid de shaol ann arís. Bhí a cháil go forleitheadúil ar fud an domhain agus meas dá réir air.[164]

(There is no point in blaming him because he didn't do this in this way or that in that way, according to those who blame him. There was no-one ever like him in Ireland who was seen with such respect and such fondness by everyone in the country or who was held in such regard as he was and there never will be again because there will never be a life like that again. His fame was worldwide and he was respected accordingly.)

In her collection of material from Kiltartan, county Galway, Lady Gregory indicated great admiration for O'Connell :

'O'Connell was a great man. I never saw him, but I heard of his name. One time I saw his picture in a paper where they were giving out meal . . . and I kissed the picture of him.'[165]

Another account is quite effusive in praise:

Dan O'Connell was the best man in the world, and a great man surely; and there could not be better than what O'Connell was . . . He was the best and the best to everyone; he got great sway in the town of Gort, and in every other place. He did good in the world while he was alive; he was a great man surely; there couldn't be better in this world I believe, or in the next world; there couldn't be better all over the world.[166]

A practical demonstration of support for Daniel O'Connell is described in an account where it is said that a man, Páid Ó Fatha, was in Waterford city one day and saw that chamber pots which had a picture of O'Connell in them were being sold in a shop there. He thought that this was an insult to O'Connell and he broke the pots. He was brought before the local Mayor who asked him if he was acquainted with O'Connell. He replied that he was and the mayor gave him money to drink O'Connell's health.[167]

During O'Connell's term as politician the newspapers published mocking cartoons and unfavourable reports about him:

For many years the entire press of England, and a large section of that of Ireland, was ceaselessly employed in denouncing him.[168]

According to at least one account in oral tradition, O'Connell was a 'wanted' man who had many enemies:

When they used to be trying to catch Daniel O'Connell, there was a notice in Eyeries barrack that anyone that would catch him, would get so much money. He used to be dressed in every kind of clothes. Sometimes he used priest's clothes and sometimes a policeman's clothes, so that the people would not know him. One day he was dressed in a priest's clothes. His bicycle got punctured and he went into the barrack, and he asked the police if they would fix his bicycle. They said that they would of course. The notice was up at the same time. So they fixed his bicycle and he thanked them and he went away. But if they knew him they would arrest him.[169]

Although the story is obviously quite incongruous as regards O'Connell and the particular adventure with the bicycle, it illustrates a highly dramatic occasion and highlights O'Connell's cleverness in evading the law. It also aligns O'Connell with the republican figure, Dan Breen, who recalled when he was a wanted man about the years 1919 to 1920, and, dressed as a priest, he asked the police in the barracks in Maynooth, county Kildare to help him repair a punctured tyre.[170] Here again, O'Connell is seen to be successful in his fight against the established system, and it is an inevitable and important part of the folk hero's life that he has enemies and manages to get the better of them.

Unfavourable Accounts

Some people disliked O'Connell intensely, either because of his personality or for some political reason. The impact of the Young Irelanders and of their policies may have contributed to this. There were particular instances of this dislike: a certain Parson Hickson in Kerry, for example, used to draw the screens over the windows to express his hatred for O'Connell. This is said to have occurred whenever O'Connell went by his house when he was out hunting with his fifty-two hounds.[171] O'Connell knew well that some people hated him and was afraid that he might be killed. Once, when he was in Bandon, in county Cork, about to deliver a speech from a hotel balcony, he ordered the balcony of the hotel to be searched beforehand in case the Orangemen had tampered with it.[172] Sir Robert Peel was a political enemy of O'Connell, but he was an enemy who had great respect for O'Connell and for his ability. We are told that Peel once said that if he were looking for an effective, well-spoken barrister, he would be very happy to employ 'this broguing Irish fellow' instead of all the other famous barristers he could engage.[173]

On occasion, attempts were made to catch O'Connell out and tricks were played on him, sometimes successfully. When the Counsellor was expected home in Uíbh Ráthach, a local man, Stephen O'Shea used to dress himself in an old shirt and torn trousers and he would go to meet O'Connell on his way home and O'Connell would give him a suit of clothes.[174] O'Connell's tenants succeeded in tricking him once when they did not feed cattle that he sent to them for fattening:

Bhí beithígh theas ag an gConallach i nDoire Fhionáin agus dúirt sé go gcuirfeadh sé ar féarach iad go Cill Mhic Ciarainn ag triail ar na tionóntaí, go ramhróidís ann. Thiomáin sé fear leo go Cill Mhic Ciarainn agus d'fhág sé ansan le cois na mbó iad agus d'imigh sé air abhaile. Ní túisce bhí sé imithe as a radharc ná thóg muintir an bhaile leo iad suas i mbun na Binne Duibhe (An Bheann Dubh, ar chúl Mhálainn – beann ard cnoic) go dtí Túirín na gCiaróg (áit atá ar an mBinn Dubh), i mbun leacan fhraoigh ann, áit ná raibh aon ní (acu) ach fraoch agus do bhuaileadar crobh-neasc fés gach aon cheann acu ansan. Bhíodar ansan gach aon lá ansan ag siolartaigh leis an ocras go dtí ná raibh iontu ach na huaithní.

I ndeireadh an Fhómhair amach ansan, dúirt an Conallach gur dócha go raibh na beithígh ramhar amach agus chuir sé an buachaill arís á n-iarraidh go dtí go mbéarfadh sé ó dheas ar aonach na Snaidhme iad. Tháinig an buachaill á n-iarraidh agus thug duine éigin scéala do mhuintir Chill Mhic Ciarainn go raibh sé ag teacht agus bhíodar anuas arís le cois na mbó acu agus gan iontu ach na huaithní – is ar éigin sioc ná seac a chuadar abhaile – bhíodar ag siolartaigh leis an ocras. 'Ó, a Mhuire Mháthair,' a dúirt an Conallach, 'cá rabhadar so ? Insa phóna a bhíodar ó shin ?' 'Ó, i mo bhriatharsa a dhuine uasail,' a dúirt an buachaill leis, 'nach ea. Bhíodar san áit is fearr i gCill Mhic Ciarainn, áit go dtugaid siad Túirín na gCiaróg air.' 'Á, más é sin an sórt Cill Mhic Ciarainn, fágfadsa slán ag Cill Mhic Ciarainn,' a dúirt an Conallach, agus do dhíol sé amach láithreach boinn ina dhiaidh sin é le Staughton.[175]

(O'Connell had cattle south in Doire Fhionáin (Derrynane) and he said that he would send them to graze in Cill Mhic Ciarainn to his tenants, and that they would fatten there. He drove a man to Cill Mhic Ciarainn and he left him there with the cows and went away home. No sooner was he out of sight than the local people took them up to the foot of An Bheann Dubh*(a hill behind Málainn)* to Túirín na gCiaróg *(a place at An Bheann Dubh),* to a heathery slope there, where there was only heather and they put a horn-and-leg spancel on each one there. They were there every day then, crying with hunger until there was nothing left but skeletons. At the end of Autumn then, O'Connell said that he supposed the cattle had filled out and he sent the boy to fetch them to bring them south to the market in Sneem. The boy came to get them and somebody told the people in Cill Mhic

Ciarainn that he was coming and they were back again with the cows, and they (*i.e.*the cattle) were only skeletons – they were hardly able to make the journey home – they were crying with hunger. 'Oh, good Lord,' said O'Connell, 'where have they been since? Have they been in the pound since ?' 'Oh, indeed sir,' said the boy, 'they have not. They have been in the best place in Cill Mhic Ciarainn, a place they call Túirín na gCiaróg.' 'Oh, if that's the kind of place Cill Mhic Ciarainn is,' said O'Connell, 'I'll say goodbye to Cill Mhic Ciarainn,' and he sold it immediately afterwards to Staughton.)

Accounts in which O'Connell is tricked are relatively rare in the extant oral material. This is probably due to the fact that material of this nature does not show O'Connell as a folk hero.

There appears to be a general reluctance to criticise O'Connell, although in one instance, at least, it was said that a certain Seán Sigerson, from the parish of An Phriaireacht, in Uíbh Ráthach, used to hold that O'Connell had no academic knowledge of the law:

> ... *ná creididh gur le feabhas léinn atá aon eolas ar dhlí aige seo (Ó Conaill). Ní hea, ach fáidhiúlacht a thug sé leis ó dhúchas ó chailleach seana-mháthar a bhí aige.*[176]

(... don't believe that he (*O'Connell*) has a knowledge of the law because of his great learning. He hasn't, but from a prophetic quality he inherited from the hag of an old grandmother he had.)

O'Connell's grandmother, Máire Ní Dhuibh, was reputed to have the gift of prophecy and was an established poet whose satirical powers were feared by many.[177] An account from Corca Dhuibhne in county Kerry also criticises O'Connell:

> *Ach is dóigh liomsa gur rógaire maith ab ea Dónall leis. Dhein sé beart ná molfainn. Dhein sé ... nuair a bhí Dónall bocht agus an saol bocht aige. Nílim a rá go raibh sé mícheart, ach measaim nuair a dh'éirigh sé suas insa tsaol gur dh'ól sé lionn agus deocha na mbodach agus na ndaoine móra, agus gur lig sé leo agus gur mhéadaigh a gcaradas leis agus gur mhéadaigh sé i gcaradas leo. Agus gurb iad ab fhearr leis, agus nárbh iad bochtáin na tíre seo. Nílimse cinnte dho. Nár lige Dia go ndéarfainnse é. Ach do bhí sé ráite poiblí gur dhaor sé triúr do mhuintir Chearnaigh chuin a gcrochta.*[178]

(But I think that Daniel was a right rogue. He did something that I wouldn't like. He did . . .when Daniel was poor and was spending his life as a poor person. I'm not saying he was wrong, but I think when he was doing well in life that he drank beer and the drinks of the gentry and the big shots, and that he let them away with things and their friendship with him grew and his friendship with them grew. And they were his favourites and not the poor people of this country.

I'm not sure about that. God forbid that I should say it. But it was said
in public that he condemned three of the Cearnaigh family to hang.)

Accounts in which O'Connell is mocked at or censured are comparatively rare, and unfavourable comments are usually in the form of
a throw-away phrase, or an addition to an account, rather than a
continuous narrative or description of misdeeds.

It is important therefore, to recognise the primary intention of the
storyteller. The nature of an account depended frequently on the way
in which it was presented by the informant. A person who wished to
impress the folklore collector with his/her connection to O'Connell
would emphasise this aspect in the oral account. If, however, the
person was more interested in presenting the information in a purely
historical context, then the emphasis would be placed on the historical
facts and events themselves, rather than on these facts and events as
experienced or understood by the informant. The personal opinions
expressed about O'Connell were probably the storyteller's own
opinions in many instances. It is also possible that an informant heard
opinions with which he/she disagreed, and that these opinions were
expressed as personal opinions because they were seen to be popular
or desirable. Opinions may have been expressed to collectors of
folklore for the simple reason that these opinions were known to be
widely held. As is the case with many aspects of folklore, the historical
lore about O'Connell was told in many instances in response to a direct
question by the collector.

People might not wish to denigrate O'Connell for fear of disapproval
or of an argument, because their opinion was seen to contradict the
general viewpoint. This may be the reason that the oral historical lore
praises O'Connell for the most part and disparages him in only a very
few cases.

The historical lore does not contain any severe personal attacks on
O'Connell as an individual or politician. In the historical lore, the most
important feature is how O'Connell is presented and the overall picture
of him which emerges from the oral material.

As regards the informants and the amount of historical lore which
was collected from them, three hundred and eighteen accounts from
the collections of the Department of Irish Folklore have been
examined. Where the gender of the informant is known, two hundred
and forty-four of these were collected from men and twenty-five from
women. Generally, in the collections of the Department of Irish
Folklore, more material has been collected from men than from
women, but in the case of historical lore about O'Connell there is
possibly a particular reason for this state of affairs. Much of the

historical lore is concerned with O'Connell's life as a public figure, with political events, with duelling or with male pastimes like hunting *etc.* in which women were not involved. A further analysis of the accounts reveals that historical lore was collected in at least twenty-eight counties in Ireland. The dates of collection – between about 1935 and 1980 – and the average age of the informants at the time of collecting – seventy-two years of age, reveal that historical lore about O'Connell has declined a great deal as a living tradition. About a hundred and fifty years have now passed since O'Connell's time, and it would appear that the tradition of historical lore about him has almost disappeared. Folk memory, however, still retains accounts of historical lore, especially in Uíbh Ráthach where the tradition was strongest.

O'Connell in Historical Lore

The historical lore about Daniel O'Connell is of great importance in relation to his development as a folk hero. Historical evidence and oral tradition certainly overlap and agree in many respects. There are elements for which historical documentation exists, which are also part of historical lore, and in many cases these form the basis for the creation of the folk character. O'Connell is a powerful person and a clever lawyer, and these traits are very important aspects of the character found in all genres of oral tradition about him. The principal characteristics which come to light in the historical lore are exceptional intelligence even as a young boy, a quick wit, cleverness as a lawyer, his skill as a duellist, his powers as an orator and his ability as a political leader. He is regarded as a champion of those who are unjustly treated. He is a person of fine appearance, who delights in hunting and he is generous. All of these traits are testified to in the historical record, but oral tradition stresses these traits above others. The traits and events which are preserved in oral tradition are those with which the rural population identified and which they respected. Oral tradition places O'Connell on a higher level than other politicians, yet includes him at the same time as part of the rural Catholic community. Many character traits are in keeping with the image of the popular leader and the person of courage – both physical and intellectual. In preserving and developing these traits, oral traditon shows that O'Connell is an exceptional character. The material is formed to suit the tradition itself.

Clearly, traditional narratives favour the concrete and the active. Opinions and political references are therefore generally omitted as they might introduce an element of uncertainty or irrelevance. The clearest example in this respect is the folk tradition about the duel with D'Esterre. The duel is important in history but it is given a significance in the historical lore beyond its actual role. There are many reasons for this. It is a narrative which has a beginning, central point and ending. It lends itself thereby to easy recall. Another reason for its importance in oral tradition is that it adds to O'Connell's image as leader and supports this understanding of his role. There are many such examples in the historical lore where a particular occasion or event is underlined. In the historical lore, in general, a description is given of a particular event or incident rather than a statement that it took place. In all of the historical lore, a sense of occasion and a sense of the specific is given to the material. The importance of the event is increased and is presented dramatically, thereby developing O'Connell as a highly 'stressed' or emphasised personality.

History is changed and formed as it finds expression in oral tradition. There is doubtless an element of idealisation of the person and of the past which removes it to an extent from the historical evidence. The result of this mingling is that a strong personality emerges who is placed on a level above that of the ordinary person. The attitudes to folklore of those who possessed and possess it, need to be borne in mind. The tradition bearers were obviously very proud of this fellow countryman who contributed to Ireland's cause. Folk tradition hardly mentions the Catholic cause. Oral tradition does not emphasise Emancipation, Repeal or political life, but stresses rather O'Connell's personality and power in relation to these events. Although accounts of his term of imprisonment have not appeared in oral tradition, it was important to the extent that it promoted the image of a type of martyr who was wrongfully imprisoned.

Folk tradition is, on the whole, faithful to the Liberator and does not censure or mock him in his advancing years and depressed spirits. O'Connell emerges in historical lore as a popular leader who is respected for his cleverness in dealing with the established government by using his quick wit, and in physical combat against the enemy as in the duel with D'Esterre. He directs the ordinary people and is accepted and encouraged in this role, thus becoming an established figurehead who affects their lives and outlook. Here he may be seen as a retrospective champion of Nationalism.

This positive image of O'Connell which emerges in the numerous and widespread accounts of historical lore is an indication both of the popularity of the accounts themselves and of the high regard in which the traditional material was held by those who gave it to the folklore collectors. It contains accounts and narratives from almost all parts of Ireland, in which O'Connell's important personality is underlined, preserved and embellished. Perhaps most significantly, the historical lore tells us not only a great deal about O'Connell, but also about the attitude of the informants to their own past.

Historical Lore: Sources
Armagh: IFC 1112:217-8; 1622:119-20; 1782:226-7; 1803:117, 145, 152-3.
Carlow: IFC 96:270-3; S903:51; S906:30-2.
Cavan: IFC 1196:62-3, 185-6; 1786:263-4; 1787:198; 1800:508; 1803:117, 120; S1005:92-6.
Clare: IFC 39:54-8; 537:498-9, 576-80; 1011:90; 1414:378-88; 2051:46-7; S585:86; S593:445-6; S598:311; S599:406; S609:494, 497-9; S610:68-9; S613:211-5; S614:164; S627:102. *Béal.* 17 1947 176. IFC Tape 1978 R. uí Ógáin from Jackie Shannon, Spanish Point, Kilfarboy, Ibrickan.
Cork: IFC 45:26; 107:456; 283:272-3; 643:104; 654:373-6; 686:355-6; 736:430-1; 779:78; 807:508-9; 808:97, 502-3; 1527:208; 1592:211; 1673:173; S275:217; S300:346; S314:45; S319:337; S344:173; S364:211; S374:85.
Donegal: IFC S1098:70-71.
Down: IFC S797:214.
Dublin: IFC 1960:184-9; 1966:262; see Joyce 1986 89, 118.
Fermanagh: IFC 1711:207-9.
Galway: IFC 257:559-62; 354:249-50, 254-6; 355:21-3; 389:456, 476-81; 404:480-81; 463:98, 121-3; 569:260-1; 634:283; 829:461-4; 1205:100; 1227:75; 1311:273-5; 1322:79-80; S18:308. de Bhaldraithe 1977 18-19. Gregory 1909 24-37.
Kerry: IFC 17:235-7; 19:235-7; 27:179-80; 125:172-3; 126:187-90, 198-202; 145:12-18; 146:230, 402, 419-22; 148:174-5, 182, 215, 264; 149:23, 40, 220, 357-60, 463-8, 696, 1011; 214:764-70; 308:202, 204, 225; 531:295; 532:109, 435-41; 557:210-11; 570:297-8, 390; 612:93-4; 621:144-51, 168-71; 658:363; 659:81-3, 290; 667:105-6, 131-3; 685:61-2; 698:89-100; 702:186; 716:3-5, 172-3, 312; 733:126-8, 295, 354-5; 768:66-70; 772:254; 777:476; 796:8-10, 12-15; 797:32-4, 68-70, 168, 201, 444, 568-71; 823:257-60, 308-9, 566-9; 833:233-9; 834:144-7; 843:139-40; 859:66-70; 862:478-9; 927:49, 132, 144-6, 228, 357; 929:326-7, 362-5, 403-5, 415-6; 930:130-4, 326-7; 936:479-81; 960:568; 961:558-61; 962:75-6; 964:367, 434-9, 517; 995:60; 996:78-81, 547-9, 585; 1003:109-116, 187-8; 1006:78, 83-4; 1007:3-4, 206, 553, 778-80; 1064:12-13, 164, 200, 308, 374; 1099:270-6; 1114:282; 1125:51, 87, 96-7, 242-4; 1146:57, 252-4, 496; 1147:201-3, 572-6; 1150:39-40; 1152:420; 1158:29; 1167:136-7, 450-3, 571-3; 1168:109, 156, 202, 392; 1186:148-9; 1198:210-11; 1200:344-5; 1225:31-3, 363-5; 1226:275-7; 1272:152-3, 157; 1312:58-60; 1341:68, 109-113, 259-60; 1357:65; 1396:238; 1421:198; 1662:120-2, 163; 1915:32; S433:49; S437:77; S444:262; S456:27; S462:285; S466:228-9, 360; S470:64; S474:125; S476:329, 422-3, 496. IFC Tape 1948 Tadhg Ó Murchú from Pádraig Stounder Ó Sé, and Pádraig (Dhónaill Óig) Ó Sé, Doire Ianach, An Dromaid. IFC Tape 1968 Bo Almqvist from Micheál Ó Gaoithín, Baile Bhiocáire, Dún Chaoin. *Béal.* 11 1937 117-25. Ó Duilearga 1948 82. Domhnall Ó Súilleabháin 1936 255-7, 263, 267-8.
Kildare: IFC S772:104-8.
Kilkenny: IFC 1660:2, 18, 108; S869:255-61.
Laois: IFC S828:219-20.
Limerick: IFC 628:17-8, 100-3, 295-6, 311; 1164:28-31; 1193:80-2, 101, 181, 310; 1194:555-7; 1276:190; S504:183-4; S507:445; S527:178.
Longford: IFC 1901:299-300; 1902:111-3 .
Louth: IFC 1503:252; 1570:136.
Mayo: IFC 134:222; 191:278; 572:287-9; 804:204-5; 810:236-7; 914:228-30; 1401:173-8, 294-6; 1534:525-6. IFC Tape 1976 Séamas Ó Catháin from Peadar Bairéad, Ceathrú na gCloch, Cill Cuimin.
Meath: IFC 497:250; 1197:120-1; 1405:237; 1535:273; S685:217; S687:328-9; S688:67-8; S703:90-2. *IO* 24.10.1936 (iii).
Monaghan: IFC 1566:80; S931:378; S942:217; S946:264.

Offaly: IFC 1677:108; 1709:175-7.
Roscommon: IFC 1574:539-40; 1639:238; S234:8-9, 70-71, 222; S238:280; S243:220.
Sligo: IFC 485:22-4; 1756:189; S171:30.
Tipperary: IFC 517:329-32; 700:118-9; 738:417; S533:231; S534:532-3; S550:33, 52; S553:186, 289-90; S582:241-2.
Tyrone: IFC 1566:80.
Waterford: IFC 152:231; 153:102-4, 199, 597-9; 1100:337-8; S638:219; S640:99-100.
Wicklow: IFC 497:250, 291-2; *Béal.* 5 1935 185-6.
Wexford: IFC 1344:112-3, 216-7; 1399:466; S900:152-3.
No Provenance: *Chapbook* n.d. 3-16. *CS* 1.6.1901 181; 3.6.1905 5; 18.11.1905 18.12.1909 6; 7.12.1912 9. *Dublin University Magazine* vol.17 1841 774. *IO* 21.1.1903 8; 22.4.1903 6; 3.1.1923 10; 14.2.1923 106-7; 16.2.1935 196; 30.7.1938 4-5; 19.11.1949 17; 17.4.1954 16; 11.12.1954 22-3; 21.7.1956 5; 28.7.1956 10; 22.12.1956 19; 29.12.1956 6. *Irish Fun* November 1919 76-7. *The Irish Packet* 11.5.1907 162-3; 18.5.1907 195; 20.3.1909 799; 15.5.1909 207-8; 12.6.1909 342. *OB* 6/1929 708-9; 8/1924:448. *The Shamrock* 1892 vol. 29 555-6. *An Stoc* 9/1918 1; 1/1919 1. Kennedy 1853 139-49. Mag Ruaidhrí 1944 101-6.

References

1. Reference is made in the *Standard Dictionary of Folklore, Mythology and Legend* to the 'pointed or proverbial quality of the anecdote' and it is precisely this type of material which is excluded from the genre of historical lore. Funk & Wagnall 1950.
2. For example John Norcot D'Esterre, Thomas Goold.
3. IFC 930:326-7. Na Teinnimh Íochtarach is a townland in the parish of Dairbhre. In this book, original placenames are given in the language of the area at the time of collecting. As far as possible, the placenames have been standardised as regards spelling. As far as practicable, quotations in Irish and English, from both manuscript and published sources have been standardised as regards spelling, and dialect forms have been preserved.
4. The use of 'Liberator' in Irish carries the meaning of the English word. The 'Liberator' is mentioned in *Ulysses*: 'They passed under the hugecloaked Liberator's form', an image in keeping with the folklore of O'Connell. Joyce 1986 77.
5. Italics, within brackets in the manuscript quotations, indicate additional information from the collector or clarifications by the author.
6. IFC 1167:136-7.
7. IFC 1193:80-82; see O'Connell 1972 vol. 1 144.
8. See Chapter 1: 3-6.
9. IFC 1341:68.
10. IFC 1007:3-4. Collected by Tadhg Ó Murchú from Liam Ó Cathasaigh, aged seventy-five, a farmer.
11. Kerry IFC 733:353-4.
12. Luby 1874 75.
13. Daunt 1848 16.
14. IFC 733:354-5. Collected in 1941 by Tadhg Ó Murchú from Pádraig Ó Carúin, aged sixty-six, a shoemaker and a farmer, Ceanna Eich, An Dromaid, barony of Uíbh Ráthach.
15. *CS* 1.6.1901.

16. See for example Thompson 1958 vol. VI; Williams 1979.
17. IFC 612:93-94. Tír Ó mBaoill is a townland in the parish of Cill Fhionáin, barony of Uíbh Ráthach.
18. Luby 1874 10; O. MacDonagh 1988 21-26.
19. Collins 1969 184.
20. IFC 777:476. Collected in 1941 by Tadhg Ó Murchú from Micheál Ó hAilíosa, aged about sixty, a farmer, Na Túiríní, parish of Cill Chrócháin, barony of Dún Ciaráin Theas.
21. O'Connell 1972 vol. 1 23-33 *passim..*
22. O'Rahilly 1950 309-10.
23. IFC 1341:68-9. Collected in 1954 by Tadhg Ó Murchú from Mairéad Ní Cheallaigh, aged seventy-two, a farmer's wife, An Rinnín Bán, parish of Cathair Dónall, barony of Dún Ciaráin Theas. An Lóthar is a townland in the parish of Cill Chrócháin, barony of Dún Ciaráin Theas.
24. IFC 148:181-82; 667:131-3; 768: 66-70. Com an Chiste, a mountain recess, is between An Coireán and Cathair Dónall in the barony of Dún Ciaráin Theas.
25. IFC 1006:83-4.
26. IFC S599:406. Collected *c.* 1936 from local people and written by Pádraig Mac Cormaic, a teacher in the primary school of Stonehall, Newmarket-on-Fergus, county Clare.
27. In Irish folklore a tradition of *ius primae noctis* has been documented. This consists of the landlord's right to have sexual intercourse with a bride on the first night of her marriage. See doctoral thesis in the Department of Irish Folklore, S. MacPhilib *The Irish Landlord System in Folk Tradition: Impact and Image* 1990.
28. IFC 1168:156. Collected in 1949 by Seosamh Ó Dálaigh from Pádraig Ó Beaglaoich, aged eighty-seven, a weighmaster at Killorglin market, parish of Kilorglin, barony of Trughanacmy.
29. IFC Disc 103-108. Collected in 1948 by Tadhg Ó Murchú from Pádraig (Stounder) Ó Sé, aged about seventy and Pádraig (Dhónaill Óig) Ó Sé, aged about sixty-seven, Doire Ianach, parish of An Dromaid, barony of Uíbh Ráthach.
30. IFC Tape R. uí Ógáin 1979. Recorded from Jackie Shannon aged about eighty, Spanish Point, parish of Kilfarboy, barony of Ibrickan, county Clare.
31. See Chapter 4, (iv) O'Connell Meets his Match.
32. This anecdote was told to the author on several occasions and in many parts of Ireland, and was said to have occurred in Rathkeale, county Limerick, in some versions.
33. IFC S900:152-3. Collected in 1938 through the National School of Rathnure, parish of Killanne, barony of Bantry, county Wexford. This account probably refers to Arthur MacMurrough (1831-1889). He was a politician (Conservative) and landlord. He was born in Borris, county Carlow and was renowned for his justice both as a magistrate and landlord. He represented county Wexford (1866-68) and county Carlow (1868-80).
34. Thomas Goold was called to the Irish bar in 1791. He was MP in the last session of the Irish Parliament.
35. Limerick IFC 1194:556-7.
36. Gwynn 1947 164.
37. IFC 1186:148-9. Places mentioned in the accounts are townlands in the parish of An Dromaid, barony of Uíbh Ráthach.
38. For example IFC S527:178. Collected in 1937-1939 through the national school of Patrickswell, parish of Crecora, barony of Pubblebrien, county Limerick, by John Ryan, Patrickswell, county Limerick.

39. M. MacDonagh 1929 334. 'John Scanlan....was hanged at Limerick for the murder of Mary Hanly by drowning her in the river Shannon.'
40. The Whiteboys were an agrarian secret society founded in Tipperary in 1761, and spread throughout Munster. They were condemned by the Catholic church and the secular authorities for atrocities against landlords, including murder, assault, maiming of animals and other forms of intimidation. Their activities continued into the nineteenth century. Among their main grievances were landlord oppression, insecurity of land tenure, tithes, wages and unemployment.
41. Charlie Houlihan was an elderly neighbour of the informant from whom he heard a number of accounts.
42. IFC 1193:80-2. Collected in 1950 by Colm Ó Danachair from Richard Denihan, aged eighty-five, a farm labourer, Gortnagross, parish of Rathronan, barony of Shanid, county Limerick. A similar tale has been published in Germany regarding a ban on importing coffee. A guard came into a railway carriage and smelled coffee. A person who had a great deal of coffee said that he had none, but that another passenger in the carriage had a large quantity of it, and so the bigger amount was left intact. Griesbach and Schulz 1962 37.
43. Doneraile is a town in the barony of Fermoy, county Cork. In 1829 four men were convicted at Cork of conspiring to murder local landlords. John Doherty was the solicitor-general who led the prosecution. O'Connell broke down the prosecution's four chief witnesses, Whiteboys who had turned king's evidence.
44. IFC 1272:152-3. Collected in 1948 by Donncha Ó Súilleabháin, Lackaroe, parish of Kenmare, barony of Glanarought.
45. See for example IFC 658:363; 796:8-10; 797:201; S374:85.
46. *IO* 30.7.1938 3-4, 17.4.1954 16; *OB* 6.1929 712; Sheehan 1950 ed., 103-77.
47. Gwynn 1947 187-90.
48. For a detailed account of the background to the duel and the duel itself, see M. MacDonagh 1929 80-87; O. MacDonagh 1988 136-137.
49. The comment that D'Esterre was or had been in the Indies may come from the fact that he was at one time a Captain in the Royal Marines.
50. IFC 621:168-171; also published in *Béaloideas* 11 1941 117-25. Collected in 1936-1937 by Seán Ó Dubhda from Seán Ó Criomhthain, a farmer, aged sixty-one, parish of Cill Maolchéadair, barony of Corca Dhuibhne.
51. IFC 1639:238. Collected in 1962 by James G. Delaney from John Kenny, aged sixty-five, a farmer, Carrowmurragh, parish of Ballybay, barony of Athlone south.
52. Pistols became duelling weapons about the middle of the eighteenth century. Previously swords or rapiers were used. In the late eighteenth century swords were still resorted to as the skill of the swordsman could be an advantage. Members of the legal profession were very much to the fore as regards propensity for duelling. Barry 1981 37.
53. IFC 1803:152-3. Collected in 1972 by Michael J. Murphy from Frank 'Wings' Campbell, aged seventy-seven, townland and parish of Forkill, barony of Orior Upper, county Armagh.
54. IFC 996:547-9. Collected in 1947 by Tadhg Ó Murchú from Dónall Ó Cúrnáin, aged about fifty-eight, a farmer, Málainn, parish of An Dromaid, barony of Uíbh Ráthach.
55. IFC 17:235-7; 214:764-70; 834:144-7.
56. Major William Nugent MacNamara was a landowner and later an MP for county Clare (1830-1852). He was a noted duellist and acted as second for O'Connell in the duel with D'Esterre; see O.MacDonagh 1988 136.
57. IFC 936:479-481. Collected in 1944 by Seosamh Ó Dálaigh from Mait Grumail,

aged eighty-two, a fisherman, An Mhuiríoch, parish of Cill Maolchéadair, barony of Corca Dhuibhne.

58. Probably refers to the fact that Major MacNamara was a 'fire-eating petty country gentleman'; O. MacDonagh 1988 136. Duellists were sometimes called fire-eaters. There are some accounts in oral tradition about MacNamara which contain no reference to O'Connell; see for example IFC 834:144-8; 936:479-481.

59. IFC 404:480-481. Collected in 1937 by Seán Ó Flannagáin from Peadar Ó hAirt, aged sixty-six, a farmer, Inse Bhuí, parish of Cill Béacanta, barony of Cill Tártan, county Galway.

60. See Chapter 4, (v) O'Connell in London: the Political Career.

61. For related motifs in folklore see MI K 1741.2, and tale types no.AT 1053, 1890, 1894.

62. IFC S772:104-8. Collected in 1936-1938 through the national school of St. Brigid's Convent, Kildrought, barony of North Salt, county Kildare.

63. IFC S614:164. Collected in 1938 through the national school of Corofin (girls), parish of Kilnaboy, barony of Inchiquin, county Clare by Mary MacNamara, from John MacNamara, aged forty, Loughtagoona.

64. IFC 1803:117. Collected in 1972 by Michael J. Murphy from Michael Rooney, Blacklion, parish of Killinagh, barony of Tullyhaw, county Cavan.

65. For references to and accounts of the duel with D'Esterre see IFC 17:235; 146:419-422; 214:764-796; 621:168-171; 667:131; 796:10; 996:548-9; 1007:778-83; 1064:374; 1112:217-8; 1150:39-40; 1167:571-3; 1399:466; 1574:540; 1639:238; 1803:117, 152-3; 1960:184-5; S610:68; S613:213-4; S614:164; S772:104-8;

66. See Chapter 3, p. 103 for example.

67. IFC S444:262. Collected in 1936-1938 through the national school of Nohaval, parish of Ballymacelligott, barony of Trughanacmy, from Pat Lacey, aged seventy-five, a farmer, Coolnadead, parish of Ballymacelligott. This account may refer to O'Connell's brother, John, who was seriously wounded in a duel with Richard Francis Blennerhassett in a dispute over Catholic Emancipation. O'Connell 1972 vol. 1 318-319.

68. IFC S171:30. Collected in 1936-1938 through the national school of Cloonacool, parish of Achonry, barony of Leyney, county Sligo, by Philomena Bradley from her father.

69. IFC 628:17-18. Collected in 1939 by Seosamh Ó Dálaigh from Johnny Roche, aged seventy-eight, a farmer, Dually, parish of Newcastle, barony of Shanid, county Limerick.

70. There are similarities in the traits displayed by O'Connell the duellist and the nineteenth-century local champion in Tipperary, Mat the Thresher, the hero of *Knockagow* C.J. Kickham 1887 359.

71. Cú Chulainn is a mythical champion who dominates the Ulster cycle. For further information on Cú Chulainn, see Ó hÓgáin 1990 131-9.

72. For details on the Clare election in song tradition see Chapter 3, p. 86 and *passin*.

73. IFC 1193:181. Collected in 1950 by Colm Ó Danachair from Richard Denihan, aged eighty-five, a farm labourer, Gortnagross, parish of Rathronan, barony of Shanid, county Limerick.

74. IFC 716:5. Collected in 1940 by Tadhg Ó Murchú from Micheál Ó Conchúir, aged ninety-four, a blacksmith, Faha, Listry, parish of Kilbonane (?), barony of Magunihy. The word 'behind' in this account, is a literal translation of the Irish word '*thiar*' meaning 'in the west' and also 'behind.'

75. de Bhaldraithe 1970 39.

76. IFC S613:213. Collected in 1936-1938 through the national school of Tamhnach,

Ennis parish of Dysert, barony of Inchiquin, county Clare, by Elizbeth O'Halloran from her father, Frank, aged forty-three, Ballygriffey, parish of Dysert.

77. IFC S585:86. Collected in 1936-1938 through the national school of Clonlara, parish of Kiltanon, barony of Tulla Lower, county Clare. Spancelhill is about two miles east of Ennis.

78. A Protestant landowner in Cahiracon, Kildysart, county Clare whose daughter married O'Connell's son, Maurice.

79. IFC 1125:87. Collected about 1945 by Dónall Ó Súilleabháin, Fearann an Tí, Cathair Dónall, barony of Dún Ciaráin Theas. O'Gorman-Mahon called himself 'The' O'Gorman-Mahon. He was a young Catholic graduate and was one of the two people deputed at an excited Catholic Association meeting to invite Major MacNamara (see footnote 56) to stand against Fitzgerald in the Clare election of 1828. Gwynn 1947 173.

80. IFC 702:186. Collected in 1940 by Seosamh Ó Dálaigh from Éamon MacGearailt, aged sixty-eight, a farmer, Lios na Caolbhuí, parish of Clochán, barony of Corca Dhuibhne. Similar occurrences happened in Waterford in relation to the Beresfords where people were driven away because they voted for O'Connell's organisation.

81. The priests supported O'Connell and urged people to vote for him. 'The only polling centre was in Ennis so that some voters had to travel long distances to get there. A number of the priests marched with groups of forty-shilling freeholders from their parishes, making a public demonstration of their determination to support O'Connell; ' Murphy 1992 80. Those who held a lease for life of a house or land, in which the lessee had an interest worth forty shillings a year, known as a 'forty-shilling freehold', were granted the vote in 1793. Catholics still could not become members of Parliament because of the Oath of Supremacy. The more forty-shilling freeholders a landlord had on his land, the greater his influence in elections and it was noted by contemporaries that landlords were now encouraged to divide their estates into even smaller holdings for that reason. However, with Emancipation, the qualification for the franchise was raised from forty shillings to £10. One consequence was to reduce the national electorate from 230,000 to 14,000; Hickey and Doherty 1989 177.

82. M. MacDonagh 1929 166-7; see Murphy 1992 80-1.

83. IFC 1125:51. Collected c. 1945, by Dónall Ó Súilleabháin, Fearann an Tí, Cathair Dónall, barony of Dún Ciaráin Theas. Other accounts of this incident appear in IFC 148:264; 733:126; 823:566-9; S466:228. 'Droichead na Leamhna' probably refers to the bridge in Killorglin over the river Laune.

84. IFC 153:599. Collected in 1936 by Nioclás Breathnach from Liam Ó Mathúna, aged eighty-four, a stone mason, Cnocán, Baile na Míolach, parish of An Teampall Geal, barony of Déise, county Waterford.

85. IFC 914:228-30. Collected in 1943 by Tomás a Búrca from Mairéad Ní Lubhóg, aged sixty-five, a farmer's wife, Dúnuibhir, parish of Acaill, barony of Buiríos Umhail, county Mayo. O'Connell was undoubtedly more deferential in reality, and folklore underlines here the daring and defiant nature of his personality.
In fact, the queen ascended the throne in 1837, some eight years after Catholic Emancipation had been achieved.

86. de Bhaldraithe 1977 19.

87. IFC 1800:508. Collected in 1972 per Thomas Barron from Jimmy Brady, aged about seventy-two, Ann St., Balieborough, barony of Clankee, county Cavan.

88. IFC 1782:226-7. Collected in 1970 by Michael J. Murphy from Frank 'Wings' Campbell, aged seventy-six, townland and parish of Forkill, barony of Orior Upper, county Armagh.

89. IFC 1622:119-20. Collected in 1963 by Michael J. Murphy from Micky Carroll, Carrickastickan, parish of Forkill, barony of Orior Upper, county Armagh. Mullaghbawn is also in the parish of Forkill.

90. IFC 843:139-40. Collected 1941-1942 by Donncha Ó Súilleabháin, Lackaroe, parish of Kenmare, barony of Glanarought, from local people. See also two published versions, Chapbook n.d. and Kennedy 1853 147. The tithe war in Kilkenny is documented in M. O'Hanrahan 1990 497, where a similar occurrence is mentioned.

91. IFC 389:456-458. Collected in 1937 by Seán Ó Flannagáin from Séamus Ó Riagáin, aged about eighty-four, a farmer, Tóin Raithní, parish of An Bheitheach, barony of Cill Tártan, county Galway.

92. See also E. Drea c. 1924 for a detailed account of the Carrickshock incident. O'Connell's role in defence of the accused in dramatic, publicised cases probably contributed to the development of his image in folk legend as defender and saviour of the opressed.

93. IFC 152:231. Collected in 1936 by Nioclás Breathnach from Peats Cotters, aged seventy-three, Cill na bhFraochán, parish of Dún Garbhán, barony of Déise, county Waterford. Cnocán na mBuachaillí is a field in Heilvic, parish of An Rinn, so called because 'Buachaillí Bána' (Whiteboys) used to hide there, but it was also said that when servant boys had an hour to spare it was there they used go. *Logainmneacha ó Pharóiste na Rinne* 1975 21.

94. IFC S550:52. Collected 1935-1939 through the national school of Templemore, barony of Eliogarty, county Tipperary, by Michael Kennedy from James Peters, aged about eighty, Barnane, barony of Ikerrin, county Tipperary.

95. Lover 1834 67-106. See also Ó Héalaí 1972 45, where a poem in Irish, dated 1836, is quoted which describes the condemning to death and burial of the tithes.

96. For detailed descriptions of meetings see O. MacDonagh 1989 224-234.

97. IFC 634:283. Collected in 1939 by Seosamh Ó Cormacáin from Patch Ó Congbailligh, aged eighy-four, a farmer, Shanclogh, parish of Kilchreest, barony of Loughrea, co. Galway. Co. Clare may have come to be 'O'Connell's native county' in this account because of his close involvement with it.

98. IFC 1786:263-4. Collected in 1971 by Michael J. Murphy from Patrick Curnyn (Paddy Pat Jimmy), Black Lion, barony of Tullyhaw, county Cavan. This is probably an example of how O'Connell made political, diplomatic and pragmatic use of the Irish language as suited the occasion. The importance of the Catholic Association and Catholic Rent is emphasised in MacGrath 1985 256.

99. IFC 354:254-6. Collected in 1937 by Seán Ó Flannagáin from Séamus Ó Riagáin, aged eighty-three, a farmer, Tóin Raithní, parish of An Bheitheach, barony of Cill Tártan, county Galway.

100. IFC S582:241-2. Collected in 1938-1939 through the national school of Bishopswood, parish of Knockavilla, barony of Kilnamanagh Lower, county Tipperary by M. Mac Cárthaigh from Denis McCarthy, Kilmore, Golden, county Tipperary. There was a major Repeal meeting held in Cashel in 1843 which O'Connell attended. O. MacDonagh 1989 225.

101. IFC S942:217. Collected in 1938 through the national school of Annalitten, parish of Muckno, barony of Cremorne, co. Monaghan by Máire Ní Sheáin, Formil, Castlemahon, county Monaghan. The account mentions a field in the townland of Fincarn, north-west of Broomfield, parish of Donaghmoyne, barony of Farney, county Monaghan.

102. *IO* 11.12.1954 22-3.

103. M. MacDonagh 1929 280-1.
104. O. MacDonagh 1989 230.
105. IFC 797:68-70. Collected in 1941 by Tadhg Ó Murchú from Tadhg Ó Súilleabháin, aged about seventy-eight, a farmer, Inse Baoi, parish of An Dromaid, barony of Uíbh Ráthach.
106. IFC S685:217. Collected in 1938 through the national school of Whitecross, Julianstown, parish of Stamullen, barony of Upper Duleek, county Meath, by Peggy Landy, Julianstown, from Ms. A.J. Flynn, Shallon, Julianstown.
107. IFC 153:199.Collected in 1936 by Nioclás Breathnach from Máire Ní Loingsigh, aged sixty-nine, a housewife, Seanaphóna, parish of Cill Rosanta, barony of Déise, county Waterford.
108. IFC 700:118-9. Collected in 1940 by Seosamh Ó Dálaigh from 'Old' Foley, aged ninety-three, a small shopkeeper, Boherclogh, parish of St.John Baptist, barony of Middlethird, county Tipperary. A meeting was also held on 25 September 1845 in Knockane, Thurles, county Tipperary.
109. IFC 497:250. Collected in 1929 by Ms. M. Healy, Bray, county Wicklow, from her father. Per Tomás Ó Cléirigh, 54 Upper Blessington St., Dublin.
110. O. MacDonagh 1988 98.
111. IFC 659:290. Collected in 1939 by Seosamh Ó Dálaigh from Seán Ó Cearmada aged eighty-nine, a fisherman, Curraghatoosane, parish of Listowel, barony of Iraghticonnor.
112. Von Pückler-Muskau 1833 385.
113. Daunt 1845 276.
114. Lyne op. cit., 84.
115. Lecky 1871 240.
116. ibid. 227.
117. Lyne op. cit., 84.
118. IFC 537:498-9.
119. An Stoc 9/1919 1.
120. IFC 1592:211. Collected in 1961 by Seán Ó Cróinín from Jerry Buckley, aged seventy-eight, (formerly) a farm labourer, Cnoc Raithín, parish of Cluain Droichead, barony of Múscraí Thiar, county Cork. The belief that English was necessary to make one's way in the world was, and still is, widespread in Irish speaking districts, where mass emigration was and is the norm. Often, the Irish language is seen to be of little use in English speaking communities by many native Irish speakers.
121. M. MacDonagh 1929 342. See G. FitzGerald 1990 70-71 for an illustration of the rapid decline of the Irish language in the relevant counties, 1771-1871.
122. IFC 1167:453. Collected in 1949 by Tadhg Ó Murchú from Seán Ó Deá, aged eighty-three, a farmer, Cinn Aird Thiar, parish of An Phriaireacht, barony of Uíbh Ráthach.
123. It is the Irish language, for example, that saves O'Connell's life in London in the best known anecdote of all, when the Irish servant girl warns O'Connell in Irish that his drink or food have been poisoned; see Chapter 4. On another occasion, his life is again saved by the Irish language according to one oral account of his duel with D'Esterre; see p. 30.
124. IFC S234:70-1. Collected in 1938 through the national school of Páirc na bhFia, parish and barony of Boyle, county Roscommon by Thomas McGarry, Shegorey, parish and barony of Boyle, from his grandfather, Patsy McGarry. In the area of public works, in 1846, earnings of a shilling a week were common, with some workers earning higher sums. Daly 1986 80.

125. IFC 149:463-8. Collected in 1936 by Tadhg Ó Murchú from Pádraig Mac Gearailt aged seventy-seven, Cill an Ghoirtín, parish of An Dromaid, barony of Uíbh Ráthach. See also Ó Faoláin 1938 152.

126. For example IFC 149:1011; 823:257-60; 1167:450-3.

127. IFC 927:132. Collected in 1943 by Tadhg Ó Murchú from Micheál Ó Téacháin, aged seventy-six, a farmer and a huntsman, Spuncán, parish of An Dromaid, barony of Uíbh Ráthach.

128. IFC 1225:31-33. Collected in 1952 by Tadhg Ó Murchú from Seán (Mhártain) Ó Súilleabháin, aged about fifty-eight, a farmer, An tImleach Mór, parish of An Phriaireacht, barony of Uíbh Ráthach.

129. IFC 733:355. Collected in 1941 by Tadhg Ó Murchú from Pádraig Ó Carúin, aged sixty-six, a shoemaker and a farmer, Ceanna Eich, parish of An Dromaid, barony of Uíbh Ráthach.

130. IFC 996:585. Collected in 1947 by Tadhg Ó Murchú from Dónall Ó Cúrnáin, aged about fifty-eight, a farmer, Málainn, parish of An Dromaid, barony of Uíbh Ráthach.

131. Mulvey in O'Connell 1972 xxiii.

132. Kennedy 1853 147-8.

133. Chapbook n.d. 14-15.

134. IFC 1167:453. Collected in 1949 by Tadhg Ó Murchú from Seán Ó Deá, aged eighty-three, a farmer, Cinn Aird Thiar, parish of An Phriaireacht, barony of Uíbh Ráthach. The Butlers were landowners in the Waterville (An Coireán) area of Uíbh Ráthach.

135. IFC 148:174-5. Collected in 1935 by Tadhg Ó Murchú from Conchúr Ó Murchú, aged about sixty, a farmer and fisherman, Rinn Iarthach, parish of Cathair Dónall, barony of Uíbh Ráthach.

136. Luby 1874 533. In many parts of Uíbh Ráthach, hunting was extremely popular, as is the case to-day. Beagles, or 'hounds' as they are called locally, were used in the hunt, mostly for foxes in the Uíbh Ráthach area. The Butler family of Waterville hunted packs of Kerry Beagles – an internationally famous breed of hound from 1818 to 1868; see Lewis 1975 71.

137. Binns 1837 346.

138. IFC 27:179-80. Collected in 1915 by Tadhg Ó Murchú, from his father, Tadhg Ó Murchú, An Coireán, parish of An Dromaid, barony of Uíbh Ráthach.

139. IFC 1167:571-3. Collected in 1949 by Tadhg Ó Murchú from Seán Ó Deá, aged eighty-three, a farmer, Cinn Aird Thiar, parish of An Phriaireacht, barony of Uíbh Ráthach.

140. IFC 1312:58-60. Collected in 1952 by Tadhg Ó Murchú from Pádraig (Thaidhg Mhóir) Ó Súilleabháin, aged eighty-two, a farmer, Barra Ceanúigh, parish of An Dromaid, barony of Uíbh Ráthach.

141. IFC 796:12-15. Collected in 1941 by Donncha Ó Súilleabháin, Lackaroe, parish of Kenmare, barony of Glanarought.

142. IFC 929:327.Collected in 1944 by Tadhg Ó Murchú from Micheál Ó Braonáin, aged seventy-seven, a farmer, Ath-Ghort, parish of An Chill (An Phriaireacht), barony of Uíbh Ráthach.

143. IFC 149:40. Collected in 1935 by Tadhg Ó Murchú from Seán Ó Móráin (Seán Jur) aged seventy-eight, Bun an Bhaile, Cathair Dónall, barony of Dún Ciaráin Theas.

144. IFC 927:144. Collected in 1943 by Tadhg Ó Murchú from Micheál Ó Téacháin, aged seventy-six, a farmer and a huntsman, Spuncán, parish of An Dromaid, barony of Uíbh Ráthach.

145. IFC 1198:210-211. Collected in 1951 by Tadhg Ó Murchú from Micheál (Pheaidí Dhean) Ó Conaill, aged eighty-three, Meall na hÓn, parish of An Dromaid, barony of Uíbh Ráthach.

146. Nic Pháidín 1987 115 defines *tropán* as a type of edible seaweed, *Alaria esculenta* , *murlins* perhaps.

147. IFC 570:390. See also Madden 1848 124-7.

148. IFC 1167:453. Collected by Tadhg Ó Murchú from Seán Ó Deá, aged eighty-three, a farmer, Cinn Aird Thiar, parish of An Phriaireacht, barony of Uíbh Ráthach.

149. IFC 1396:238. Collected in 1955 by Tadhg Ó Murchú from Séamus Ó Clúmháin, aged eighty-five, a shoemaker and a farmer, Cathair na mBan, parish of An Fhaill Mhóir, barony of Uíbh Ráthach.

150. Von Pückler-Muskau 1833 384.

151. Chapbook: The Life and Times of Daniel O'Connell, Esq., Dublin. Published in 1847, a month after O'Connell's death.

152. Kohl 1844 145.

153. Edwards 1975 71.

154. Kohl 1844 147.

155. IFC 107:456. Collected in 1935 by Tomás Ó Ciardha from Tomás Ó Ríordáin (An Caist) aged seventy-nine, a farm labourer, a poacher and a *spailpín*, Araglin, parish of Kilworth, barony of Condons and Clongibbon, county Cork.

156. Kennedy 1853 148-9.

157. IFC 1787:198. Collected in 1971 by Michael J. Murphy from Michael Rooney, Blacklion, parish of Killinagh, barony of Tullyhaw, county Cavan.

158. IFC 964:367. Collected c. 1945 by Tadhg Ó Murchú from Pádraig (Óg Liath) Ó Súilleabháin, aged eighty-four, a farmer, Muing Uí Dhubhda, parish of An Phriaireacht, barony of Uíbh Ráthach.

159. IFC 927:357. Collected in 1943 by Tadhg Ó Murchú from Micheál Ó Téacháin, aged seventy-six, a farmer and a huntsman, Spuncán, parish of An Dromaid, barony of Uíbh Ráthach.

160. Gregory 1909 67.

161. Murphy 1992 85.

162. IFC Tape R. uí Ógáin 1979. Recorded from Jackie Shannon, aged about eighty, Spanish Point, parish of Kilfarboy, barony of Ibrickan, county Clare.

163. IFC 39:54-8. Contributed in 1931 by Seán MacMathúna, Luach, parish of Cill Eidhle, barony of Corcomrua, county Clare. Seán Mac Mathúna collected folklore in his home district for the Irish Folklore Institute in the early 1930s until 1935. He collected for the Irish Folklore Commission until 1947. The use of the word *'Saoirseoir'* in this account, instead of the usual word 'Liberator' may be due to the fact that the collector is making a general comment on the tradition, as he sees it.

164. IFC 1125:97. Collected c. 1945 by Dónall Ó Súilleabháin, Fearann an Tí, Cathair Dónall, barony of Dún Ciaráin Theas.

165. Gregory 1909 66.

166. Gregory 1926 74-5.

167. IFC 153:102-4. Collected in 1936 by Nioclás Breathnach from Pádraig Ó Loingsigh, aged sixty-five, a farmer, Seanaphóna, parish of Cill Rosanta, barony of Déise, county Waterford.

168. Lecky 1871 224.

169. IFC S275:217. Collected in 1936-1938 through the national school of Urhin (boys), parish of Kilcatherine, barony of Bear, county Cork by Seán Ó Ceallaigh from his mother, Caherkeen, parish of Kilcatherine.

170. Breen 1993 76-7.
171. IFC 995:60. Collected in 1945 by Tadhg Ó Murchú from Micheál Ó Conaill, aged seventy-seven, a farmer, Imleach Mór, parish of An Phriaireacht, barony of Uíbh Ráthach, county Kerry. The person in question may be a certain Samuel Murray Hickson, a local enemy of the O'Connells and 'of the Catholic clergy,' whom O'Connell especially requested should not be appointed sheriff of county Kerry. O. MacDonagh 1989 130. O'Connell's correspondence contains a letter to Lord Mulgrave imploring him not to appoint Hickson sherriff in Kerry and 'not to inflict on this county so decided an enemy of the Reform party and of the Catholic clergy and of the present ministry' as Hickson. M. O'Connell vol. v 347.
172. IFC S314:45. Collected in 1938 through the national school of Bandon, parish of Kilbrogan and Ballymodan, barony of Carberry East, county Cork, by Gregory Burke, Bridge St., Bandon from Cornelius Donoghue, aged sixty-five, Shannon Street, Bandon.
173. Chapbook n.d. 15.
174. IFC 308:204. Collected in 1936 by Tadhg Ó Murchú from Pádraig (An Chasúir) Ó Súilleabháin, aged seventy-two, a farmer, Muing Uí Dhubhda, parish of An Phriaireacht, barony of Uíbh Ráthach.
175. IFC 532:438-441. Collected in 1938 by Tadhg Ó Murchú from Dónall Ó Cúrnáin, aged about fifty, a farmer, Málainn, parish of An Dromaid, barony of Uíbh Ráthach. The name 'Staughton' mentioned in the account refers probably to Thomas Stoughton, who died in 1862, Ballyhorgan, Listowel, county Kerry and who was high sheriff for that county in 1839. Another ms. account says that the cattle were tied up in Cill Mhic Ciarainn for fear O'Connell would raise the rent if he saw that they were well fed (Kerry IFC 1007:553).
176. IFC 667:105-6. Collected in 1941(?) by Tadhg Ó Murchú from his father, An Coireán, parish of An Dromaid, barony of Uíbh Ráthach.
177. uí Ógáin, 'Máire Ní Dhuibh' *Sinsear* 1981 101-7.
178. IFC Tape Collected in 1968 by Bo Almqvist from Micheál Ó Gaoithín (An File), aged seventy, Baile Bhiocáire, parish of Dún Chaoin, barony of Corca Dhuibhne. The Kearneys were hanged in 1816 for conspiracy to murder John Kinlan, a steward of Ponsonby Shaw of Friarstown, parish of Tallaght, barony of Uppercross, county Dublin. O'Connell was asked for his advice on having the Kearneys arrested under the then new 'Conspiracy to Murder Act'. O'Connell said the men could thus be arrested and, according to Malachi Horan: 'the country round here never forgot and never forgave Dan O'Connell for that – the only bad thing he ever did.' Little 1976 ed., 38-9.

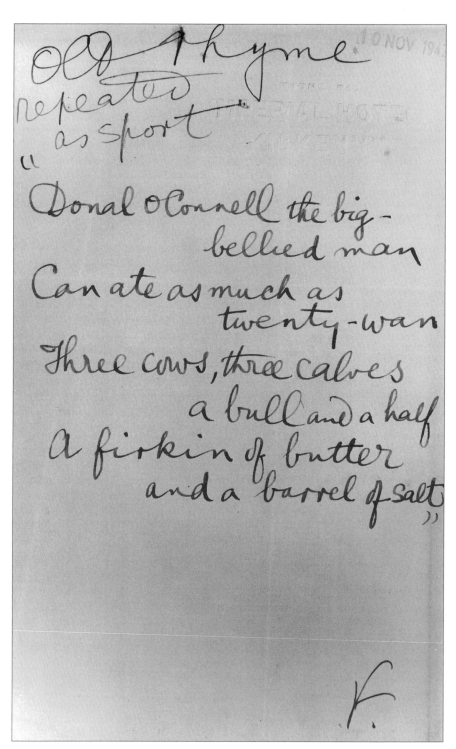

Old Rhyme
repeated
"as sport"

"Donal O'Connell the big-
belled man
Can ate as much as
twenty-wan
Three cows, three calves
a bull and a half
A firkin of butter
and a barrel of salt"

F.

Rhyme collected by Fionán MacColuim in 1942 probably from county Kilkenny (IFC Box 16).

Carhen, the reputed birthplace of Daniel O'Connell (Ríonach uí Ógáin 1993).

Hearth, Cill an Ghoirtín, An Dromaid, Uíbh Ráthach (Caoimhín Ó Danachair 1947).

Bóthar an Chunsailéara (The Counsellor's Road), Fearann Iarthach, Cill Chrócháin, Dún Ciaráin Theas (Ríonach uí Ógáin 1993).

"Reading 'The Nation'" by Henry MacManus (National Gallery of Ireland).

THE O'CONNELL CENTENARY RECORD.

O'Connell's duel with D'Esterre (The O'Connell Centenary Record).

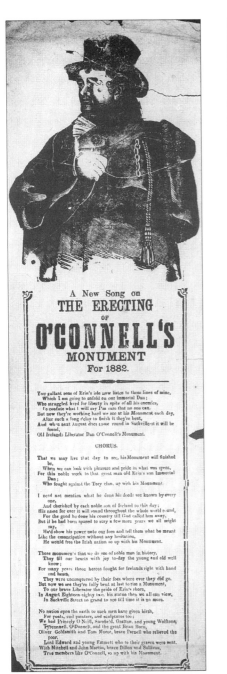

'A New Song on The Erecting of O'Connell's Monument For 1882'. A broadsheet ballad, from The Folk Music Section, The Department of Irish Folklore.

'A New Song on The Procession For the Unveiling of O'Connell, and Opening of the Exhibition'. A broadsheet ballad, from The Folk Music Section, The Department of Irish Folklore.

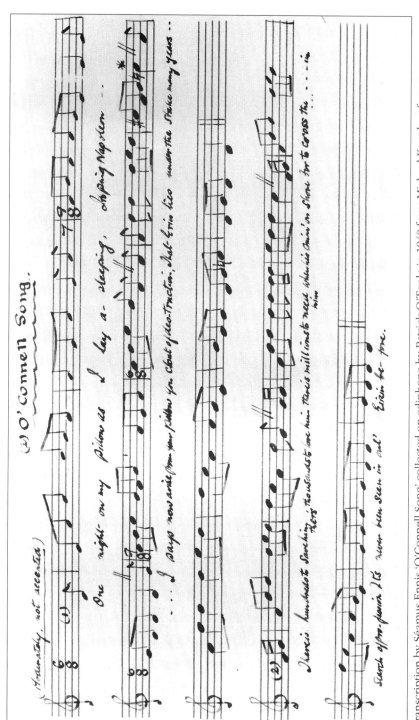

Transcription by Séamus Ennis 'O'Connell Song' collected on ediphone by Patrick O'Toole in 1940 from Michael Keogh, a farmer, Aughavannagh, Aughrim, county Wicklow, from the Irish Folklore Collection.

Dónall Binn Ó Conaill

Music transcription of a verse of the song 'Dónall Binn Ó Conaill'. Collected by Ciarán MacMathúna from Cáit Ní Ailíosa, An Dromaid, Uíbh Ráthach. *Music from Clare and Kerry* RTÉ MC 102, Dublin, 1987.

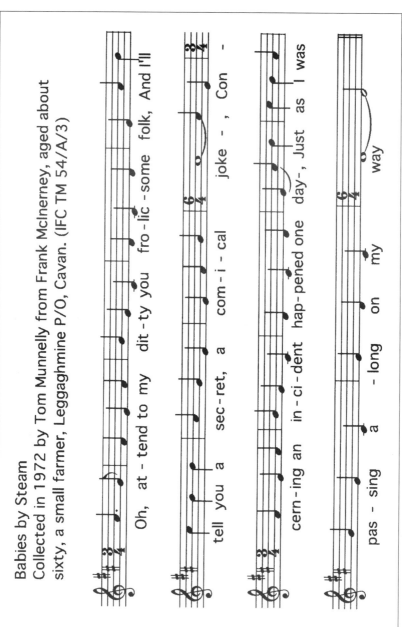

Babies by Steam
Collected in 1972 by Tom Munnelly from Frank McInerney, aged about sixty, a small farmer, Leggaghmine P/O, Cavan. (IFC TM 54/A/3)

Music transcription of a verse of the song 'Babies by Steam' collected in 1972 by Tom Munnelly from Frank McInerney, aged about sixty, a small farmer, Leggaghmine P/O Cavan.

coimisiún béaloideasa éireann

conntae _Garraíǧe_ .... barúntaċt _Corca Duibne._

paróiste _Mártan._ ....

Ainm an Sgríobnóra ... _Seósam Ó Dálaiġ._

Seolaḋ an Sgríobnóra ... _baile Biocáirṡe . Dún Caom._
Daingean Uí Cúsa.

Do reníobar ríor an... _7. eairdd_ ...... ro ar an... _edifin. Feabra 1947._

ó béal-airnír... _Muiris Ó Conċubair . (Maurice Seán Connor)_

Aor... _77_ ...gairm-deaċa... _feameóra beag_ ...aċá in a ċoṁnuí

i mbaile feaspainn... _baile Bovrín._

aġur a raoluioḋ aġur a tóġaḋ i... _Nán dur idútra ._

Do cuala ré (f) an _7. eairra_ _ó na Seandaoṁe ar an baile._

.... _blian ó ṁn ó._

.................(Aor an uair ṡin.............) a ḃí in a ċoṁnuí an uair ṡin

[_Tobac ó ṡál mo coṡe dtí barra mo ċluaiṡe._]

[_Tosai fráin 187._]

Bí bean boic ruḋó ann 7 ḃr ṡ ṡual muiġín
beag . ǧcóir an donaiġ áir cúnaṁ beag éiġmr dí
féin 7 ḃí buaċaull éiġie ṡual i n-fear aice 7
ní raiḃ ṡé ró- ċruṁn dá faḋ 7 ṁai ṡé lei a
muiġín ar an donaċ 7 má ċuaiḋ do ḋi mrg d'
muiġín ar neaṁ-ní ǧan do ní buaiġ di ruḋ ai
deaṡa ré mar túrpé 'n-a ḃréuġán beag do
leanḃ . Nuair a ṫóṁ ṡé 'baile, "Zá ǧo mavi

Tadhg Ó Murchú, An Coireán, with ediphone and cylinders (Photographer: Séamus Ó Duilearga, around 1938).

Probable site of the duel between Daniel O'Connell and John Norcot D'Esterre, Oughterard, County Kildare (Ríonach uí Ógáin, 1995). My thanks to Mr Martin Kelly, Celbridge for helping me locate the site.

Detail of drum of O'Connell monument, O'Connell St., Dublin (courtesy of Paula Murphy). Monument by John Henry Foley, erected in 1882. The detail shows Éire holding the Catholic Emancipation Act in one hand and pointing up to O'Connell with the other hand.

Chapter 3

The song tradition

The term 'song' is applied here to poetry and verse which was sung to an air or, in some cases, may have been recited. The song material was composed, for the most part, by contemporaries of O'Connell, and it is of particular importance because it reflects O'Connell as seen by those who were immediately and directly influenced by him. An indication of the date of composition is provided in many of the songs themselves, and they sometimes contain a commentary on political events at the time. Many of the songs were probably composed for a particular occasion – for example, in celebration of O'Connell's 1828 election victory or of Emancipation.

Songs expressing the hope of some future great achievement by O'Connell were more than likely composed during his lifetime when he was at the height of his popularity. Although most of the song material is anonymous, the authors of some of the songs are known, and this information helps to date the composition.[1]

The literary, manuscript tradition in Irish existed alongside the oral tradition during O'Connell's lifetime and for some time afterwards. This literary tradition contains a number of songs or poems about O'Connell, but the literary tradition seems not to have become a part of the oral tradition to any significant extent. The language of the songs in the literary tradition is a good deal more formal and structured than that found in most of the songs in the oral tradition. Nevertheless, song-makers with a taste for heightened language were found in many areas. However, as is to be expected, the sentiments in both traditions are identical in that O'Connell is praised throughout, sometimes to excess.

Typical of the kind of dramatic, exaggerated, praise lavished on O'Connell is:

Is é Dónall binn Ó Conaill caoin
An planda fíor den Ghaelfhuil,
Gur le feabhas a phinn is meabhair a chinn
Do scól se síos an craos-shliocht;[2]

(Gentle, kind Daniel O'Connell, Is the true scion of the Gaels, With his excellent writing and intelligence, He has flayed the greedy breed.)

And typical of praise, in English, is:

> He still commands a million hands,
> What monarch can exceed him?
> His throne is part of each Irish heart,
> Except the worthless traitor.[3]

Such compositions are the result of the composer working within a communal consensus. That these compositions represent contemporary feeling is evidenced by their entry into oral tradition, for compositions by an individual were not absorbed into the traditional repertoire unless the verses struck a chord in the collective consciousness. Topicality could be the reason a song would be made, but only conformity within the tradition would ensure its survival.

Though some topical squibs from the pages of contemporary magazines, such as *Punch,* are quoted among the following examples, these would not generally be ascribed to the pen of a songwriter. All songwriters are poets, but not all poets are songwriters. A poem may be sung or spoken, yet performance is not its invariable *raison d'être* as is the work of the songwriter. The latter always writes for the extended audience of the home, street or concert hall, while the former can be happy to target the solitary eye or mind. In the case of Irish songs about O'Connell, most of them would seem to have been the result of spontaneous individual inspiration. This would also be true for the greater bulk of songs in English relating to O'Connell. However, it must be remembered, particularly in the case of English language songs, that it was common practice among broadsheet printers to commission songs and ballads relating to the sensational stories of the day, in the manner in which the tabloid newspapers of our time seek stories of this kind to increase their sales. These songs were printed on ballad sheets and sold throughout Ireland at fairs, markets and other public gatherings. Some ballad sheets had verses in Irish, mostly in macaronic or bilingual form, where English orthography was used.[4] Ballad sheets were very common in Ireland until the first quarter of this century, and were 'printed but dispensable accessories' to the oral tradition.[5]

With regard to the songs which were created during O'Connell's lifetime, their function has changed since the time of their composition. When O'Connell was alive, the songs served to emphasise and popularise certain of his character traits. They served to immortalise him, or to commemorate a particular occasion or event. Some of the songs of praise served to promote his popular image and took the form of propaganda material for his political beliefs. The songs of Tomás Rua Ó Súilleabháin, for example, expressed support for O'Connell and for his policies.

Some of the poets did not conceal their own political beliefs. Songs of praise were composed expressing at the same time firm political beliefs which were certainly not in keeping with O'Connell's stated political ideals.

People were exhorted to prepare to fight, and the hope was expressed in many songs that foreign troops would travel by sea to free Ireland. Local politics and political feeling were reflected:

> The Irish speakers, through the verses of their poets saw politics in an immediate local and largely, sectarian context. In this they were fully in tune with the dominant themes of O'Connellite political action – civil rights, power and patronage.[6]

After O'Connell's death, although some of the obvious currency and immediate relevance of the songs disappeared, the posthumous idea of O'Connell still had a relevance idealistically and politically, like Napoleon and Parnell who also survived in song.

It is easy to identify and isolate the song material about O'Connell. Verse is clearly a genre not only in appearance and form but also in approach and, to a lesser extent, in content. The songs are more formal in style and in approach than the narrative material. There are other distinctive features in the folk-song material about O'Connell. It is highly dramatic and often quite stereotyped as the composition of an individual. While a song is being sung, the singer does not have the opportunity or the freedom which a storyteller has to adapt the material to suit personal opinions or beliefs. Tales and anecdotes which were popular before O'Connell's time were 'O'Connellised' because they mirrored the character in oral tradition. This 'O'Connellisation' rarely happened in the case of the songs, presumably because song material in general is not flexible and because the songs about O'Connell were, for the most part, composed specifically about him. Exceptionally, 'The Little Fife And Drum', often called 'The Female Drummer', usually concludes with a toast to the King or Queen, but in one version, the final verse is:

> Here's a health to O'Connell; another unto you,
> And to every Irish girl that wears the colours true.
> If O'Connell wants for more men before the War is o'er,
> I'll put on me hat and feather and fight for her (*sic*) once more.[7]

The songs reflect the oral-formulaic technique prevalent in international ballad and song tradition where composers and singers rely on certain formulae, phrase groups and images in creation and performance.[8] There is little variation in versions of songs, whereas legends and anecdotes tend to vary a good deal from version to version. Apart from the possible variation of an air, the only changes to the songs are minor textual changes: the verses may be sung in a different order, or some singers may include or exclude verses of a particular version of a song.

Although he is denigrated or mocked in a small number of songs, the vast majority of them are positive towards O'Connell. The oral narrative tradition also contains a very small proportion of negative accounts about O'Connell. In general, the historical lore is closer to recorded historical fact than is the song material; however, the songs tend to establish or confirm history, and concentrate on the duel with D'Esterre, the Clare election and Emancipation – focal points which are also emphasised in the historical lore. Many references are made in the song material to O'Connell's great deeds, but emphasis is placed for the greater part on O'Connell's heroic image, and the poet uses imagination and established and accepted poetic formulae to that effect. This results in a linguistic style which is very different from the style of the narrative material. Stereotypical phrases are used, along with metaphors and similes which are certainly removed from historical reality. Jan Vansina's observation about panegyric poems suggests their relationship to historicity:

> A poem of praise is certainly not composed for the purpose of recording history. Poetry of this kind is composed either during the lifetime of the person concerned, or immediately after his death. It is a category of poetry which is strictly bound by rules of the poetic art, and its outstanding characteristic is a liberal use of stereotype phrases indicating the exceptional virtues of the person who inspired the poem . . .It is obligatory to use a large number of stereotype phrases in this category of poems. So the poems serve as a source of information about the social ideals prevalent at the time when they were composed.[9]

Although folk-song as a genre does not demand compliance to rules of this kind as set out by Vansina, it would appear that certain stock devices are used in folk-songs of praise. O'Connell is separated from the image portrayed in history and another character is created who is above the ordinary, but the character is created within the context of historical events. The songs contain motifs which were current at the time, and do not deviate from this style, particularly as regards those in Irish. It was perhaps for this reason that Seán Ó Faoláin believed that the folk mind was not helpful from a historical point of view, and curses the 'Gaelic songsters' who were composing songs, and who made use of classical mythology to create visions and images expressing hopes for Ireland's freedom.[10] Ó Faoláin lamented that the composers did not tell of their own personal troubles.

Some of the O'Connell songs reflect the patronage of poets by wealthy Gaelic families like the O'Connells. This tradition of the poet composing verse in praise of the leader of a 'Big House' has been well documented.[11] As a genre, laments were traditionally made as a gesture of respect following the death of an important person. O'Connell does not appear to have been lamented in this specific way in song, but is lamented rather as a leader of the Irish people.

In Irish and in English, the picture of O'Connell presented by the poets is consistent. The difference is one of language and style. The language of the Irish songs is more austere and formal than their English counterparts. In the songs in Irish, the metaphors and alliteration of adjectives reflect the influence of the literary tradition in Irish, as illustrated in the following verse which is part of a composition dated 1836 by Pádraig Phiarais Cúndúin:

> *Taoiseach tréitheach, tréadach, treasúil,*
> *Líofa, laochta, i maodhmaibh machaire,*
> *Le claimhe, le gaithibh, le gaisce, le gártha,*
> *Ar cuthach chum catha is a tháinte treon.*[12]

(A talented, pastoral, rebellious leader, Polished, heroic, in battles on the plains, With swords, with spears, with armour, with shouts, Eager for battle with his hosts of strong men.)

By comparison, the English verses are less literary, less alliterative and less subtle in style.

> But all were daunted by the tyrant's frown,
> Till one arose before men and angels ,
> His mind as mighty as the ocean's wave,
> It was noble Dan repealed her dangers.[13]

While style may differ, the songs in both languages reflect the same attitudes and themes about O'Connell. In song tradition, O'Connell emerges as a hero. Clearly, then, the bulk of the song material is in praise of O'Connell, frequently to an exaggerated degree which denies credibility – an exaggeration common in song tradition in general. It is unlikely that the songs have been altered to any great extent with the passage of time. Many of the songs were very popular in the living tradition and may never have been published during O'Connell's lifetime. Other songs were published either during O'Connell's lifetime or since his death, and have enjoyed immense popularity. O'Connell's popularity is also reflected in tune titles. Few dance tunes in Irish traditional music have historical associations but a number of tunes incorporate mention of O'Connell's name and political activities.[14] Tunes which can be heard at traditional music sessions to-day include 'O'Connell's Farewell to Dublin' which is a set dance[15] and also a reel,[16]

'O'Connell in Clare' and 'O'Connell's Trip to Parliament'[17] which are both reels. A jig, which is said to be very popular around Woodford in county Galway is known as 'O'Connell's Jig on Top of Mount Everest'.[18]

One poet who wrote poems in praise of O'Connell was Tomás Rua Ó Súilleabháin, as mentioned above. Tomás was born near Doire Fhionáin in county Kerry, around 1785, and was a contemporary of O'Connell. The poet's first language was Irish and he held it in great regard. In his compositions he:

> fearlessly expressed his belief in a Gaelic-speaking nation liberated and rejuvenated by the great Iveragh leader.[19]

Tomás used to work as a postman for the O'Connell family in Doire Fhionáin. They were very generous towards him, and he wrote several songs in praise of O'Connell. Apparently, O'Connell was instrumental in sending Tomás to Dublin for his education; the college is not named, however, and Tomás wasn't happy there. He became ill, and after three years, he came home and settled down in Doire Fhionáin.[20] Two other Munster poets who were contemporaries of Daniel O'Connell, and who included him in their compositions, were Máire Bhuí Ní Laoire and Pádraig Phiarais Cúndúin. Máire was born in 1774 in Múscraí Thiar, county Cork, where she lived until she married a horse-dealer from Skibbereen, Séamus de Búrca, in 1792, and they lived very comfortably. She could not read or write but her love for Ireland and Irish culture emerges in her poetry. The exact date of her death is not known, but she is thought to have died about 1846.[21] Pádraig Phiarais Cúndúin, 1777-1856, was from the Baile Mhac Códa district, barony of Uíbh Mac Coille, east Cork. He emigrated to America at the age of fifty-seven and never returned to Ireland.[22]

To-day, folk-song tradition about Daniel O'Connell is neither strong nor widespread. In this regard, it is important to emphasise that the songs were sung to an air, and so formed part of a very popular pastime.[23] The songs about O'Connell which survive in contemporary singing tradition have the function of recall and of pleasure. Most songs about O'Connell are part of a tradition which has almost disappeared over the last sixty years or so, however. Although O'Connell's political goals and beliefs may now be irrelevant to rural and urban population alike, there is still a local and a historical relevance in the songs about O'Connell in Uíbh Ráthach, where the songs of Tomás Rua are still sung. The song 'Babies by Steam' has also survived in singing tradition. Perhaps the reason for its popularity is the fact that it is a lighthearted, comical song, and is relevant more for its amusing content than for any expression of support, or lack of support, for O'Connell's policies.

It is impossible to say which song types were the most popular during O'Connell's own lifetime, but if the songs collected in the 1930s can provide a yardstick, the vision poetry appears to have attained great popularity, as it was still widespread at that time. Its survival may be due to the expression of hope contained in this kind of song, or it may be due to the inherent aesthetic quality of the vision songs, which were regarded by many singers as a particularly beautiful song form. This is seen in the number of vision songs and poems about O'Connell, in Irish and in English, collected by the earlier song collectors like A.M. Freeman in the Cork *Gaeltacht* in 1914,[24] right up to the current collecting work of Tom Munnelly with the Folk Music Section of the Department of Irish Folklore. We are very fortunate that such a sizeable collection has been gathered over the years, as it offers an insight into O'Connell's importance and popularity in oral tradition. Material which was published during O'Connell's lifetime is contained in songbooks and broadsheets, and these also constitute an invaluable source which provides scores of songs about O'Connell.

The Clare Election
In the Irish and English songs alike, the Clare election is heralded as an important victory for O'Connell. This is consistent with the historical picture. The Galway poet, Antoine Raiftearaí, was so impressed that he wrote a song entitled *'Bua Uí Chonaill'* (O'Connell's Victory). He says in the song that O'Connell has gained the upper hand over the enemy, and he holds great hope for the future:

> *Gunnaí is lámhach is tinte cnámha,*
> *Beidh againn amárach, is tá sé in am,*
> *Ó fuair Ó Conaill bua ar an namhaid.*
> *Aibeoidh bláth is beidh meas ar chrann.*
> *I gContae an Chláir, tá uasal is ardfhlaith*
> *Ag craitheadh lámh is ag déanamh grinn,*
> *Ach bog faoin gcárt go n-ólam sláinte*
> *Na bhfear ó Árainn go hInis Uí Chuinn.*[25]

(We will have guns and firing and bonfires Tomorrow, and it is time, Since O'Connell conquered the enemy. Flowers will ripen and trees will bear fruit. In county Clare there are noblemen and high princes, Shaking hands and having fun, But go for the quart, so that we can drink the health, Of the men from Aran to Ennis.)

Before the election took place, hopes were high that O'Connell would be elected a Member of Parliament for Clare:

> Our worthy brave O'Connell, says the *Shan Van Vogh,*
> To have you in we're longing, says the *Shan Van Vogh*
> Sure you we well have tried,
> And you're always at our side,
> And you never tuk a bribe, says the *Shan Van Vogh*[26]

Tomás Rua Ó Súilleabháin also understood the significance of the Clare election, and interpreted it in song as a very hopeful sign for the future. He said: *'Sin mádh agat ó Chlár'* (That is a trump card you have from Clare).[27] In another song, entitled 'The Three Women's Conversation', a Clare woman tells with pride of O'Connell's connections with her native county and she extols his virtues:

> Miss Clare replied and she deeply sighed,
> Saying: 'He was from Kerry, I don't deny,
> But he did cross over the Shannon water
> And the men of Clare made their first reply.
> Likewise the women they fought courageous
> And in twenty-eight they gave him the chair,
> For he being a Catholic and son to Gráinne
> In the House of Commons they thought him queer.'[28]

There are references in song and in documented history to the bonefires which were lit to celebrate O'Connell's victory, and one song entitled 'As I Roved Through the Town' tells us that in county Kildare bells were ringing on this joyous occasion:

> O'Connell was in from Clare and all the bells were ringing.[29]

The hope was expressed that O'Connell would meet with great success when he took his place in Parliament. Here the poet speaks to O'Connell, wishes him well, and places great confidence in him:

> Farewell dearest Danyel Hibernia's confidential frind,
> Our blessin go along wid you unto the british shore,
> Nobility and Gintery to Parliamint will you attind,
> Likewise be accompanied with The blessings of the Poor.
> Our foes within the house as mute as any mouse,
> To see the Agitator Triumphantly arrange, . . .[30]

The Tithes

Other aspects of O'Connell's political career are mentioned in a few songs. We are told, for example that the tithes have been removed:

> *Tá na deachmhaithe buaite orthu agus ministrí ag fáil a gcirt.*[31]

(The tithes have been defeated and justice being meted to ministers.)

Events like the tithe-war did occur, but conventional time reckoning is telescoped here, as happens in a great deal of folklore.

The events of Carrickshock[32] are remembered in a song entitled 'The Battle of Carrickshock,' about which it was said:

> In support of the application for the postponement (*of the trial*) the
> crown submitted a copy of a seditious ballad called 'The Battle of

Carrickshock', which had been found in Kilkenny in the posession of
John Redmond (from near Enniscorthy in county Wexford), who had
been found singing it to a crowd opposite the Tholsel.

The ballad singer was arrested.[33] 'The Battle of Carrickshock' contains
the following verses:

> Then the Peelers did fall without murmur or bawl,
> Then their guns and their bayonets were shattered,
> How sad was their vase, when their eyes nose and face,
> When their lives and firelocks were battered......

> Three cheers now I crave for O'Connell the brave,
> For our Patriot King who is your guardian,
> So boys, don't be afraid, for the Tithes are all paid,
> Before Patrick's day in the morning.[34]

James Kean, the man who was said to have briefed the Carrickshock
men and who was a hedge school master, had to leave Ireland. 'Kean's
Farewell to Ireland' expresses his sorrow and also his faith in O'Connell:

> Farewell I say for ever to my native Irish home.
> I do implore my friends at home to agitate and petition,
> The tithes arears ne'er to pay and let them support their own,
> Obey the law and shun discord and let them seize your property,
> Depend on brave O'Connell to meet them for their doings,
> He will bring home to Erin's shore your parliament depend on it.[35]

Although it was a popular belief that all throughout his legal and
political career attempts were frequently made to bribe him, in the
spirit of the hero in folkore, O'Connell could not be bought:

> For eighteen years in Parliament Old Erin he did represent,
> For all the gold was in the mint, as you may now suppose,
> They could not buy that hero brave who now lies in his silent grave.[36]

Emancipation

As regards Emancipation and the Clare election, O'Connell's triumphs
are again reflected in folk-song. The achievement for which O'Connell
is most frequently remembered in song is Catholic Emancipation. The
songs and verse are more than likely a reflection of the aspirations of
O'Connell's supporters and an attempt by them to rally support for
him. For example, the song called 'Election *na Gaillimhe*' (The Galway
Election), appears to have been composed by the poet Raiftearaí to
urge Irish people to support O'Connell's policies and to vote for Sir
John Bourke in the 1833 election:

> *Tá* Jumpers *go deacrach is gach baile faoi bhuaireamh*
> *Nár dhéana Dia trua do lucht bíoblaí bréag.*

Ba bheag acu sinne a bheith tuirseach faoin ualach,
Ó scríobh Mártan Liútar i mbliain a seacht déag.
Imríodh an cluiche is bhí an muileata in uachtar,
Ó Conaill is a chúnamh a chuir ceann ar an scéal;
Ach cuiridh sa gcathaoir dúinn Sior Seán de Búrca
Is labhróidh sé cliúthúil i bhfabhar na nGael.[37]

(The Jumpers are difficult and every town is anguished, May God show no mercy to those of the false bibles, They cared little us to be weary and burdened, Since Martin Luther wrote in the year seventeen. The game was played and the diamond was on top, O'Connell with his assistance finished the matter; But put Sir John Bourke in the seat for us, And he will speak honourably in favour of the Gaels.)

The struggles involved in attaining Emancipation are also mentioned:

Who wrought Emancipation
Against the tyrants, made a stand.[38]

In song, Emancipation is regarded as a major event in historical terms, and is mentioned in the same breath as the battles of Waterloo and Fontenoy in one composition, where a beautiful woman asks the poet about famous Irishmen:

Tell me if you're able who gained the day at Waterloo?
Who gained the day at Fontenoy, wasn't it a son of Erin too?
With ruin and desolation, our fertile country overran,
Who gained the Emancipation, wasn't it an Irishman?

Speak of the Emancipation, the man that took the noble part,
Was held in veneration in every honest Irish heart.[39]

O'Connell, after his death, is remembered as the patriot who achieved Emancipation:

In memory to the friends that are gone, boys gone,
Here's the memory of O'Connell that is gone.

In the year '29, I remember well the time,
The immortal O'Connell like a dawn,
The emancipation gained, and the clergy freed from chains,
But old Ireland's liberator he is gone, boys gone
May his soul rest in heaven – he is gone.[40]

Emancipation has freed Irish Catholics from the tyranny and injustices which they suffered. 'Brave Dan O'Connell' has gained Emancipation for them 'From base submission and servile chains.'[41] In one song, O'Connell himself speaks and, in listing his achievements, he refers to Emancipation as one of his greatest triumphs:

Oh, remember the year so glorious he cried,
When I Emancipated poor Erin.[42]

In a small number of songs, England is thanked for granting Emancipation. On one occasion, King George IV is applauded because he 'rectified our cause', and mention is made of Ireland's union with England, where O'Connell is said to have conquered the enemy:

Green Erin it will flourish
And friendship will abound,
In praises of King George the Fourth,
Who will all bigots keep down.
There is worthy Peel and noble Steel
That's worthy of applause,
Long live these noble gentlemen,
That rectified our cause.

Now we are emancipated,
And Catholics are free,
Returning thanks to heaven,
We gained our liberty.
The shamrock wore in highest state,
In union with the rose.[43]

Elsewhere, the same poet accepts this union and is happy to see it continue, although he hopes that Ireland will be a nation some day and not a 'petty province':

Let the whiskey go round whilst our shamrock we'll drown,
Toast to Dan and the friends of old Granua;
Though the Tories combine to blast our design,
We'll stand loyal to the crown of Britannia.
A resident parliament is Erin's demand,
But no separation from Great Britain's land.[44]

Usually however, England is seen as Ireland's enemy, and the gratitude expressed to O'Connell is due in no small measure to the belief that he would rout the villains who are treating the Catholic population unfairly. The Catholics in Ireland are looking for equality with the English and all of this will happen when O'Connell achieves Emancipation:[45]

Emancipation *a theacht faoi shéala,*
Cead ag Gaeil bheith chomh hard le Gaill.[46]

(Emancipation will come in a sealed charter, The Gael will have equal standing with the English.)

A woman from county Kerry talks to her friends and praises O'Connell for his achievement of Emancipation:

And in twenty-nine he did blindfold them
And Emancipation to us did bring.[47]

In Ballintra, county Donegal, there was a riot when people celebrating Emancipation were attacked by the local Orange yeomanry, and this gave rise to a contemporary composition, 'Easter Monday 1829', which the informant said 'was circulated orally':

> On Easter Monday morning in the year twenty-nine
> When the Catholics of Drumhome together did combine;
> They went into the chapel on that eventful day,
> And Father Kelly warned them to shun the threatened fray.
>
> He said unto these young men: 'There's bound to be a fight,
> I beg of you, my children, to stay at home tonight.'
> These bold undaunted young men did not fear being cut down,
> And boldly did adventure, and went into the town.
>
> And when they reached Hugh Walls's they gave a loud huzza,
> Saying: 'Granua's sons without their guns will conquer Ballintra',
> Just inside one half hour the Orangemen flocked round,
> With guns and swords and bayonets to drive them from the ground.[48]

Repeal is mentioned optimistically in many of the songs in anticipation that O'Connell would achieve it, just as he has achieved Emancipation. This is expressed in the songs in both English and Irish. A Kerry poet called Sylvester O'Shea lived at Brackhill Cross, which is quite close to the Castlemaine Railway Station. He flourished at the time O'Connell was making his great effort to repeal the Union and was, it is said, a personal friend of the Liberator. He praised O'Connell and said that he would win Repeal despite opposition:

> And now in spite of fate, he'll win
> Repeal for Paddy's Land.[49]

A version of the song *'Síle Ní Ghadhra'* also expresses the conviction that Repeal will be realised.[50] In one of his compositions, Tomás Rua praises O'Connell and confirms his faith and trust that Repeal will come to pass:

> *Is é Dónall Ó Conaill an t-óigfhear cumais*
> *Planda ceart de Ghaelaibh,*
> *Mar is é do chuir an scéal ar bun,*
> *Agus tabharfaidh sé an Repéil leis.[51]*
>
> (Daniel O'Connell is young and able, The rightful scion of the Gaels, Because he has taken charge And he will gain Repeal.)

Agitation for Repeal should be sustained and O'Connell ensured of support if he is to be successful, according to one song.[52] O'Connell is closely associated with Repeal and is exhorted to continue his good work in the song 'When Erin's Green Banner's Unfurled'.[53] The songs expressing optimism about Repeal cannot for the most part be dated with total accuracy, but they were probably composed a short time after Emancipation, when spirits and hopes were high. Support for the Repeal movement is illustrated in the song 'As A Gallant Tar, Pat Braved The Stormy Ocean':

> In our gallant ship Repeal,
> Pat instantly set sail
> Now she scuds before the gale,. .
> At our helm Dan appears,
> With his Irish Volunteers,
> Hailed by a nation's cheers,
> Singing yo, heave ho![54]

Monster Meetings and Repeal

O'Connell's popularity also emerged in songs relating to the monster meetings he held all over Ireland. His power and appeal as orator and leader were reflected in the song 'On The 15th Day Of August In The Year Of '43', describing the meeting held on the hill of Tara in county Meath that year:

> A burst of acclamation rose that rent the voltic skies,
> When the mighty Liberator approached unto the Hill,
> Each heart in exultation and with joy each bosom filled,
> To see that moving structure going to mount his royal throne,
> With vistery smiling on his brow, to Irish hearts was shown.[55]

Another song recalled the same meeting:

> On the Royal Hill of Tara,
> Irish thousands did prevail
> In union's bands
> To join their hands
> With Dan for the Repeal.[56]

These meetings were considered in folk-song as the stepping stones to Repeal. People were exhorted to continue with the agitation and to support O'Connell:

> By the speech from the throne we're denied of our own,
> We're branded for seeking separation,
> We're told to our face we disturb public peace,
> By Reform and Repeal Agitation.
> The Cabinet shook, they have schemed a long time
> The friends of the people they fain would divide.
> Dan and Sheils stand blunt to pull down Tory power,
> Helped on by the champion brave Feargus O'Connor,

To his noble ancestors his conduct and honour
Down with tithes, let Repeal decorate Erin's banner,
On Patrick's Day in the morning.
But religious contentions it never should do,
Paddy's sons to divide, were we loyal and true,
We'd complete the grand object that Dan had in view.[57]

Some of the measured dramatic appeal of the Repeal meetings is indicated in the piece 'The Repealers' Trumpet Call', in which isolated drums and trumpets take part, as well as a band.[58] Apart from an occasional reference, no importance is attached in song to O'Connell's appointment as Lord Mayor of Dublin in 1841. At the height of the Repeal movement, O'Connell was arrested and sentenced to a year's imprisonment because of the Repeal agitation. His term of imprisonment served to increase his popularity and added to his role as folk hero. The image of the incarcerated hero appealed to the folk mind and did not reflect the excellent treatment which O'Connell actually received during his term of imprisonment. There was great celebration on O'Connell's release from prison, and hopes were high once again that he would take charge of the Repeal movement. Michael Moran (1794-1846), or 'Zozimus', as he was called, was a well-known Dublin street-singer. He composed a song about O'Connell's time in prison and about his release. T.B.C. refers to T.B.C. Smith, Chief Counsel for the Crown:

Ye boys of Old Hibernia, attend unto me,
Whilst I give you the story of young T.B.C.;
Unlike his father, who stood by Father Maguire,
He prosecuted O'Connell, with spite like hell's fire.[59]

He also composed a different song on the same subject which is yet another parody of the *'Seanbhean Bhocht'* (Poor Old Woman):[60]

Oh! Dan did you get out?
Says the T.B.C.,
Or did you get up the spout?
Said the T.B.C.,
There were locks both great and small,
Did you dare to break them all,
Or did you scale the prison wall?
Said the T.B.C.[61]

Regardless of how O'Connell left the prison, his freedom placed him at the helm of the Repeal movement again:

You put up your proclamation
Says the Dan Van Vought,
To agitate Paddy's nation,
Says the Dan Van Vought;

You put me in a cage,
The people to enrage:
But I am once more on the stage,
Says the Dan Van Vought.[62]

The welcoming home of O'Connell from Parliament is a recurring theme. He probably exploited this ritual, and the result is partly folk tradition and partly a pragmatic exercise by O'Connell in public relations. He was welcomed on his arrival to address a meeting in one song, 'Thrice Welcome Brave O'Connell'.[63] Tomás Rua welcomed him with 'Fáilte is Fiche is Tuilleadh ina nDeoidh'[64] (A Welcome And Twenty And More Besides). A relative of O'Connell, Seán Ó Conaill, a poet, welcomed him on another occasion in a poem entitled 'Chum Dónaill Óig Flaithiúil Fíoruasail Uí Chonaill Ó Dhoire Fhionáin' (To Young, Generous, Truly Noble Daniel O'Connell from Doire Fhionáin):

Fáilte is dá fhichid tar mhíltibh laoch
Do bhláth na seabhac nach íseal méin.[65]

(Welcome and two score more, above thousands of heroes To the prince of hawks of noble bearing.)

In this poem, O'Connell is identified with the Catholic Church and its martyrs:

Atá báidh led' sheasamh ag an fháidh Dónall
Tháinig slán ó uaill na leon;
Na hapstail de shíor ar tí thú shaoradh,
Is an dá fháidh cheannasach, Eoin is Seán;
Gach ardfhlaith eile d'fhuiling an bás
Le grá do Chríost, a nguí id' pháirt;
Sin saoire ceapaithe
Ag Rí na bhflaitheas
Do naimhde leagadh gan chairde!

Thy stand is dear to the prophet Daniel,
Who came safe from the fury of the lions;
The apostles ever ready to free thee,
And the two mighty prophets, the two Johns;
Every high chief else who suffered death
Through love of Christ, praying on thy behalf,
Behold a holiday
Appointed by the King of heaven,
To overthrow thy foes without quarter.[66]

Local Pride

A large proportion of the folklore and song about O'Connell was collected in his native county Kerry and particularly in that part of the Uíbh Ráthach barony where O'Connell's presence was most in evidence. The songs illustrate a strong sense of local pride in the Liberator. Tomás Rua makes frequent reference to O'Connell's birthplace and to his home in Doire Fhionáin. He describes in one song how there will be great celebration when O'Connell returns home to Kerry from the Parliament. He will be welcomed along the entire journey but a special welcome awaits him in Uíbh Ráthach:

> Beidh tinte cnámh in Uíbh Ráthach romhat
> I mbaile cois trá mar a mbeidh báire is ceol,
> Ar Dhoire Fhionáin aerach mar a dtriallfaidh slógh
> Ar bhruach an Chalaidh sin, Carraig Uí Chróin.[67]

(There will be bonefires before you in Uíbh Ráthach, In the town near the strand where there will be games and music, In pleasant Doire Fhionáin where the crowds will come, To the edge of that harbour, Carraig Uí Chróin.)

O'Connell was a hero and his home district claimed some of his fame. The barony as a district, or identified area, appears a great deal in the songs in Irish and is used by the poets to express a strong cultural identity. The acceptance and use of the 'county' as a unit of local pride appears to be more recent.[68] This may indicate a later date of composition for the song entitled 'Misses Limerick, Kerry and Clare,' where pride in the county comes to the fore. Here, in a conversation between three women, one from Limerick, one from Kerry and one from Clare, historical events are discussed to discover which of the three counties is the most noteworthy. The bone of contention between the women is the strength of O'Connell's connection with each county. The Kerry woman claims that O'Connell was born in her county:

> Oh, Miss Kerry blushed then and spoke quite hasty:
> 'Is this my son that you're speaking on?
> Was he not from Kerry, the great Liberator,
> From that noble place they call Derrynane?
> Where he got birth and good education
> Until he was fit to go before the king.'

The woman from Clare says that it was people from her county who elected O'Connell, and adds that there is a statue of O'Connell in Ennis, the largest town in Clare.[69] But the Limerick woman claimed that the city of Limerick also boasts a statue of O'Connell:

> But the man you're meaning, the great Liberator
> We have his statue in Limerick town.[70]

The following is from a song by a poet, Dan Murphy, who lived at Geata an Uisce, half a mile east of Kilgarvan. The collector said Dan lived 'a generation ago':

Farewell to county Kerry, for it's there I do reside,
And from it that all Irishmen first raised their heads with pride.
It reared brave Dan, who led the van; through British laws he tore;
Oh, *grá mo chroí*, I'd love to see Old Ireland free once more.[71]

A different song, entitled '*Grá mo chroí*, I'd like to see old Ireland free once more' contains the following verse:

Its true we had brave Irishmen,
As everyone must own,
The Liberator, O'Connell, true,
Lord Edward and Wolfe Tone.[72]

Doire Fhionáin assumes great importance in song as the birthplace of O'Connell:

Or can you equal Derrynane men
The birthplace of immortal Dan.[73]

O'Connell as Leader

O'Connell inspired great hope in the poets of the day that he would achieve Repeal. This hope was often closely connected with the poet's desire to see Ireland free and England vanquished. Seán Ó Braonáin placed great hope in O'Connell as Liberator. Ó Braonáin was born between 1780 and 1790 in Baile Mhic Aindriú, parish of Cill Mhaoile (Kilmoyly) in county Kerry. He spent some time as a travelling teacher in east Kerry and some of his songs were popular in oral tradition. In a song he composed for O'Connell, he says O'Connell will destroy the unjust laws which have been imposed on Ireland by the English, and Irish people will be free. It is said that the poet stood apart and sang this song for O'Connell one day near Ardfert, where a crowd had gathered to meet the Liberator:

Suífidh Conaill géille gan mhaill i bhFéis na Sagsanach.
Brisfear ris is réabfar na dlíthe claona cheapadar.
Glaofar rí d'fhuil Ghaeil arís
I réimheas chríochaibh Banba
Agus réx do shíolrach Shéamais chríonna
A' rialú ríocht na Breataine.
Is beidh clanna Gaeil gan spleáchas re hálmhach na n-allachon.[74]

(The authoritative O'Connell will sit without delay in the English Parliament, He will break down and destroy the unjust laws they invented, And a king descendant of wisdom, Séamas, Ruling the kingdom of Britain, A king of Gaelic blood will be invoked again, In authority over Banba's land, And Gaels will be independent of the foreign brood.)

While O'Connell is away from Ireland looking after the interests of the Irish Catholics, the people of Munster are told to take heart.

A mhná na Mumhan éistigí liom,
Tá an cás ar chúl gan súil le filleadh,
Táim gan fonn do mo chrá is do mo bhrú,
Líontar chugainn piont is gloine.
Tá Wellington sínte agus Peel go tréith
Tá tinteacha cnámh ar gach ardchnoc sléibhe,
Beidh Éire arís ag síor ól tae,
Is é rá na naomh go bhfuil an téarma caite,
Éigse na Mumhan éistigí liom
Tá an báire chugainn ar bharr na toinne,
Tá petition *scríofa ag teacht ón Róimh*
Sin rianta ar chúrsa Dhónaill Uí Chonaill.[75]

(Oh, women of Munster listen to me, The case has receded without hope of return, I am without inclination, being tormented and crushed, Let glass and pint be filled out for us. Wellington is dead and Peel is weak, There are bonefires on top of every mountain, Ireland will once again drink tea constantly, The saints say that the term is ended. Sages of Munster listen to me, The contest is coming to us, on the crest of the waves, A petition has been written and is coming from Rome, These are the traces of Daniel O'Connell's work.)

Tomás Rua sees O'Connell's election in Clare as a great sign of hope. He foresees that the English will be overcome and the people of Ireland will regain their status and independence:

San bhfómhar so chughainn is ea dóighfeam púirf[76]
Le glór an Údair Naofa,
Beidh Seoirse dubhach gan choróin, gan chlú,
Gan sólás búird, gan féasta.
Ólfam lionn is beoir le fonn,
Is comhsheinfeam tiúin den Ghaedhilg.
Beidh bróga dubha ar gach óigfhear chlúmhail,
Cé gur ró-fhada dhúinn dhá n-éagmais.[77]

(Next autumn we will burn the harbours, Supported by the voice of the holy writer, King George will be sorrowful without crown or honour, Without good things to eat, without a feast. We'll drink ale and beer with good humour And we'll join in an Irish tune. Each young man of honour will wear black shoes, Although we have been too long without them.)

In another composition by Tomás Rua, he says that O'Connell will lift this great sorrow from Ireland, that he will take his rightful place and that he will conquer the English enemy.[78]

The Clare election was a triumph, not only for O'Connell, but for the Irish people as a whole, and it was the direct result of the support they had given to O'Connell. One song counsels Irish people to be united and steadfast in their pursuit of freedom. If they follow this advice, according to an unnamed poet, O'Connell will be able to gain freedom:

Má bhíonn sibh buan-tseasmhach is seasamh le chéile
Beidh agaibh Éire aris faoina réim,
Tiocfaidh Ó Conaill agus claimhte Chionn tSáile,
Is ní scarfaidh go brách go mbí saoirseacht againn féin.[79]

(If you are steadfast and stand together, You will control Ireland again under his power, O'Connell will come with the swords of Kinsale, And will never part until we have our freedom.)

In 'Thrice Welcome Brave O'Connell,' we are told about the stance O'Connell took against the enemy, and that he will succeed in achieving Repeal despite the unfavourable circumstances.[80]

The *Aisling*

The *aisling* or vision poetry is a form frequently used to portray O'Connell. This particular *genre* is well documented in Gaelic literary tradition.[81] The main theme in the earlier literary *aisling* is the restoration myth where Ireland will be restored to her former glory. However, it is used here to speak of O'Connell and his promises. The nineteenth century *aisling* is an example of the use of a traditional *genre* for contemporary persons and events, and O'Connell takes his place alongside Bonnie Prince Charlie and Napoleon Bonaparte as the prophesied Saviour of Ireland. The *genre* is used to portray Ireland's condition and O'Connell's power to improve it. The vision poetry, which includes songs about O'Connell, uses the formula where the poet is asleep beside a river or is walking along in a rural setting, lost in thought; he hears a girl's voice as she appears before him. She is inevitably the most beautiful woman he has ever seen. He asks her what her name is – is she Helen or Venus or someone else? She replies that she is Ireland, and says that O'Connell will perform great deeds for Ireland, or that he has already done so. The vision poems in English and in Irish are similar in many respects. Established formulae are used to start and end the poems. Nature is introduced at the beginning as a setting for the dream or vision. At the end of the composition, the person who has been asleep wakes up and/or the beautiful lady disappears. There appears to be a tendency in the material in Irish to describe Ireland's wretched situation, whereas the material in English tends to list and describe O'Connell's achievements. Vision poetry and song are examples of a literary phenomenon which existed during

O'Connell's time and was adapted in folk-song tradition to portray O'Connell as folk hero.

In one example of a vision poem, the beautiful girl says that matters can be left in O'Connell's capable hands. He will free the Catholics from oppression by a foreign church and Irish people will no longer be obliged to pay high taxes. Revenge will be achieved for the harm brought to Ireland by English rule.[82]

In another vision song, the poet complains that the woman has suffered injustice for a long time, and that there is no-one to plead her case for her. The woman refers to O'Connell and to the great achievements he has already attained:

'A rí-bhean shultmhar, bhéasach atá faoi chumha gan chéile,
Ag tál go búch ar bhéaraibh gan féasta ná só,
Is fada dhúinn gan faoiseamh ná ceart i gcúirt dá phlé dhúinn
Fá ghallasmacht tax is claonchur gan daonnacht inár gcóir.'
D'fhreagair sí: 'Ná daor mé, ó tharla chugat i m'aonar,
Gan gharda groí do m'éileamh i gcéin mar ba chóir.
Gurb é Dónall múinte léannta do thóg an ceo seo d'Éirinn,
Do réidh gach snaidhm is géarcheist do Ghaelaibh go deo.'[83]

(Oh, royal, pleasant, well-mannered woman, who is lonely, without a companion, Who is gently suckling the bears without feast or comfort, We have been a long time without relief or our rights being discussed in court, Under foreign rule, tax and deceit without humanity is our lot.' She replied: 'Do not condemn me since I have come to you alone, Without a great guard demanding me in foreign parts as should happen, Daniel who is civil and learned, lifted this gloom from Ireland, He has solved every problem and difficulty for the Irish forever.')

There are seven verses in this *aisling*, each eight lines in length. Characteristically, O'Connell is mentioned in one or two lines only in the vision poems. In 'Maidin Álainn Gréine' (One Beautiful Sunny Morning), the poet asks the lady who she is. She replies that she is Ireland. The poet is hoping for relief from rent and from taxes. She tells him not to worry, that O'Connell will save the day.

Ná ligse feasta de do dhánta, ní do ghá duit bheith buartha,
Gí fada dhúinn ag trácht air tá an cairde linn buailte,
Is cúileann mhaiseach mná mé do tháinig le tuairisc,
Go bhfuil Ó Conaill ó Uíbh Ráthach is an lá aige siúd buaite.[84]

(Do not give up your verses, you need not worry, Although we have spoken of it for a long time, respite is here, I am a beautiful fair maiden, who has come to report, That O'Connell from Uíbh Ráthach has won the day.)

'Síle Ní Ghadhra' is a widely sung song found in several variants. In the versions of the song in English, 'Síle' is not always a beautiful woman, but in versions of the song in Irish she appears inevitably to play this part in the tradition of vision poetry. In one of the versions in Irish, a stately woman visits the poet as he lies in bed. In reply to his question about her identity, she says that she is Síle, or Ireland, whose churches have been destroyed by the English. They have hunted her priests and Mass is now read in ditches and by hedges. She has waited patiently until it is time for Daniel O'Connell, her son, to take command. Many of the songs treated here were gathered by collectors unskilled in musical notation and before the days of mechanical recording. Consequently, not many airs survived. Fortunately, this is one of the few songs, of which the air was written down. It is said to have been composed in the period 1820 to 1830 by Fr James Veale, PP of Kill and Newtown in county Waterford.[85]

In 1843 or 1844, Diarmuid Ó Mathúna from west Cork composed a vision poem 'Spéirbhean ag Trácht ar Reipéil' (A Beautiful Woman Talks about Repeal). She is Banba or Ireland, and each verse is followed by the chorus saying that Repeal will be attained and that Daniel O'Connell has Ireland's interest at heart.[86]

Tomás Rua Ó Súilleabháin composed a song in which he asks a beautiful woman, Úna, if O'Connell is preparing for battle as the Catholics are getting ready for war.[87] The imagery here illustrates the overlap of religion and politics as found in the traditional *aisling*. Here, Catholics are ready to support O'Connell and to follow his lead:

> Tá an Catoilic trúp ina bhfoirinn i dtiúin,
> Ag feitheamh ar chuntas éigin,
> Ó íochtar na cúige go huachtar Mumhan,
> Chum preabadh go humhal le chéile.

> (The Catholic troop have assembled in form, Waiting for some report, From the north of the province to the south of Munster, Dutifully, to spring together.)

Many of the same motifs and themes which are found in the vision poetry in Irish are also found in the vision poetry in English which extol Daniel O'Connell. In 'Madam Pray Have Patience', also known as 'Who Gained The Fame For Erin's Isle?', a girl in a green cloak comes to visit the poet who is sitting beside a river. She asks him who attained fame and renown for Ireland:

> Was it not a son of Erin too
> When ruin and desolation
> Our fertile country over-ran,
> Who gained Emancipation?
> Oh, say it was an Irishman.

The poet agrees and names other famous Irishmen like Grattan, Burke and Davis. Then he continues:

> Speak of Emancipation,
> The man who took that noble part
> Is held in veneration
> By every honest Irish heart.
> The brightest star that Erin raised
> Or from her fertile valleys sprang,
> He was called the Kerry eagle
> Or otherwise immortal Dan.[88]

A beautiful woman appears to the poet in a dream in 'Erin's Green Shore' and, when asked who she is, she tells the poet:

> I am a daughter of Daniel O'Connell
> And from England I lately came over
> I have come to awaken my brother
> That slumbers on Erin's Green Shore.[89]

One vision poem tells how a son of O'Connell is asleep and O'Connell speaks to him, describing his own great achievements and instructing the son to remember these historic events:

> One night as old Granua reclined to rest,
> And dame Nature in her soft couch slumbered,
> The moonbeams from heaven shown (shone) forth from the west,
> And the sky had bright stars without number.
> I laid myself down for to rest without fear,
> When an angelic vision to me did appear,
> And thus spoke heroic saying: 'Son lend an ear,
> To your father's advice, brave O'Connell.'[90]

There are seven further verses which recount O'Connell's bravery, his feats and his fame. The song concludes by expressing the hope that O'Connell's dream will be realised. 'Granua' enters the vision poem and she speaks to O'Connell and his son and tells them of her difficulties.[91]

Mummers' Plays

O'Connell is treated in a fairly lighthearted way when he is introduced into songs in mummers' plays.[92] In a play from county Wexford, we are told that there was a conversation between Wellington, Saint Patrick and O'Connell. Saint Patrick describes how the English have destroyed the true faith in Ireland and have downtrodden the Catholics. Wellington says to Patrick that King George is a friend of Patrick's:

> Saint Patrick answers:
> 'To hold my tongue proud Wellington, great pain lies in my breast,
> For Dan O'Connell is the man that knows my temper best.'[93]

O'Connell then speaks and says that he himself is from a brave and famous family. In another version of this mummers' play, O'Connell is given one of the leading roles and he gives a detailed description of himself and of his achievements:

> Here I am the great O'Connell, from a knightly race I came,
> My royal habitation lies in ancient Derrynane.
> I am the man they call brave Dan, your friend on each occasion,
> And the first MP that ever sat of the Catholic persuasion.
> For my country's wrongs I deeply felt, they filled me with vexation,
> And our cruel foes for to oppose I formed an Association.
> It is certain sure, the Church most pure, should persecution bear,
> But the Penal yoke was lately broke by electing me in Clare;
> To Parliament straight away I went, in hopes to free our nation,
> Wellington and Peel, I made them yield and grant Emancipation.
> That stillborn pact, the Stanley Act, supplants the Church's ambition.
> Those vexatious tithes I have laid aside, by a total abolition.
> The Catholic rent I underwent, to break and wreck in twain;
> Those tyrants' chains from off our plains, that bound us with disdain.
> For thirty years, it plain appears our rights they us denied,
> They may regret they have borne away their Union as their pride.
> And from that time in chains we were bound, for justice we appealed.[94]

O'Connell then goes on to say that he intends to liberate Ireland. The inclusion of O'Connell as a central character in the mummers' play places him firmly with others of world renown, such as Wellington, Napoleon, Julius Caesar and Nelson.

Laments

The lament is fairly well represented in the song tradition about Daniel O'Connell. In general, O'Connell is portrayed as a hero in folk tradition, insofar as he performs great deeds and has supernatural powers, but in death he does not conform to the image of the hero who meets a glorious end which ensures his immortality. Although O'Connell dies of natural causes, as a dispirited old man, he is still lamented as someone of great importance. In 'Erin's King' (a lament for Daniel O'Connell), people could hardly believe that Ireland's 'King' was gone:

> When I heard the news, I was much confused.
> I myself excused when I thus did say:
> 'Is O'Connell gone, old Erin's son,
> The brightest lord that e'er stood the day?'[95]

Around the turn of the century, Seán Mhicil Ruiséal, a Kerryman and son of the informant, Micheál Ruiséal, from Corca Dhuibhne, emigrated to America where he spent twelve years, having travelled as far as Alaska. He came home and settled in Corca Dhuibhne. While he was in Montana, he composed a poem decrying emigration, and said that if O'Connell were still alive, his own situation would not be so pitiful. He also says that he misses O'Connell a great deal:

> *Dá mairfeadh Ó Conaill arís i gceannas,*
> *Ba shocair suairc an lá dhúinn,*
> *Mar do dhéanfadh sé íde ar gach* Tory *galair,*
> *Is bheadh* Home Rule *againn gan spleáchas,*
> *Ach mo thrua insan uaigh é, mar tá sé meata,*
> *Is an Pairnéalach sínte lámh leis,*
> *Is gan againn ina ndéidh ach dríodar danair,*
> *Nach fiú iad do chur go Parlaimint.*[96]

(If O'Connell were alive again and in charge, It would be an easy, happy day for us. Because he would deal with every worthless Tory, And we would have Home Rule without subservience. But sadly, he is in the grave because he has perished, With Parnell lying beside him. And all we have left are foreign dregs, That are not worth sending to Parliament.)

Seán Mhicil Ruiséal called the poem '*An Spailpín Fánach*' (The Wandering *Spailpín* (Spalpeen), and said that two other emigrants from Baile Uachtarach, Dún Urlann, Corca Dhuibhne, helped him to compose it.

Several versions of 'The Youth That Belongs To Milltown' have been collected. This song, and the song 'Babies by Steam', are the most popular O'Connell songs to have survived into recent oral tradition. A Kerryman who is in England recalls O'Connell's achievements for Ireland. He is told that O'Connell spent some time in England:

> We had a man here from your country and that was the year '29
> Whether right or wrong be the question, he'd try for to jink out the game.
> Daniel O'Connell they called him, from Derrynane in Kerry he came.
> Says the youth: 'He was born in Carhen, the old ruins are yet to be seen,
> Just at the brink of the waters convenient to Cahirsiveen.
> He once was the king of our country, with the harp and the shamrock as crown,
> May God rest his soul, he is in heaven,' says the youth that belongs to Milltown.[97]

In 'There's A Dark Cloud Hanging O'er Us For Many A Weary Year', Ireland's heroes are listed, among whom Charles Stewart Parnell is given the most important position and others mentioned are Michael

Dwyer, Robert Emmet, Lord Edward FitzGerald, Wolfe Tone and then O' Connell:

> He was a hero of Ireland, he played a hero's part,
> His body lies in Ireland, to Rome he willed his heart,
> He loved the Irish people, and adored his native sireland,
> Though dead to day I'm proud to say, that he was a hero of Ireland.[98]

Irish people hope that other brave men will fight Ireland's cause, just as O'Connell has done in 'You Sons Of Erin's Isle, Who Bear Sorrow With A Smile'.[99]

Emotional, sentimental language is used in many of the songs, and in the laments in particular.[100] Some of the metaphors emphasise the image of O'Connell as an essential part of Ireland's past and of the Irish people, and he can never be forgotten:

> The harp it is hung in Tara's Hall sad and lonely,
> By him it was strung, ah, by him and him only,
> And worthy we were such a man to be given,
> For angels declare they have crowned him in heaven.[101]

A few songs were composed about monuments built in commemoration of O'Connell. One song of this kind was composed when the foundation stone of one particular monument in Dublin was laid, and the importance of the public occasion is stressed:

> On Monday last the Trades did walk in order to repair,
> Unto the Liberator's house, south side of Merrion Square,
> Then by the Corporation with all the clergy at their head,
> Through the streets of this great city in procession they were led.[102]

This song is entitled 'A New Song On The Procession To Lay The Foundation Stone Of The O'Connell Monument' in one broadside and it is said to have been 'written by a patriotic Protestant', who is proud of the composition. In 'Rejoice Ye Irish Patriots', we are told that the monument in question will perpetuate O'Connell's memory when the statue is erected for all to see and his special status is emphasised:

> When he'll be elevated on his pillar tall and high,
> A ring of heavenly angels will salute him from the sky
> With golden harps resounding they will chant his deathless praise,
> For the good he done his country up from his cradle days.[103]

The song 'We Meet To-day As Brothers Should' was composed for the fifteenth of August 1882, the day on which one such monument was to be unveiled:

> In unity and peace,
> To honour Dan, the brave, the good,
> Defender of our race

O'Connell's name and glorious fame
Forever shall live on
And we to-day a tribute pay,
To Erin's chieftain gone.[104]

In 'Prepare You Gallant Irishmen', we are told how well O'Connell has merited this commemorative monument.[105] An Orange songmaker was unhappy with the Sackville St. monument however, and composed the following 'On the Intended O'Connell Monument, in Lower Sackville Sreet, Dublin':

Yet now, in servile ranks behold them;
To honour him who thus cajoled them,
They march in state through Dublin town;
And in a most seditious manner,
Emblazon on their broad green banner,
A yellow harp without a crown.

In Sackville Street, midst Bishops solemn,
They've laid the stone for Daniel's column.[106]

Song and Narrative

There are a few O'Connell songs which occur also as tales or anecdotes. This is not unusual as the same stories are often found in parallel prose and song traditions.[107] In the O'Connell prose/song tradition, O'Connell emerges the victor either on a verbal, legal or practical level. 'The Tinkers' Hotel' is one such example, where O'Connell takes 'action' against an English hotel owner who has insulted him or another Irishman. The other Irishman is frequently said to be a tinker. O'Connell gives money to some tinkers to buy expensive clothes and stay in a hotel in England. They make noise with hammers and tins. The other residents leave the hotel because the tinkers refuse to leave as they have paid their money, and so the owner of the hotel loses his custom. The hotel then gets a bad name and no-one goes to stay there any more. As a folktale, 'The Tinkers' Hotel' appears to have been quite popular, and at least fifty-eight versions have been collected in several counties.[108] The tinkers' behaviour is described in song in the following way:

It was for four days they kept up the hammering,
The landlord he charged them on the first day,
Ten pounds but was glad to bestow them four hundred,
Before he could get those damn tinkers away.[109]

Another anecdote is usually included as part of the song about the tinkers' hotel. It tells of O'Connell being stopped in the street by an Englishman who shows O'Connell a note of money, and asks him if it is 'good'. O'Connell takes the money and says that it is worth five pounds. He then pockets the note, saying that he is taking it as a fee for the information.[110] Almost every version of these anecdotes is set in London, and they illustrate the English trying to mock O'Connell and catch him out. This is seen in comments which form part of the tale, such as: 'The English used to try to make a game of Dan'[111] or 'They made him out to be a mope when he went to London first.'[112] In another version, they mock O'Connell's brogue: 'Here comes the great Irish Counsellor O'Connell, a fine speaker but with a most amusing brogue.'[113] The anecdote again illustrates O'Connell the trickster and his ability to use his cleverness to help the less fortunate. The song is entitled 'You Sons Of The Shamrock Give Ear To My Ditty':

> One day through the street as brave Daniel was walking,
> A party of Cockneys for to view him they stood
> In order to humbug the monarch of Ireland,
> One pulled out a note and said: 'Sir, is that good?'

> For to answer the question brave Dan was not lazy,
> The note to his pocket he conveyed in a thrice;
> When asked to return (it) he says to the fellow:
> 'Sir, I'm a counsel that's paid for advice.'[114]

According to the historical record, there was a certain Fr Tom Maguire who was champion of Roman Catholic militants and was renowned for his oratory. A great debate was arranged between Maguire and a Protestant preacher called Pope, and was held in the Dublin Institute in Sackville St., from the nineteenth to the twenty-fifth of April 1827. The hours of debate were from 11.am to 3.pm each day and O'Connell acted as one of the Catholic chairmen. There was intense public interest. In honour of his victory there, O'Connell gave Maguire a silver plate worth a thousand pounds. Late in 1827 Maguire was in court defending himself against a Protestant innkeeper from Drumkeeran in county Leitrim, who claimed that Maguire had seduced his daughter and that she was pregnant by him. The child was said to have been born dead while Maguire was carrying on his polemical activities in Dublin. O'Connell defended Maguire in this suit in which costs of six pence were awarded against the defendant.[115]

In oral tradition, O'Connell plays the role of clever lawyer in a version of the tale which tells of a girl who has been bribed by a Protestant minister to give evidence against a Catholic priest who is accused of having made her pregnant. O'Connell arranges that a James McGourty, a clever poet, should swear in court that it was he who had the relationship with her. He does so and the case is dismissed against the priest who, at the time, was not long home from college:

To impart his knowledge to Christianity,
In famed Drumkeeran he reigned content,
And preached the gospel to young and old,
Until a female Judas named Anne McGarraghan,
Swore hard against him for the love of gold.

It was Luther's faction got up this compaction
To take an action against the divine,
That he in vestments no more would shine.
But O'Connell's bravery freed him from slavery
When the McGarraghan's knavery did fail to put him down.[116]

A certain Fr William Plunkett is said to have been assisted by O'Connell when accused of being the father of a child by a girl who is not named:

It was in the month of April in the year 1831,
She took an oath against me and said I was the man,
The father of her baby of which she had so long concealed,
She swore I was an outlawed man and then I was sent to jail.

The song relates that Fr Plunkett was in Cavan prison under sentence of death, which was commuted to deportation to New South Wales. The bishop wrote to O'Connell who came to his assistance, and the priest was freed and became 'a clergyman once more in Kingscourt town'.[117]

In a similar tale of alleged paternity, which does not appear to be part of the song tradition, O'Connell arranges that the girl is robbed on her way to the court. The robbers, whom O'Connell has employed, steal a forged note from the girl. The note, which has been arranged by O'Connell, contains an offer of money from a Protestant minister to the girl if she gives evidence against the priest. O'Connell reads the note in court. The priest is set free, and the minister and the girl are sentenced.[118]

In Praise of O'Connell

As we have already seen, O'Connell is a man of noble character who has never taken a bribe:

Mo ghrá mo phrionsa Dónall
Córach nár breabadh riamh,
Mar gur fhág sé galar dóghach,
Orthu go deo lena saol,
Mar go bhfuil ministrí gan deacha ann
Agus cléirigh a deireadh 'áiméan' leo
Leagaithe ina bpá.[119]

(The just prince, Daniel, is my darling Who was never bribed, Because he left them melancholy, For the rest of their lives, Because there are ministers without tithes, And clerics who would say 'amen' to them, Are lowered in their pay.)

His sense of justice is praised:

> He never made distinction between colour, class, or creed,
> His motto was in every place, stern justice to each man.[120]

And in the same song we are told:

> He was the first in battle and the last to leave the field.

Irish people can trust him because he will fight for his country:

> For Ireland's rights, with voice like thunder,
> He woke the echoes of Tara's Hill.
> In weal or woe he never violated,
> The several confidences his nation gave.[121]

His qualities as a statesman are praised:

> For statesmanship, eloquence and judgement,
> The name of O'Connell, in italics bold,
> Is written in history, so our ancestry,
> Proves Irishmen's glory brighter than gold.[122]

He was good to the poor and to the church, and he used his power with justice.

> The orphans he cared for and the widows protected,
> And our clergy most dear by his counsel was directed,
> The army does fear his majestic great power,
> To his laws did adhere at his voice they did lower.[123]

He is neither deceitful nor untrustworthy:

> The heart of O'Connell is upright and sound,
> Not a grain of deception is there to be found,
> Through the medium of law may he alter the scene.[124]

O'Connell is praised highly in a composition of eight verses which drink to his health. Here, probably because it is a lighthearted, straightforward piece, with no exhortations or political complaints, there is no specific mention of O'Connell's political achievements. He is praised as a patriot, but no reference is made to Emancipation or to Repeal:

> Fill high the flowing bowl -
> Fill high for Erin's boast -
> Drink deep each free-born soul,
> 'Tis O'Connell's health we toast.
>
> O'Connell! glorious name!
> Oh, how dear to freedom's cause!
> Ye that burn with patriot flame,
> Swell the tribute of applause! ... .

Then millions shall adorn
Their Liberator's fame
And infants yet unborn
Lisp and bless O'Connell's name![125]

Mockery and Denigration

Not all the songs about O'Connell are complimentary however. A small number of songs poke fun at him or belittle either his political activities or his personality. An amusing song called 'Babies By Steam' or 'I Crossed Over The Moor And I Met An Old Woman' is widely sung in Ireland. In oral tradition generally, O'Connell is said to have been a womaniser.[126] This is an important part of O'Connell tradition and it again conforms to the picture of the hero as possessing extraordinary sexual prowess. It finds expression here in a song of praise which at the same time mocks O'Connell and blames him. The song takes the form of a conversation between a tinker and an old woman who mocks O'Connell, and his 'children by steam'.[127]

The use of the word 'steam' to symbolise O'Connell's promiscuous reputation may have its origin in the discovery, about the year 1850, that chicken-hatching could be carried out by steam.[128] Although the song is basically a comical one, there is a strong element in it which rejects O'Connell's policies and popularity.

Predictably, O'Connell is mocked and despised in songs which were composed outside the Catholic, nationalist tradition. In an Orange songbook, the Orangeman says that he will have to leave Ireland:

A stout worthy Orangeman surely am I
And now as I see that the system's gone by,
Rigedum diro dee.
Since Dan and his clan then I see did prevail,
Then off to Vandiemans I mean to set sail,
My goods I shall auction and that on the nail.
Rigedum diro dee.

Spoken: Yes, gentlemen, I am going, and going with a broken heart, that infernal cirvumventing, demagogue, O'Connell never quit until he completed our ruination .[129]

One Orange song tells of O'Connell in purgatory and says that orders have been given from Rome that Masses should be said for his release. The song appears to scoff at the Roman Catholic church more than at O'Connell and seems to use O'Connell as a vehicle for this mockery:

Oh, hard's his fate if he must stay,
Like other beggarmen I say,
For Gratis-prayers on All Saints' Day

O, let that never carry.
Sell scapulars, crosses, cords and beads
And all green sashes and cockades,
All Irishmen – do lend your aid
For Dan in Purgatory.[130]

'Old Father Dan' deals once again with the subject of O'Connell in purgatory, and mocks him:

Now ould Father Dan was the rarest ould sprig
That Ireland ever did see,
For the most of his wit, och! it lay in his wig,
And he long kept the rent-box key.

Chorus:
Then square up your shovels in a row,
Tumble up the sods with the hoe boys O;
There is no more rent for ould Father Dan,
He's gone where the rest all will go.[131]

O'Connell's death seems to have afforded an opportunity for derision to his adversaries, perhaps some of it in relief:

Oh, heard ye yon harper
Play Danny's departure,
My Boghilanbwee, dear Boghilanbwee.
The great liberator, the fam'd agitator,
No more proves the traitor,
Sweet Boghilanbwee.
For he's gone! sure he's gone!
The dear Boghilanbwee,
To the regions unknown, to give up his repealing.
Despairing, whilst Erin swears his double-dealing
Was that which still murdher'd her Boghilanbwee.[132]

During O'Connell's time, some newspaper reports took the form of forceful attacks in which O'Connell is accused of being a slave to the Catholic church and of using the money of the poor to further his own ambition or simply to provide him with a lavish standard of living. The following was published in *The Times*, the twenty-sixth of November 1835:

Scum condensed of Irish bog!
Ruffian, coward, demagogue!
Boundless liar, base detractor!
Nurse of murders, treason's factor!
Of Pope and priest the crouching slave,
While they lips of freedom rave,
Of England's fame the viprous hater,

Yet wanting courage for a traitor.
Ireland's peasants feed thy purse,
Still thou art her bane and curse.
Tho' thou liv'st, an empire's scorn,
Lift on high thy brazen horn.
Every dog shall have his day,
This is thine of brutish sway.
Mounted on a Premier's back,
Lash the Ministerial pack;
At thy nod they hold their places,
Crack their sinews, grind their faces . . .

Spout thy filth, effuse thy slime,
Slander is in thee no crime . . .

Then grant the monster leave to roam,
Let him slaver out his foam;
Only give him length of string,
He'll contrive himself to swing.[133]

And once again he is censured in the following verses, also in *The Times*, for his misuse of the money of the poor:

Hark, hark to the begging box shaking!
For whom is this alms-money making?
For Dan, who is cramming
His wallet, while famine
Sets the heart of the peasant a-quaking.

The priest from the altar inveigles
The peasant, reluctant, yet higgles;
His children's support
Is bagged. A year's sport
Is in store for the Darrynane 'beagles'. . .

The land is all blighted with famine!
The land is all blighted with famine!
Yet still doth he crave,
And, like Ghoul at the grave,
Rakes rottenness, rooting for Mammon![134]

The Orange tradition states that O'Connell deceived many people in a song entitled 'The Royal Irish Blackbird':

O'Connell did his thousands dupe, did fob the
rent, and fail to them,
What was he but a Mocking Bird, when promising
'Rapale' to them?
Sing boys, sing, *etc.*[135]

An Orange 'Anti-Repeal Song' does not name O'Connell, but implies that those who are promoting Repeal will suffer:

Shall they from punishment be free
Who agitate repeal?

And let the end rebellion be
Their threatenings we disdain
The Legislative union we
Shall with our lives maintain.
Ye valiant loyal northern men
Shall die with bond to seal
The well-shot guns of Ulster then,
Shall thunder 'No Repeal'.[136]

In all, there appears to be only a very small body of songs in which O'Connell is censured, and these have been recorded in the published rather than in the oral tradition. It is hardly likely that these songs of censure, such as were published in journals like *Punch*, found their way to the oral singing tradition. On the whole, the songs in Irish do not mock or scoff at O'Connell in the lighthearted way in which many of the songs in English seem to mock him. He is, however, called to task in one song in Irish for his misuse of the clergy in collecting money from the poor for his political cause, and for his constant use of the English language:

Nach mór i gceist Ó Conaill againn is a chuid argóinteacht Bhéarla,
Nach fada ag súil ag clanna Gaedheal go ndéanfadh sé dóibh cabhair,
Is é a bhfaca muid dhá mhaith ariamh seanchas agus Béarla,
Agus na sagairt ag cruinniú déirce dhó fhéin le haghaidh n-a chíos.[137]

(O'Connell is being discussed a great deal, and his English argumentations, Irish people have long hoped that he would help them, All we have seen as a result was talk and English, And the priests collecting charity for him for his rent.)

This song 'Amhrán Shéamuis Bheartla' (Séamus Bheartla's Song), was composed in praise of one Séamus Mac Donnchadha or Séamus Bheartla, who lived in Ros a Mhíl, in county Galway, and who was known for his generosity. He is said to have died about 1898, aged over eighty.

Language and Imagery in the Songs
Many of the songs emphasise O'Connell's victory over the enemy. Most of the traditions dealing with the restoration myth employ a vision which is both violent and apocalyptic. O'Connell's victory, as expressed in the song tradition, is political, but the language in the songs often

gives the impression that violence and bloodshed are part of this victory, although these tactics were contrary to O'Connell's beliefs.

In a version of '*Sliabh na mBan*' in Irish, swords are mentioned as a weapon to be used against the enemy when O'Connell is in power, and it is said that O'Connell will trounce the English down to hell:

> *Dónall Ó Conaill ó Dhoire Fhionáin, ós aige a bhí an teanga líofa,*
> *blasta dóibh,*
> *Do labhair sé leo go líofa bíodh is gan aon bhladar leo,*
> *Gheobhaimid le toradh claímh é is cloífimid na Sasanaigh,*
> *Beidh na Sasanaigh i dteannta is beimid á bplancadh siúd go*
> *hifreann.*[138]

(Dónall Ó Conaill from Doire Fhionáin, since he can talk to them fluently and smoothly, He spoke to them fluently although not flattering them, We will get it with a sword and we will subdue the English, The English will be in difficulty and we will be trouncing them to hell.)

In his songs, Tomás Rua makes frequent reference to O'Connell's bravery and to overpowering the enemy. He says he will be very pleased when O'Connell wins the day and the foreigners are routed, although of the five songs of praise composed by Tomás Rua about O'Connell, three of them do not mention battle.[139] However, '*Is ea chuala tré mo Shiúltaibh*' (I heard as I was walking), describes O'Connell with his sword of blood in his hand, ready for the slaughter:

> *Tá an scafaire Dónall i bhfoirm is i gcóir,*
> *A chlaíomh fola ina dhóid chum éirligh,*
> *Is do dhearbhaigh a bheol sara rithfidh an fómhar,*
> *Go dtógfadh an brón de Ghaelaibh.*[140]

(Dónall, the strapping fellow is in form and ready, Is sword of blood is in his fist ready for slaughter, And his mouth affirmed that before the end of autumn, He would lift the sorrow from the Irish people.)

We have already seen that Pádraig Cúndún praises the warriorlike traits in O'Connell's character, and the idea of the fighting hero. He mentions swords, spears and O'Connell's willingness to do battle.[141] Tomás Rua says that O'Connell is conquering the followers of Luther and Calvin:

> *Tá Ó Conaill ag fiach ar na diabhalaibh le fada*
> *Anois nó ariamh tá dá stialladh is dá stracadh.*[142]

(O'Connell has been hunting the devils for a long time, Now and forever lacerating them and tearing them apart.)

The language and images in the songs are very vivid, and indicate O'Connell's physical power to overcome the enemy. This type of warlike imagery is used in the songs in Irish more than in the songs in English, and the conventions and imagery of the compositions must be considered. As L.M. Cullen has said:

> The dislike of foreign intruders emerges strongly in the Gaelic poetry of the seventeenth and eighteenth centuries; it accounts for the most violent language of the period; it, rather than religious animosity in its own right lies behind the rather abstract antipathy towards the Reformation and to the reformed churches.[143]

In the English songs, reference is made to his victory but it is seldom implied that blood will be shed. A typical example in a contemporary song in English is:

> Success to the great O'Connell,
> That beat our daring foes.[144]

Sometimes the words imply that physical violence is used, although this is not specified. In keeping with a violent picture of O'Connell is the way in which his duel with D'Esterre is preserved in song tradition.[145] In one song in Irish, we are told that O'Connell overcame D'Esterre on the Curragh of Kildare:

> *Dónall Ó Conaill den bhoirbfhuil aird ab fhearr,*
> *Is gur i gCurrach Chill Dara do threascair sé*
> *Stairs (sic) ar lár.*[146]

> (Dónall Ó Conaill of the best, noble, fierce, blood, And it was on the Curragh of Kildare he vanquished D'Esterre.)

In a song called 'You Hearty Gay Fellows Draw Near Me Till I My Adventures Relate', a character, Jack, tells of all the famous places he has visited and says:

> And making for Dublin city, I bought on the Curragh Kildare
> The handful of slugs that O'Connell stuck in the guts of D'Esterre.[147]

The songs and reality do not coincide here, as the place where the duel was fought was in Bishopscourt, county Kildare. A broadsheet song recalls O'Connell's bravery in the duel:

> His foes could never him affright, to end his days was their delight,
> When D'Esterre did challenge him to fight, undaunted he was found,
> While MacNamara he did stand, as second for our noble Dan,
> He fell the proud D'Esterre quite lifeless to the ground.[148]

O'Connell the Saviour

Many of the songs refer to the help O'Connell has received, or will receive, from God in his righteous pursuit of freedom. Even at his birth, there was rejoicing in Paradise in celebration of the arrival of a great person: 'The angels sung sweet hymns of joy the night he got his birth.'[149]

God and the Catholic church are on his side, and they will guide him in his efforts to conquer the enemy. Prayers are included in the songs, seeking protection for him:

> To guide famous Dan, we implore the protection,
> Of God and Saint Patrick, this morning.[150]

In verses in Irish, the poet prays that O'Connell will be protected by Heaven and by the Church. He says O'Connell is the guardian of the faith, a branch that has been strengthened by the holy Trinity, he is beloved by the Pope, by cardinals, bishops, priests and brothers.[151]

It is said that God sent O'Connell to assist Ireland in her cause:

> Come all you Roman Catholics
> Raise your voices all,
> For God has said our holy church
> Will never sink or fall.
> He lit a lamp in Munster
> To let the world see,
> Which crossed the deepest channels
> To gain our liberty,
> The bondage of those Israelites,
> Our Saviour he did see,
> He then commanded Moses,
> To go to set them free,
> And in the same we did remain
> Suffering for our own,
> Till God has sent O'Connell
> To free the Church of Rome.[152]

In the foregoing lines, O'Connell is compared to Moses and just as the Saviour sent Moses to lead the Israelites to the promised land so he has sent O'Connell to take care of the Irish people. In a song in Irish, it is said that Mary's only son is by O'Connell's side to help him with his difficult task:

> Gurb é Dónall Ó Conaill athair na clainne,
> Péarla den chine daonnacht
> Do chuaigh thar uisce agus do bhuaigh ar ríthibh,
> Bhí an tAon-Mhac Muire taobh leis.[153]

(Dónall Ó Conaill is the father of the family A pearl of the human race, Who traveled over the sea and conquered kings, The Only Son of Mary was beside him.)

Celebrating O'Connell's victory in Clare, Diarmaid na Bolgaighe Ó Sé, a contemporary of O'Connell's and a south Kerry poet, says that grace from the Holy Lamb will assist him and keep him safe from the enemy:

Bíonn grásta an Uain Naofa gach lae aige agus cumhacht ina láimh..

(He has grace from the Holy Lamb every day and power in his hand)[154]

Tomás Rua believes that the Lord has O'Connell's interests at heart and that He will take good care of the Liberator. He exhorts his supporters to pray for O'Connell who will benefit from the prayers of his Catholic followers to help him towards success:

A chomharsana, comhairle dhíbh tugaim,
Agus tógaidh go háirithe é;
Bígí cóirithe i gcóir is i bhfoirm
Ag cur guidhe i láthair Dé;
Bhur gCoróin Mhuire ghlórmhar bíodh agaibh
Is an salm breá fós dá léamh,
Ar son Dónaill ghil chróga mhic Mhurchadha,
D'fhilleadh is a námhaid go tréith![155]

(Neighbours, I give you advice, And be sure to take it, Be equipped, ready and in form, Saying prayers to God; Have your rosaries, And read the fine psalm as well, For bright brave Dónall son of Murchadh, That he will come home and his enemies weakened.)

The songs state that the Catholic Faith is the true one and that it will overcome the Protestant faith.

O'Connell is often called the saviour of the Irish people, a motif which has obvious biblical conotations and coincides very well with the idea of a Christlike figure who leads his people. Here, O'Connell is both political and religious saviour. The biblical motif occurs throughout the folklore material about O'Connell and would appear to be part of the messianic tradition about him as the chosen one, the person sent from heaven with the express purpose of coming to the assistance of the Irish and saving them. Against the gloomy picture of Ireland's political situation at the time, the importance of O'Connell's role is apparent:

In the days of old, when the fierce enslaver,
With rod of iron, kept poor Erin down,
In vain she called to her sons to save her,
But all were daunted by the tyrant's frown,
Till one arose before men and angels,
His mind as mighty as the ocean's wave;
It was noble Daniel repealed her dangers.[156]

In several songs, he is described as the king who has command over his people as is illustrated in the following description of the monster meeting in Tara on 15 August 1843, a meeting at which about half a million people were assembled:[157]

> The mighty Sovereign of the Hill, you all do understand,
> Advanced to the platform hailed by each succeeding band,
> With flags and banners hoisted on high on Tara's lofty plain
> Each sounding tone said: 'We'll bring home our Parliament again.'[158]

Comparisons

O'Connell is often compared to famous characters of history – those of proven courage and also those established in victory. He is like Napoleon, for example, and is said to be his equal in fame. It is mentioned that O'Connell will be king just as Bonaparte was:

> *Agus dá dtagadh suaitheadh bheart insan tír seo,*
> *Agus go bhfillfeadh an* fleet *isteach,*
> *Agus go gcruinneoidíst inár dtimpeall,*
> *Mar dhíon don fhathach inár measc,*
> *Go dtroidfimíst go dílis iad*
> *Ar chlaíomh nó ar phúdar ceart,*
> *Agus go ndéanfaimíst Ard-Rí de,*
> *Insan tír seo mar Bhonaparte.*[159]

(If there were a disturbance of affairs in this country, And the fleet were to return in here, And that they would gather round us, As protection for the giant in our midst, We would fight them faithfully, With sword or with proper powder, And we would make him High King, In this country, just like Bonaparte.)

O'Connell's enemies hate him so much that they would rather see him dead than see Napoleon dead:

> *B'fhearr leo marbh é ná Bón, is go mbeire orainn beo,*
> *Chum go bhfeicfeam na crónphoic traochta!*[160]

(They would prefer him dead than Bonaparte, and may he find us living, To see the swarthy bucks (often applied to the foreign invaders and settlers) subjugated.)

Tomás Rua Ó Súilleabháin compares O'Connell to Moses, and says that Irish people are like the people of Israel and will be led across the Red Sea by their own Moses, Daniel O'Connell.[161] In an oration delivered by the Kerry poet, Sylvester O'Shea, a contemporary of O'Connell, he is again called Moses:

> He spoke at a meeting in Milltown in favour of some candidate whom O'Connell put forward; in the opening words of his speech he said: 'Cheers for the great Liberator and the Moses of his day.'[162]

When he is compared to Aristides, his favourable traits of character are listed:

Like great Aristides of old,
His soul was proof 'gainst sparkling gold.
Pure, patriotic, firm and bold,
His neck he would not bend
In tame submission to the chain.[163]

In the same vein, he is likened in an Irish poem to the *Fiannaíocht* hero Oscar.[164]

Imagery from nature is a device frequently utilised by songmakers throughout the world and, not surprisingly, it is also used to praise O'Connell. He is often compared to a plant or to an animal. No matter what trait of character is being extolled, he excels above others. Tomás Rua often refers to him as a branch or a tree:

A bhile de rás na nGaedheal . . .
A bhile bhoig, álainn, shéimh, . . .
Is é an planda cumasach, curanta, cóir . . .
Is é an bhile fé bhláth do b'áilne snódh . . .[165]

(Scion (sacred or historic tree) of the Gaelic race. Gentle, beautiful, calm scion . . . He is the powerful, heroic, just, scion (plant), . . . He is the flourishing scion, of most beautiful appearance . . .)

He is compared to a lion in a song collected in county Clare:

Nuair a chlois an tAthair Vinsí (Vincent),
An leon croí úd do bhí le teacht,
Do ghléasadar cathaoir dó.
Agus sheinneadar suas an band.
Bhí ministrí cloíte ann
Ag baint fees *amach is an deichiú beart,*
Seolfaimid san loing iad,
*Agus bead díbeartha go h*Isle of Man.[166]

(When Fr Vincent heard, About that lion heart who was to come, They prepared a chair for him, And the band started to play. There were subdued ministers there, Taking fees and tithes, We will put them in a ship, And they'll be driven to the Isle of Man.)

And Tomás Rua says that the 'lion' has travelled from Doire Fhionáin:

Fáilte is fiche is tuilleadh ina ndeoidh,
Óm' chroí is ea cuirimse roimis an leon.[167]

(A welcome and twenty and more besides, From my heart I place before the lion.)

The king of the animals is used to portray O'Connell's power and stature and his public leadership. Tomás Rua also calls him a dragon.[168] He is called the 'Kerry eagle' in one song,[169] and in another he is called a cock:

These lovely hills some time ago
They were possessed by tyranny,
But the 'Kerry Cock' that is lying low
He gained the day for Bantry.[170]

O'Connell is seen to be a star who will guide the Irish people through these troubled times. He is called 'Our guiding star through bondage drear',[171] and:

The brightest star that Erin raised
Or from her fertile valleys sprang.[172]

The various metaphors and similes used in the songs to describe O'Connell underline his popular image, and distinctive aspects of nature are used in O'Connell comparisons. This symbolism occurs in the songs in Irish and in English alike. It was a well-established practice in the broadsheets in English that animals were used to represent men:

We often find animals symbolizing men. A large number of Irish political broadside ballads celebrate heroes under the guise of birds. We are not astonished to find the imperial eagle, the image of faith, courage, and supreme power, representing O'Connell.[173]

In one song O'Connell is called 'Erin's Green Linnet', a bird which is not in keeping with the warlike image of the eagle, dragon or lion. Zimmerman explains that this comparison with the linnet is based on an influence from the love-songs.[174]

O'Connell's nobility and proud ancestry are emphasised in the songs in Irish, in particular. This is to be expected, as the Gaelic poetic tradition has always emphasised the importance of noble genealogical descent. Only a man of his noble blood would have the ability to be leader:

Den ráibfhuil do b'fhearr ar bith síoladh.[175]

(Descended from the best champion blood).

In addition to the references to nature and to animals, O'Connell's leadership is represented by the poets in other ways. He is called the prince, and the pearl of the Irish people. The imagery used in the songs dramatises and exaggerates O'Connell's role as leader.

After his death, it was said that he holds a place of great importance in heaven: 'At the high throne of Heaven his fame does extend.'[176] His immortality is given recognition in lines like the following:

Round the vault where you sleep at the tomb of Glasnevin,
A train of bright angels surrounds you from heaven,
While songs of applause to your memory is given,
By all the true bards on your own native shore.[177]

Dramatic images of comparison are used in describing O'Connell:

As Sol – when from the eastern sea
He slowly rises – darts his ray
Oe'r lands far thence, and drives away
The lowering clouds of night,
So Dan, by unremitting zeal -
The glowing truths he did reveal
Illumed the road to Erin's weal
And man's undoubted right.[178]

O'Connell in the Song Tradition

The picture that emerges from the record is that there are over twice as many songs in English as in Irish, either about O'Connell specifically, or songs in which he is mentioned. As well as this, more versions of songs in English were collected, or were available to the collectors, than were versions of songs in Irish. This is surprising as significantly more collecting was done in Irish-speaking areas than in those areas where the English language predominated. As might be expected, counties Kerry and Cork were the most productive areas due to O'Connell's close connections with Uíbh Ráthach, and due also to the strength of the vision poetry tradition in Munster.

Although O'Connell songs appear for the most part to have been sung for popular entertainment, it occurred in at least one instance that they were viewed with apprehension when, at a fair in Toomevara, in county Tipperary in 1828, a clash took place between police and people, after the police had ordered away a ballad singer who had 'sung all day about O'Connell'.[179]

We are left to deduce a great deal about the song tradition of O'Connell, as much of the available material was collected at a time when its currency had practically disappeared. In terms of literary merit, the songs of Tomás Rua were seen to be of high quality, but none of the O'Connell songs entered the Irish imagination in the same way as those of Thomas Davis and 'The Nation', where music and song were seen as a 'duty' or mission:

Music is the first faculty of the Irish, and scarcely any thing has such power for good over them. The use of this faculty and this power, publicly and constantly, to keep up their spirits, refine their tastes, warm their courage, increase their union, and renew their zeal, is the duty of every patriot.[180]

Sir James Graham, who was Home Secretary in 1843, considered the national songs published in 'The Nation' to be *very mischievous and exciting,* and in an attempt to diminish any threats to British rule in Ireland, Sir Robert Peel ordered a prosecution of the authors of seditious articles, ballads and speeches. This order did not produce the desired results however.[181] To mention a few examples of the best-known songs which have survived from 'The Nation', there was 'A Nation Once Again', 'Step Together', and 'The West's Asleep'. Davis's songs were used as a powerful form of political education, and are emotionally intense, whereas the songs about Daniel O'Connell appear to have been primarily a form of popular entertainment, and were not created with the same conscious use in mind as the compositions in 'The Nation'.

Having said that, however, songs like 'The Youth From Milltown' and 'Babies by Steam' have survived in oral tradition long after most of the songs of 'The Nation' have disappeared.

The Song Tradition: Sources
Armagh: IFC 1782:225-8.
Carlow: IFC 96:270-3.
Cavan: IFC 212:240-4; 1786:38-43; 1806:230-1; 1891:14-19; 1893:114-6; S1010:122; IFC Tape 1972 54/A/3 TM from Frank McInerney, Leggacumine P.O.; 1976 498/2-3 TM from Packie Reilly, aged sixty-seven, Brusky, Corrigan.
Clare: IFC 41:320-1; 54:317-8; 90:142-3, 154-6; IFC Tape 1974 323/A/1 TM from Tom Lenihan, Knockbrack, Miltown Malbay; IFC Tape 1978 R.uí Ógáin from Jackie Shannon, Miltown Malbay, Kilfarboy.
Cork: IFC 219:495,497-501; 220:329-30; 283:168-9; 334:505-9; 476:116-9; 736:263; 737:147-50; 789:538-40; 1591:364-6; 1592:232-3,442-5; 1680:67 (S.Ó Cróinín Tape 11b); 1790:191-4, 195-7; *Béal.* 7 1937 28-31; de Brún 1972,98-9; Ó Donnchú 1932 59-60; Ó Foghludha 1932 68-70; Ua Duinnín 1912-13 16-18.
Donegal: IFC 1854:23.
Dublin: Zozimus 1871 24-30.
Fermanagh: IFC 1711:27-8, 207-9, 212-4, 256-7.
Galway: IFC 160:423-4; 305:304-8; 354:331-2; 607:5-9; 630:385-91; 633:535-7; 634:283-6,289-91; 645:94-5; 970:578-80; 1205:100; 1311:511-13; de hÍde 1935 118-23; Ó Coigligh 1987 99-100.
Kerry: IFC 14:115-7; 95:18-19; 121:326-7, 386-8; 125:287-8; 570:367-8; 667: 199-202; 782:43-5, 195-7; 797:26-7; 823:56-7, 359-60; 927: 300-2; 928: 52-5; 999:489-94; 1064: 39-43, 374; 1125:244; 1147:184-7; 1167:137-8; 1530:341-5; 1915:33; S433:49; S474:124; S475:165-70; *CS* 7.12.1907; Fenton 1922 10-11, 56-60, 78-9, 95-6, 108; RTE MC 102 1987; D. Ó Súilleabháin 1936 268-75; S. Ó Súilleabháin 1937 32-4, 45-7.
Kilkenny: IFC 96:164-231.
Leitrim: IFC 512:552-4; 559:276-8;1404:570-6.
Limerick: IFC 98:19-23; 629:114-6,431-3.
Longford: IFC 1795:123; 1901:257-9,299-300.
Mayo: IFC 249:186-8; 665:352-3,441-4; 804:204-5; 1534:526-7; 1775:355.
Meath: IFC 921:462-4.

Monaghan: IFC S960:128-35.
Offaly: IFC 1796:235-6.
Roscommon: IFC 1795:118-9.
Sligo: IFC 444:83-4.
Tipperary: IFC 1060:392-3.
Tyrone: IFC 1216:151-7.
Waterford: IFC 85:333-4; 86:94-8; 150:543-7; 183:116-7; 259: 711-2; 275:413-4.
Wexford: IFC 412:26-7; 481:318-21; 493:55-77; 1564:30-46; 1859:166-73; S900:380-81.
No Provenance:
Aberystwyth Mss.A24 NL W MS 5342. *Broadsheets, Songbooks and Chapbooks* in IFC and NL. *Broadsheets* Michael O'Hanrahan, Kilkenny Archaeological Society. *Maynooth College* Mss 6,9,60(a),131,202,203,487. *RIA* Mss. 63,35 v (No. 25), 1651.18; 64,119; 117(b),6; 333,187i; 373,403; 495,171,172,173; 552,246; 569,23,24; 594,511; 602,71m; 654,483; 659,(222) (224); 769,395i,396i,397; 899, 66,144,147; 942,1,169m,172,175; 1185,68; 1254,II,8; IV,(4). *Torna* Mss UCC T X 1 ii 42.

References

1. Fenton 1922. Ó Donnchú 1933.
2. Standardised from Fenton 1922 95. The songs in Irish are in *amhrán* metre for the most part, a metre which is based on vowel assonance as opposed to syllabic metre.
   There is a vast number of songs, and versions of songs about O'Connell. Therefore, only relevant quotations and verses from songs are included here in the body of the text. Appendix A consists of full texts of a selection of the songs.
3. BB NL 28: Broadside (or broadsheet) ballad, printed on a single sheet of paper. Usually, several ballads were printed on this sheet which were then cut into single slips for sale by the ballad seller. These song sheets are notorious for their mis-spellings and misprints and are presented here without alteration. Where a reference number is not available for library/archive broadsheets, the title/first line of the ballad is given here.
4. See for example BB NL 326: 'Maddan erin a'len er bara Knuch glonna ait lehas' *(sic)* which transposes: *Maidin (Maidean) aoibhinn álainn ar barra Chnoc Glinne ait lehas (?)*.
5. Shields Dublin 1990 139.
6. Ó Tuathaigh 1974-5 33.
7. IFC 1795:124-5. Collected in 1956 by James G. Delaney from Patrick Mulligan, Cloncowley, parish of Killoe, barony of Longford, county Longford.
8. Dorson 1972 38.
9. Vansina 1965 149.
10. Ó Faoláin 1945 229.
11. Corkery 1967 ed., 42-67. See also Cullen 1969 7-47.
12. Standardised from Ó Foghludha 1932 68.
13. BB NL 329: 'You mourning sons of our afflicted nation' (O'Connell's Grave). English words like 'Repeal' which contain 'ea', were pronounced to sound 'Repale' (*Reipéil* in Irish).
14. See Breathnach 1971 66; O'Neill [1922?] 30.
15. Ceol an Chláir vol. 1 LP CCÉ CL 17.
16. Breathnach 1976 231.
17. Breathnach 1985 93,179.

18. Jack and Charlie Coen: 'The Branch Line' Topic LP 12 TS 337.
19. Fenton 1922 10.
20. Fenton 1922 12.
21. Ó Donnchú 1933 introduction.
22. Ó Foghludha 1932 introduction.
23. Due to the lack of reference to song airs in many publications, we have little indication of the airs to many of the songs, although in recent years Tom Munnelly has collected, on sound recording, a number of O'Connell songs.
24. See Journal of the Folk-Song Society 23-25 1920-21 London.
25. Ó Coigligh 1987 30. cf. de hÍde 1935 118-123. Inis Uí Chuinn (Inchiquin) is about seven miles from Ennis town but it is very possible that Ennis was in the poet's mind as the centre of the election.
26. Lover 1899 219.
27. Fenton 1922 56.
28 IFC 305:304-8. Collected in 1936 by Liam Mac Coisdeala from Martin O'Donnell, aged seventy, a farmer, Derrybrien, parish of Ballinakill, barony of Loughrea, county Galway. Another version Tape TM 323/A/1 1974. Collected from Tom Lenihan, Knockbrack, Miltown Malbay, county Clare and he called it 'Misses Kerry, Limerick and Clare'.
29 IFC 823:359-60. Collected in 1942 by Tadhg Ó Murchú from Bríde Ní Néill (Bean Philib Uí Mhurchú), a farmer's wife, Cúil, parish of Dairbhre, barony of Uíbh Ráthach.
30. Lover op.cit. 220.
31. Standardised from D. Ó Súilleabháin 1936 272.
32. The Carrickshock incident was one of the notable incidents of violence at the time, when in 1832 eleven policemen were killed, and O'Connell acted for the defence in the subsequent trial. See Chapter 2: Tithes.
33. O'Hanrahan 1990 500.
34. BB O'Hanrahan. Part of another song about Carrickshock is 'You Gallant Sons of this Irish Nation' in IFC 1660:109-10 collected in 1932 (?) by Seán Ó Ceallaigh from Johnnie Maher, Bodal, parish of Dungarvan, barony of Gowran, county Kilkenny. See also O Lochlainn 1965 180-1,191.
35. BB O'Hanrahan. 'Farewell unto the shamrock shore I am gone for evermore'.
36. BB NL 'Come All You Sons of Erin's Land And Mourn The Loss Of Noble Dan' (O'Connell ...).
37. Ó Coigligh 1987 100, 180-1. See de hÍde 1935 118-23.
38. IFC S433:49. Collected 1934-1939 through the national school of Castlemaine, parish of Kiltallagh, barony of Trughanacmy by Peggy Sullivan, Ballinamona, from William Hanafin, aged seventy, Laharan, parish of Kiltallagh.
39. IFC 54:317-8. Collected in 1934 by Tomás Ó Ciardha from Tomás Ó Ríordáin (An Caist), aged seventy-eight, a pensioner, Airglinn, parish of Cill Uird, barony of Condons and Clongibbons, county Cork.
40. BB NL (By Memory Inspired And The Love Of Country Fired).
41 BB NL 75.
42. BB NL 327; The Mitchell Library, Glasgow.
43. Chapbook NL 1830.
44. Chapbook NL 1830.
45. Fenton 1922 95-6.
46. Ó Coigligh 1987 99. See de hÍde 1933 118-23.
47. See footnote 28.

48. IFC 1854:23. Contributed in 1975 by Hugh Deery, Ballintra, parish of Drumhome, barony of Tyrhugh, county Donegal.

49. IFC S433:49. Collected 1934-1939 through the national school of Castlemaine, parish of Kiltallagh, barony of Trughanacmy by Peggy Sullivan, Ballinamona, from William Hanafin, aged seventy, Laharan, parish of Kiltallagh.

50. *IG* IV 1899 [1890] 25-6..

51. Standardised from D. Ó Súilleabháin 1936 269; also Fenton 1922 95.

52. Chapbook NL 1830.

53. BB NL (Hurrah for O'Connell, Meagher and Repeal).

54. BB NL 389.

55. BB NL 61. For details of the Tara meeting see O. MacDonagh 1989 229-231.

56. Chapbook NL 1830.

57. Chapbook NL 1830. 'Sheils' probably refers to Richard Lalor Sheil (1791-1851) who joined O'Connell in forming the Catholic Association. He was indicted for seditious libel but a change of prime minister led to the prosecution being dropped. Between 1831-1851 he was MP variously for county Louth, Tipperary and Dungarvan. O. MacDonagh 1988 317. Feargus O'Connor (1794-1855) was Chartist leader. He founded the central committee of radical unions in 1866 and the London Democratic Association in 1837. He established *The Northern Star*, a weekly radical paper in 1837. In 1840 he was found guilty of seditious libel and imprisoned for eighteen months. In 1846 he inaugurated the 'Chartist Co-operative Land Company' and in 1847 a journal called *The Labourer*. O. MacDonagh 1989 359.

58. *Ballads and Songs by the Writers of the Nation* Dublin 1845 296-7.

59. Memoir of Zozimus 1871 24-30. For Fr Maguire, see pages 95-6.

60. See p. 75.

61. *ibid.*

62. *ibid.*

63. IFC 1167:137-8; Collected in 1948 by Tadhg Ó Murchú from Liam Ó hAinifín, aged seventy-five, a farmer, Laharan, parish of Kiltallagh, barony of Trughanacmy. Also in IFC S433:49. Collected 1934-1939 through the national school of Castlemaine, parish of Kiltallagh, barony of Trughanacmy by Peggy Sullivan, Ballinamona, from William Hanafin (possibly the same informant as IFC 1167 above) aged seventy, Laharan, parish of Kiltallagh.

64. Fenton 1922 56-60.

65. 'His kinship with O'Connell is evidently no small source of satisfaction and inspiration to the author, of whom, beyond his name, we know nothing.. . The poem was probably written not long after the passing of the Emancipation Act. It contains no reference to the Repeal agitation.' Standardised from *IG* V 1894 121.

66. *ibid.* including translation 122.

67. Fenton 1922 59-60. Fenton explains in a footnote that the rock called Carraig Uí Chróin is south of Doire Fhionáin (Derrynane).

68. Nolan 1982 6,13.

69. Although no date of composition is given for the song, the Ennis monument was inaugurated on 3.10.1865.

70. See footnote 28.

71. IFC 630:85-9. Collected around 1935 by Margaret Gallivan, Kilbanow, parish of Kilgarvan, barony of Glanarought.

72. O Lochlainn 1939 126.

73. BB IFC O'Leary 49/28.

74. de Brún 1972 9-18, 98-9,138. The song appears to have been composed between July 1828 and February 1830, when O'Connell had been elected but had not yet taken his seat.

75. IFC 219:495. Collected in 1936(?) by Pádraig Ó Conaill from Seán Mac Cárthaigh, aged sixty-five, a farmer, Achadh Tobair Mhóir, parish of Cill Fachtna Beag, barony of Cairbre Thoir, county Cork.

Arthur Wellesley, Duke of Wellington (1769-1852) was chief secretary for Ireland 1807-9 and prime minister 1828-30, Nov.-Dec. 1834. O. MacDonagh 1988 319. Sir Robert Peel (1788-1850) was chief secretary for Ireland 1812-18. He prepared the three bills relating to Catholic Emancipation. He was prime minister 1834-5, 1841-6. O. MacDonagh 1988 315. Edward Stanley (1799-1869) was chief secretary for Ireland 1830-3, and prime minister 1852,1858-9,1866-8. O. MacDonagh 1989 361. His outstanding achievement in Ireland was the creation of a system of National Education on a non-denominational basis. However, the system moved away from this.

76. Hopes were high that the French would come to help Ireland. They would burn the ships in harbours to prevent the English putting out to sea.

77. Standardised from Fenton 1922 95-6.

78. *ibid.*, 78-9.

79. IFC 645:94-5. Collected in 1939 by Máirtín Ó Mainnín from Máirtín Ó Duithche, aged fifty-nine, a farmer, Dubhachta, parish of Conga, barony of Ros, county Galway.

80. IFC S433:49. Collected 1934-1939 through the national school of Castlemaine, parish of Kiltallagh, barony of Trughanacmy by Peggy Sullivan, Ballinamona, from William Hanafin, aged seventy, Laharan, parish of Kiltallagh.

81. Corkery 1967 126-145. For an account of particular relevance see Zimmermann 1967 introduction, especially pages 54-8.

82. IFC 14:115-7. Collected in 1933 by an Br P.T. Ó Riain from Micheál Grumail, Cathair Scoilbín, parish of Cill Maolchéadair, barony of Corca Dhuibhne.

83. IFC 1790:191-4. Collected *per* Pádraig Ó Conaill, Bréan Trá, An Sciobairín, barony of Cairbre Thiar, county Cork.

84. IFC 1790:197. Collected *per* Pádraig Ó Conaill, Bréan Trá, An Sciobairín, barony of Cairbre Thiar, county Cork.

85. *IG* IV 1889 [1890],24-6. See Appendix A, A Selection of Songs.

86. Ua Duinnín, '*Spéirbhean ag trácht ar Reipéil,*' *Gadelica 1* 1912-13 16-18. The song was first written down apparently by the composer's grandson.

87. Standardised from Fenton 1922 78-9.

88. IFC 1592:442-5. Collected in 1961 by Seán Ó Cróinín from Jerry Buckley aged seventy-eight, a former farm labourer, Cnoc Raithín, parish of Cluain Droichead, barony of Iar-Mhúscraí, county Cork. See also Cork IFC 54:317-8.

89. IFC 633:535-7. Collected in 1939 by Máirtín Ó Mainnín from Áine Ní Loideáin aged twenty-nine, a small farmer, Corr na Móna, parish of Conga, barony of Ros, county Galway. Áine was originally from An Gleann Mór, An Cheathrú Rua, barony of Magh Cuilinn, county Galway, where she learned the song from her father. This a version of Laws Q27 as catalogued in the catalogue of types of British broadside ballads traditional in America; see Laws 1957 286.

90. BB NL 327 One Night As Old Granua Reclined To Rest. This seems to be based on the song 'Napoleon's Dream' which is sung by Sam Larner on 'A Garland for Sam' Topic LP 12 T 244 and on 'A Soldiers Life for Me', vol. 8 in the 'Folksongs of Britain' series, Topic 12 T 196. See also Healy 1969 160-2.

91. For further examples of vision poetry and song about O'Connell see IFC 14:115-7; 47:66-7,73-6; 1147:184-7; BB NL 326: Maidin (Maidean) Aoibhinn Álainn ar Barra Chnoc Glinne ait lehas (?) (One Pleasant Beautiful Morning On Top Of Cnoc Glinne).

92. Mummers' plays are performed predominantly in the east and north of the country around Christmas time. The folk drama involves the death and resuscitation of the hero and is usually followed by music and dancing.

93. IFC 96:164-231. Contributed in 1929 by Mrs. Kavanagh, The Rower, county Kilkenny.

94. IFC 1859:166-73. From a written copy lent to N.A. Huddleston by John Pierce of Rosslare Harbour in 1958. The play was performed until about 1914 'and appears to date from about 1820-50' which means that O'Connell was probably alive at the time of its original composition. For a note on Wellington and Sir Robert Peel see footnote 75.
The 'act' mentioned in the song may refer to Robert Peel's reduction of the tithe agitation by an act which made composition of the tithe for money payment compulsory.

95. Breathnach 1977 29. This is quoted by Breathnach to illustrate the 'borrowing' of assonance or vowel rhyming, from Irish versification. See BB IFC Simon O'Leary 121.

96. IFC 121:386-8. Collected about 1927 by Seán Ó Dubhda from Micheál Ruiséal, a farmer and a poet, Coimín, parish of Cill Maolchéadair, barony of Corca Dhuibhne. Micheál's age is not given, but the account implies that he was an old man when he died in 1929. One of his sons was Tomás Ruiséal, a nationalist and a teacher in Carraig an Chobhaltaigh, county Clare who was killed by British soldiers there on Palm Sunday 1918.

97. IFC 782:195-7. Collected in 1941 by Larry O'Brien from P.J. O'Sullivan, aged sixty-five, a stonemason, Keel, Anascaul, parish of Ballynacourty, barony of Corca Dhuibhne.

98. BB NL 579.

99. BB NL (Wrongs of Ireland).

100. For further examples of laments see BB NL: 'You Gallant Sons of Erin's Isle, I Hope You'll Give Consent' (O'Brien's Advice to the Irish People); BB NL 328: 'You Heavenly Muses, You Angelic Vision'; BB NL 37: 'Dear Erin, Your Hopes Are Now Nearly Blasted'.

101. BB NL 328: You Heavenly Muses, You Angelic Vision.

102. BB IFC 24b. The foundation stone for the monument was laid in Lower Sackville Street, (now O'Connell St.) on 8 August 1864.

103. BB IFC 27; NL 32,46.

104. BB NL 94.

105. BB IFC 28; NL 57,203.

106. Archer 1869 218. BB IFC 28; NL 57, 203.

107. The wellknown ballads 'Captain Wedderburn's Courtship', 'King John and the Bishop' and 'The Boy and the Mantle' for example are also found in oral narrative form.

108. See Armagh IFC 1112:218; 1803:142-3; Cavan IFC 1195:127-32; 1837:183; Clare IFC S613:211; Cork IFC 107:645-6; 203:283; 334:505-9; S282:292; S364:265; Donegal IFC 186:563-6; 454:210-2; 694:378-80; S1111:529-30; Galway IFC 373:359-60; 404:573-8; 471:35-6; 630:344-8; 739:532-4; 785:211-5; 829:38-40; 851:272; 869:538-42; 970:446; 1311:175-8; 1322:78-9; 1354:331-4; S16:84-5; S22:147-9;

S40:399-40; S82:39,137; S272:16-7; Gregory 1909 24-5; Kerry IFC 306:381-3; 475:351-4; 632:363-5; 772:69-71; 796:4-5; 979:625-7; D. Ó Súilleabháin 1936 260-1; Limerick IFC 628:27-30; Longford IFC 1399:513; 1486:403(i); 1901:301-3; Mayo IFC S144:148-50; Monaghan IFC S960:128-32; Roscommon IFC 1551:173; 1709:216-7; S238:247-9; S243:27-8; Sligo IFC 512:464-8; S234:202-3; Tipperary IFC 517:339; Tyrone IFC 1216:151-4; Waterford IFC 152:332-3; 275:486-7; 1239:23; *IO* 26.8.1950 20.

109. IFC 334: 500-509; Collected in 1937 by Eoghan Ó Súilleabháin from Pádraig Ó Súilleabháin aged sixty, a farmer, Rothum, An Gleann Garbh, parish of Cill Cascán, barony of Béara, county Cork.

110. For versions of the anecdote see Armagh IFC 1112:217; 1803:149-50; Cavan IFC 1196:384-5; 1787:201-2; Kerry IFC 621:143; 685:38; 1064:153; 1150:38-9; Cork IFC 107:664; 334:500-1; 789:539-40; 1543:47-8; S372:216; Limerick IFC 628:82; 507:587; Longford IFC 1399:513; Mayo IFC Tape 1976 Séamas Ó Catháin from Peadar Bairéad, Ceathrú na gCloch, Cill Cuimin; Monaghan IFC S960:128-32; Waterford IFC 275:486; S646:48; Sligo IFC 485:20; Tyrone IFC 1216:151-4; *IO* 11.2.1950, 21; 26.8.1950,20. No provenance *Irish Independent* 4.10.1945, 2.

111. Longford IFC 1399:513.

112. Louth IFC 1112:217.

113. Limerick IFC S507:587.

114. IFC 334:500-509. Collected in 1937 by Eoghan Ó Súilleabháin from Pádraig Ó Súilleabháin, aged sixty, a farmer, Rothum, An Gleann Garbh, parish of Cill Cascán, barony of Béara, county Cork.

115. Bowen 1978 106-9.

116. IFC 1891:15-19. Collected in 1977 by M.J. Murphy from Philip Dolan, aged seventy-seven, Black Lion, parish of Killinagh, barony of Tullyhaw, county Cavan. For other references to this incident and to the song and also for narrative accounts see Cavan IFC 1787: 208-9; 1803: 130; 1806:229-231; 1893:114-6; Kerry IFC 702:220-1; 834:171-5; 963:99-106; 967:207-10; D. Ó Súilleabháin 1936 265-6; Meath IFC 557: 577-87. Also mentioned in a verse of BB IFC 28: 'Prepare you gallant Irishmen – prepare without delay'.

117. IFC 782:43-5. Collected in 1941 by P.J. O'Sullivan from Patrick Daly, aged seventy, a farmer, Annascaul, parish of Ballynacourty, barony of Corca Dhuibhne.

118. Versions are to be found in Cavan IFC 1787:208-9; 1803:130; 1806:229-31; Kerry IFC 702: 220-1; 834:171-5; 963:99-106; 967:207-10; D. Ó Súilleabháin 1936 265-6; Meath IFC 557:577-87.

119. IFC 823:359-60. Collected in 1942 by Tadhg Ó Murchú from Bríde Ní Néill (Bean Philib Uí Mhurchú), a farmer's wife, Cúil, parish of Dairbhre, barony of Uíbh Ráthach.

120. BB NL Come All You Sons Of Erin And Mourn The Loss Of Noble Dan (O'Connell ...).

121. BB NL 329; You Mourning Sons.

122. BB NL 128; Poets May Pen The Fame Of Each Nation.

123. BB NL 75; You Heavenly Muses.

124. BB NL 80(?): John Bull Be Easy (The Repeal of the Union).

125. Chapbook NL 1830.

126. See Chapter 2 p. 23.

127. See Appendix A, A Selection of Songs.

128. An account of this dramatic invention is given in *A Guide to Glasgow Fair* where it is said in an account of the patent hydro-incubator:

'For hatching eggs. This is a most novel and interesting exhibition, and cannot fail to excite and enlist the reflective faculties of every beholder. Chicken-hatching by steam! who could have believed that such a mysterious triumph would be added to that other wonderful achievement of this subtile element. Watt could never have dreamt of such a result, when experimenting on its power in the construction of the steam engine.' There follows a descriptive account of the hatching of one of the chickens and how he is 'apparently as happy as if he came in the legitimate way of generation'. The account concludes with an invitation to all to visit this phenomenon at the Glasgow Fair. 'The admission is only One Penny, and cannot fail to interest every body.' *A Guide to Glasgow Fair* Glasgow n.d., 10-11, The Mitchell Library, Glasgow..

129. Songbook NL no date.
130. *Collection of Orange Songs* Toronto 1895 21.
131. BB IFC O'Leary 52a/98; The Mitchell Library, Glasgow. This may be a parody on the minstrel song 'He's Gone Where the Good Niggers Go'.
132. BB The Mitchell Library, Glasgow. 'Boghilanbwee' is the Irish *buachallán buí* meaning yellow ragwort or ragweed.
133. M. MacDonagh 1929 231-2; O. MacDonagh 1989 125.
134. M. MacDonagh 1929 345-6.
135. Archer 1869 105.
136. Collection of Orange Songs Toronto 1895 9.
137. IFC 607:5-9. Collected *c.* 1938 by Brian Mac Lochlainn from Seosamh Mac Donnchadha, Ros a Mhíl, parish of Cill Cuimin, barony of Magh Cuilinn, county Galway.
138. IFC 98:19-23. Collected in 1932 by Patrick Burke from Denis Condon aged about eighty, Galbally, barony of Coshlea, county Limerick. Denis was from Gleann na gCreabhar or Anglesborough in the parish of Kilbeheny, barony of Coshlea, and was one of the last native Irish speakers in this district.
139. Ó Héalaí 1972 55.
140. Standardised from Fenton 1922 78-9.
141. Ó Foghludha 1932 68-70.
142. Standardised from Fenton 1922 58.
143. Cullen 1969 26.
144. Chapbook NL 1830.
145. For narrative accounts of the duel with D'Esterre see pp. 26-31.
146. IFC 927:300-2. Collected in 1943 by Tadhg Ó Murchú from Micheál Ó Téacháin, aged seventy-six, a farmer and a huntsman, Spuncán, parish of An Dromaid, barony of Uíbh Ráthach.
147. BB NL 384.
148. BB NL; Come All You Sons Of Erin And Mourn The Loss Of Noble Dan (O'Connell ...).
149. BB IFC 27; NL 32, 46 Rejoice Ye Irish Patriots, You Lived To See The Day.
150. Chapbook NL 1830.
151. *IG* V 1894 121.
152. Chapbook NL 1830.
153. IFC 928:52-5. Collected in 1944 by Tadhg Ó Murchú from Pádraig Ó Conaill aged eighty-six, a river steward and a farmer, Ceapa na gCrann, parish of An Dromaid, barony of Uíbh Ráthach.
154. Standardised from S. Ó Súilleabháin 1937 45-7.

155. Standardised from Fenton 1922 56-7.
156. BB NL 329 You Mourning Sons Of Our Afflicted Nation.
157. For details of this meeting see O. MacDonagh 1989 229-30.
158. BB NL 61: On The Fifteenth Day Of August In The Year Of Forty-Three.
159. IFC 41:320-1. Collected in 1933 by Seán Mac Mathúna from Micheál Mac Connól, Baile Pháidín, Inis Díomáin, barony of Corcamruadh, county Clare.
160. Standardised from Fenton 1922 79.
161. Fenton 1922 58.
162. IFC S433:49. Collected 1934-1939 through the national school of Castlemaine, parish of Kiltallagh, barony of Trughanacmy by Peggy Sullivan, Ballinamona, from William Hanafin, aged seventy, Laharan, parish of Kiltallagh.
163. Songbook NL no date. The Athenian general, Aristides lived around 484 BC, a person of great temperance and virtue which procured him the surname of Just.
164. *IG* V 1894 121. Oscar is a leading warrior in the Fianna cycle.
165. Standardised from Fenton 1922 56, 59.
166. IFC 41:320-1. Collected in 1933 by Seán Mac Mathúna from Micheál Mac Connól, Baile Pháidín, Inis Díomáin, barony of Corcamruadh, county Clare.
167. Standardised from Fenton 1922 59.
168. *ibid*. 95-6.
169. IFC 1592:442-5. Collected in 1961 by Seán Ó Cróinín from Jerry Buckley aged seventy-eight, former farm labourer, Cnoc Raithín, parish of Cluain Droichead, barony of Iar-Mhúscraí, county Cork.
170. IFC S900:380-1. Collected 1936-38 through the national school of Rathnure (girls), parish of Killanne, barony of Bantry, county Wexford. An explanatory note to the song in the manuscript says: ' "The Kerry Cock" refers to Daniel O'Connell in the poem, who won the lawsuit for the farmers against, Mr Kavanagh, Borris, the landlord'. See Chapter 2 pp. 23-24.
171. IFC 1167:137-8. Collected in 1948 by Tadhg Ó Murchú from Liam Ó hAinifín, aged seventy-five, a farmer, Laharan, parish of Kiltallagh, barony of Trughanacmy.
172. IFC 1592:442-5. Collected in 1961 by Seán Ó Cróinín from Jerry Buckley, aged seventy-eight, former farm labourer, Cnoc Raithín, parish of Cluain Droichead, barony of Iar-Mhúscraí, county Cork.
173. Zimmermann 1967 56.
174. *ibid*. 57.
175. Standardised from Fenton 1922 56-7.
176. BB NL 37 Dear Erin Your Hopes Are Now Nearly Blasted.
177. BB NL 191 On Tara's High Mount On The Ninth Of September.
178. Songbook NL n.d., Full Many A Chief In Erin Rose.
179. Murphy 1992 86-7.
180. See *Ballads and Songs by The Writers of 'The Nation'* Dublin 1845 in which the Preface describes the outstanding popularity of the ballads and songs published in 'The Nation' since 1842.
181. McCaffrey 1966 152.

Chapter 4

The tales and anecdotes

Tales and anecdotes constitute the most widespread and most frequently recorded folklore *genre* about O'Connell, within which the jocular tale or anecdote is very much to the fore. This chapter is concerned with these tales and anecdotes of which well over a hundred separate types have been documented.

Folklore is of its nature in a process of constant change, and in the area of anecdotes and tales, as elsewhere, its fluctuation becomes apparent. Factors such as the storyteller's mood, the audience and the environment will affect the content of a tale. No tale will be told in the same way on any two occasions by a storyteller. Various themes and motifs will be ordered, emphasised, included or omitted on each occasion.

Constant features in all of the O'Connell tales, however, are the comical element and the fact that O'Connell is the focal point. Often, his behaviour or verbal dexterity constitutes the comical element in the tales. This material may sometimes have its origins in historical circumstances, but it exists primarily because it is ideally suited to oral narrative and to the image of O'Connell within that narrative form.

Some of the tales documented here are also to be found in international folklore, and may have been included in the international folktale classification system.[1] These tales are told in many instances about prominent individuals in other countries and similarly, Daniel O'Connell is the hero in some of the international tales in this country. Many of these tales probably became 'O'Connellised' during O'Connell's own lifetime. All of the international tales told in Ireland about O'Connell are found in Irish, and some have been recorded in Irish only.

In the context of the folklore about Daniel O'Connell, these international tales are of great importance because they establish him firmly as a folk hero for whom time and place are almost immaterial. Here, the historical character of O'Connell has almost disappeared, although there may still be a connection in some instances between the folktale and historical events. For the most part however, in these tales,

O'Connell has become a mythical character who is not bound by place or time.

To date, only a small number of international tales told in Ireland about O'Connell have been identified and classified, and further tales will doubtless come to light as research progresses.[2] O'Connell is associated primarily with those international tale types which involve a clever response or trick, or a circumvention of a legal situation.[3] It is possible to date some of the international tales, or at least to trace their existence to a time before that of O'Connell. These particular tales then, were obviously adapted to portray O'Connell and thus became 'O Connellised'. In most cases, however, it is difficult to say when the tale was created. Indeed, some of the stories must have been known to storytellers during O'Connell's lifetime, but O'Connell would have had to achieve the status of folk hero, before he could appear in such tales and legends.

The longer tales and anecdotes appear far more frequently in Irish than in English. Irish predominates in the shorter jocular anecdotes as well, although in accounts which describe or refer to his clever repartee, much of the story is in English only. Most of the stories come from county Kerry although a sizeable number were also collected in county Galway. Certain tales and anecdotes have been recorded in one or two counties only, like, 'A Woman Swears Against her Husband'[4] or 'The Bribed Judge', which are found, to my knowledge, in the Kerry *Gaeltacht* only, or 'Some Things Not For Sale', which is found in Galway and Mayo only. There are completely isolated examples of some tales, but this is quite rare. For example, a collector in county Galway was told a story about O'Connell when he was in London, and how he helped make a success of a business venture for an Irishman who was struggling to make ends meet there.[5] Although no other versions of this tale have been collected, it may well be a part of a more widespread tradition which simply did not come to light in the course of the collecting work.

Consideration must be given here to the history of collecting and of storytelling in Ireland. A review of the recorded material and its distribution must take into account the nature of the areas where the colllecting was done, the attitudes of the storytellers to the collectors and many other social and linguistic factors. For example, as the tales and anecdotes about O'Connell are in Irish, for the most part, the material from the Irish-speaking districts of Kerry and Galway is particularly strong, as we might expect. There were, however, full-time collectors of folklore working in the Irish-speaking districts of Clare and Cork and yet the same wealth of material is not found in these counties. Similarly, because of the Clare election, we might expect more anecdotal material about O'Connell from that county, than has in fact been recorded. A point also worth noting is that certain tales are told about O'Connell in counties far removed from his native district, although no versions of these tales have appeared in the collections from, for example, Kerry, his home county which is rich in other tales about O'Connell.

The type of anecdote told about O'Connell illustrates the close linkage between popular entertainment and popular culture. The tradition is primarily an oral one, with transmission of the tales occurring in most instances from parent, or older neighbour or relative, to a member of the next generation. At the time the tales were collected from the storytellers, approximately between 1935 and 1975, the storytellers told the collectors that they had acquired the stories orally, and this occurred probably in an intimate, domestic situation where people were visiting in local houses. The audience would thus have included neighbours and relations, and the situation would not have involved any form of 'public performance' to a large audience. A very small number of O'Connell tales have been published in English or in Irish, and there was a relatively small reading public in the Irish language at the time when many of the storytellers probably first heard tales about O'Connell, towards the end of the nineteenth century.[6]

The tales and anecdotes were told primarily for entertainment, but they also reveal attitudes to O'Connell as well as something of the storyteller's attitudes to other things and his or her own sense of humour. Oral tradition gives recognition to O'Connell's status in the tales, where he is elevated above the level of the ordinary and is conferred with particular talents. O'Connell's status in the tales is the result of a conscious decision, as well as being a product of the unselfconscious, natural growth of a tradition in which O'Connell is given the leading part. The most important character trait portrayed in the stories is O'Connell's cleverness and his agile, witty speech. The political situation of the time is mirrored by the other characters in the tales and anecdotes – Protestants, Englishmen and landlords on the one hand, and the poor, downtrodden Catholic Irishmen and women on the other hand, whom O'Connell avenges or saves. O'Connell invariably wins court cases and wagers. Some of the tales emphasise his cleverness as a young boy or illustrate that his own children are as clever as he himself is reputed to be. His heroicism as portrayed in the tales and anecdotes is due to the gift of cleverness rather than learned skills or legal qualifications, but the final picture which emerges is that of a skilful lawyer. This particular trait is of great significance in the creation of the folk hero.

Many of these anecdotes are not true, although the historical

O'Connell appears to have had a number of amusing adventures. Most of the comical anecdotes are unbelievable narratives often called 'tall tales'. Some of the anecdotes told about O'Connell are also told about other historical characters in Ireland, such as John Philpot Curran or Dean Swift.[7] They are also told about other well-known characters without any great change to the tale itself. They are not bound by history, or by any one particular date, place or character.

The anecdotes in this chapter have been arranged thematically and according to the 'pointed or proverbial quality of the anecdote'.[8] This is by no means a hard and fast division, as themes and motifs overlap constantly in the tales. Versions of tales also vary a great deal and so the criteria used here in the tale classification are based on the general thrust or emphasis of each tale. This is not to say that each tale belongs to one category only. Most tales could be included in several categories. For example, a number of the tales depicting O'Connell's cleverness in the courtroom could also be included in the section on tales which illustrate O'Connell's assistance to a poor Irishman. Equally, clever verses said to have been composed by O'Connell could be categorised either as a display of O'Connell's cleverness, or as a quick reply to an insult. In most cases the stories describe a single event which includes a number of motifs.

Humour is certainly a primary reason for the prominence of these tales in oral tradition, and many have survived to the present day because of the fact that the amusing anecdote is suited to many occasions and many different types of audiences.[9]

Many of the tales about O'Connell were collected in clusters, of perhaps around six stories, where one O'Connell tale appears to lead into another, and once a storyteller had told one anecdote about O'Connell, it frequently brought another to mind.[10] The fact that the tales have not only a hero in common, but also common motifs and themes, helps the storyteller to recall and narrate the stories either individually or in clusters. There is no difference in construction, thrust or theme between the classified AT tales and tales which have not been thus classified.

(i) Successful Resolutions of Cases

The Prisoner Will Not Hang

Bhí Éireannach istigh i saloon i Sasana lá agus d'éirigh na Sasanaigh chuige agus má dh'éirigh, bhuail sé duine acu le buile ghloine agus do mharaibh sé é. Ach bhí Dónall ag faire i gcónaí orthu. Ach chonaic sé fear ar an sráid go raibh aithne agie air trí lá roim lá na cúirte.

'Imigh ort isteach,' ar seisean, 'go dtí an mbartender san istigh agus féach an dtairriceodh sé anuas an tÉireannach a mharaibh an Sasanach istigh ann.'

D'imigh agus tairricíodh anuas é. Do tháinig sé amach aríst. Dúirt sé le Dónall é.

'Seo fiche punt duit,' ar seisean 'agus téir isteach agus cuir na fiche punt leis ná crochfar, ná é.'

D'imigh an fear eile isteach. Tairricíodh anuas aríst é.

*'Is dócha,' ar seisean 'go gcrochfar é,' leis an m*bartender.

'Dhera, cad ina thaobh ná déanfaí?' arsa an bartender.

'Cuirfidh mé fiche punt leat,' ar seisean 'ná déanfar.' Buaileadh síos an t-airgead ar lámh dhuine éinteach eile. Do tháinig sé amach agus dúirt sé le Dónall é go gcuir sé na fiche punt ar láimh duine bhí istigh.

*'Alright,' arsa Dónall, 'mise an cunsailéir anois,' ar seisean, 'beidh ar tí é sin a shaoradh agus i dteannta an atornae bheidh aige agus má tá,' ar seisean, 'ar do bhás bí i dtigh na cúirte an lá san agus fiafródsa den m*bartender *bhfuil aon ní aige á bhuachtaint le é seo chrochadh. Déarfaidh sé ná beidh agus abairse go bhfuil fiche punt curtha síos agat fhéin leis ná crochfar é.*

Ach lá na cúirte bhí an fear a chuir síos na fiche punt leis ag éisteacht leis.

'Deirimse go bhfuil,' ar seisean 'agus rud buaite agat leis. Chuiris fiche punt liomsa,' ar seisean, 'go gcrochfaí é agus chuireas-sa leat ná déanfaí.'

'Anois,' arsa Dónall, 'cad athá le rá agat? Cad é mar sórt finné tusa bheith ag cuir geall síos go gcrochfaí an fear bocht san, bhí á shaoradh fhéin, nuair a bhí an iomarca acu chuige. Bí amuigh as tí na cúirte,' ar seisean, 'is ná faighim isteach inti tú faid a bheadsa i mo chunsailéir anseo.'

*Do thug sé an tÉireanach free*áltha *agus d'imigh sé amach agus d'fhág sé ansan iad.*[11]

(There was an Irishman in a saloon in England one day and the English people went for him, and if they did he hit one of them with a blow of a glass and killed him. He was taken and put into prison. But Daniel was watching them all the time. He saw a man he knew in the street, three days before the court.

'Go in,' he said, 'to the bartender in there and see if he mentions the Irishman who killed the Englishman in there.'

He went in and mentioned it. He came out again. He said it to Daniel:

'Here is twenty pounds for you,' he said, 'and go in and bet him twenty pounds that he won't hang.'

The other man went in. It was mentioned again.

'I suppose,' he said, 'that he will hang,' he said to the bartender.

'*Dhera*, why wouldn't he?' said the bartender.

'I'll bet you twenty pounds,' he said, 'that he won't.'

The money for the bet was witnessed by someone else. He came out and he said to Daniel that he had placed the twenty pounds in the hand of someone who was inside.

'Alright,' said Daniel. 'I'm the counsellor now,' he said. 'I will free him, and together with the attorney he will have, and as that is so,' he said, 'on your life, be in the courthouse that day and I will ask the bartender if he has anything to gain if this man hangs. He will say he doesn't and you say that you have bet twenty pounds with him that he won't hang.'

But the day of the court, the man who made the bet of twenty pounds with him was listening to him.

'I say that you have,' he said, 'and that you have gained something by it. You made a bet of twenty pounds with me,' he said, 'that he would hang and I bet you that he wouldn't.'

'Now,' said Daniel, 'what have you to say? What kind of a witness are you to make a bet that that poor man would hang and he was to have been released but there were too many people after him. Get out of the courthouse,' he said, 'and don't let me find you in it again, as long as I am a counsellor.')

Within the anecdotes, the most frequent theme as regards O'Connell relates to his cleverness in the courtroom. This is sometimes based on evidence which he has pre-arranged. A very popular tale, 'The Prisoner Will Not Hang', recounts O'Connell's bet with the chief witness against the accused that the prisoner will not hang. When the case comes to court O'Connell asks the witness if he has bet money on the hanging of the prisoner, and when the witness admits that he has, the case is dismissed.[12]

The number of recorded versions of this legend indicates its popularity in oral tradition. Twenty-one versions have been collected in Irish and eight in English. As is the norm, the setting of the scene varies a good deal from version to version. The event is variously said to have taken place in Castlebar, Listowel or Cork. Murder is the crime committed in all accounts except one. The characters belong to O'Connell's era – landlords, peelers[13] and English people, characters who appear constantly in the folklore of O'Connell. O'Connell returns to the scene of the crime, in heavy disguise in most cases, and involves the owner of the hotel or the person who has witnessed the crime in a bet that the accused will or will not hang.

In 'Perjurers Identified,' as champion of the Irish, O'Connell proves how biased the English legal system is and succeeds in identifying perjurers. O'Connell kills his own horse, and he brings the hotel manager with him as witness to the killing. In court, O'Connell discredits the evidence of five Englishmen who have sworn against an innocent Irishman who has been arrested for the crime.

Of the nineteen versions of this story known to me, twelve are in Irish and seven in English. The places mentioned as the location of the tale are Dublin, London, England, Ennis, Kilkenny and Macroom. In fifteen versions, a horse or horses are killed by O'Connell, or by others at his direction. In three accounts, O'Connell breaks a number of windows in the presence of witnesses and in one of the Mayo versions, he gets permission from the Queen of England to break the windows in the Houses of Parliament. Five thousand pounds is the reward offered for the capture of the offender in this instance. Four Irishmen are arrested for the crime with seven witnesses to swear against them. The Queen of England is O'Connell's chief witness, however, and so the prisoners are freed. O'Connell inevitably employs as witnesses those who are held in high esteem and will be believed, such as lawyers, judges, the Queen or other members of nobility or gentlemen.

In a few versions of this story, a reason is given for the false oath. In the version about the Queen of England, for example, we are told that the Queen wanted O'Connell to prove that bad laws are made in the Parliament in England which allow hundreds of Irishmen to be exiled. In another version of the story, from Cork, it is stated that a man called Malachy Duggan swore against innocent people in Macroom, and that they were to hang. O'Connell is employed to act on their behalf. He tells two fellows to shoot a horse for which he offers them two hundred pounds. Duggan swears that two others committed the crime, and so his false swearing is brought to an end.

Once again, O'Connell manages to achieve the desired verdict in the case of the stolen pig, where O'Connell and the accused divide and share the pig before the case comes to court, and in court O'Connell can honestly say that the accused 'ate no more of that pig than I did'.[14]

In only two versions of this tale, 'Half of the Pig', is a reason given for the theft. In one instance, it is said that the thief makes his living by thieving.[15] On the second occasion, a man has been treated unjustly and O'Connell tells him to steal the pig and to divide it in two. The man does so, and when the owner of the pig goes to feed it the following morning:

> ... *fuair sé, an mhuc a fuair sé inné, bhí sí greadaithe.* Report *áileadh é, an fear seo, ar tugadh an mhuc uaidh, a choinneacas a gabháil soir agus anoir an bóthar ar feadh an lae agus cuireadh fios ar na gardaí. Agus fritheadh leath na muice crochta istigh ag an gcréatúr. Rugas air agus cuireadh isteach i bpríosún é.*[16]

> (... he discovered that the pig was gone. This man was reported, the man who was seen going up and down the road all day long. And the guards were sent for. And half the pig was found hanging inside the poor creature's house. He was arrested and thrown into prison.)

Subsequently the prisoner is freed following O'Connell's presentation of the case in court. There the case rests, with one exception where O'Connell advises the prisoner to sue for defamation of character after the court case, since he has been grievously insulted. The thief in this instance gets hundreds of pounds compensation.[17]

In another story, the judge is forced to let the prisoner go in a case which rests a good deal on O'Connell's credibility and high character as he claims to have known the witness 'Since his Shoes Cost Fourpence'. In three of the recorded versions of the story, the location is in England. In one instance, the incident is said to have occurred in Cork and in another, in Dublin. Usually, the crime committed is not very serious. It may be theft, as is the case in two Galway versions of the story. In some versions, we are told that a child committed the crime, possibly to reduce its seriousness. In two versions, however, the crime is more serious, involving murder, in one case.[18] In the other, it is simply stated that the crime was very serious.[19]

In most instances, O'Connell gives the accused fourpence, or another sum of money, and tells him to buy shoes for himself. The accused is invariably set free. In one version of the story, O'Connell deals with the situation somewhat differently. In this version, a man comes to O'Connell asking him to defend him, and O'Connell deals with it in the following manner:

> Chuir sé isteach i gcliabhán leinbh é, agus bhain luascadh as an gcliabhán ar feadh scaithimh bhig, agus dúirt glaoch air chum teisteiméireachta a thabhairt do os comhair an bhreithimh agus choiste. Do ghlaoigh. 'Cad é do theistiméireacht air?' arsan breitheamh. 'Tá,' arsa an Conallach, 'nár dhéan sé aon ní riamh as an slí ar éinne chomh fada agus atá aithne agam air.'
>
> 'An fada é sin?' arsa an breitheamh. 'Ó bhíos dhá luascadh sa chliabhán,' arsa an Conallach.[20]

(He put him into a child's cradle, and rocked the cradle for a little while, and said to call him to testify before the judge and his jury. He did so. 'What is your testimony of him?' said the judge. 'Well,' said O'Connell, 'he has never done anyone any harm as long as I know him.'

'Is that long?' said the judge.

'Since I used to rock him in the cradle,' said O'Connell.)

In the tale 'A Woman Swears Against her Husband', a woman sees her husband killing sheep and sees the owner of the sheep catch her husband in the act, but O'Connell manages to have the husband freed. He advises the woman before the trial that she should wink at the owner of the sheep in court at every opportunity, implying thereby that she shares some secret with the owner. This is to be done in full view of the judge, and she should also swear that she has seen her husband killing the sheep. In court, O'Connell is then able to 'prove' that the owner of the sheep and the woman had plotted to have the woman's husband convicted.

In 'The Miser is Convicted', which has been recorded, to my knowledge, in the northern half of Ireland only, O'Connell's good name and his arranged evidence also win the day for him. He advises a poor man to wear a wig while stealing from a miser, and to make peculiar faces during the theft. The poor man does so, and in court O'Connell wears the same wig and makes similar peculiar faces, so that the miser claims that O'Connell carried out the theft. This is such a ludicrous suggestion that the case is dismissed.

The location of the tale is given in two versions only, when Sligo and Roscommon, respectively, are mentioned as the place where the action is placed. Shirts or linen are stolen in most cases, but a hat and a piece of cloth are mentioned also. Usually no reason is given for the theft, but in one instance it is said that the theft is to help a widow to pay the rent,[21] and in another version it is said that two Englishmen left a watch on the ground so that an Irishman would pick it up and be arrested.[22] In two versions, O'Connell, in disguise, commits the crime.[23] Half of the versions are in Irish and in one of these, it is said that the thief's 'trade' is stealing:

Well, *bhí ógánach fear ann agus is é an* trade *a bhíodh aige ag goid éadaigh agus ag goid léinteacha agus gach aon sórt a gheobhadh sé amuigh. Ach bhí fear ann a raibh dosaen léinteacha aige aon* heat *amháin amuigh ina gharraí agus bhí crúca beag aigesean; chaitheadh sé isteach é agus bheireadh sé amach na léinteacha. Tháinig an fear air – tháinig an fear air. D'imigh eisean (an gadaí) agus na léinteacha leis agus bhí marc aige ar na léinteacha ar an bhóna nach raibh ag duine ar bith.*[24]

(Well, there was a young man and his trade was stealing clothes and stealing shirts and anything he could find around. But there was a man who had a dozen shirts once, out in his field, and he (the thief) had a little crook and he would cast it out and take out the shirts. The man found him – the man found him. He (the thief) went off, with the shirts, and he had a mark on the collar of the shirts that no-one else had.)

In the international tale of 'The Lawyer's Mad Client' (*AT 1585*), a man sells the same oxen to several people. On the advice of the judge (lawyer) he feigns insanity when brought to court. When his fee is demanded he still feigns insanity.[25] In the 'O'Connell' versions of the tale, O'Connell is, naturally, the lawyer. In one Kerry version, Eoghan Rua Ó Súilleabháin plays one of the main characters in the tale. Eoghan Rua (1748-84) was a Munster poet celebrated for his wit, and about whom a number of tales survive.[26]

The nonsense phrase, or non-contextual phrase, to be used by the accused, varies from version to version, but it is always in English, with one exception, where he says: '*Fág mar sin é!*' (Leave it so!). Otherwise the phrase may be 'Bow-wow-wow,' (Donegal), 'Would you eat a scallion?' (Armagh and Cavan), or 'Well done, judge, and that's your payment' (Kerry). The tale has been recorded in Ireland in several versions where the main character is not O'Connell, but someone else. As told about O'Connell, it is one of the few examples of a situation in which O'Connell is outwitted by someone with a clever tongue. The tale itself is a great deal older than O'Connell's time. 'The Lawyer's Mad Client' was the basis for a medieval French comedy, entitled 'Maître Pathelin'.[27]

Of the seventeen recorded versions in which O'Connell plays the principal role, six are in Irish and eleven in English. In almost all instances, the clever reply given to the judge and then to O'Connell is nonsense – made up of nonsense syllables, or of a combination of words or a phrase which make no sense in the context. The crime committed varies from sheepstealing to murder. In all accounts, the defendant is released on the grounds of insanity and, when O'Connell requests payment from him, he is given the same reply as was given to the judge.

In another story, a device used by O'Connell in court is that of arranging for a second verdict for the one offence, resulting in the lighter sentence being imposed.[28] In most versions of 'The Second Verdict', O'Connell advises his client to throw a handful of sand at the judge and hit him between the eyes to make him angry. This is done just as the death sentence is about to be passed. In anger, the judge attempts to pass a second sentence, and as this is seen to exceed the law, the prisoner is dismissed.

Another alleged case takes place when a widow's son is accused of stealing horses. O'Connell is in court just to give an opinion, as he said himself. In court O'Connell said that he would hang the boy who was working for Lord Gore 'despite all the Lord Gores in the county Leitrim.' When Lord Gore heard that, he said he would take the boy back into his service, just to spite O'Connell.[29]

There is a single version of a story in Irish which tells of a law which was being made in England to commit confessions to paper. O'Connell signed such a paper and his son threw it in the fire. O'Connell said he would fine the son a hundred pounds and a gentleman who was present said the son must hang. O'Connell said he could not fine his son and hang him at the same time, and his son was saved.[30]

The tithe-related story, 'The Minister is Tricked', underlining the religious divide, has been recorded in county Kerry only. Of the fourteen recorded versions, only two occur in English and one of these is introduced in the following manner:

> Daniel O'Connell was a powerful smart man. He couldn't be beaten. He was an attorney, you know yourself, and he saved many a one from being hung, and transported, and so on. Like Pat O'Shea, the time … They used be carding that time – carding wool – and the carders were like curry-combs, you know, for cleaning cows and horses, and so on. Well, here was a custom that time, the parsons could raise so much on the Catholics, and of course the Catholics wouldn't want it at all, and it used to cause a lot of trouble.[31]

The story continues with an account of how a group of men attack a parson in south Kerry. He is stripped naked and his flesh is torn off with a carder. The culprits are masked, but the mask falls off one of the group and the parson recognises him. The man, sometimes called Seán Ó Sé, goes to O'Connell asking for help as he is afraid he will hang:

> 'Dá mba é toil Dé é ba bhreá an scéal dom bás breá glan d'fháil ar mo leaba dom féin seachas mé a chrochadh,' arsa Seán. 'Pé acu toil Dé nó duine é níl aon dul eile ón gcroich agat ach bás d'fháil,' arsa an Conallach leis.
>
> 'Beidh an breitheamh anseo le mo chois-se ar a n-osclóidh an Seisiún agus ba mhaith an bhail ort dá gcailltí thú agus é ann. Tabhair do bhóthar anois ort agus feicim marbh thú roimis an Seisiún.'[32]

> (If it were God's will I would like to die a fine, clean death in my own bed instead of hanging,' said Seán. 'Whether it is God's will or man's will it is only by dying that you can avoid hanging,' O'Connell said to him. 'The judge will be here with me before the Session opens and it would be a good plan for you if you were to die while he is here. Away with you now and let me see you dead before the Session.')

The man pretends to die and O'Connell brings the judge to his wake, but they do not stay very long because of the smoke and the darkness at the wake. However, the occasion makes its mark in the judge's mind. In court, the case is dismissed as the accused is dead and has been thus seen by the Judge. O'Connell has advised Seán Ó Sé not to be seen for a while, as he is supposed to be dead, but the minister or parson becomes very frightened when he sees Seán Ó Sé some time later and thinks he has seen a ghost.

Often, O'Connell's success in solving a case, either in the courtroom or outside it, is due to his quick reaction and practical, astute reasoning in relation to the particular case in hand, an example of which is the following tale:

The Man Who Lost his Eye (AT 1593)

Beirt fhear a bhí amuigh ag iascach i mbád agus thit duine acu amach thar bord agus chuaigh sé go tóin poill. Ar a theacht aníos dhó arís rug an fear a bhí sa mbád ar an gcroisín agus thug stracadh faoin bhfear a bhí amuigh, ach barr ar an donas, cá gcuirfeadh sé an t-iarann ach isteach ina shúil, ach mar sin fhéin d'éirigh leis a thabhairt isteach sa mbád, agus a shábháilt ón mbá. Tar éis an tsoighleas ar fad a rinne fear an bháid bhí an ceann eile le buille agus le báine, dhá rá gur as an riocht a chuir sé an chroisín ina shúil. Dúirt an fear eile nárbh ea, ach ní raibh maith dhó leis an bhfear eile, ná a bheith ag cur ar a shon fhéin leis.

Chinn sé ar na comharsanaigh sa mbaile an cás a réiteach agus ba é a dheireadh an chúirt.

Nuair a chuaigh lucht an dlí thríd an gcúis ó bhun go barr bhíodar féin trína chéile agus séard a dúirt an breitheamh go gcaithfí an chúis a chur siar nó go ndéanfaidís staidéar maith ar an gceist eatarthu féin. Ní raibh ag dul thart ó bhéal go béal ach an chúis dlí. Is é a bhíodh ina ábhar comhrá ag fear is bean, ag óg agus sean go dtí faoi dheireadh go raibh na páistí scoile féin ag plé na cúise. Bhí Dónall Ó Conaill ina scorach beag ag teacht abhaile ón scoil an lá seo agus scata dhá chomhaoiseanna in éindí leis, agus tharraing duine acu cúis na n-iascairí anuas. Ba shin an chéad uair a chuala Dónall aon trácht ar an dlí agus chuir sé gach uile thuairisc faoi rith na cúise, agus hinsíodh dhó ó bhun go barr.

'Tá sé éasca go leor an chúis sin a phlé,' a deir Dónall. 'Tugtar amach an fear sin arís san áit chéanna agus caitear amach thar bord ann é agus más féidir leis teacht isteach uaidh féin arís, tá an fear eile ciontach. Thosaigh na buachaillí eile ag bualadh bosa agus ag bladhrach ag rá go raibh an chúis dlí réitithe ag Ó Conaill. Bhí fear mór dlí ag dul thart ar a chapall agus nuair a chonaic sé an éirí in airde a bhí faoi na gasúir d'fhiafraigh sé dóibh céard a bhí orthu. D'inis siad dó céard a tharla agus cén freagra a thug Dónall ar réiteach na cúise. Chuir an marcach tuairisc cá raibh Dónall agus tugadh ina láthair é. D'ardaigh sé leis ar mhuin a chapaill é go dtug abhaile é agus gur iarr ar a mhuintir é a scaoileadh leis faoi dhéint lucht an dlí.

Thoiligh a mhuintir é a scaoileadh leis, agus ba ghearr go raibh sé i láthair lucht ceannais an dlí. hInsíodh do lucht an dlí faoin réiteach a bhí tugtha ar an gcúis ag an mbuachaill óg, agus d'aontaigh siad d'aon fhocal go mba breith réasúnach í agus go mba shin breith na cúise.

Cuireadh fios ar an toirt ar an mbeirt a raibh an dlí eatarthu agus tugadh an bhreith. An fear a thit sa bhfarraige a thabhairt amach arís agus a chaitheamh le fána san áit chéanna agus cead aige a theacht slán dhá mbeadh sé in ann ach nach mbeadh cead ag aon duine aon chabhair a thabhairt dhó agus mara mbeadh sé in ann theacht slán cead aige a dhul síos, ach dhá dtiocfadh go leanfaí an fear eile faoin

130

tsúil a bhaint as. Bhí an fear a rinne an lot an-tsásta leis an mbreith ach ní thiocfadh an fear eile sa gcontúirt an bhreith a thriall. Tar éis na cúise sin thug an fear dlí a chas ar Ó Conaill ag teacht ón scoil leis é agus chuir ag staidéar dlí é don chéad uair.[33]

(Two men were out fishing in a boat and one of them fell overboard and sank. When he came to the surface again the man in the boat grabbed the hook and hauled in the other man, but unfortunately, where did he put the hook only into the man's eye, but nevertheless he managed to bring the man into the boat and to save him from drowning. After the good turn the man in the boat had done, the other man was furious, saying that he had disfigured him putting the hook into his eye. The man said he hadn't, but there was no point talking to the other man (who had been saved), nor trying to convince him.

The neighbours at home failed to solve the case, and in the end it came to court.

When the lawyers examined the case from top to bottom they were confused, and the judge said that the case would have to be postponed until they studied it properly among themselves. There was talk only of the court case. It was the topic of conversation of men and women, of young and old until at last, even the school children were discussing the case. Daniel O'Connell was a young lad coming home from school one day with some of his companions, and one of them started to talk about the case of the fishermen. That was the first time Daniel had heard of the law and he got every account about the course of the case, and he was told from start to finish.

'It is easy enough to decide that case,' said Daniel. 'Let that man be brought out again to the same spot and let him be thrown overboard there and if he can come in of his own accord, the other man is guilty.' The other boys started to clap and call out saying that O'Connell had solved the legal case. An important legal man was passing by on his horse and when he saw the excitement among the boys, he asked them what was happening. They told him what had happened and the answer Daniel had given for the solution of the case. The rider asked where Daniel was and he was brought to him. He lifted him up on his horse and took him home and asked his parents to let him go to meet the lawyers.

His parents allowed him to go with him and it wasn't long before he was in the presence of the leading legal people. The legal people were told about the judgement the boy had given in the case and they all agreed that it was a reasonable judgement, and that that was the judgement for the case.

The two who were contesting the case were sent for immediately and the judgement was given. The man who fell into the sea was to be brought out again and thrown overboard in the same place, and let him save himself if he could, but no-one was allowed to give him any help, and if he couldn't save himself, let him go under. If he survived, the other man would be pursued for taking his eye out. The man who had done the damage was very happy with the judgement, but the other man wouldn't risk testing the judgement. After that case, the legal man who met O'Connell coming from school, took him away with him and sent him to study law for the first time.)

This tale is called 'The Ungrateful Serpent Returned to Captivity' (AT 155) in the international classification, where it is said: 'An Irish by-form tells how a drowning man who loses an eye at the hand of his rescuer, sues him for damages.' The form of this tale, as told about O'Connell, is very similar to AT 155, but as similar tales about other animals, people and beings have been classified and numbered under different headings, and as it cannot be established for certain that there is a generic relationship between the international tale (AT 155) and the present story, it may be better to classify the tale under humour and humourous tales of a clever man. The tale is therefore classified here under AT 1593 (see AT 785A and AT 921).[34]

The story occurs as far back as the thirteenth century, at least, when it was treated in verse in the French *fabliaux*. The medieval version and the version told about O'Connell are quite similar, as is apparent in the following summary of the *fabliaux*:

> The court was quite at a loss when it came to deciding the rights of the case, but a fool who was present at the time said to them: 'Why this hesitation? Let the first speaker be thrown back into the sea on the spot where the other man hit him in the face and if he can get out again the defendant shall compensate him for the loss of his eye.'[35]

The tale has also been recorded in Schleswig-Holstein in Germany.[36] In Ireland, the basic elements do not vary; O'Connell seems to have been interpolated into an existing tale which was altered to suit O'Connell in that he is sometimes the judge in charge of the case, sometimes the lawyer for the defence, or else the child who suggests the solution to the case. Sometimes it is O'Connell's child who provides the solution. In this case, O'Connell may recognise the child as his own because of his cleverness, and O'Connell – or the judge or lawyer – gives money to the child.[37] Of the forty versions of the story about O'Connell, twenty-eight are in Irish and twelve in English. He plays the role of lawyer or judge in twenty-eight versions in all. In eleven versions O'Connell is the clever boy who provides the solution.

As regards the geographical distribution of the tale and its motifs, it has been recorded in Kerry more than in any other county. In five versions from Kerry, two from Cork and in the only recorded Wexford version, O'Connell recognises that the clever child is his own son. In the western counties, the most frequent version is that of O'Connell as the clever boy. In one Mayo version, it is said that O'Connell was 'clever and knowledgeable. He conducted a case when he was seven years old, that many judges had failed to solve.'[38] Here, O'Connell displays a trait of the classical or epic hero. It is a feature of the heroic life-pattern that the hero 'reveals his strength, courage or other particular features at an early age.'[39] It is thereby intimated that O'Connell will achieve fame because of his cleverness.

The structure of the tale is consistent throughout the various versions, as are the themes and the order of the themes. The story is also told in Ireland about other famous characters, such as Dean Swift and John Philpot Curran, and several versions have been recorded where no proper names are mentioned. In the stories about Dean Swift, the Dean gets advice from young scholars about the case.[40] In the Curran stories, we are told that Counsellor Curran, probably John Philpot Curran, is the boy who provides the clever solution in one instance,[41] or that Counsellor Curran is the lawyer who sends the clever child to school.[42]

A very popular tale of astute questioning is a story entitled 'The Name in the Hat', where O'Connell pretends in court that he is reading the name of the accused from a hat which was found at the scene of the crime by a policeman who is being cross-examined. There is no name in the hat but O'Connell persuades the policeman to say that he has also seen the name of the accused in the hat, and the case then has to be dismissed as none of the policeman's evidence can be believed.

The places mentioned in relation to this anecdote are Cork, Kerry and Limerick. The crime committed is usually a murder but in the one Mayo version it is robbery. In one version we are told that the man was accused of murder, but the narration implies that he was wrongfully accused.[43] In most cases it is quite clear that the accused is guilty of murder, although an excuse is sometimes given for the crime. For example, a poor man from Kerry has spent some time away from home working as a *spailpín* (seasonal worker) and is making his way back to his wife and family. On his way he goes into a house for his supper and there acquires a spade. He sets off again and is accosted by a man who has an iron pistol and who demands his money. In self defence, and in protection of his wages, the *spailpín* commits murder.[44] Some other versions also give a reason for the killing. These include an account of a boy killing another with a stone while they are playing,[45] and an account of O'Connell giving a boy five pounds and a gun to kill a minister – O'Connell then makes a bet with a shopkeeper that the boy will not hang.[46] In other versions the killing may take place during a drunken fight.[47]

Usually, the name that O'Connell pretends to spell from the hat is S-é-a-m-u-s or, in the versions in English, J-a-m-e-s. In a Wexford version, O'Connell buys a hat exactly like that found beside the body, and he asks the witness if the hat belongs to the accused.

By extremely clever cross-examination, O'Connell manages to destroy the evidence of the witness in some instances. One such example is a murder case which is depending chiefly on the evidence of one principal witness for a conviction, where a character named Darby is being cross-examined. All the versions of this anecdote are quite similar, where the witness admits to being drunk at the relevant time. It is mentioned in some versions that the crime involved is murder.

Another story of clever cross-examination describes how Daniel was counsel in a case against a false will. One of the principal witnesses swore that there was life in the man when the will was signed. O'Connell asked if it was not a live fly that was put in the dead man's mouth in order to be able to swear that life was in him. The witness admitted that this was indeed the case, and O'Connell's clever questioning in this instance is said to have made him quite famous.[48]

In some versions, the background to the court case is given and it is said that the dead man had married again after the death of his first wife. He had a son from the first marriage and other children from the second marriage. When the eldest son was away from home his father was ill, but the second wife didn't send his letters to the son. The father died and a witness said in court that there was life in the father when a will was written whereby everything was left to the second wife. The tale is also told about John Philpot Curran,[49] and about other unnamed lawyers, whose cleverness in proving a will to be false is illustrated. A number of published versions of the tale have been noted numbering fifteen in all, of which eleven are in English and four in Irish.

The tale 'Chickens from Boiled Eggs' (AT 821B), is described in the following way in AT: 'The Devil as Advocate: Boiled peas may grow as soon as chickens can be hatched from boiled eggs. Many years after the guest has eaten them, a host demands an enormous sum for eggs claiming that by this time they have hatched out chickens who have in turn laid eggs etc. The devil as advocate comes in and demands that the host cook his peas for planting. "Boiled peas may grow as soon as chickens can be hatched from boiled eggs." The devil carries off the judge.'[50]

As told about O'Connell in Ireland, O'Connell takes on the devil's role of advocate in the story. This tale was recorded in India and in the Orient as early as the fifth century.[51] It has the title 'George Buchanan and the Eggs' as told in the *Dictionary of British Folktales*.[52] The description of George Buchanan, the man who throws the peas on the floor of the courthouse, is very similar to the accounts of O'Connell in Irish oral tradition. Buchanan wins his case by 'natural shrewdness' rather than by legal knowledge, a trait which is also to be found in several tales about O'Connell. Nasreddin Khoja, a similar type of character in the folklore of Turkey, plays the role of lawyer in versions of the tale from that part of the world.[53]

The tale is also told in Irish tradition with no mention made of O'Connell.[54] Of the ten 'O'Connell' versions at my disposal, five are in Irish and five in English, and the plot, characters and their roles are similar in all versions.

In some stories, the court or judge is brought to rule in favour of the accused by clever, often devious means. One such tale, 'The Bribed Judge' tells how a man in county Kerry bribed a judge to transport the accused for life, or to hang him. The bribe he received was a quantity of wine, a measure which contained about ninety gallons. At the trial, things seem to go against the prisoner and O'Connell pretends to fall asleep. The judge wakes him and O'Connell says he has been dreaming that a very fine horse has drowned in a pipe of wine. The judge realises that O'Connell is aware of the bribe and he releases the prisoner.[55]

In another court case, O'Connell is defending a man who has committed a serious crime, such as multiple murder for example, thus underlining the fact that O'Connell is a great lawyer. It is also said that no other lawyer would take the case, emphasising O'Connell's courage and self-confidence. In court, he asks the judge if he might have a few words with his client in private. The judge replies that he may, and tells O'Connell to 'Do All You Can For the Prisoner'. Outside the court, O'Connell tells the man to run for his life and not to stop. Inside the courtroom, O'Connell explains that he was doing all he could for the prisoner and that was to let him have his freedom.[56]

By clever interpretation of events, O'Connell solves the problem of 'The Elder Twin' in a case where money is left to the younger of twin brothers. A great deal of the money went on legal costs, trying to work out which of the twins was the younger. Eventually it came to the Four Courts in Dublin, where O'Connell said that the last of the twins to be born was the elder because the first corn that went into the sack was the elder.[57]

(ii) Helping the Underdog

Tobacco to the Tip of his Ear

Well, there was a man from Westport – he was a pig jobber – he went over with a wagon of pigs, over to England. There was no lie in this. This happened anyhow. And he was going up the streets of Liverpool with them, walking them up, and this shopkeeper came out and he asked him how much for the best and the worst of them, of the pigs. And the man thought it was the best pig and the worst that he was wanting.

He said so much and he gave the pig jobber the money he asked for two pigs, for the best and the worst one. And he sent out his men and drove every one of them. He had them all gone.

But the poor jobber, he hadn't the cost to bring him home, to his own place and he was in an awful way. Someone told him about Dan, Dan was in such a hotel, to go to him. He went and told his story to Dan. Dan listened to him, anyhow. And he brought him into a room and he took a lance and he cut a small tasteen of the skin, the top of the skin, of his right ear. And he wrote a letter and he asked him where he lived. And he mailed it back to the far west in Ireland.

'You'll go now,' he said, 'and I'll give you plenty of money. And go in to that man,' he says, 'the man that took the pigs from you.'

And there was that pig-tail tobacco. It was thin and long. An ounce of it would nearly be a foot long or more.

And he asked him how much would he charge him for as much tobacco as would go from the top of his toe to the top of his ear.

And the shopkeeper looked at the size and he said so much. A good price! The pig jobber handed him out the money. And a young lawyer was sent in with him to witness it. Handed it out to him.

'My good man!' says the lawyer, 'you'll pay well for the drove of pigs you bought from this man,' he says, 'yesterday.'

'All the tobacco,' he says, 'in England,' he says, 'wouldn't go to where the top of that man's ear is buried beyond in Westport,' he says, 'in Ireland.'

He gave him three times the price of the wagon of pigs to settle with him. That's what he did with him. [58]

This is a version of an extremely popular tale in which the problem is solved by O'Connell without going to court, and the poor Irishman makes his fortune as a result of O'Connell's plan. In terms of popularity, it is second only to the tale and verse, 'A Dhónaill Uí Chonaill an dTuigeann tú Gaeilge?', which tells of an attempted poisoning of O'Connell in London, from which he is saved by an Irish-speaking servant girl. Of the seventy-nine recorded versions of 'Tobacco to the Tip of his Ear', forty-nine are in Irish and thirty in English. O'Connell's role does not vary throughout – he succeeds invariably in helping the innocent man to get his revenge on the person who has tricked him.

In all the versions of the story, a man goes to a fair or a market, usually trying to sell pigs or possibly cattle. He is said to be a *spailpín* (seasonal worker), a huckster, a jobber or a harvestman, and his encounter with the buyer takes place in different locations such as

Abbeyfeale, Ballinrobe, Bantry, Bristol, Cork, Dingle, Dublin, Galway, Kenmare, Killorglin, Liverpool, London, Tralee or York. A feature of many folk legends is their tendency to become localised, and this is something that can be easily achieved. In our story here, like so many others, the particular place in Ireland which is mentioned is often in the storyteller's own district. If the tale is situated in England, then very often it is said that the poor man left the storyteller's own district to go to England. The poverty of the jobber is sometimes emphasised by saying that pigs are his only posessions, and we are sometimes told that his mother is a widow. In every version, a shopkeeper plays the trick on the Irishman, and in almost every case, the trickster is an Englishman. A phrase with a double-meaning is the reason for misunderstanding when the shopkeeper is trying to make the bargain: *'Cé mhéid ar an rogha agus ar an díogha?'* ('How much for the best and the worst?'), *'ar an olc agus ar a mhaith de na muca?'* ('for the bad pigs and the good ones?') *'...from the smallest to the biggest?', 'ar an muic bhán le cois na muice duibhe?'* ('...for the white pig along with the black pig?')[59] In these instances the person selling the pigs thinks that he is selling only some of the animals, and accepts money for only some of them. The buyer, however, insists that his question included the entire amount.

In eleven versions, the Irishman loses his money because of a bet, rather than a trick. In these versions, which are all from Galway, with one exception from Mayo, an Irishman goes into a shop, usually in England, and makes a bet with the shopkeeper that he doesn't have a case for his reaping hook. The shopkeeper gives him a cow's horn and it fits the hook.[60]

Well, *bhí* harvestman *i Sasanaí, agus tháinig sé isteach go siopa. Bhí sé ag faire sa tsiopa thart agus ní raibh sé ag iarraidh dada, ná ní fhaca sé an rud a bhí sé a iarraidh sa tsiopa. D'fhiafraigh fear an tsiopa dó céard a bhí sé ag dearcadh ina dhiaidh, nó céard a bhí ag teastáil.*

'Ó,' ar seisean, 'níl mé dhá iarraidh, ná ní fheicim agat i do shiopa é,' ar seisean.

'Cuirfidh mé geall leat go bhfuil,' arsa fear an tsiopa, ar seisean, 'cuirfidh mise geall leatsa,' ar seisean.

'Cén geall a chuirfeas tú?'

'An méid atá saothraithe i mbliana agam.'[61]

(Well, there was a harvestman in England and he came into a shop. He was looking around the shop and he wasn't asking for anything, nor did he see what he wanted in the shop. The shopkeeper asked him what he was looking for, or what he wanted.

'Oh,' he said, 'I'm not looking for it, and I don't see it in your shop,' he said.

'I bet you it's here,' said the shopkeeper, he said, 'I bet you,' he said. 'What will you bet?'
'All I have earned this year.')

In two versions of the story, the shopkeeper insults Daniel O'Connell and this is the reason for O'Connell's revenge.[62] In other accounts, a poor man doesn't have enough money to pay for what he has drunk, or an Englishman refuses to give a piece of bread to a poor man, or an Englishman is mocking a 'Paddy'. In some versions, a stupid man is trying to get 'the highest penny' for his pigs, and he sells the pigs when a penny is held up high. At this point, O'Connell enters the tale, if he is not already a part of it, and offers advice to the losing party. In forty-four versions, a piece is taken off the top of the man's ear; in twenty-seven versions, a piece is taken off his toe: in three versions, a piece is taken from a horse's tail: in two versions, a piece is taken from a finger, and in one version from a toe-nail.

In all versions, tobacco is the unit of measurement used to seal the bargain with the shopkeeper, and in all versions, the question is asked 'How much would it cost to get as much tobacco as would reach from the top of the ear (toe) to the top of the foot?' In all versions, the poor man receives compensation, money in most cases, and usually worth far more than the price of the animals. In a few cases, he gets tobacco, and sometimes he gives a share of it to O'Connell. O'Connell inevitably emerges as the hero of the tale. He treats the poor Irishman gently, for example: 'O'Connell cuts the top of his ear off and posts it to Cork. He bandages the man's ear.'[63] This image is in keeping with the humane O'Connell who is ready to help the person who has been tricked and who treats him gently. Although a few versions of the tale do not refer to O'Connell, there is no evidence that the tale was ever told about other named characters. From the number of international motifs which form part of the basic structure of the tale in the versions found in Ireland, however, it is likely that the tale itself existed before O'Connell's time.

Appearing as saviour of the downtrodden and the mistreated Catholic and as their champion, Catholic supremacy and virtue are underlined as O'Connell wins the day. In the stories, public support is demonstrated for O'Connell and for his politics. In most of the O'Connell tales, the enemy is the political and personal enemy of the cause of the Irish Catholic. One tale, 'Tomorrow Never Comes', underlines O'Connell's support of the clergy. The story describes how O'Connell persuades a landlord to allow his tenants – Catholic priests, monks or nuns – to stay until 'tomorrow'. He gets this permission in writing. The following day the paper which the landlord has signed is shown to him again by O'Connell and he realises that he has allowed the tenants to stay as long as they like.

In four instances, it is stated where the tale takes place. In a Longford version, it is said to occur in a convent in Multyfarnham which is in that county. The convent belongs to a wealthy gentleman and he is trying to evict the nuns. They go to Daniel O'Connell for assistance.

In two accounts from Kerry, the lands of Mount Melleray in county Waterford are the matter of contention.[64] The people about to be thrown off their land are inevitably priests, brothers or nuns, with only two exceptions, both from county Cork, where O'Connell helps lay people to postpone the payment of rent until 'tomorrow'.

The basic motif of this story is very old – that is, the clever use of words in legal proceedings to avoid payment of rent. A similar motif has been documented in early Irish literature: King induced by saint to remit tribute till *Luan*.[65]

In one example of the story 'Once Bitten, Twice Shy', Dan advises a poor Irishman how to get money. He tells him to go into a Jew's shop or a bank, and to put his hand down into the gold, and then to run out but not to bring any gold with him. The Irishman does so, and the shopkeeper or the man in the bank sends for the police, but nothing can be proven against the Irishman as no gold is found on him. The Irishman subsequently wins a legal case for defamation of character.[66] Afterwards, O'Connell advises him to go into the bank again and to take the gold with him on this occasion. This time no-one stops him.[67] Of the thirteen recorded versions of this tale, eleven are in Irish and three in English. In six versions, it is said that the incident takes place in a Jewish shop, and in three versions the action takes place in a bank. The insult to the Irishman is emphasised when he is chased by the shopkeeper as he shouts for the police to arrest the thief. In one instance, a man called Seán Ó Murchú from Cathair Saidhbhín gets so much compensation that he is able to return to Ireland and settle comfortably there.[68] In another case, a man from Conamara gives some money to O'Connell out of his compensation and is still able to buy land and a fine house for himself in Ireland.[69]

In 'The Devil in Disguise', we are told that O'Connell helps a man whose money is being kept unjustly from him. O'Connell goes to the trickster's house, dressed in animal skin and horns and it is thought that he is the devil. The priest is summoned. O'Connell says he will leave the house if the money owing is repaid.

In most versions of the story, a person is given money to mind and when the time comes to repay the money, there is no trace of it. The person who keeps the money is by no means poor. On the contrary, it is always a minister, a shopkeeper or a rich Protestant who already has money, and who wants to increase his wealth. The crime is, of course, made all the worse by the fact that the money is taken from a shoemaker, a servant boy, a poor Catholic or a widow.

When O'Connell reaches the trickster's house, he pretends he is an Englishman, a beggar or a traveller, in order to gain admittance to the house and spend the night there. Sometimes, he brings the animal skin and the horns in a bag in preparation for the morning, and the servant girl thinks he is the devil when he appears dressed in this disguise. When the minister fails to get rid of the devil, the priest is summoned. The power of the priest in this instance is seen to be greater than that of the minister, thus conforming with popular ideas about clerics of different denominations, and their respective powers.

In some versions, it is said that a conversation takes place between the priest and the devil in Latin, and this increases popular respect for O'Connell's learning. Of eleven recorded versions of the story, eight are in Irish, and the tale appears to be associated, on the whole, with county Donegal and the north-west of Ireland.

In another tale, 'A Shave for Two', of which we have at least ten versions, the barber (who is sometimes an Englishman) is cruel and unjust, and overcharges a customer (who is sometimes a poor Irishman in London) for a haircut. In a less common version of the same tale, O'Connell helps a little boy who has been mistreated, to get his revenge on the barber.

In one version only, O'Connell himself is the person who is over-charged by the barber for the haircut.[70] In a few versions, it is said that the Irishman had drink taken and that in this way the barber succeeded in overcharging him.

An isolated account, in Irish, tells of O'Connell helping a poor man who has been duped. The man has three piglets and spends a long time fattening them. Eventually, he brings his three pigs to the fair and sells them to a shopkeeper. The shopkeeper takes the pigs and says that he has bought them for his brother, a priest. The poor man goes to the priest to get his money and discovers that the priest doesn't know the shopkeeper. O'Connell comes to the rescue when he finds the shopkeeper and engages him in conversation about the price of pigs that day. The poor man appears and challenges the shopkeeper for sending him to a priest who had never heard of him, and had never wanted to buy pigs. O'Connell tells the shopkeeper to pay the poor man fifteen pounds for the pigs and says that if he doesn't do so, he will eventually have to pay a great deal more.[71]

A tale entitled, 'Some Things Not For Sale' (AT 1559C*), is noted in Irish tradition only. It tells of a man who enters a huge shop where everything is said to be available. He bets with the owner that there are some things he cannot supply. The bet is accepted. The man then asks for six pairs of spectacles for his geese, a saddle for a frog, three sailfuls of wind to drive his sailing boat *etc*. He wins the bet.[72] Of twelve versions of the story from Ireland, O'Connell appears in three of them. In those versions where O'Connell is not named, another Irishman is involved who may be named 'Paddy'. Sometimes 'Paddy' has emigrated to England and been tricked by a shopkeeper in the past, or he may be an Irishman who is described as being 'clever'. On other occasions, the trickster in the story may be a local person with a reputation for cleverness, as occurs in the case of a certain Kerryman called Diarmuid Ó Bric, about whom a number of stories are told.[73] As told about O'Connell, the tale appears to be found in Irish only, with two versions collected in county Galway and one in Mayo. In the Galway versions, the incident takes place in England and is a vivid example of O'Connell's assistance to an emigrant Irishman.

The Irish version of the tale 'Payment With the Clink of Money' (AT 1804B) tells how a man paid, by jingling coins in his hands, for a poor meal which he had only smelled. Only three versions have been documented, in which O'Connell plays the part of advisor to the fellow who is asked to pay for what he has smelled. Two of these versions are in Irish and one is in English. The tale dates from at least the fifteenth century. It appeared in printed sources such as chapbooks as early as 1480, and its appearance in many languages in similar publications indicates its popularity and suggests a strong influence on oral tradition.[74] It occurs also in the Italian Novella or tale in prose, which is at least three centuries old, where a man is sued for payment for the enjoyment of the smell of meat when roasting.[75] As told about O'Connell, there are only minor differences between the various versions. In an account from Tipperary, the owner of the house demands payment and, when approached about the problem, O'Connell says: 'When the smell of the meat did him, the jingle of the money should do the man of the house.'

In the Kerry versions, six fellows ask for a meal and are given meat. One of the fellows does not want the meat and eats bread instead. The woman who gave them the meal steals his hat because he refuses to pay for the meat. O'Connell is passing by and hears the argument. The woman says the fellow did not need to eat the meat because the smell of it filled his stomach. O'Connell takes some money from his pocket and puts it in his hat. He holds it out to the woman and tells her to put her nose into it and to fill her stomach with its smell.

O'Connell is often depicted as not taking kindly to mocking or jeering, and in the tales he usually gets his revenge on those who make fun of him. This happens in the tale of 'The Laughing Horses'. In this story, a trick is played on O'Connell when bundles of oats are stuck into the rear end of his horse and the culprits say to O'Connell that his horse is so stupid that he is eating oats through his rear end. O'Connell, or his servant boy, retaliates by slashing the sides of the tricksters' horses and saying then that their horses are breaking their sides laughing at O'Connell's horse. The tale is also told about Jack, Dean Swift's clever servant boy.[76] It would appear in this case, that an older tale became 'O'Connellised', to suit the Liberator's role as folk hero.

In the tales, O'Connell is sometimes mocked by the English, and he helps other Irish people who are similarly ridiculed, especially in London. In a tale called 'A Chimney Sweep and a Barber', we are told that a poor Irishman, the sweep, was in London. The barber used stand at his door and say: 'There's a smell off you! Look at the dirty thing!' O'Connell advised the Irishman to wash his face and to get a good suit of clothes and new shoes and a hat, and to go into the barber. So the sweep cleaned and dressed himself and went into the barber and asked the barber if he would shave him. The barber said he would. There were five or six others in the shop and the barber brought him in and he shaved him.

The man told the barber that there were three big hairs on his behind, and he asked the barber to shave these as well. The barber did as he was asked. The man paid the barber with a fine, yellow farthing, and the barber simply put it in his pocket, because he thought it was a sovereign. The next day, the sweep appeared again and he was as black as soot. The barber was mocking him again when the sweep said to him that he had shaved him yesterday, and shaved his behind for a farthing. At that, the barber put his hand into his pocket and pulled out the sovereign and, of course, it was only a farthing. The barber didn't mock him any more after that.[77]

In another story O'Connell arranges to rob the rich and helps his fellow countrymen to have a better quality of life. In the tale entitled, 'Tar on a Saucepan', a poor Irishman is described as a young fellow, a beggar or a shoemaker, who takes sovereigns out of a bank, attached to a tar-covered saucepan. In one instance, the adventure is said to have taken place in England where the Irishman is unable to get work.[78]

(iii) Bets

The Night of the Wisps
Dan O'Connell made a bet of a hundred pounds that he would rouse Ireland in one night; in twenty four hours. I heard old Ann Graham of Cornagee say she minded 'The Night of the Wisps' well; she said their

house was knocked up ten times and more in the night with ones running to leave a wisp.

It was a wisp of straw. O'Connell started it down in Athy, I think, and give four wisps to four men and told them to leave a wisp in four different houses, and the people of that house would have to run and leave a wisp in four more. O'Connell said that if they didn't, a terrible plague would come upon them and the whole country was running mad, running to houses where there were wisps and then running to others. And he won his bet.[79]

Some accounts describe bets or wagers in which O'Connell gets the upper hand. Sometimes, he sets out to prove that his political adversaries, or other people in authority, are too proud and are not prepared to acknowledge his cleverness. O'Connell is not a man to refuse a challenge of any kind, and he takes on bets when they are put to him. Often, it is O'Connell himself who offers the challenge.

In the anecdotal material, the most dramatic and historically verifiable bet of all is one which is known as 'The Night Of The Wisps'. O'Connell said he would rouse Ireland within twenty-four hours.

In the Donegal versions of the story, O'Connell is in the Houses of Parliament in England and the deputies are mocking him, so he makes a bet with them that he will rouse Ireland in twenty-four hours. In one account, the reason for the 'Night of the Wisps' is simply because O'Connell wants to send a message as quickly as possible from Dublin to Sligo.[80] The message is urgent and so O'Connell puts a note inside a straw, attaches the address on the outside, and the straw is sent from house to house. It reaches Sligo far quicker than the postal delivery. Some of the versions of the story in English refer to stones which are brought from house to house.

In most cases, O'Connell sends a message from house to house to warn of a plague of typhus or some other disease. In a few accounts, no reference is made to O'Connell's part in the event. This happens in an Antrim version, for example, where it is stated that the 'Night of the Wisps' took place before 1798. On this occasion, wisps were brought from house to house during the organisation of a rising. The collector of this account wrote: 'Other narrators seem to agree it was 1798 – The Year of the Turn-Out.' The second version in which O'Connell is not mentioned is from Wicklow, where it is said that the people of the Glen of Imaal thought that Ireland was to be attacked, and that people were warned of this by bringing bread from house to house. No date is given here – it is simply stated that it happened 'Long, long ago'.

These exceptional cases, where no mention is made of O'Connell, are in contradiction to the recall expressed in other accounts. In an account from Donegal, for example, the storyteller says it was his own father who went to Mín an tSionnaigh, in the barony of Kilmacrenan, with the last wisp.[81] In another Donegal version, it is said that Pádraig Ó Gallchobhair from Cró na Sléibhe, Na Gleanntaí, had to travel twenty miles to bring his wisps to the houses.[82] And in Donegal again, the storyteller's neighbour, who was called Cathal Ó Sidheáil, remembered the occasion well as he was one of those who was running.[83] In county Down, a man called McKevitt said he would run although he had no stones to bring with him, and he said if he didn't do so: 'Somethin' 'll bound to happen to me before morning.'[84] One woman said that her mother took part in it: 'My mother saw it done and she had a hand in it.'[85] One storyteller said that a Mrs McAniff in Cavan remembered the night well, and she had told him that people were coming to her house again and again to find out if the wisps had been brought there.[86] The story is so well-known in Donegal that there is a saying there in Irish *'Chomh gnóthach is dá mbeadh oíche na sifíní ann.'* ('As busy as if it were the night of the wisps').[87]

Accounts of 'The Night of the Wisps' have been recorded for the most part in the northern counties, with only one version each from counties Kerry, Wicklow and Galway. Sixteen of the twenty-three recorded versions are in English.

A related episode of historical origin occurred in 1832 when there was a threat of cholera in Ireland. At that time, the Blessed Virgin was said to have appeared in a church in Charleville in county Cork, and she is said to have left ashes on the altar which were the only protection against the disease. She is said to have requested people to behave in the following manner:

> She ordered that small packages of the ashes should be taken to neighbouring houses, and that the owner of each house was then to take four parcels of ashes out of his own chimney and bring them to other houses, giving the same instructions to each family.[88]

Fear and panic were widespread as the ashes were taken from place to place. As this incident is said to have occurred when O'Connell was at the height of his fame it is in keeping with folk tradition and with the popular dramatisation of O'Connell that this incident should be connected to him.

In a number of other anecdotes, O'Connell wins a mundane type of bet. A man tells him that no blacksmith could ever make more than three nails at one time. O'Connell retorted that there was a blacksmith, Tadhg Ó Murchú in Uíbh Ráthach, who could 'make seven nails at a go'. Tadhg made the seven nails and the Counsellor won his two hundred pounds, from which Tadhg was given ten pounds for drink.[89]

In some stories, O'Connell gets the upperhand of, or revenge on, the

English. Many of these anecdotes illustrate the opposite of the modern ethnic jokes in which 'Paddy' plays the role of the fool. For example, because of his understanding of the Irish language O'Connell is able to win a bet which he makes with some English people. At a dinner, O'Connell claims that he knows someone who can eat seventeen turkeys at one sitting. He brings in an Irish boy who eats twelve turkeys and then says:, *'A mháistir, ní thig liom níos mó a ithe'* ('Master, I can't eat any more'). O'Connell says that the boy has said he would eat as many more again. The English people refuse to let him eat them, however, so O'Connell wins the bet.[90]

There is a relevant isolated version of the international tale 'Weeping and Laughing' (AT 1828*) in which a parson preaches so that half the congregation weeps and the other half laughs because he is without breeches.[91] This tale is not included in TIF, and the only Irish version of it, which is told about O'Connell, describes how O'Connell made a bet that he could make half the crowd laugh and half the crowd cry. He succeeds in doing so by delivering a sad speech to the crowd in front of him so that they are moved to tears. At the same time, he has no seat in the back of his trousers so that the crowd behind him are laughing.

As summarised in AT, the tale of 'The Cat and the Candle' (AT 217) tells of a man who has a cat trained to hold up lighted candles on its head. The king has a mouse let loose, however, and the cat drops the candle and chases the mouse.[92] Although forty-seven versions of this tale have been documented in Irish tradition, O'Connell is mentioned in only three of them – two in Irish from Donegal and one in English from Sligo. In other versions of the tale recorded in Ireland, where O'Connell does not appear, the characters in the tale include a king and a scholar, a captain and a farmer, an Englishman and an Irishman and a poor scholar and a minister. The tale is used in many versions to illustrate the Irish proverb: *'Is treise dúchas ná oiliúint'* ('Nature is stronger than training.')[93]

In another story, O'Connell was being mocked once at a dinner in London, and he bet a hundred pounds that he would prove on the following day that the English were fools. He filled a box with brand new gold sovereigns and stood at Westminster Bridge shouting: 'Brand new sovereigns at a penny each.' Nobody bought one as they didn't believe him, and thought he was crazy. He won his bet and the stakes were doubled. The story continues:

> He went to an apothecary that he knew next morning early and got three dozen empty pill boxes. Then he went to an Irishman that was fattening pigs outside of London and got the boxes filled nicely with fresh pig-dung.

Back with him to Westminster Bridge, he got up on the box and began to shout out the merits of the wonderful foreign concoction he had for the complexion – 'only 2/6 a box.' Arra man, he had to run out of the place before 10 o'clock. They had all his stock bought up. I tell you, you coudn't be up to Dan.[94]

'The Uglier Foot' (AT 1559B*) is the title of a tale in which a travelling man comes to a house and gets a meal. He shows his foot to the owner and lays a wager that there is a foot even uglier than it in the house; the owner wagers that there is not. The traveller then lays bare his other foot, which is much uglier than the first, and wins the bet.[95] The tale can be traced to at least as early as the thirteenth century.[96] There is only one 'O'Connell' version of this tale, and it provides a further example of the 'O'Connellisation' of material. There are several versions in Irish tradition told about other characters, such as, for example, Seán Ó Móráin, Morgan Fahy or Paddy Sheils. As told about O'Connell, the tale is another example of him being insulted by an Englishman and managing to turn the tables. As is the case with other versions of the tale, the O'Connell version has two characters, one 'ranking lower in the social scale and having deformed feet'.[97]

The version about O'Connell was told in direct response to a query by the collector asking if anyone in the district knew the Liberator, or remembered him. The informant replied that his father knew him well, and then started to tell the tale of the uglier foot.

(iv) O'Connell Meets his Match

The Goose With the One Leg (AT 785A)

Dan and his servant were going the road one frosty morning and there was a goose and it standing on one leg at the edge of a pond.

Some time previous the servant had served a goose to Dan and it had only one leg, because the servant had the other one. Dan scolded him for eating the leg and the servant kept saying that the goose had only the one leg.

'Now,' says the servant, when he saw the goose standing on the one leg, 'there's a goose, now, with only one leg.'

'Hush!' says Dan to the goose, and the goose put down her other leg.

'Now, hasn't she two legs?' says Dan.

'Now why didn't you do that to the other goose?' says the servant.[98]

On one of the rare occasions when O'Connell meets his match, the tale 'The Goose With The One Leg' (AT 785A) tells of a thief who is accused of eating a goose's leg, and maintains that the goose has only the one leg. The goose is, in fact, merely standing on one leg. The master, O'Connell, confounds the rascal by frightening the goose which then uses both legs.[99]

In Irish tradition, this tale is more frequently told about Dean Swift and his servant boy than about Daniel O'Connell. The folklore accounts of Swift and O'Connell have a great deal in common, and it is precisely this kind of tale which is told about each of them. Both were public figures and were seen to support the downtrodden. The anecdotes and tales about them are humourous, and the humour is based a great deal on quick wit and repartee. In folklore, verses are attributed to both of them. They are both figures of authority and are at the same time very popular. They are perceived as being shrewd. Tales of the 'master-servant', in which the servant proves himself to be cleverer than the master, are told about both O'Connell and Swift.[100] In the 'O'Connell' versions of the 'master-servant' tale of the goose with one leg, O'Connell is not in the role of trickster but rather as the 'tricked', that is the role of master. There are eleven recorded versions of the story, in which Dean Swift and his servant boy are the main characters, and three versions which have O'Connell as the master.

The tale is found in Bocaccio's Decameron of the fourteenth century and it occurs in a number of oriental collections and also in many other early collections of jokes and anecdotes.[101] It has been known in the English language since at least the seventeenth century. A version of it was published in 1693 in a book of comical tales entitled *Jests Refin'd and Improved*.[102] The tale appears to have attained great popularity in early chapbooks and jestbooks in many languages.[103] The widespread availability of chapbooks and penny books in Ireland and their influence on oral tradition is a subject which requires further examination. It is certainly true that a great deal of narrative, and of anecdotes and comical tales in particular, became part of folk tradition in Ireland through these publications.

Even on occasions when O'Connell is beaten by a client or by someone else, he has initially shown his cleverness. This occurs, for example, in the tale entitled 'An Abduction', when he gives advice to a young man as to the best way to get a girl's hand in marriage from her reluctant father. O'Connell advises him to take the woman and to put her in front of him on his horse and to go around the four corners of the town announcing that the woman is abducting him. In this way, it will not be suspected that the man is in fact the abductor. The couple follow his instructions and go away, and it transpires in some versions that the girl is actually the Counsellor's daughter.[104]

O'Connell's advice is so good in this instance, that in advising the procedure for abduction, he cannot pursue the abductor on a point of law. In a Donegal version of the story, it is the butler who falls in love with O'Connell's daughter. In a Cork tale, the girl in question is not O'Connell's daughter, but the daughter of a nobleman who is in love with a servant boy. And so it appears that the boy is usually of lower social standing than the girl. In a Mayo version of the story, the boy is named as Cearbhall Ó Dálaigh, a famous romantic poet about whom a great deal of folklore exists, much of it portraying him as a folk hero.[105] A Galway version appears as part of a series of tales and anecdotes told about O'Connell, and it would appear that there is again here some confusion between John Philpot Curran, the famous lawyer,[106] and Daniel O'Connell.

In the tale 'O'Connell Recognises His Own Child', O'Connell meets a child who asks him for money. When O'Connell gives it to him and promises more the next time they meet, he recognises the child to be his own because the child is clever and has taken a short cut to meet O'Connell quickly again. The tale contains motifs which are found in versions of AT 873 'The King Discovers his Own Son', AT 921 'The King and the Peasant's Son', and also in AT 875 'The Clever Peasant Girl' II – The Tasks.[107]

In sixteen of the twenty-two versions of the story noted about O'Connell, the clever boy is O'Connell's son. In one instance, it is a daughter of O'Connell who is shown to be clever, or the child may otherwise be described as an unrelated 'clever child' in some versions. As regards the clever boy motif, Dean Swift's servant boy is also said to have been clever.[108] In all the 'O Connell' versions of the story, the child shows the ability to perform impossible, or near impossible, tasks, a motif which is well established both in Irish and in international folklore. In a few versions, the tale is interwoven with the tale 'The Man who Lost his Eye' (AT 1593), also told about O'Connell.

The tale illustrates the belief that, as the father is clever, so also will the child inherit this gift and be recognised as his father's son because of it. In versions of at least one other tale, 'Hospitality Won by a Trick', it is also shown that O'Connell's child is clever and has inherited the same kind of cleverness associated with his father.[109]

In most versions of 'O'Connell Recognises his Own Child', the child shows his cleverness by taking a shortcut and meeting O'Connell again before he is expected to do so. In one account, O'Connell asks a girl for her name and she says she does not know, except that she hears her mother say she is a daughter of Daniel O'Connell. She also takes the shortcut and meets O'Connell again but he says he doesn't want to meet her while she is wearing linen or wool. Her mother tells her to go to the bog, to get bogcotton, and to knit a suit for herself. She comes then to meet O'Connell and has fulfilled his conditions. She also fulfills a condition which is not imposed by O'Connell, that is, she does not come by the road or on a path, but over the fences. This version of the story[110] is obviously closely related to the 'impossible tasks' motif, found in many other tales, for example in the Fenian tale of Diarmaid and Gráinne.[111]

In some stories, a clever boy catches O'Connell out by interpreting a word in its literal meaning. Sometimes, the boy is a widow's son, a type who is portrayed in folklore very often as an exceptionally clever lad, or else who evokes pity if his cleverness is not illustrated.[112] In one example of the story entitled 'Literal Meaning',[113] O'Connell manages to get his revenge on a person who has tricked him. He makes a bargain with a woman that she will provide him with goose dung. She then has to pay him ten pounds when O'Connell proves that the dung contains gander and goose dung. O'Connell's own respect for cleverness is shown in a version of the story where he goes to the mother of a clever boy, and asks if he can take the boy away and make a lawyer of him.[114]

In the tale of 'The Geese and the Ganders,' O'Connell pays a boy for a flock of geese which is to be delivered to him the following day. The boy removes the ganders from the flock and delivers the geese only.

On another occasion, a fellow called Seán Bán is accused by a woman of having abducted her, but she proves to be too clever for O'Connell when he tries to catch her out. In one version of the story, O'Connell arranges to have a box of lice walk on the jacket of the girl's counsellor the day of the trial, and the lawyer is highly embarassed and leaves the court. Of the ten recorded versions of this tale, only two are in English and, from its distribution, the tale appears to be a Kerry one. Seán Bán is usually the name given to the person who is convicted. His surname is given as Ó Murchú, Moriarty or Brewer and, in one instance, the storyteller said that he knew the woman in question – Cáit Bhán.[115] When the tale occurs in English, the conversation between O'Connell and the girl still takes place in Irish.

In another story, we are told that O'Connell was caught out once when he went to a shoemaker and asked to have shoes made for him. The shoemaker had no leather and O'Connell gave him ten pounds towards the leather, saying that the man who has the money must always buy the drink. The shoemaker pays back two-and-sixpence, and later five shillings towards the ten pounds, saying to O'Connell that the man with the money must buy the drink. O'Connell eventually tells him to keep the rest of the money owing or it would all be drunk. It is said that the shoemaker was the first man ever to play tricks on Daniel O'Connell.[116]

Continuing with tales of shoemakers and shoes, O'Connell met his match when he went to have a side-patch put on a shoe in the tale 'The Shoemaker Outwits O'Connell'. Here, when O'Connell says that he has never paid such a high price for a patch on his shoe, the shoemaker says that he has never before put a patch on a counsellor's shoe.

(v) O'Connell in London: the Political Career

'A Dhónaill Uí Chonaill, an dTuigeann Tú Gaeilge?'

Bhí Dónall Ó Conaill ag féasta i Sasana uair amháin i measc na Lordanna móra i Londain. Bhí an dearg-ghráin acu ar Dhónall ach níor mhaith leo a ligean orthu fhéin leis, ach shocraigh siad plean chun é a chur dá chois. Fuair siad deoch nimhe agus chuireadar trína chuid tae é. Bhí cailín aimsire ag obair sa gcuairt ina raibh an féasta le bheith agus bhí togha aithne aici ar Ó Conaill. Ar a thabhairt faoi ndeara don chailín go raibh nimh dhá chur sa dí do Dhónall, labhair sí agus dúirt:

> *An cailín: 'A Dhónaill Uí Chonaill, an dtuigeann tú Gaeilge?'*
> *Ó Conaill: 'Tuigim, a chailín, céard sin is léar dhuit?'*
> *An cailín: 'Tá nimh ar do chupán, cuir thart é más féidir.'*
> *Ó Conaill: 'Más fíor sin a chailín, is maith í do spré-sa.'*

Níor thuig éinne dhá raibh sa láthair céard a bhí ar bun idir an bheirt agus sin a bhí uaidh Dhónall. Ní dhearna sé ach an fáinne óir a bhí ar a mhéir a scaoileadh ar an talamh agus nuair a chrom na boic mhóra a bhí leis síos chun a thógáil, d'athraigh seisean a chupán leis an té ba ghaire dó, agus bhí an báire leis.[117]

(Daniel O'Connell was at a feast in England once with the big Lords in London. They hated Daniel intensely but they didn't want to let on to him, and they made a plan to get rid of him. They got a poisonous drink and they put it through his tea. There was a serving girl working in the mansion where the feast was to be held and she knew O'Connell well. When the girl saw that poison was being put in Daniel's drink, she spoke and said:

> The girl: 'Daniel O'Connell, do you understand Irish?'
> O'Connell: 'I do, girl, what do you see?'
> The girl: 'There is poison in your cup, send it around if you can.'
> O'Connell: 'If that is true for you, girl, you will get a good dowry.'

No-one there understood what was going on between the two of them and that was what Daniel wanted. He let the gold ring on his finger fall to the ground and when the gentlemen bent down to pick it up, he exchanged his cup with that of the person nearest to him and he was fine then.)

The best-known and most widespread of all of the O'Connell anecdotes is the one quoted above, which tells of an unsuccessful attempt to poison him, and describes how he is saved by a servant girl who warns him in Irish not to take the poisoned drink. The story is entitled *'A Dhónaill Uí Chonaill, an dTuigeann Tú Gaeilge?'*

At least one hundred and forty-four versions of this tale have been documented from oral tradition, of which forty-two are in English. One reason for its popularity must be that it lends itself to easy recall because of the short, straightforward verse. In addition, it is highly dramatic and so keeps the listener's attention. Although the tale was often told in English, the verse was nearly always recited in Irish. In some versions, however, the message in the verse was given in prose form in English.

As recently as 1948 a version of this story was collected in Irish in county Tipperary.[118] The following extract from a Wexford version, however, collected in English, shows how an attempt has been made to render the Irish rhyme into verse:

> 'Daniel O'Connell do you understand Irish?'
> 'Yes, my dear girl, I can both read it and write it.'
> 'There's salt in your porridge, and mind it.'[119]

In areas outside Irish-speaking districts, although the storyteller often says that he does not speak Irish himself or that he doesn't understand the verse, the verse itself is sometimes given in English orthography of the words in Irish, as in:

> Dónall Ó Conaill dig-in-thoo *(an dtuigeann tú)* Gaelic
> Ta colleen jass*(Tá cailín deas)* the brim-a my hat-a.[120]

> (Dónall Ó Conaill do you understand Irish?
> Yes, nice girl, the brim of my hat *(?)*)

The storyteller in this instance went on to explain that the verse meant that the drink contained a hatful of poison. As with several other anecdotes about O'Connell, this incident takes place in London, or in some part of England. The people at the dinner are described as Englishmen or Protestants. In one instance, O'Connell is in Scandinavia;[121] in three versions, he is in Dublin;[122] in one version, he is in the centre of Ireland,[123] and in another version he is invited to Dunboy Castle.[124]

In most cases, the poison is put in O'Connell's drink, but sometimes it is put in his dish or in his porridge. The girl tells O'Connell, in different ways, that he is being poisoned. She may say '*Tá ... deoch (salann) i do chupán,*' ('There is a drink (salt) in your cup'), '*rud ar do shoitheach*' ('something in your dish') '*piobar sa phraiseach*' ('pepper in your porridge'), '*oiread ar do ghloine*' ('as much in your glass'), '*a mharódh na céadta*' ('that would kill hundreds'). In the versions in English, she says: 'The herring isn't caught with bait,' or 'There's salt in your porridge.'

O'Connell promises the girl a dowry when she reveals the situation to him. He lets something – a knife, a ring, or money – fall on the floor and he, or the girl, quenches the lights. While this is happening, he exchanges his own glass with that of the person next to him. Usually, that person is not named, although it is implied that the person is a

Protestant, an Englishman, a member of Parliament, or at least a very important gentleman. It may happen that O'Connell spills his drink while directing the attention of the guests out the window so that he need not drink the poison. One rather unusual version tells how O'Connell explains that the custom in Ireland is for people to exchange glasses. O'Connell's enemy refuses to recognise this custom and he drinks his own drink. O'Connell then pretends that he has drunk the poisoned drink and he runs from the room to vomit the poison.[125] In most cases, however, O'Connell succeeds in exchanging drinks, the enemy dies on taking the poisoned drink, and O'Connell and the girl get away.

The anecdote is popular not only for its dramatic effect, but also because it illustrates that while O'Connell is credited historically with encouraging the use of English, it is the Irish language that saves him in this instance.

As this anecdote is the one which is most frequently told about O'Connell and is also the most widespread, a few examples are given here of the anecdote from different parts of Ireland:

> *Bhí fear ann darb ainm Dónall Ó Conaill agus shíl na hAlbanaigh go raibh drochdhlí aige. Chuir an bodach seo faoina choinne. Tháinig sé agus chuir siad nimh ina chupa. Bhí cailín Gaelach insan teach. Dúirt sí: 'A Dhónaill Uí Chonaill an dtuigeann tú Gaedhilg?' 'Tuigim a chailín is dadaidh is léar leat?' 'Tá oiread ar do chupa is mhuirfeadh na céadtaí.' D'athraigh sé an cupa. D'ól bodach an cupa agus thit sé marbh. Thug Dónall Ó Conaill an cailín leis ar a chúlaibh.*[126]

(There was a man called Daniel O'Connell and the Protestants thought his laws were bad laws. This churlish fellow sent for him. He came and they put poison in his cup. There was an Irish girl in the house. She said (in Irish):

'Daniel O'Connell do you understand Irish?'

'I do, my girl, what do you see?'

'There is as much in your cup as would kill hundreds.'

He exchanged his cup. The churlish fellow drank the cup and he fell down dead. Daniel O'Connell took the girl away behind him on his horse.

In one version,[127] O'Connell is referred to as Dónall Ó Conchúir, but the story's origin is betrayed by a reference to the 'members' who are attending the dinner. In a Galway version, O'Connell isn't mentioned at all,[128] but we are told that an Irish king and an English king are eating a meal together. The Irish king is getting the better of the English king. There is an Irish girl working for the English king and he tells her to put a spoonful of poison in the Irish king's cup. The girl warns the Irish king in Irish. The Irishman exchanges cups with the Englishman

152

who falls dead when he takes the drink. The Captain, as the Irish king is called, brings the girl away with him and they are married. In the versions told about Daniel O'Connell it is not stated that O'Connell and the girl are married.[129] In one version, however, it is said that O'Connell brought the girl home to Ireland with him.[130]

It happens in two versions that the girl is singing as she waits on the table, so that the guests will not notice that she is addressing O'Connell directly.[131] In two Galway versions, the girl pinches her child to make it cry. The woman of the house tells the girl to bring the child upstairs to where the gentlemen are eating, and that the child might stop crying, and the girl gets her chance then to tell O'Connell about the poison in his drink.[132] In a version of the story from Louth, the girl speaks to O'Connell in English but her information is discreetly hidden. She says: 'The herring isn't caught with bait.'[133]

Apparently, this anecdote 'A Dhónaill Uí Chonaill, an dTuigeann Tú Gaeilge?' is told only about Daniel O'Connell and not about other named characters, although there is another tale which has some of the same basic characteristics as 'A Dhónaill Uí Chonaill, an dTuigeann Tú Gaeilge?' which was collected in county Donegal. Here it is said that a man called Cathal Ó Colla is staying in an enemy's house when the servant girl tells him it is time for him to go. When he asks her what she sees, she says that she sees his life is in danger if he remains there.[134]

His knowledge of Irish saves O'Connell once again in another story when he is told he will be killed if he fails to complete a building in nine days. O'Connell says he needs to have a tool brought from Ireland in order to finish the work. He says, in Irish, that the tool is called 'Restrain him Until he Comes for the Tool Himself'. A messenger is sent for the tool, and he comes to O'Connell's wife. He says he has been sent for something which O'Connell calls 'restrain him until he comes for it himself':

> Smaointigh an bhean léi féin go raibh rud éigint suas agus go raibh Dónall i ngéibheann. 'Tá sé anseo sa chombra mór,' a deir sí, 'agus is faide láimh atá ort féin ná ormsa chun é d'fháil.' Chuaigh sé dá(?) choinne chuig an chombra. Bhrúigh Bean Uí Chonaill síos san combra é agus bhuail sí glas air. 'Fanfaidh tú ansin anois go dtaga Dónall Ó Conaill abhaile.' Scríobh sí ansin chuig an duine uasal, go raibh a mac gafa aici agus ní ligfeadh as sin é go dtagadh Dónall Ó Conaill abhaile.[135]

(She thought to herself that something was up and that Daniel was in captivity. 'It is here in the big chest,' she said, 'and your arm is longer than mine to get it.' He went to the chest to get it. Mrs O'Connell pushed him into the chest and locked him in. 'You will stay there now, until Daniel O'Connell comes home.' She wrote to the gentleman to say she had captured his son and that she wouldn't let him go until Daniel O'Connell came home.)

The trick referred to in this story is one of the central motifs in a tale about *An Gobán Saor,* who was a renowned craftsman in Irish legend.[136] The stories and traditions attached to *An Gobán Saor* are no doubt much older than traditions about O'Connell and we may take it that the O'Connell story is a loan from the *Gobán Saor* tradition.

Because of his acute perception, O'Connell survives another attempt on his life, when he is given a treacherous present, according to another story. The gift which is given to O'Connell varies from version to version of the story. It may be a horse with a revolver or some explosive hidden under the saddle, or a box containing an explosive – in which case O'Connell asks the boy who has brought the present to open the box. In a Kerry version, for example, a servant boy brings a present of a horse to O'Connell and O'Connell tells him to sit up on it:

Is amhlaidh a bhí an revolver socair san iallait, faoi mar bheadh trap roimh frannncach. Nuair a shodaraíl an capall; d'éirigh sé san iallait, is nuair a thit sé anuas arís uirthi d'imigh an piléar tríd suas. Bhí san le fáil ag Dónall; is bhí an duine uasal suite in airde ar a chathaoir sa ghrianán chun go gcífeadh sé Dónall á mharú, is do bheadh pléisiúr air, ach is amhlaidh a bhí tráthnóna brónach aige.[137]

(The revolver was set in the saddle, like a trap to catch a rat. When the horse started to trot, he got up in the saddle and when he came down again on it, the bullet went up through him. That was meant for Daniel; and the gentleman was sitting above on his chair on the balcony to see Daniel being killed, and he would be very happy, but he had a sad evening.)

In one of the Galway versions of the story, O'Connell is sent a pair of slippers containing poison:

Thriáileadar (na Sasanaigh) babhta eile leis – péire slipéaraí a thabhairt dó (do Dhónall Ó Conaill) le bheith ag damhsa, agus bhí nimh sna slipéaraí. Ach bhí Ó Conaill tapaidh go leor dóibh. Thug sé péire slipéaraí dá chuid féin leis. Níor chuir sé air ar chor ar bith na cinn a fuair sé uathusan.[138]

(They (the English) tried another time as well – to give him (Daniel O'Connell) a pair of slippers for dancing, and there was poison in the slippers. But O'Connell was quick enough for them. He brought a pair of his own slippers with him. He didn't put on the ones he had got from them at all.)

O'Connell's parliamentary activity, career, and life were quite far removed, both physically and psychologically, from the lives and experiences of most of the storytellers. There was a vast distance between the ordinary rural people in Ireland at the time and Westminster. However, a few tales of parliamentary life have entered the oral tradition. One of these, 'Wearing his Hat Three Times', is especially popular. In the story, O'Connell succeeds in having a law changed in Parliament by wearing his hat there on three consecutive occasions. Thirty-six versions of this story have been collected, eighteen in Irish and eighteen in English in thirteen different counties. The plot appears to be the same in English and in Irish, although in one Irish version, the tale has a somewhat dramatic ending, when O'Connell has been allowed to wear his hat three times in Parliament:

> *Choinnibh sé air a hata, agus choinnibh an fhaid a bhí sé i bPárlaimint – gach aon duine ceann-nochtaithe ach é.*
> *Chrom sé ar a bheith ag féachaint timpeall ansan agus dúirt duine éigint ar deireadh leis:*
> *'Conas a thaitníonn an tigh seo leat?'*
> *'Taitníonn an tigh go maith liom,' ar seisean, 'ach tá ana-iontas orm,' ar seisean, 'ná titeann sé anuas is ná sceitheann na fallaí fé – aon áit go bhfuil* perjur*éaraí istigh ann.'*
> *Bhí an fear a thug a leabhar i gcomhchlos leis, is d'éirigh sé amach is d'imigh sé amach don* yard *is do lámhach sé é fhéinig.*[139]

(He kept his hat on and he kept it on while he was in Parliament – everyone bareheaded except himself.
He started looking around then, and someone said to him in the end:
'How do you like this house?'
'I like the house well enough,' he said, 'but I am very surprised,' he said, 'that it doesn't fall down or that the walls don't crumble – anywhere there are perjurers present.'
The man who had sworn (that if O'Connell sat in Parliament he would shoot himself) was within earshot, and he went out into the yard, and he shot himself.)

According to tradition, O'Connell was not treated with courtesy in Parliament and on one occasion, his son, Maurice, used forceful means and produced a pair of pistols to put an end to the disrespectful coughing which went on while his father was speaking, as we are told in the story 'Coughing in Parliament'. Once again, as in the case of 'Wearing his Hat Three Times', this tale is unusual in that it represents a part of O'Connell's parliamentary life – an aspect of his more formal life which seems to appear only on rare occasions in oral tradition.

There is an isolated tale, or possible version of a tale, which tells of O'Connell using the parliamentary system to free some Kerry fishermen who were to be sentenced for life, or to hang, for smuggling. O'Connell wrote a pardon for the men on a piece of paper which he hid in the tip of his sword. In Parliament, he had the sword passed all round the house and, as the pardon had then been carried through the Parliament, it became law and the men were pardoned and let home free.[140]

(vi) Wit and Repartee

Kissing his Backside

When Daniel O'Connell was over in England 'twas very hard for him, they used always make games at him or try to be doing it, and he was walking down the street one day and he stood on an orange peel and if he did he slipped, the poor man, and he fell on his backside down on the ground.

'Oh, Connell,' says the prime boys, 'the flags of London are too grand for you to walk on them.'

'Begor, then though grand they are,' says Daniel, 'I'll make them kiss my backside.'[141]

This anecdote is found in at least fourteen versions. It exemplifies the large number of short items which are included in this section. Most of them consist of only a few lines. They all share one feature, however: they illustrate, yet again, O'Connell's witty, clever speech. Many of them border on the joke.[142] O'Connell is portrayed as an exceptionally clever lawyer in the anecdotes, legends and folktales about him and as such his power of expression plays a crucial role in the stories. As a Catholic Irishman, he is constantly depicted as getting the better of his opponent in clever speech, despite the latter's attempts to outdo O'Connell in wit. As a folk hero, O'Connell inevitably has the last word.

Some of the anecdotes show O'Connell putting his enemy in his place with a vulgar or insulting statement, or with a verse. Few would therefore wish to incite O'Connell's anger for fear of his sharp, sarcastic tongue. These traits in O'Connell bear close similarity to the traits of the poet in Irish tradition. The poet was held in high regard; he was a leader in his own right and renowned for clever speech and creativity. O'Connell was also well-respected and held in awe. His power is understood in terms of Irish tradition. It is often said of the poet that he has natural and supernatural gifts.[143] The poet can be vulgar and uncouth. These traits are, of course, part of witty or ready speech – of 'deisbhéalaíocht' as it is known in Irish. O'Connell uses these features a great deal, in particular if attempts are made to mock him or to scoff at him.

In the following examples O'Connell himself is the victor. He is not fighting a case for a poor prisoner or trying to help someone else who is in trouble. He is describing or answering someone who has tried to catch him out, or he may be indulging in wordplay. The material included here is without a particular plot or narrative thread. Very often, O'Connell wants merely to put someone else in their place, or he may be trying to influence his audience.

O'Connell is said to have been particularly adept at insulting his enemies. Oral tradition tells us that he once insulted Thomas Herbert, a landlord, in the following way:

> If I had the five, knave and ace,
> I couldn't straighten the nose on Herbert's face.[144]

In folklore, O'Connell intensely dislikes being insulted. In the course of the election battle between himself and Fitzgerald in county Clare, one of O'Connell's tenants met 'sallow Butler' from Waterville.[145] Butler said that O'Connell had no more chance of going to Parliament in England than Butler's big lump of a dog called Rover. O'Connell heard what Butler said and when Butler invited him to dinner one day when he was home on holidays from Parliament, he asked O'Connell about the wonders he had seen in Parliament. O'Connell replied:

> 'Do chonac,' a deir Dónall, a deir sé, 'mórán ionadh ann gan aon doubt, ach más ea, ní fhaca aon radharc ar Rover ann!'[146]

> ('I have,' said Daniel, he said, 'seen many wonders there without a doubt, but even so, I haven't seen trace of Rover there!')

O'Connell was quick to rebuke the insulters in the following account:

> Daniel O'Connell was going across to England, and when he landed, there were a lot of corner-boys watching him. One of them said: 'I'll have a joke on this Irish fellow now.' So he walked up to Daniel and said to him: 'Do you know the latest?' 'No,' says Daniel, 'what is it?' 'The devil is dead,' says the Englishman. Daniel put his hand in his pocket and drew out a penny and offered it to the Englishman. 'What is that for?' says the Englishman. 'That's the way we assist the orphans when the head of the house is dead,' says Daniel.[147]

On another occasion, an Englishman said that a person talking in Irish was like a dog barking.

> Dúirt an Sasanach gur cuma nó madra ag amhastraigh, duine ag labhairt na Gaolainne. 'D'airíos madra ag amhastraigh thall in Éirinn agus is é an rud a dúirt sé ná – "D'ith damh dubh ubh amh ar neamh"' (mar a bheadh madra ag amhastraigh). 'Is bacach an argóint atá ar siúl agat,' arsa Dónall. 'Ná fuil a fhios agat gur chuir na Sasanaigh scéith i gcroí na ndaoine agus fiú amháin gabhair Chiarraí go léir le chéile.' 'An amhlaidh airís gabhair Chiarraí ag labhairt Béarla?' arsa an Sasanach. 'D'airíos agus do thuigeas.

D'airíos gabhair á rá le bean a bhí ag gabháil an bóthar – "Peg, I beg a big egg"' *(ag déanamh aithris ar ghabhair ag meigeallaigh). Do stop an argóint.*[148]

(The Englishman said that a person speaking Irish was like a dog barking. 'I heard a dog barking over in Ireland and he said – *"D'ith damh dubh ubh amh ar neamh"'* (sounding like a dog barking) ('a black ox ate a raw egg in heaven'). 'That is a weak argument,' said Daniel. 'Don't you know that the English have terrified people and have even terrified all the goats in Kerry?' 'Did you hear Kerry goats speaking in English?' said the Englishman. 'I did and I understood them. I heard a goat say to a woman who was going along the road – "Peg, I beg a big egg"' (imitating a goat bleating). The argument was over.)

One day, a minister was trying to catch O'Connell out and asked Dan what a miracle was:

After some time he got the minister turned around and then he drew and gave him a good kick in the arse. 'Did you feel that now?' says O'Connell to him. 'I did,' says the minister. 'Well,' says Dan to him, 'it would be a miracle if you didn't.'[149]

On another occasion, O'Connell was very quick to answer an Englishman who insulted him:

And there was another thing; he was coming on the train ... on the train, and there were two Englishmen sitting opposite him, and he was swallowing all they were talking about. But he had the paper upside down, in his hand. This fellow looked over and he says:
'You're an Irishman,' he says.
'I am,' says Dan. 'Why?'
'Well,' he says, 'you're listening to our crack,' he says, 'and the paper upside down: you couldn't read it.'
'If I turned it the other way,' he says, 'an Englishman could read it.'
And he turned round and he read his own speech backways out of the paper, Dan O'Connell.[150]

O'Connell did not take kindly to being insulted on his own home ground either:

Long ago a stranger came to Dublin for a holiday and he asked Daniel O'Connell to show him the principal buildings in Dublin. So one morning Daniel and himself set off to see the buildings. When they came to Nelson's Pillar Daniel said: 'this is one of Dublin's principal buildings.' 'O my! O my!' said the stranger, 'you would get a bottle of stout in England twice bigger than that.' Then they came to another fine building. 'O my! O my!' said the stranger, 'you would get a sandwich in England twice bigger than that.' Daniel was getting very sick of the stranger, when a huge train came up (into?) the city carrying on top of it a half a mile of rail for a railway. 'O my! O my!' said the stranger, 'what is this Daniel?' 'Well,' said Daniel, 'they are building a new factory outside the city and today they are bringing in the kitchen poker.' So the stranger walked off very vexed![151]

Sometimes, O'Connell replies to insults in an impudent, rude way, as occurs when the English belch in Parliament to insult him as they interrupt his speeches. O'Connell asks a little boy to come in and to break wind in order to upset the English. O'Connell then says to them: 'That is going downwards but you are sending it out of your mouths.'[152]

O'Connell sometimes replied both verbally and practically when he was insulted, as the following three anecdotes illustrate:

At this time O'Connell was one if not the most famous Counsellor in Ireland. A leading draper got a bust of O'Connell in every handkerchief he stocked in his shop. The handkerchiefs sold like hot buns. Very good. A leading Counsellor, a rival of O'Connell's, pulled out one and blew his nose into the bust saying at the same time: 'high and low and every race can blow their noses in Daniel's face.' 'Rich and poor and every class can stick their noses in Daniel's arse,' was the reply.[153]

Some Lord invited Dan over to his place in England one time, and they used to be all trying to take a rise out of him when he'd be in England. This morning some of them put jalap (a purgative drug) in Dan's tea and then they brought him out for a drive in the coach. A couple of times they had to pull up and Dan went into some house to relieve himself. So Dan got fed up with this and the next time he got the call he just stuck his arse out of the coach window. The Lord was very annoyed. 'Mr O'Connell,' he says, 'I'll be disgraced. Everyone knows the carriage with the coat of arms on it.'

'Everyone knows the carriage,' says Dan, 'but no-one knows the arse.'[154]

Daniel O'Connell was at a feast one night, and the other people present wanted to kill him. They were all Englishmen. They had a roast 'piggy riggy' (pig?) for supper, and Daniel had to carve it. 'Whatever you do to that animal,' says one of the Englishmen, 'I'll do the same to you.' 'All right,' says Daniel. He went up to the pig, and stuck his finger up under its tail, and brought down some of the stuffing and ate it. He then took down his breeches and says to the man. 'Will you do that to me?' That finished the story.[155]

This is how O'Connell distinguished between the sexes on one occasion:

Whether it was for bets or what I don't know, but he had to tell the difference between the man and the woman. They were dressed alike. There were apples in the house and he dropped a few into his pocket. So O'Connell says: 'Would you care for an apple?'

They said they would. And he threw one apiece to them. I'll hold he wasn't long then in finding which was which. To catch the apple the man put his legs together; but if you ever remarked it, a woman widens her legs. And Dan had her. (Was thus able to distinguish).[156]

In the story of Huckleberry Finn, when he is dressed as a girl, a woman guesses that he is, in fact, a boy in disguise, when she throws a lump of lead to him, and he catches it by clapping his legs together on it. Later, she explains to Huck that a girl would throw her knees apart to try catching anything in her lap.[157]

O'Connell's rude reply put an English lady in her place one time when she insulted an Irishman:

There was a mason one time in England, an Irishman, and this lady used pass every day and she used say: 'Mortar to your stones for I know you're a mason,' and he was annoyed from her. He met O'Connell one day and he told him about her. O'Connell went with him the following day and he was tending the mason by-the-way (pretending to tend the mason?) on the scaffold. The lady came.

'Mortar to your stones,' she said, 'for I know you're a mason.'

'Stone to your belly,' says O'Connell, 'for I know you're in sason (season)'. She didn't come any other day.[158]

Obviously, O'Connell would not have liked Irish people to be insulted. The following anecdote may be told about Irish people, as in this version, or about coloured people or about Catholics. It is told about O'Connell, and it has also been documented in the folklore of Dean Swift:[159]

When Daniel reached the place of the feast, he noticed there was writing on the gate. He went over to it and this is what he read: 'No Irish pigs allowed in here,' and Daniel wrote under it:

'Whoever wrote this wrote it well
For the same is written on the gates of hell.'

So Daniel walked away and did not go to the feast.[160]

O'Connell was said to be able to compose *ex tempore* verse as suited the occasion:

Bobby Burns, the Scotch poet, was one time overtaken with drink and he got very sick. He was walking down the road at the time and he worked himself as far as a bridge, spanning a river, and in the meantime he was very sick, every now and again.

Some time he was very sick Dan O'Connell came the way, and the moans of Bobby attracted his attention. He went over to him and asked him what was wrong with him.

'I understand,' says Burns, 'that you are Dan O'Connell and you're a very clever man and you'll be able to tell me what to tell the doctor. I don't want to tell him, I filled myself with whiskey.'

'I want your name,' says Dan.

'My name is Robbie Burns from Innerleith.'

'I'll tell you what you'll tell him,' says Dan.

'My name is Robbie Burns,
I come from Innerleith,
I lost the key of my arse
And I'm shitting through my teeth.'[161]

On another occasion, O'Connell replied in verse to a man who tried to catch him out:

There was a batch of Councillors standing in one bunch on the shore, waiting for this ship to land and Dan O'Connell was in another bunch, nearhand the first one. One of them in the first bunch thought himself clever and wanted to take a rise out of Dan, and he says to his comrades: 'Watch,' he says, 'I'm going to take a rise out of Dan before everyone,' he says, 'and I'll go down and ask him up to our crowd.'

Very well; he went down to where Dan was standing. They saluted each other, himself and Dan. At this time the millionaire's ship had landed and there was a tender going out to meet her. 'Mr O'Connell,' he says, 'might I trouble you to answer me a question?'

'By all means,' says Dan, 'ask whatever you like.'

'Will you come up a few steps more,' he says to Dan, 'more would like to hear this besides you and I.' So they moved up to where the other group was.

'Supposing now,' says this fellow to Dan, 'you see that tender going out to the big ship?' he says.

'I do,' says Dan.

'Well, supposing, now,' he says, 'Mr O'Connell, when that tender is coming in again, and a naked woman walked up the strand, what plan would you have not to make the people laugh at her?' and Dan said:

'If such a thing, it came to pass,
And that your nose was stuck in her arse,
Then every time she'd give a stir,
It's at you they'd laugh and not at her.'[162]

Not all of O'Connell's verse compositions were rude, however, as the following anecdote illustrates:

One day Daniel was passing a shop in London and up on the glass was written:

'In this beehive we're all alive
And whiskey makes us funny.
If you are dry, come in and try
The flavour of our honey.'

Daniel's answer was:

> 'If I went in the bees would sting
> Because I have no money.'[163]

O'Connell once made a clever verse about an elderly judge:

> 'But about his pretence of supreme innocence
> There will be just a suspicion of fudge,
> For the baby unborn is not such a greenhorn
> As the octogenarian judge.'[164]

Daniel O'Connell passes sarcastic comments in some instances in oral tradition. In a discussion about Irish people, for example, O'Connell says that if you put an Irishman on a spit, you'll get another Irishman to turn it.[165] Once, O'Connell and a young Irish patriot are admiring the view from Killiney Hill in county Dublin. The young Irishman says how happy he is that there is not a trace of anything British to be seen. O'Connell points out to the sea, where there is a warship at anchor. He says: 'A speck of British power.'[166]

It is said that when O'Connell was elected the first Catholic Mayor of Dublin since the so-called Reformation he was not allowed by law to attend Mass in State robes, and he passed the comment: 'Yes – the Lord Mayor may be a Catholic but his robes are Protestant.'[167]

Sometimes, O'Connell simply makes a witty statement or comment, as is illustrated in an account which describes how O'Connell and his companion meet a funeral on the road on one occasion. The mourners recognise O'Connell and give a cheer. This surprises his English companion, but O'Connell says: 'The corpse would have doubtless cheered lustily too, if he could.'[168]

It was said as well that Daniel O'Connell's order to his party in the British House of Commons to abstain from voting was: '*ná bac leis*' ('pay no heed to it').[169] This last comment is yet another example of O'Connell's pragmatic use of Irish, although he was opposed to its use in general.

A very famous debate, the tale of 'Biddy Moriarty' is said to have taken place between O'Connell and a woman who was a huckster, near the Four Courts, in Dublin. In the battle of words between them, O'Connell won the day. In some instances, the debate was said to have been instigated as a result of a bet. O'Connell's method of confounding the woman verbally was to use terms in geometry which baffled Biddy. This account has appeared in both published and oral sources, and the published versions are more complete. Some of the oral accounts mention the fact that the event took place but do not include the actual conversation.

O'Connell is said to have made puns sometimes as the following example illustrates:

In the year 1822 Sir Anthony Hart is appointed Lord Chancellor. Plunket[170] wanted the appointment but he could not be spared from the Parliament in England. Sheil[171] asks O'Connell, when the new judge takes up his position for the first time, how Plunket appears, as he says: 'How does Plunket look this morning?' O'Connell replies: 'Oh, very sore at Hart.'[172]

And in a Scottish chapbook, an account of his wordplay was based on his legal career and reputation:

Mr O'Connell, who is remarkable for the successful verdicts he obtains, having been lately robbed of his wardrobe, replied to a friend that was lamenting his loss: 'Never mind, my dear Sir, for surely as I have gained so many suits, I can afford to lose a few.'[173]

Only one example has come to light of word play in Irish by O'Connell:

Bhí sé lá i mBaile Átha Cliath – an Liberator *agus dhá bhullán a bhí fén gcóiste aige, dhá bhullán a bhí fén gcóiste a bhí á tharrac. Ach dúirt duine éiginteach leis gur mhór an t-ionadh ná faigheadh sé dhá chapall in ionad an dá spreota bullán sin. 'Ó, is fearr liom iad so,' a dúirt sé, 'mar is de* bhreed *na mbullán ab ea mo mháthair.' (de mhuinitr Mhaoláin ab ea a mháthair.)*[174]

(He was in Dublin one day – the Liberator – and he had two bullocks pulling his coach – two bullocks drawing the coach for him. But someone said that it was a wonder he didn't get two horses instead of those two useless bullocks. 'Oh, I prefer these,' he said, 'because my mother was of the same breed as the *bullán* (bullock).' (His mother's family name was *Maoláin*, similar in pronounciation to *bullán* in the grammatical structure used here).

One of the best-known anecdotes which illustrates O'Connell's ready tongue, sarcasm, and sense of irony, as well as his direct approach, centres on the reply O'Connell gives to a man who is breaking stones by the roadside at the time of the Clare election:

When Dan O'Connell found that he was elected for Clare he slipped away from all followers and supporters and went out the country road for a quiet stroll by himself. When he was about two miles outside the town, he came across a poor old man breaking stones on the side of the road. The old man flung the hammer aside and jumped up and asked Dan:
'Could you tell me was O'Connell returned, sir?'
'It's all equal to you who was returned or who wasn't. You'll have to break the stones no matter who gets in. O'Connell was elected.'

'Thanks be to God and his holy mother,' and the poor old man ran home with the news.[175]

Of the twelve recorded versions of this story, only one is in Irish and this is from Uíbh Ráthach. It is the only account where the stone-breaker is named. The background to the tale is given as follows:

Bhí seanfhear thoir ansan ar thaobh an bhóthair, i nGleann Chárthaigh, go dtugaidís Seana-Mhaitéas air, de mhuintir Mhurchú, bhí sé ar thaobh do lámha cléithe nuair a bheifeá ag dul síos go Droichead Bhéal an Lá (Doirín Áiríoch) agus nuair a bhíos-sa i mo gharsún ag dul go Cill Orglan i dteannta m'athar, do bhíodh sé ar thaobh an bhóthair agus do bhíodh sé féin agus m'athair ag caint, agus iniseadh sé mórán cúrsaí dho i dtaobh an tseana-shaoil. Bhí contract bhóithre aige agus nuair a bhíodh an Conallach ag gabháil soir is anoir ann, bhíodh sé (Maitéas) ag cuir tuairisc Shasana air. ... Ach an tráthnóna so do háirithe á raibh sé ag gabháil anoir, stop Maitéas é agus é ag gabháil anoir an bealach agus do chuir sé tuairisc Shasana air, faoi mar a dheineadh i gcónaí. 'Á,' a dúirt sé, 'is cuma dhuitse cad tá ar siúl i bhFeis Shasana, ach tabhair aire do do ghnó féin! Bí ag briseadh na gcloch san ansan, agus ní bheidh a mhalairt agat go brách pé ní a dhéanfaidh Feis Shasana ná aon Fheis eile acu!' Bhí an neamhmhaithí i gcónaí ag gabháil leis an gConallach.[176]

(There was an old man living to the east there at the roadside, in Gleann Cárthaigh who was called Seana-Mhaitéas, of the Ó Murchú family, he was to your left hand side as you go down to Béal an Lá Bridge (Doirín Áiríoch). And when I was a boy, going to Cill Orglan with my father, he would be at the roadside and he and my father used to talk and he would tell him many things about life in the olden times. He had a contract for the roads and when the Counsellor was coming east and coming back, Maitéas used ask him about England. . . . But one evening when he was coming from the east, Maitéas stopped him and asked him about England, as he always did. 'Ah,' he said, 'it doesn't matter to you what's going on in Parliament in England, but look after your own affair! Break those stones there, and you won't ever have anything else, no matter what the English Parliament or any other Parliament does!'
O'Connell always had the hard word!)

The account in Irish is the only one in which O'Connell is criticised for his remark. In the accounts in English, O'Connell's reply is praised, with comments like:

I tell you that he always had a ready answer![177]

The Image of O'Connell in the Legends and Anecdotes
The legends and anecdotes describe O'Connell in very definite terms. His generosity to his fellow countrymen and women, and his support

of their achievements, knows no bounds. He acts on their behalf, but is on occasion generous in a more passive way.

O'Connell provides his services free of charge in many cases, especially in those instances where the 'poor Irishman' is looking for help. Once, O'Connell was given some advice, in lieu of payment. He successfully defended a man charged with stealing a cow, and as the man couldn't afford to pay O'Connell, he advised him how to steal a cow that a butcher would be likely to buy:

> 'Go into the field on a cold night and the cow that's farthest out from the fence is your cow.'[178]

O'Connell is seldom portrayed as a man who is set to improve his own lot. However, in one tale '(Supper) Hospitality Won by a Trick' (AT 1526A), he does just that.[179] Over fifty versions of the tale have been included in TIF, and of those in which O'Connell appears, three versions were collected in Irish and one in English. All four 'O'Connell' versions are from the south-west of Ireland. In these stories, O'Connell may, for example, burn his clothes and money as well as those of his companion, and then cause a rumpus the following morning and ensure that he receives compensation. In one version, it is O'Connell's son who plays the trick and is praised by the hotelier for this clever and successful ruse.[180] Naturally, as O'Connell is clever, so then might one expect his children to be clever. His clever child is a feature of folk tradition, as is also O'Connell's high regard for cleverness. There may have been a certain reluctance in this instance on the part of the storytellers to state explicitly that O'Connell was believed to have children outside of marriage but the motif as found in the tales 'Hospitality Won by a Trick' and 'O'Connell Recognises His Own Child' was clearly popular.

From the point of view of the historical lore about O'Connell, these tales are important. They reflect the apparently popular belief in folk tradition that O'Connell was the father of children outside of his marriage, and that O'Connell himself acknowledged this, and took pride in the child's cleverness.

In addition to the insight the legends and anecdotes afford into the creation and development of the folk image of O'Connell, the stories illustrate the widespread use of the amusing tale for popular entertainment. The amusing tales about O'Connell reveal a great deal about the people who told them and about those who, as passive bearers of tradition, enjoyed them and kept them alive. Although the stories are not in the realm of politics or of documented history, opinions and emotions about O'Connell, and popular expectations of the time are indicated in them. O'Connell succeeds in overcoming the political and religious enemy and thus helps the Irishman to regain his lost self-respect. These were certainly in keeping with the aspirations of many Irish people during O'Connell's lifetime.

References

1. See Aarne and Thompson 1973; Ó Súilleabháin and Christiansen 1963.
2. For a list of O'Connell tales, including international tales, see Appendix D.
3. The titles of the tales included here have been taken from the Aarne Thompson index (AT), or the Types of the Irish Folktale (TIF), where appropriate. In other cases, the stories have been given titles by the author.
4. Because of the vast number of anecdotes, and versions of anecdotes about O'Connell, it has been possible to include in the body of the text, only a small number of illustrative examples. Appendix C consists of texts of a number of the tales.
5. IFC 851:353-4.
6. See Chapter 1 for comments on literacy.
7. Philpot Curran (1750-1817), born in Newmarket, Cork, was a lawyer, orator and wit. He was called to the bar in 1775 and became a King's Counsel. He was Master of the Rolls from 1807 to 1814. Jonathan Swift (1667-1745) was Dean of St. Patrick's Cathedral in Dublin from 1713 and is best known for his writings in English. Because of his satires against the English establishment, he became very popular with the ordinary Irish people.
8. Funk and Wagnall 1950 56. As short, pointed, pithy narratives, anecdotes were an early development of the literature of the people, whether gratifying the popular taste for gossip and scandal or employed for edification or entertainment.
9. Although there are similarities between an anecdote and a joke, they are not identical or interchangeable terms. The anecdote is on a higher intellectual level than the joke. For a description of the similarities between the anecdote and the joke see Röhrich 1977 6.
10. For examples of tale clusters see Cavan IFC 1915: 71-9; Roscommon IFC 1506: 486-9.
11. IFC 979:598-600. Collected in 1946 by Seosamh Ó Dálaigh from Muiris Mac Gearailt, aged seventy-six, a farm labourer, Baile an Fheirtéaraigh, parish of Dún Urlann, barony of Corca Dhuibhne. Other versions: Clare IFC S610:69-70; Cork IFC 1674:95-110; Donegal IFC 186:544-6; 454:212-15; 694:383-6; Galway IFC 404:493-501; 645:315-8; 868:290-4; 1025:303-9; 1311:263-6; 1354:329-30; 1765:396-8; Gregory 1909 26; Kerry IFC 146:450-3; 149:661-6; 796:6-8; 858:307-20; 984:444-51; 1272:154-5; 1342:170-4; 1493:107-15; S478:143-7; IFC Tape 1968 Bo Almqvist from Mícheál Ó Gaoithín, Baile Bhiocáire, Dún Chaoin, Corca Dhuibhne; Longford IFC 1457:359-60; Mayo IFC 333:179-84; S101:3242-5; Roscommon IFC 1709:213-5; Waterford IFC 246:63-83.
12. MI J 1150 cleverness connected with the giving of evidence; K 170 deception through pseudo-simple bargain; MI N O wagers and gambling. Versions: Clare IFC S610:69-70; Cork IFC 1674:95-110; Donegal IFC 186:544-6; 454:212-5; 694:383-6; Galway IFC 404:493-501; 645:315-8; 868:290-4; 1025:303-9; 1311:263-6; 1354:329-30; 1764:396-8; Gregory 1909 26; Kerry IFC 146:450-3; 149:661-6; 796:6-8; 858:307-20; 979:598-600; 984:444-51; 1272:154-5; 1342:170-4; 1493:107-15; S478:143-7; IFC Tape 1968 Bo Almqvist from Mícheál Ó Gaoithín, Baile

Bhiocáire, Dún Chaoin; Longford IFC 1457:359-60; Mayo IFC 333:179-84; S101:324-5; Roscommon IFC 1709:213-5. Waterford IFC 246:63-83.

13. Policemen were so called because of the establishment by Sir Robert Peel in 1814 of a police force called the Peace Preservation Force.

14. Limerick IFC S483:141.

15. Donegal IFC 186:547-8.

16. IFC 1322:582-5. Collected in 1953 by Proinnsias de Búrca from Ciarán Ó Súilleabháin, aged sixty-eight, a farmer, from Loch Conaortha, parish of Carna, barony of Baile na hInse, county Galway.

17. Galway IFC 1322:582-5.

18. Cork IFC 779:16-7.

19. D. Ó Súilleabháin 1936 266-7.

20. D. Ó Súilleabháin 1936 267.

21. Sligo IFC S155:496.

22. Longford IFC S762:227-8.

23. Galway 663:438-40; Sligo IFC 485:46-50.

24. Donegal IFC 186:549-51. Collected in 1936 by Liam Mac Meanman from Neddy Ua Muighe, aged eighty-one, a farmer, Glaiseach Beag, parish of Cill Taobhóg, barony of Rathbhoth Theas, county Donegal.

25. MI J 1190 cleverness in the law court; J 1210 clever man puts another out of countenance; K 1655 the lawyer's mad client.

26. See Ó hÓgáin 1990 346-8.

27. See Rotunda 1942 119-120, also S. Prato 'La scène de l'avocat et du berger de la farce Maître Pathelin' see *Revue des traditions populaires* 1894 537-8.

28. MI J 1179 clever judicial decisions; J 1184 no second punishment for same offence; K 453 cheating through knowledge of the law.

29. IFC 1480:46-7. Collected in 1956 by James G. Delaney from James Kenny, aged seventy-four, a blacksmith, Knockawalky, parish of Templemichael, barony and county of Longford. Other versions: Galway IFC 158:46-9; 867:265-8; Wexford 591:255-8.

30. Donegal IFC 561:266.

31. IFC 632:365-9. Collected in 1939 by Liam Shine from Paddy Sweeney, aged seventy, a farmer, Tarmons, Tarbert, parish of Kilnaughtin, barony of Iraghticonnor. Other versions: Kerry IFC 125:363-6; 126:207-12; 148:187-94; 632:365-9; S420:638-40; S428:169-71; S468:222,227-9; S470:241-3; S473:483-5; S475:280-1; S478:155-7; *CS* 16.8.1902, 388; D. Ó Súilleabháin 1936 257-60.MI J 1130 cleverness in the law court; K 1860 deception through feigned death (sleep).

32. D. Ó Súilleabháin 1936 257-60.

33. IFC 645:369-73. Collected in 1939 by Colm Ó Finneadha from Pádraig Ó Flaitheartaigh, aged fifty-one, a farmer, Lochán Beag, parish of Cill Ainthinn, barony of Maigh Cuilinn, county Galway. Other versions: Cavan IFC 1787:196-8*; Clare IFC 695:117-21; S607:14; S609:496-7*; S618:71-2. Cork IFC 535:30-31; 808:496-8; Donegal IFC 233:4031-3; S1073:22-3. Galway IFC 232:478-83*; 525:531; 669:566-8*; S48:54-5; *Béal* 5 1935 258; Kerry IFC 256:168-72; 304:44-7*; 338:429-36; 386:338-43; 534:1-5; 658:368-9; 659:419-20; 936:475-7; 979:600-601; 1152:420-1*; 1168:393-4; 1513:228-30*; S426:472; S472:333; IFC Tape 1968 Bo Almqvist from Mícheál Ó Gaoithín, Baile Bhiocáire, Dún Chaoin*; Longford IFC 1480:45-6*; 1486:411-12*; Mayo IFC 693:22-3*; S101:28; S138:158-9; Tipperary IFC S552:159-61; Waterford IFC 152:330-331; Wexford IFC 543:552-4*.

An asterisk indicates that this particular version has yet to be included in TIF.

34. MI J 1123 wisdom of child decides lawsuit; king in disguise sees child's game which represents the case; J 1179 clever judicial decisions.
35. Rickard 1973 2-3.
36. Selk 1979 79.
37. See AT 921.
38. Mayo IFC S138:158-9 (translation).
39. de Vries 1963 214.
40. Mayo IFC 227:254-60.
41. Limerick IFC 628:14-6.
42. Kerry IFC 984:11-15. For information on Curran and Swift see footnote 7.
43. Cavan IFC 1196:185-6.
44. Kerry IFC 1475:331-5.
45. Galway IFC 349:427-31.
46. Galway IFC 1018:207-8.
47. Kerry IFC 796:5-6.
48. Versions: Donegal IFC 1619:126; Kerry IFC 149:656-61; 796:4; S477:344-50; Mayo IFC 693:16-7; Meath IFC 557:420-4; Roscommon IFC 1506:487; Tipperary IFC 517:344; no provenance: *IO* 20.5.1903 5; *The Irish Packet* 11.5.1907 162; *OB* 6.1920 238; 6.1929 711; Kennedy 1853 143; M. MacDonagh 1929 50. MI J 1140 cleverness in detection of truth; K 362.7 signature forged to obtain money.
49. Kerry IFC 149:656-61. See footnote 7.
50. MI J 1160 clever pleading; J 1191.2 suit for chickens produced from boiled eggs; J 1530 one absurdity rebukes another; K 1600 deceiver falls into own trap.
51. Almqvist in Murphy 1975 166.
52. Briggs 1970 Part A vol. 2 100. Buchanan (1506-82) was an author and a man famous for his learning, who was tutor to James VI of Scotland, and to the Admiral Crichton. Tradition has chosen to make him into the King's Fool, though crediting him with great natural shrewdness. Various well-known folk anecdotes clustered round his name. His character is invariably a good one.
53. Walker and Uysal 1966 236.
54. For example Kerry IFC 858:122-8; 1492:352-60. For a detailed study of AT 821B, see Almqvist 1986 134-152
55. Versions: Cork IFC S364:212-3; Kerry IFC 273:134-43; 858: 325-33; Leitrim IFC S217:37-8. MI J 1147 detection through feigned dream; J 1192 bribed judge; J 1195 judge frightened into awarding decision.
56. Versions: Down IFC 1619:107-8; Galway IFC 232:485-8; 1016:37; 1236:326. MI J 1193: clever interpretation of judges's statement.
57. Versions: Louth IFC 1691:134-5; Murphy 1975 53. MI H 255 test of which of twins is elder; J 1179 clever judicial decisions.
58. IFC 1709:218-20. Collected in 1966 by James G. Delaney from William Rourke, aged eighty, a farmer, Cloonkeen, parish of Kilkeevin, barony of Castlereagh, county Roscommon. Other versions: Cavan IFC 1787:203-4; 1837:205-6; Clare IFC 39:369-70; 2050:99-100; Cork IFC 779:17-8; S282:172-3; S364:258; Donegal IFC 694:380-3; Galway IFC 10:70-6; 232:121-7; 236:123-5; 346:74-8; 373:355-8; 404:484-93; 563:214-20; 578:138-45; 606:578-80; 607:220-3; 633:16-27; 634:394-7; 784:78-9; 785:205-11; 867:270-3; 931:575-7; 970:445; 1133:238; 1311:267-73; 1322:77-8,585-9; 1833:64-5; S4:225-6; S16:96-7; S26:49; S32:388-9; S46:227-8; S66:241-2; S74:432-3; S77:415-6; *Béal.* 5 1930 257-8; Kerry IFC 12:333-5; 37:454-8; 149:453-62; 338:365-9; 358:269-72; 597:248-53; 796:10; 982:158-61; 114:278-9; 1124:220-3; 1150:34-7; S473:120-3; Leitrim IFC S206:613-4; Limerick IFC 628:24-7; 658:148-51; Longford IFC 1457:361-2; 1901:253-6; Louth IFC 1569:163; Mayo IFC

71:90-3; 195:461-3; 333:221-4; 523:556-63; 803:89-93; 1401:171-4(i); 1636:42-6; S116:31; Roscommon IFC 1506:488-9; S238:267-8; Sligo IFC S172:41-3; Tipperary IFC 517:332-4,339; 738:224-5; Waterford IFC 86:12-20; 152:367-9; 1239:23; Wexford IFC S871:436-8; no provenance: *An Stoc* 7/1926 7; Kennedy 1853 43-6. MI J 2469 fool follows instructions literally; K 170 deception through pseudo-simple bargain; K 195 a ribbon long enough to reach from ear to ear. The rascal has had an ear cut off in a distant city; Pauli (ed. Bolte) no. 713; K 475 cheating through equivocation; K 493 dupe betrayed by asking him ambiguous question; K 1600 deceiver falls into own trap; N 0 wagers and gambling; Q 38 deeds punished, miscellaneous.

59. A tale with close parallels appears in Kerry IFC 967:225-7 where the point or thrust is in the dual meaning of the word '*ceann*' in Irish, meaning 'a head' or 'one'.

60. See also AT 1559C*.

61. IFC 1401:171-4(i). Collected in 1954 by Seán Ó Moghráin from Antoine Ó Loingseacháin, aged eighty, a servant, Bun an Chorraigh, parish of Acaill, barony of Buiríos Umhaill, county Mayo.

62. Cork IFC S364:258; Tipperary IFC 517:332-4.

63. Limerick IFC 658:148-51.

64. Kerry IFC 796:10; 1272:157.

65. *Luan* may mean Monday or doomsday; see K 2319.7 Cross 1952.

66. This tale is mindful of a modern urban legend concerning a man who, late one Friday evening, goes into one of only two specialist car dealers in Dublin and buys an expensive model for which he pays by cheque. He then goes to the second dealer to sell the car which he has just bought. The second car dealer is suspicious and phones the first dealer to check up on the customer. The first dealer panics and phones the bank to stop the cheque. On Monday morning, the cheque is honoured and the customer later sues the car dealer, from whom he bought the car, for defamation of character.

67. Versions: Armagh IFC 1803:148; Cork IFC 686:358-9; Donegal IFC 143:2177-9; S1046:127-9; Galway IFC 563:221-30; 829:465-9; 1833:153-7; Kerry IFC 306:282-92; 834:166-70; 979:594-7; 1114:279-81; S423:614-7; S439:181-5. MI K 170 deception through pseudo-simple bargain; X 610 jokes concerning Jews.

68. Kerry IFC S423:614-7.

69. Galway IFC 563:221-30.

70. Kerry IFC 823:571-2.

71. Kerry IFC 934:260-8.MI J 1510.

72. MI N O wagers and gambling.

73. Kerry IFC 966:33; see TIF 277.

74. Bolte ed. 1972 268.

75. Rotunda 1942 42.

76. Jarrell 1964 107.

77. Waterford IFC 153:315-7. MI J 1210 clever man puts another out of countenance; J 1500 clever practical retorts.

78. Mayo IFC 693: 240-2.

79. IFC 1806:227-8. Collected in 1972 by Michael J. Murphy from Philip Dolan, aged seventy-four, Black Lion, parish of Killinagh, barony of Tullyhaw, county Cavan. Other versions: Antrim IFC 1359:11; Cavan IFC 1786:136; Donegal IFC 185:277; 186:542-3; 374:323-6; 799:422-4; Down IFC 1567:15-6; 1619:110; Murphy 1975 55. Galway IFC 161:144-5; Kerry IFC S475:157; Leitrim IFC S209:439-41; S210:487-8; Louth IFC 1570:135; Roscommon IFC 1573:215; S231:299; S232:35; Sligo IFC

S159:133-4; Wicklow IFC S914:438; *IO* 6.8.1919 92; no provenance: *Irish Independent* 4.10.1945; *The Irish Packet* 21.8.1909. MI N 0 wagers and gambling.

80. Roscommon IFC S231:299.
81. Donegal IFC 185:277.
82. IFC 374:323-6.
83. IFC 799:422-4.
84. IFC 1567:15-6.
85. Leitrim IFC S209:439-41.
86. Cavan IFC 1806:227-8.
87. IFC 374:323-6.
88. Ó hÓgáin 1985 116.
89. Kerry IFC 148:505-7.
90. Mayo IFC 1208:301-4. Another version: Kerry IFC 797:172-3. For further examples of bets by O'Connell see Kerry IFC 149:806-8; 304:306-40; 532:503-6; 834:556-62; S439:186-7; Mayo IFC 803:83-8; Roscommon IFC 1574:540(i).
91. Roscommon IFC 1506:487-8*. MI N O Wagers and gambling.
92. MI N O wagers and gambling.
93. See Appendix C.
94. IFC 517:341-2. Collected in 1938 by Peadar Mac Domhnaill from Tom Flood, aged fifty, a farmer, Toem, parish of Toem, barony of Kilnamanagh Upper, county Tipperary.
95. MI N O wagers and gambling.
96. For an analysis of the tale see Almqvist 1991 82-113.
97. For other versions of the tale see *ibid.* 190-216.
98. IFC 1480:107*. Collected in 1957 by James G. Delaney from James Rogers, aged seventy-three, a farmer, Derrycassan, parish of Columbkille, barony of Granard, county Longford. Other versions: Donegal:IFC 1619:109*; Kerry IFC S436:89-90*.
99. MI J 1114 clever servant; J 1340 retorts from hungry persons; K 402.1 the goose without a leg.
100. Ó hÓgáin 1985 86-99.
101. See Aarne and Thompson 1973 AT 785A for references to other versions.
102. Jarrell 1964 101-2, 114-5.
103. For background information on early occurrences of this tale see Lee 1909 177-9. The tale of the one-legged crane appears in the Decameron, day six, novel four, and it is one of those that is to be found in the jests told of the fourteenth century Turk, Nasreddin Khoja where it is told of a goose, not a crane. It is also told, as in the Decameron, in Pauli's 'Schimpf und Ernst' no. 57. It forms part of a play called 'Chrisis', written about 1444, by Enea Silvio Piccolomini, afterwards Pope Pius II. Here again, it is a greedy cook who steals the leg of a crane and tells his master they only have one.
104. Versions: Cork IFC 203:281; Donegal IFC 186:560; Galway IFC 155:102-4; Kerry IFC 929:326-7; Mayo IFC 195:453-7. MI J1180 clever means of avoiding legal punishment; J 1510 the cheater cheated.
105. See Ó hÓgáin 1990 334-6.
106. See footnote 7.
107. MI H 530 riddles; see H 1050 paradoxical tasks; H 1051 coming neither on nor off the road (comes in the rut or ditch at side of road); J 1111.2 illegitimate daughter of trickster inherits father's ability to dupe others; Q 91 cleverness rewarded; U 121 like parent, like child; H 1054.4 task coming neither in softness nor in hardness (comes clad in garments of mountain down) (Cross 1952). The Munster poet Eoghan Rua Ó Súilleabháin (1748-84) is also said to

have recognised his child by the child's cleverness; see Ó hÓgáin 1990 346-8.

108. For example IFC 227:254-60; 166:536.

109. Kerry IFC 823:306-7.

110. Kerry IFC 11:212-4.

111. In the *fiannaíocht*, or fenian lore, Diarmaid eloped with Fionn's woman, Gráinne, and the couple had many adventures; see Ó hÓgáin 1990 161-3. When Diarmaid refuses to go with her, he says to Gráinne: 'I will not go with thee, I will not take thee in softness and I will not take thee in hardness, I will not take thee without and I will not take within. I will not take thee on horseback, and I will not take thee on foot,' said he.

She was between the two sides of the door on a buck goat, 'I am not without, I am not within, I am not on foot, I am not on a horse; and thou must go with me,' said she. Schoepperle 1913 402.

In another account of this tale of Diarmaid and Gráinne, there is a description of Gráinne's clothes: She however went to a fairy woman and got garments made from mountain down. She came with this garment on, riding on a he-goat in the dusk of the evening, when it was neither light nor dark; and thus it could not be said that she was clothed or unclothed, on foot or on horseback, in company or without and consequently was deemed free from the spell laid upon her.

These motifs are found in Grimm's 'Die Kluge Bauern Tochter' (No. 94). In Irish tradition these tasks, or similar tasks, are often associated with *An Gobán Saor* (The Master Builder) as he sets tasks for his prospective daughter-in-law (Ó Súilleabháin 1970 875). The tale as told about O'Connell then, is evidently an 'O'Connellisation' of much older material. In one account about O'Connell, he and a boy are sheltering from the rain and O'Connell asks the boy why he doesn't mend the thatched roof so that it wouldn't let in the rain. The boy says that he couldn't mend it when it is raining, and that there is no need to repair it when it is dry as there is no leak. O'Connell says he is as clever as if he were his own son (Kerry IFC 659:417-9). The tale is also told about Dean Swift (IFC 480:412).

112. Galway IFC 271:152-3.

113. Galway IFC 970:324-6.

114. Galway IFC 271:152-3.

115. IFC 960:37-40.

116. Galway IFC S3:100. MI J 1210 clever man puts another out of countenance.

117. IFC 645:313-4. Collected in 1939 by Colm Ó Finneadha from Pádraig Ó Flaithbheartaigh, aged fifty-one, a farmer, Bearna, parish of Ráth Úin, barony of Gaillimh, county Galway. Other versions: Armagh IFC 1782:228; 1803:151-2; Cavan IFC 1787:202-3; S964:105; Clare IFC S609:494-5; S610:68-9; S618:177,247; S622:356; Cork IFC 283:81; 369:266-72; 437:401-2; 536:97; 596:65; 686:357; 789:536-7; 808:99; 1224:223-6; 1543:48-9; 1592: 212; 1596:461; 1673: 113-4; S275:213-4,215-6; S326: 207; S328:264-5; S338:60-1; S382:58; Donegal IFC 186:557; 366; 333-4; 454:220-1; 561:265-6; 694:387-8; S1062:42; S1070:131; S1073:22; S1081:330-1; S1111:530; Down IFC 1619:106-7; Dublin *Béal.* 12 1942 185; Galway IFC 113:24-5; 236:96-7,65-70, 369-70; 287:37; 354:59-61,250-1; 355:26-8; 394:4-5; 471:37-8; 474:365-6; 569:26-7; 578:106-7; 605:268-70; 627:367-8; 829:37-8; 851:266-7; 867:268-70; 869:537-8; 1133:300; 1236:395; 1311:278-9; 1322:76-7; 1764:400; S32:346-8; S42:16; S46:248; S59:493; S81:344; S82:37,134-5; *Béal.* 5 1935 144; de Bhaldraithe 1975 35; Gregory 1909 27-8; Kerry IFC 7:236; 306:393; 630: 105-6; 658:369-70; 685:29-30; 717:16; 796:3; 908:108-10; 1064:608; 1067:262-3; 1150:37-8; 1152:419-20; 1158:29; 1168:392; 1272:151-2; 1278:31; S437:77-8; S457:38-9; S456:1; S472:39-40; S475:156,186-7; S478:29-30; IFC Tape 1968 Bo Almqvist from Mícheál

Ó Gaoithín, Baile Bhiocáire, Dún Chaoin, Corca Dhuibhne; D. Ó Súilleabháin 1936 261-2; Limerick IFC 407:283; S520:63; S527:194; Longford IFC 1480:105; Louth IFC 1569:162; 1570:135; Mayo IFC 76:309-10; 734:238-42; 836:612-3; 1208:303-4; 1229:432; 1401:176; S120:202; S132:371-2; S142:223; IFC Tape 1976 Séamas Ó Catháin from Peadar Bairéad, Ceathrú na gCloch, Cill Cuimin; Offaly IFC 1709:181-2; Roscommon IFC 1771:19-20; Sligo IFC S159:132; S173:283-4; Tipperary IFC 3328:188-9; 517:340; 738:418, 493; S583:194; Disc 1948 Caoimhín Ó Danachair from Micheál Ó Maoldomhnaigh, Cnoc Maoldonn; Waterford IFC 152:332; 153:51-4,313-4,598; 275:485-6; 1100:335-6; S642:313; *OB* June 1922 361; Wexford IFC 1399:88-9; no provenance: *CS* 8.6.1901; *IO* 21.10.1933 528; *Irish Independent* 4.10.1945 2; *The Irish Packet* 26.6.1909, 415; *OB* April 1920 203; *Tír na nÓg* July 1947 3. Mag Ruaidhrí 1944 105.

118. IFC Disc 1948 Caoimhín Ó Danachair from Micheál Ó Maoldomhnaigh, Cnoc Maoldonn.

119. IFC 1399:88-9. Collected *c.* 1955 by James G. Delaney from Mrs Elizabeth Byrne, aged eighty-seven, a housewife, Milltown, Grange, parish of Killann, barony of Bantry, county Wexford.

120. IFC 1803:151-2. Collected in 1972 by Michael J. Murphy from Frank 'Wings' Campbell, aged seventy-seven, townland and barony of Forkill, barony of Orior Upper, county Armagh.

121. IFC 369:266-72. Collected in 1937 by Eoghan Ó Súilleabháin from Máire Ní Bhraonáin, aged seventy-two, a farmer's wife, Drom Garbhán, parish of Cill Cascán, barony of Béara.

122. Galway IFC 1236:395; 1322:26-7; Donegal S1081:330-1.

123. Kerry IFC 1272:151-2.

124. Cork IFC S275:215-6. The account probably refers to a castle in Killaconenagh, barony of Béara, county Cork.

125. Galway IFC S46:248.

126. IFC 561:265-6. Collected in 1938 by Liam Mac Meanman from Peigí Nic an Bhaird, aged eighty-three, a housewife, Seanmhín, parish of Inbhear, barony of Banach, county Donegal.

127. Donegal IFC 186:557-8.

128. IFC 869:537-8.

129. Tipperary IFC Disc 1948 Caoimhín Ó Danachair from Micheál Ó Maoldomhnaigh, Cnoc Maoldonn.

130. Kerry IFC S465:1.

131. Sligo IFC S173:283-4; *OB* 4/1920 207.

132. IFC 355:26-8; 605:268-70.

133. IFC 1569:162. Collected in 1962 by Michael J. Murphy from James Loughran, Anaverna, Ravensdale, parish of Ballymascanlon, barony of Lower Dundalk, county Louth.

134. IFC 391:45-6.

135. IFC 1133: 299-301. Collected *c.* 1937 by Cáit Ní Bhriain, Gleannabéil, Béal Átha Glúinín, parish of Tuaim, barony of Clár, county Galway. MI J 1112 clever wife; K 170 deception through pseudo-simple bargain.

136. See Ó hÓgáin 1990 241-3.

137. IFC 621:142-3. Collected 1936-37 by Seán Ó Dubhda from Seán Mac Criomhthain, aged sixty-two, a farmer, townland and parish of Cill Maolchéadair, barony of Corca Dhuibhne.

138. IFC 287:39. Collected in 1931 by an tAth. P.E. Mac Fhinn in Greallach, parish and barony of Liatroim, county Galway.

139. IFC 621:140-1.Collected 1936-37 by Seán Ó Dubhda from Seán Mac Criomhthain, aged sixty-two, a farmer, townland and parish of Cill Maolchéadair, barony of Corca Dhuibhne.

140. Kerry IFC Tape 1968 Bo Almqvist from Mícheál Ó Gaoithín, Baile Bhiocáire, Dún Chaoin.

141. IFC 628:81-2. Collected in 1939 by Seosamh Ó Dálaigh from Johnny Roche, aged seventy-eight, a farmer, Dually, parish of Newcastle, barony of Glenquin, county Limerick. Other versions: Armagh IFC 1803:144; Cavan IFC 1803:118; Cork IFC 437:402; 686:357-8; Galway IFC 354:248-9; 1833:64. Kerry IFC 658:371; 796:3; 908:110; 1150:38; 1168:392-3; 1272:67, 156; Limerick IFC 628:81-2.

142. They all contain the international motif MI J 1250 clever verbal retorts (repartee).

143. See Ó hÓgáin 1982 chapter 1.

144. IFC 1064:168-9. Collected in 1943 by Donncha Ó Súilleabháin, Lackaroe, parish of Kenmare, barony of Glanarought. Thomas Herbert was a landlord in Muckross, Killarney, county Kerry. For further examples of insults see Waterford IFC 153:314-5; Kerry IFC 659:210-1; 1147:201-2.

145. The Butlers were landowners in the area of An Coireán (Waterville), in Uíbh Ráthach.

146. IFC 667:202-4. Collected 1938-39 by Tadhg Ó Murchú from his father, An Coireán, parish of An Dromaid, barony of Uíbh Ráthach.

147. IFC 871:11-12. Collected 1934-40 by Máire Ní Sheasnáin from Mrs Margaret Fleming, Ballalley, Carrick on Suir, parish of Carrick, barony of Iffa and Offa East, county Tipperary. Another version Kerry IFC 685:38-9. MI J 1300 officiousness or foolish questions rebuked.

148. IFC 45:86-7. Collected in 1933 by Éamonn Ó hArgáin from Conchúr Ó Duinneacha, aged ninety, a tailor, Cluain Droichead, parish of Maigh Chromtha, barony of Múscraí Thiar, county Cork.

149. IFC 259:650-1. Collected in 1936 by Nioclás Breathnach from Jacky Ryan, aged fifty, a worker, Bóthar na Trá, parish of Dún Garbhán, barony of Déise, county Waterford. MI J 1350 rude retorts; J 1500 clever practical retorts.

150. IFC 1803:143. Collected in 1972 by Michael J. Murphy from Frank 'Wings' Campbell, aged seventy-seven, townland and barony of Forkill, barony of Orior Upper, county Armagh.

151. IFC S372:215. Collected 1937-39 through the national school of Clenor, parish of Clenor, barony of Fermoy, county Cork by Ena FitzGerald from Mrs Fitzgerald, aged forty-five, Lisanisky, parish of Mallow, barony of Fermoy. MI J 1300 officiousness or foolish questions rebuked. For further examples of Replies to Insults see Donegal IFC 454:221-2; Galway Béal. 5 260; Kerry IFC 308:239; 796:15; 823:570-1; 1167: 210-11; Limerick IFC S507:589; Mayo IFC 1401:175; Kennedy 1853 146.

152. IFC Tape Séamas Ó Catháin 1976 from Peadar Bairéad, Ceathrú na gCloch, Cill Cuimin, county Mayo (summary in translation). MI J 1350 rude retorts; J 1500 clever practical retorts.

153. IFC 796:5. Collected in 1941 by D. Ó Súilleabháin, Lackaroe, parish of Kenmare, barony of Glanroughty. Other versions: Kerry IFC 1272:68,156. MI J1350 rude retorts.

154. IFC 1506:488. Collected in 1958 by James G. Delaney from John Stoker, aged fifty-eight, a farmer, The Grove, parish of Kilteevan, barony of Ballintober, county Roscommon. Another version: Waterford IFC 153:312-13. MI J 1350 rude retorts.

155. IFC 871:10-11. Collected 1934-40 by Máire Ní Sheasnáin from Mrs Margaret

Fleming, Ballalley, Carrick on Suir, parish of Carrick, barony of Iffa and Offa East, county Tipperary. Another version Tipperary IFC 517:342-3. MI J 1500 clever practical retorts. For further examples of Rude Statement or Reply see Donegal IFC 186:415-6; Galway IFC 1322:589-95.

156. IFC 1569:162-3. Collected in 1962 by Michael J. Murphy from James Loughran, Anaverna, Ravensdale, parish of Ballymascanlon, barony of Lower Dundalk, county Louth. MI J 1500 clever practical retort.

157. Twain 1955 edition 70, 72.

158. IFC 658:559. Collected in 1939 by Seosamh Ó Dálaigh from Seán Ó Cearmuda, aged eighty-nine, a fisherman, Currach an tSusáin, parish of Lios Tuathail, barony of Oidhreacht Uí Chonchúir. MI J 1350 rude retorts.

159. Jarrell 1964 108.

160. IFC S372: 216. Collected 1937-39 through the national school of Clenor, parish of Clenor, barony of Fermoy, county Cork by Ena FitzGerald from Mrs Neenan, aged seventy, Dromroue, parish of Caherduggan, barony of Fermoy. Another version: Kerry IFC S439: 240. Also told about Dean Swift where he added two lines to the advertisement for employment which said 'No Catholic need apply.' Louth IFC 1112: 217.

161. IFC 1480:9. Collected in 1956 by James G. Delaney from Patrick Hetherton, aged seventy-five, a farmer, Derreenavoggy, parish of Columbkille, barony of Granard, county Longford.

162. IFC 1480:7-9. Collected in 1956 by James G. Delaney from Patrick Hetherton, aged seventy-five, a farmer, Derreenavoggy, parish of Columbkille, barony of Granard, county Longford. MI J1300 officiousness or foolish questions rebuked; J 1350 rude retorts.

163. IFC S462:285-6.Collected about 1938 through the national school of Leithead, parish of Tuath Ó Siosta, barony of Gleann na Ruachtaí by Neil O'Sullivan from his mother Mrs Mary O'Sullivan, aged forty-four, Bunaw (?). The verse in the shop window is in keeping with a published account where it is stated: 'Certain old-time inns used to have for a sign a board bearing a picture of a bee-hive with its denizens in full activity, and inscribed with the lines:
"Within this hive we're all alive;
Good liquor makes us funny.
And if you be dry, come in and try
The flavour of our honey!"
There is a Beehive Inn on the Lucan road near Dublin, where – with the conservatism of the Pale, in some things more true to tradition than the remainder of the country – the sign is still (or was until 1923) in position.
There is a Beehive Inn seven miles from Clonmel on the Dungarvan road, but the sign has disappeared.' Béal. 15 284 1945. Collected by Patrick Lyons from Patrick Condon, Clonmel.

164. IFC 843:217. Collected in 1942 by Donncha Ó Súilleabháin, Lackaroe, parish of Kenmare, barony of Glanarought. For further examples of verse said to have been composed by O'Connell see Kerry IFC 1064:61, 315; 1272:171; Sligo IFC S167:268-9.

165. Kerry IFC 796:10-12.

166. Chapbook.

167. IFC 796:15. Collected in 1941 by D. Ó Súilleabháin, Lackaroe, parish of Kenmare, barony of Glanarought. Another version: Kerry IFC 1064:167. For further examples of Sarcasm see Kerry IFC 843:147a; 1064:166-7; S463:153; *The Irish Packet* 22.5.1909 252.

168. Chapbook, n.d., summary. Another version: *OB* 6/1929 679.
169. Kerry IFC 843:197. For further examples of a statement or a reply see Cavan 1196:385; Kerry IFC 797:68-9; Wexford IFC 1399:465; *OB* 6/1929 679; Luby 1874 242.
170. Probably Baron William Conygham, lawyer and member of the Conservative party.
171. Richard Lalor Sheil (1791-1851) was a lawyer and politician. He became a member of the Catholic Board and was closely associated with the fight for Catholic Emancipation. He was active in the Clare by-election. He was amongst the first Catholics to be appointed to the Inner Bar.
172. *IO* 29.7.1903 1. Sir Anthony Hart was appointed solicitor general to Queen Charlotte in 1816. He was vice-chancellor from April to November 1827 and lord chancellor of Ireland from 1827 to 1830.
173. Chapbook n.d. Scotland.
174. IFC 1148:311. Collected in 1949 by Tadhg Ó Murchú from Seán Ó Fóghartaigh aged sixty, Slachaigh, parish of An Dromaid, barony of Uíbh Ráthach. For other examples of puns by O'Connell see Kerry IFC 685:37; 796:13; *IO* 11.2.1903 2.
175. IFC 517:328-9. Collected in 1938 by Peadar Mac Domhnaill from M. Renehan aged forty-seven, a farmer, Knockaun parish of Toem, barony of Kilnamanagh Upper, county Tipperary. Other versions: Armagh IFC 1782:227; 1803:149; Dublin IFC S797:214; Kerry IFC 1147:202-3; Clare IFC S613:213; Galway IFC S18 308; Limerick IFC 1194:556; Longford(?) IFC 1933:49; Mayo IFC 227:54-5; Monaghan IFC 1566:80; Roscommon IFC 1506:487; 1574:539(i); Tipperary IFC 517:328-9; Tyrone IFC 1566:81. MI J 1250 clever verbal retorts (repartee).
176. IFC 1147:202-3. Collected in 1949 by Tadhg Ó Murchú from Micheál Ó Móráin, aged eighty-six, a stonemason and a farmer, Caol an Phréacháin, parish of An Dromaid, barony of Uíbh Ráthach.
177. IFC 1194:556. Collected in 1950 by Colm Ó Danachair from Richard Denihan, aged eighty-six, a farm labourer, Gortnagross, parish of Rathronan, barony of Shanid, county Limerick.
178. IFC 1164:29. Collected in 1949 by Colm Ó Danachair from Richard Denihan, aged eighty-five, a farm labourer, Gortnagross, parish of Rathronan, barony of Shanid, county Limerick. Other versions: Cavan IFC 1196:383-4; Clare IFC S613:212; Kerry IFC 1064:308; no provenance *IO* 11.2.1950 21; 12.7.1922,27; *The Irish Packet* 20; Luby 1874 239. MI J 1250 clever verbal retorts.
179. We are told in the index of international tales that as well as supper, other advantages may be included here.
180. Kerry IFC 823:306.

Statue of Daniel O'Connell by John Hogan in City Hall, Dublin. The statue was unveiled in 1843 (Sarah Cully, Audio-Visual Centre, UCD, 1995).

Chapter 5

The emergence of the folk hero

Throughout Irish oral tradition, Daniel O'Connell is unquestionably a folk hero. He appears as such in historical lore, in the traditional song material, in the international tales and in the legends and anecdotes. O'Connell emerges as a person of strong and remarkable traits of character which earn him the respect of the community. Among these traits are his ability as a lawyer, his cleverness and wiliness, his quick wit and his gift for composing verse. Because he is held in great esteem, Daniel O'Connell's fame is thereby increased, and the achievements of both the historical and the folk character are exaggerated to create a mythical, heroic figure.

This chapter presents and examines some of the oral material which illustrates Daniel O'Connell as folk hero. The emergence of the folk hero may be viewed as the ultimate step in the development of the folk character, which in turn is a development of the historical character.

Heroicism

A hero is a person perceived as being apart from the ordinary. There are particular characteristics that place such a person on a different level from the rest of the human race. These characteristics earn admiration and respect from the community. While 'ordinary people' earn respect for the good deeds they perform and for their praiseworthy traits, they do not necessarily become folk heroes. They must have something more: to become a hero, the historical character must live in suitable times and must have unusual qualities. In this study of the folk hero, the classical hero is seen as one who conforms to established heroic forms. These forms consist of patterns or rules which are based on the classical heroic traditions of Greece and Rome. Supernatural traits or powers are among the essential characteristics of the classical hero. These supernatural traits can be seen in both the Gaelic heroes, such as Fionn Mac Cumhaill and Cormac Mac Airt, and in a classical hero such as Hercules.

Daniel O'Connell has a number of supernatural traits attributed to him in Irish folk tradition which confirm his ranking as a hero according to classical forms. O'Connell therefore takes his place in oral tradition beside both the great Irish and classical heroes.

When viewed in a broader context, the heroic material about Daniel O'Connell is a small but vital part of the general body of oral tradition about him. Without this heroicisation process, O'Connell would not have achieved the highest rank of folk character. There were many historical factors which contributed to O'Connell's suitability to the heroic role.

He possessed all the necessary requirements of the hero. There was no one comparable to him in his time. He was of noble background, like the kings and heroic figures of history. His uncle owned a big house and the O'Connells ranked among the well-off in the community. Young Daniel O'Connell was sent to be fostered for some years as a child and was later sent to school abroad. This was unusual for most Irish people at that time. He was a good scholar. He earned his qualifications as a lawyer and his academic success was esteemed. Education and academic success were held in high regard in Irish tradition as is evident from folklore and from the tradition of hedge schools and from the manuscript tradition. O'Connell was famous at home and abroad and became known for his cleverness and his witty speech. He won many court cases. He also had powerful enemies such as Robert Peel, and he once killed a man in a duel. He had power in the court of law and he had political power in addition to this. He had power over his tenants. Little wonder that some people were afraid of him.

This combination of events and character traits were the cornerstone for Daniel O'Connell's emergence as a folk hero. They provided the raw material which was developed in the popular imagination.

During his lifetime, the historical facts about Daniel O'Connell were developed and changed in Irish oral tradition. This is particularly clear in the historical lore, where the requirements for a hero were emphasised more than were the historical facts. For example, it emerges in the historical lore that the most important single event in O'Connell's career was the duel with D'Esterre, and the fact that Daniel O'Connell killed his opponent. This was the only violent act known to have been committed by O'Connell during his lifetime, and apparently he himself wished to forget it. But the people did not. Not only was it not forgotten, but it was embellished until it became a symbol for O'Connell's heroism.

O'Connell as Classical Hero

The Gaelic heroic tradition is related to the international classical heroic tradition, and O'Connell is a part of both of these major strands in

Ireland's folk culture. The life pattern of the classical and of some of the Gaelic heroes has been studied in detail. For example, in *Heroic Song and Heroic Legend* (1963), Jan de Vries outlines the classical heroic pattern; in *The Heroic Biography of Cormac Mac Airt* (1977), Tomás Ó Cathasaigh illustrates how Cormac Mac Airt fulfills the Gaelic heroic pattern by conforming to a number of the prerequisites for the classical hero.

Daniel O'Connell does not emerge as a classical hero in the same way in which Hercules or Cormac Mac Airt are perceived, however. O'Connell did not live in a time of 'antiquity'. He is a comparatively recent figure in history, and so the reality of his existence cannot be forgotten as long as the folk memory retains accounts of him.

Only certain traits, or progressive steps, of the heroic life are found in the O'Connell of Irish folklore.[1] These are traits which are perceived to exist because of supernatural intervention. The following are apparent in an examination of O'Connell's heroic life pattern:
1. The conception and birth of the hero
2. The youth of the hero
3. The way in which the hero is raised
4. The invulnerability of the hero
5. The victory and power of the hero
6. The death of the hero

The following accounts illustrate these various episodes, all of which have a supernatural element and which bring O'Connell to the level of folk hero:

1. The Conception and Birth: Prophecies of Greatness[2]

In the legends of Daniel O'Connell's birth, it is often said that it was a miraculous event. One such legend tells how a Protestant man and woman were married but had no children although they longed to have a child. The man contributed a great deal of money to help the local Catholic priest build and furnish a church. The priest was very grateful and the Protestant said to him that he had no-one to whom he could leave his money. The priest replied that he would not say that in nine months time, that he would have someone to whom he could leave his wealth. And so O'Connell was born, an event which was regarded as a miraculous occurrence.[3] The following is part of a Conamara account of the incident where the Protestant is telling the priest that he has no-one to whom he can leave his wealth:

> '*Á, well,*' *a deir an Prostastún leis anall ar ais,* '*sin rud,*' *a deir sé,* '*ní fheicfidh mé,*' *a deir sé,* '*deireadh mo chuid airgid caite go brách. Agus níl aon nduine agam,*' *a deir sé,* '*a bhfágfaidh mé an t-airgead i mo dhiaidh aige,*' *a deir sé,* '*ach ag gach uile dhuine,*' *a deir sé,* '*a phunt*

féin agus a chúig phunt agus a dheich bpunt féin aige,' a deir sé. 'Á,
muise,' a deir an sagart, a deir sé, 'ní bheidh sin le rá agat,' a deir sé,
'faoi cheann trí ráithe. Más féidir liomsa a dhéanamh,' a deir sé, 'ná
toil Dé. Beidh duine agatsa a bhfágfaidh tú do shaibhreas aige ar ball
i ndeireadh do shaoil.' Ach chuir sé láimh ina phóca agus rinneadar
thart ar theach an phobail. D'íoc an Protastún amach gach uile shórt
leis an sagart a theastaigh uaidh, gur réitíodh amach teach an
phobail, go raibh sé in ann ag gach uile dhuine a thíocht isteach ann.
Bhí sin ag gabháil thart. Faoi cheann trí ráithe bhí mac óg ag an
bProtastún, ag an mbean. Ar ndóigh ba mheasa leis an bProtastún
mac óg a bheith beirthe dhó ná a sheacht n-oiread agus a bhí caite
aige.[4]

('Ah, well,' said the Protestant back to him, 'that is something,' he
said, 'that I won't see,' he said, 'all my money ever spent. And I have
no one,' he said, 'to whom I can leave the money after me,' he said.
'Ah, well,' said the priest, he said, 'you won't have that to say,' he
said, 'at the end of three seasons. If I can arrange it,' he said, 'or the
will of God. You will have someone to whom you can leave your
wealth later, at the end of your life.' But he put his hand in his pocket
and they went to the church. The Protestant paid him any money that
the priest wanted, until the church was put in order, so that it could
hold everyone who went in there. Time passed. At the end of three
seasons the Protestant, his wife, had a young son. Of course the
Protestant would rather have a young son born to him than seven
times the amount of money that he had spent.)

Apparently, reference in oral tradition to O'Connell's father being a
Protestant is found in county Galway only. In other counties, the
accounts indicate that his father is believed to be a Catholic, or else no
mention is made of his father's religion. Of the twenty-three recorded
versions of this event, seventeen are in Irish and six in English. In three
versions, it is said that the infant was born in a particular place, such as
Carhen or Cahirsiveen in county Kerry, or in an unspecified place in
county Limerick. In most accounts it is said that the mother had a
difficult labour, and that the father helped to build a church or to re-
roof it, or that he gave money towards this work. And so the couple
earned the gratitude of the priest and of the local community. In a few
accounts it is said that they earned this gratitude in another way, when
they gave shelter to some members of the Roman Catholic clergy and
were rewarded by the birth of a child, Daniel O'Connell.

In four of the accounts consulted it is said that O'Connell's father
was a minister. Sometimes, the miraculous aspects of the conception
and birth are emphasised by the fact that his parents are quite old. For
instance, in one account, it is stated that his father was seventy, and his
mother sixty, when O'Connell was born.[5]

In a few instances, the power of prayer is mentioned, where the couple were praying for a number of years that they might have a child. The account says that Daniel is sent in answer to these prayers. And so the involvement of the supernatural finds expression in that a child is conceived and born in a way which can only be explained by some form of miracle.

In tradition, O'Connell's birth was an exceptional one. It was not the birth of an ordinary mortal. It was a birth which was decided by God. When he was born, people were aware of the great event:

> A story from Baile Bhuirne in West Cork claims that at his birth an echo was tossed back and forth between the mountains of Kerry, so that not a man or woman but did not know that some great thing was after happening.[6]

Prophecies were made, before and after his birth, about the child's future and about his importance for Ireland. A bishop came to bless the church which was built with money donated by O'Connell's father, and he said to the father that he had 'the best plant that ever grew in Ireland'.[7] In another account, the parish priest to whom O'Connell's father had given shelter said: 'There will be an heir born to O'Connell. He will be remembered while grass will be growing or water running.'[8]

In a number of versions, it is said that the infant bore some mark on his back, or some other sign to indicate that he was exceptional and had a remarkable future ahead. The influence of mythology can thus be seen both in the unusual circumstances of O'Connell's conception, and in the physical sign of his future greatness. In nineteen versions, it is said that O'Connell was born with a cross on his back, or on his breast, or in both places. The cross was said to be like the cross on an asses back, or like a crucifix, and it was also sometimes said that it resembled a rope of hair on his back. The following is from county Armagh:

> He had a plait, a rope of hair across his chest, and it was a cross over his breast. And they said that he was an ass: that he was born an ass: born with the Cross of Christ on him. Well, those were their words.
>
> Well, the cross of Christ, there's nothing in the world ever carries it only the ass; and he must be a black ass.[9]

O'Connell is not the only one believed to have had such a birthmark. In Irish oral tradition, a prophecy was made in relation to Judas Iscariot when as an infant, a black cross was seen on his back. A poor scholar who happened to be in the house said that he had an exceptionally difficult future ahead.[10] A prophecy based on the existence of a black cross seems then to indicate a significant personality: the birth of a human being who will be a powerful force and who will be remembered for all time.

Certain parallels may also be drawn between the conception and birth of Christ, and Daniel O'Connell's conception and birth. Prophecy plays an important role in both cases: the conception is miraculous, involving divine intervention. During the birth there are signs from nature that a wonderful event is taking place: echoes are heard in each case. And a Saviour is born in each case.

In Irish folklore, the cross on O'Connell's back is said to give him special powers. In one instance, it was said that the cross was the reason for his cleverness.[11] Elsewhere, it was the sign that this was the infant chosen by God to liberate the Catholics,[12] or – as simply stated in a Galway version – that O'Connell was 'born holy'. In an account from Kerry where it was said that he was born by God's will, a man called Laoire Fíodóra, who was said to work for O'Connell, claimed that he often saw the cross on O'Connell's back.[13]

The messianic tradition of the medieval crusades is reflected very strongly in the power and aims of O'Connell. The belief was wide-spread, for example, in relation to Charlemagne, that he was a heroic warrior 'who would not only annihilate the infidel but also succour and raise up the lowly'.[14] This is very much in keeping with the Irish rural community's trust in O'Connell, their Saviour. During the crusades it was the *pauperes,* or poor people taking part in the crusades, who grasped the symbol of Charlemagne as the Saviour, and as the Last Emperor to save the people. It was firmly believed that Charlemagne also bore the traditional sign of divine election, *i.e.* the cross on or between the shoulder-blades.[15]

Elsewhere, we find further evidence of the cross as a sign of leadership. Frederick II, ruler of Thuringia (1314-1323), was also said to have such a cross: 'It was widely believed that he bore the miraculous birthmark – the luminous gold cross between the shoulder-blades.'[16]

This image of leader and Saviour is very much in keeping with the folk image of Daniel O'Connell in Irish tradition. Despite having a Protestant father in some of the folklore accounts, it was said in many of these accounts that O'Connell's father promised that he would have the child baptised in the Catholic Church. In one account he was called Daniel after the parish priest.

In a few versions, it is said that O'Connell's career suffered because he was said to be the son of a Protestant. In one instance, for example, he was to become a priest, but it was discovered that his father was a Protestant and so he became a counsellor instead.

The motifs concerning the conception and birth of O'Connell and related prophecies, certainly pre-date Daniel O'Connell as a historical character, and are introduced to the folklore of O'Connell to place him in a different sphere from, or on a level above, that of ordinary human beings, and to heroicise him in oral tradition. Although he is not an epic hero, his character is attributed some traits which are found in the epic hero's life. These traits are selected because they are in some way in keeping with the heroic folk image of O'Connell.

2. The Youth of the Hero

The tales and legends which describe various events in O'Connell's youth also set him apart from other people. His cleverness as a boy is revealed in tales such as 'The Man Who Lost his Eye'. Here, the hero proves at a young age that he is exceptionally talented and that he will have a great future. In one version of 'The Man Who Lost his Eye', it is said that O'Connell made the judgement when he was only seven years of age. This is the accepted age of reason, but Daniel O'Connell was obviously more advanced than others of the same age.[17] These indications are, of course, in keeping with the prophecies made at O'Connell's birth.

3. The Way in which the Hero is Raised

According to folklore, Daniel O'Connell was not reared at home in his parents' house but was fostered, which was a custom at the time for those who were comparatively wealthy. This is reminiscent of other great heroes like Fionn Mac Cumhaill. It is often a part of the epic hero's youth that he is raised away from home.

Following the period of fosterage, O'Connell was sent abroad to school. While Fionn Mac Cumhaill was taken from home to protect him from enemies, O'Connell was fostered because it was the custom at that time to do so:

> The curious old Irish custom of having the children of the gentry, immediately after birth, suckled and reared by healthy young matrons of the peasant class, known as 'fosterage', still prevailed in West Kerry and accordingly the infant O'Connell was sent to the wife of his father's herdsman, who lived in a cabin on the Iveragh mountains.[18]

So we see here how historical circumstances form the background for O'Connell to be introduced into the heroic life pattern.

4. The Invulnerability of the Hero

It was believed that Daniel O'Connell could not be killed: this was not dependent on his cross or on any other physical sign. It is a trait of the classical hero that he cannot be killed, or that he can be killed only in a particular spot. O'Connell is said to have been invulnerable, except in his heel, like Achilles, although this may be an isolated account.[19] In one account, his invulnerability is conferred on O'Connell in a special way, where it is said that a shirt was made for the infant Daniel in one night, and that it had the power to ensure that he would never be killed.[20]

5. The Victory and Power of the Hero

Power over Enemies

In Irish tradition, as elsewhere, the heroes were warrior-like and brave men, like Cú Chulainn. They were immortalised because of their achievements in battle. O'Connell, of course, lived in a different era and his warfare was one of constitutional nationalism. As is evident from many of the tales and legends about O'Connell, he was a leader and a kind of Robin Hood figure in oral tradition, but he was not violent. The D'Esterre incident is the only known violent deed he committed. O'Connell's victory was intellectual and moral. He conquered Protestants and Englishmen verbally, and this is doubtless symbolic of his political victory. O'Connell was held in high regard because of his power over the enemy, and the regard was for O'Connell, the Irish Catholic. O'Connell encouraged peaceful agitation throughout his life.

Nevertheless, he had enemies, and this is emphasised in much of the oral material. The existence of enemies, and his victory over them, in whatever way, further underlines his role as hero and leader. As befits the hero, O'Connell risked his own life and survived the danger.

Healing Powers

There are traditional accounts in which O'Connell is said to have cured people. The accounts of this healing power are closely connected to the accounts of O'Connell's birth, where it is often said that he had some special power, although the power is not specified. In some cases, the power is said to come from the cross on his back or on his chest. In one account, belief in O'Connell's power to cure can be traced to influence from the New Testament. The account says:

> Éinne go mbeadh aon mháchail air agus go mbuailfeadh
> sé ar a bhrat, bheadh sé leighiste.[21]

> (Anyone who had any injury and who touched his cloak, he would be cured.)

In this association with the power of Christ to cure, merely by touching his clothes, O'Connell is again likened to the Saviour. In another account, we learn that a woman told O'Connell that she heard if she rubbed against him three times her imprisoned husband would be set free.[22] Although this instance does not involve a cure, it is nonetheless of importance in identifying O'Connell as a hero with supernatural power.[23]

In another account, it is said that O'Connell's mother was ill and O'Connell said to her: *'Go mba fearr amárach thú!'* ('May you be better to-morrow.')[24] The following day she had recovered. Although the account does not state that O'Connell caused the cure, the implication is clear. The laying on of hands by O'Connell had a beneficial effect as well, apparently. We are told that on one occasion he visited Kells, county Meath and laid his hand on the head of a little girl called Anna Smith. Although it is not actually stated in the account that it was this laying of hands which caused Anna Smith to see seven generations during her lifetime, it is implied that the laying of hands was a particular gift in itself.[25]

Poetry

O'Connell proved on several occasions that he was a gifted poet, according to oral tradition. This gift increased O'Connell's standing in the community. He inherited the gift from his grandmother, Máire Ní Dhuibh, and it was not something he learned or acquired during his lifetime. Poetry was usually regarded in folk tradition as a supernatural gift, and this in turn had implications regarding the power of the poet.[26] In the case of O'Connell, his talent for composing *ex tempore* verse undoubtedly helped to develop his image as a folk hero.

6. The Death of the Hero

Daniel O'Connell did not die the bloody, warlike death of the hero: he died an ordinary death. But there is evidence of supernatural forces at work, and suggestions of the classical hero in an account from Kerry which describes certain events on the day he died:

> The day Daniel O'Connell was born, they planted a tree at Carhen bridge and it grew, and when he died it began to wither away and there was a piece of it there all the time, and it took the form of a man.[27]

So O'Connell's death affected nature, and nature expressed its sorrow at his death. It gave a sign that someone exceptional had died. It is relevant here to recall the New Testament reference to the death of Christ, where the world was in darkness for three hours and the light of the sun was obscured.[28] In Irish tradition, when Art Ó Laoire died, nature grieved at the sorrowful event and the animals were silent.[29] It is, of course, also in keeping with the *caoineadh* and the traditional songs of lamentation in Irish that nature is seen to be grieving.

The Heroic Life of Daniel O'Connell

It is difficult to say when the realm of the supernatural was introduced into the folk tradition about Daniel O'Connell. Certainly, it happened at a time when his political and historical career had been well established. Many of the songs, legends and anecdotes about Daniel O'Connell were created during a particular period in time, probably when he was at the height of his power and popularity, although it is also possible that much of the heroicisation may have occurred after his death. A further development then took place when the supernatural elements, and thereby the heroic life pattern, were introduced into the oral traditions about O'Connell. This heroic life pattern and the associated supernatural elements are, of course, rooted in a far older tradition than that of Daniel O'Connell, as we have seen.

The Folklore Material

Folklore about O'Connell is naturally not as vibrant to-day as it was fifty years ago. The fact, however, that certain areas seem to have a shortage of material about Daniel O'Connell may not necessarily mean that the material did not exist there at some time – it may merely reflect the contemporary collecting situation.

On the whole, more material has been collected about Daniel O'Connell in Irish than in English. This is due in some measure to the history of folklore collecting during the 1930s and 1940s, when most of the material about Daniel O'Connell was recorded. But even taking this into consideration, the fact remains that most of the material about O'Connell is in Irish, and much of it exists in Irish only. In the song tradition about O'Connell, for example, virtually none of the songs were translated from Irish to English or vice versa, as part of a living singing tradition. Traditional songs have rarely crossed the language divide in Ireland, possibly because of the comparatively rigid nature of their composition. On the other hand, however, some of the most popular tales and anecdotes about O'Connell were part of the living narrative tradition in both Irish and English. In any case, and regardless of the language of the material, the sheer amount of folklore available about O'Connell is evidence in itself of his important role in Irish folk tradition.

The various genres of folklore about O'Connell coincide in their presentation of him as folk hero. For example, the songs concentrate on his praiseworthy traits and elevate Daniel O'Connell very much above the ordinary people. Although the songs praising O'Connell might often tend to exaggeration, they do not contain certain traits which are very much to the fore in the anecdotes and tales. These traits include, for example, vulgarity and repartee. We are also told that accounts of his philandering were not told on certain occasions. One storyteller said that, as a child, he was put out of the house when: 'That crack was going on, in Irish: you were put out of the house altogether!'[30]

O'Connell traditions were created and kept alive for the most part by a comparatively poor, rural community. Many of the original storytellers were contemporaries of O'Connell, and he held a great fascination for them. The vast majority of the storytellers would not have known O'Connell personally, and their impressions of him would have been at least at second-hand. Some of them may have been tenants of the O'Connell family, but it would appear from the folklore collections that none of the storytellers were on the same social level as O'Connell himself. Interestingly, very few women gave accounts or told tales or legends about Daniel O'Connell. This is probably partly a result of the way in which folklore was collected in the 1930s and 1940s, at least, *i.e.* largely by men and from men. Because of lack of sufficient evidence, however, it is not possible to state categorically that women had folklore about Daniel O'Connell which was not collected from them, for whatever reason. Still on the subject of gender, it may be worth mentioning that one man, for example, had twelve tales and legends about O'Connell, while, of the few women who did tell stories about Daniel O'Connell, they usually told one or two. Women must have been familiar with lore and tales about O'Connell, however, and they must have heard a great deal of talk about him.

The Functions of O'Connell Folklore

The functions of the folklore of Daniel O'Connell operate on both the conscious and subconscious levels. On a conscious level, the songs, stories and lore all provided entertainment. The recounting of historical lore was not for educational purposes, but rather because it was seen to be interesting material. Thus, it became part of oral tradition. The characters in the tales and legends are always characters with whom the Irish rural population of the time could easily identify – farmers, labourers, *spailpíns* and fishermen. These are the people O'Connell so readily helped in the tales. Often, it was stated that he was helping a poor Irish Catholic who was suffering unjustly because of landlords, Protestants or Englishmen. In this way, O'Connell was immortalised as Saviour of the Irish Catholic, and conqueror of British rule, thus providing a source of hope and pride, at both conscious and subconscious levels, for a desperately poor people.

The Immortalisation of O'Connell in Folklore

It is no accident that such a large amount of folklore about Daniel O'Connell exists. The historical O'Connell was a fascinating person.

Some of the historical traits have become part of the folklore about him, and additional traits have been introduced to suit the folk character that has been created. O'Connell's importance in folk tradition in general is seen in the number of words used to describe him – *Cunsailéir*, Liberator, Counsellor, King and Leader and also in certain phrases used in everyday speech, such as: *'Bhuafá ar Dhónall Ó Conaill féin!'* ('You would beat even Daniel O'Connell'), which is said in praise of someone.[31] Another phrase said to someone who has a ready tongue, is: 'More power, O'Connell!'[32] His name is immortalised in folklore in other ways also – for example, in Kerry a very fine breed of horse is said to have been named after O'Connell.[33]

All of the expressions and accounts combine to make O'Connell a towering figure in Irish folk tradition. In the case of some of the legends and anecdotes, it is possible that some of them may have been immortalised by O'Connell telling them about other people, and that oral tradition then gave O'Connell the leading role in these stories. The O'Connell of Irish folklore could then assume a more active role than that of storyteller.

It is also possible that some of the metaphors used in the songs, and in some of the other material, came to be taken literally. For example, in the song 'Rejoice, ye Irish patriots', the line 'the angels sang at his birth' may have come to be interpreted in a literal sense, and become entangled with the idea of the Saviour from God.

Apart from the many stories in which O'Connell's cleverness is portrayed, phrases are also used throughout the folklore material in praise of O'Connell. For example, O'Connell's cleverness is underlined by mention of the fact in many of the tales that the most clever lawyers available had failed to solve a certain case until Daniel O'Connell came along. Similarly, at the end of a tale describing some successful court case, or a piece of clever repartee on Dan's part, the storyteller may say something to the effect that O'Connell was 'a great man and was the first man to get their rights for Irish people'. This type of comment is, of course, in keeping with Daniel O'Connell's role as conqueror of the English. Such a comment is introduced frequently at the beginning of a tale, or added to the end of it, as occurs in one version of 'The Tinkers' Hotel':

> Among the old people the name of Dan is highly honoured. These old men talk proudly of the great fight Dan had put up for Catholics.[34]

In 'The Man who Lost his Eye' a version in Irish says:

> *Níor chuaigh sé riamh ag daoradh ach ag saoradh i gcónaí.*[35]

> (He never went to condemn, but always to make free.)

188

Despite its appearance here in printed form, folklore about O'Connell is oral in origin, and its traditional life form is essentially oral. It was and is designed to be heard, not to be read. The style of singing and of storytelling is suited to a listening audience. Each informant may then make his or her own of the account, tale or song, and this adds to the free, natural style, which is intrinsic to the material. The folklore of Daniel O'Connell is an example of the great richness of traditional material which can exist about a historical character. It reveals attitudes to O'Connell which may not be revealed in more conventional historical studies. Most importantly, it shows how, during O'Connell's lifetime, people grasped certain traits in his character and developed them to create a folk hero who was a very real and important part of their lives.

References

1. de Vries 1963 211. For further examples of the heroic life see Dundes 1965 144.
2. MI f 546.3 star (cross) on breast; H 71.5 cross between shoulders sign of royalty; M 312 prophecy of future greatness for youth; T 510 miraculous conception; T 548.4 charity rewarded by birth of child.
3. Versions: Armagh IFC 1803:154; Cork IFC 879:540; S300:346; *The Irish Times* 17.4.1975; Donegal IFC 322:455-60; Galway IFC 73:297-306; 355:20-1; 389:449-56; 627:368; 802:519-21; 868:289-90; 1236:333; 1322:579-82; 1764:392-4; Gregory 1909 23-4; Kerry IFC 498:27-8; 621:172; 908:104-7; 929:101-5; 1168:266-7; IFC Tape Bo Almqvist from Mícheál Ó Gaoithín, Baile Bhiocáire, Dún Chaoin; Louth IFC 1691:163; Mayo IFC 665:473; IFC Tape Séamas Ó Catháin from Peadar Bairéad, Ceathrú na gCloch, Cill Cuimin.
4. IFC 1322:579-82. Collected in 1953 by Proinnsias de Búrca from Ciarán Ó Súilleabháin, aged sixty-eight, a farmer, Loch Conaortha, Maoras, barony of Baile na hInse, county Galway.
5. Galway IFC 73:297-306.
6. *The Irish Times* 17.4.1975.
7. Galway IFC 929:101-5 (translation).
8. Kerry IFC 1168:266-7.
9. IFC 1803:154. Collected in 1972 by Michael J. Murphy from Frank 'Wings' Campbell, aged seventy-seven, townland and parish of Forkill, barony of Orior Upper, county Armagh.
10. Galway IFC 73: 297-306.
11. Mayo IFC Tape 1976 Séamas Ó Catháin from Peadar Bairéad, Ceathrú na gCloch, Cill Cuimin; Galway IFC 868:289-90.
12. Galway IFC 389:449-56.
13. Kerry IFC 621:172.
14. Cohn 1974 72.
15. *ibid.* 73.
16. *ibid.* 143.
17. Larousse 1973 232. In Irish mythology, Setanta's name was changed to Cú Chulainn because he displayed his courage and bravery by a particular deed at that age. Setanta's deed was warlike, and O'Connell's intellectual, but in each case it is an indication that a great future lies ahead.

18. M. MacDonagh 1929 8-9.
19. *The Irish Times* 17.4.1975.
20. Kerry IFC 1168:266-7.
21. IFC 858:324. Collected in 1943 by Seosamh Ó Dálaigh from Mícheál Ó Gaoithín, aged about forty-five, Baile Bhiocáire, parish of Dún Chaoin, barony of Corca Dhuibhne.
22. Galway IFC 78:99-101.
23. Toynbee 1950 1-14. Apparently, it was the custom at one time to believe in the curative powers of royal people and others of great importance and power who were not holy people or saints. In an article which describes this phenomenon, known as 'the miracle of the royal touch' Charles I, who lived during the first half of the seventeenth century was said to have had the power to cure what was known as *The King's Evil*. Biblical material was introduced in this case when it happened, after the death of Charles I, that a woman's daughter was very ill. It happened that she came upon a handkerchief dipped in his blood. 'And as she was going home she lamented his death, for, by the good report she had heard of him, he had been converted, and believed him to be a saint. And thereupon the 19th Chapter of the Acts came into her mind, how that from St Paul were brought handkerchiefs and aprons to the sick and they were cured. She thought to herself 'Why might not his cloth do my daughter some good?'. Therefore, as soon as she came home, she wiped her child's eyes with the cloth, and in less than three weeks she was perfectly well, and nobody can perceive that ever she was ill.'
24. IFC Tape 1976 Séamas Ó Catháin from Seán Ó hEinirí, Cill Ghallagáin, parish of Cill Cuimin, barony of Iorras, county Mayo.
25. IFC S703:132. Collected in 1937-38 through the national school of the Convent of Mercy, townland and parish of Ceannanas Mór (Kells), barony of Upper Kells, county Meath, by Christina Heary.
26. Ó hÓgáin 1982 364-415.
27. IFC 1168:226. Collected in 1949 by Seosamh Ó Dálaigh from Seán Ó Ríordáin, aged eighty-six, a farmer, Curraheen, parish of Glanbehy, barony of Uíbh Ráthach.
28. *The Holy Bible,* London Catholic Truth Society London 1966 Matthew 27:45.
29. Ó Tuama 1961 42.
30. IFC 1803:145. Collected in 1972 by Michael J. Murphy from Frank 'Wings' Campbell, aged seventy-seven, townland and parish of Forkill, barony of Orior Upper, county Armagh.
31. Kerry IFC 149:220.
32. Wicklow IFC 497:291-2.
33. Kerry IFC 772:254.
34. IFC S1111: 529-30. Collected in 1939 through the National School of Sr. Oran's, Buncrana, parish of Fahan Lower, barony of Inishowen west, county Donegal, by Annie McLaughlin, Ballymagan, parish of Fahan Lower.
35. IFC 256:169. Collected in 1936 by Seosamh Ó Dálaigh from Pádraig Mac Síthigh, aged sixty-nine, a farmer, Baile an Teampaill, parish of Dún Chaoin, barony of Corca Dhuibhne.

Appendix A

Aréir is Mé go Déanach

Aréir is mé go déanach cois abhann geal an Ghaorthaidh
Ar gcríochnú an téarma, bhí ag béaraibh ar só,
Chun tinte lasadh ar thaobh chnoic, in éineacht chun spóirt,
Do rith an liú gan traochadh ar feadh críocha Inis Éilge
Agus adharca acu dá séideadh go saor, sultmhar, sóch,
Cantain suilt ag éanlaith go binn i mbarr gach géige,
Gur scuab ár bprionsa Gaelach an chraobh leis ina dhóid.

Do stadas seal go faonlag ar bhruach an doire féar glas,
Ag machnamh ar an dtréanghuith is gach saor shiolla cheoil,
Gur dhearcas taoibh liom réalthann, ba bhreátha gnúis ná aon bhean,
A luaitear den drong daonna agus caomhchruit ina dóid,
Do phreab mo chroí is m'aon toil chun páirt is grinn léi in éineacht,
Dob áthas foinn go héag liom bheith tréimhse ina comhar,
Is í spreagadh phort ar théadaibh go binn do bharr an fhéara,
Go raibh búir an fhill gan féasta ná braon puins le n-ól.

Ba bhúclach, fáinneach, péarlach, táclach, trinseach, néamhrach,
Scáineach, cíortha a céibhfholt ag teacht léi go feor,
Ba bhreá a braoi is a claonrosc, a bráid is a clí le chéile,
Ná an bháb i siege na Trae thoir (?), thug caorlasair smóil,
Ná an bhánchnis mhín rug Séadna ina bhárc ón mbinn de thréanrith,
D'fhág fá scíos a céile i mbéimeannaibh gleoidh,
Aoife chur a gaolta, ar shruith na Maoile géire,
Ná Niamh do scíord thar tréanmhuir is thug daorbhitim slóigh.

D'fhiosaras go séimh di i gcomhrá cliste in éineacht,
Ar bhean bhí ar strae í nó cad é fáth a spóirt,
Mar go dtáinig sí chomh déanach gan garda groí dá haoireacht;
Arbh í Juno, Pallas, Véineas í nó Cearnait i gcló,
Do labhair sí gan bhréag liom: 'Ní ceachtar dhíob dár léighis mé,
Ach cráin bhocht chnaoite chéasta, atá ag béaraigh do mo dheol,
Go bhfuil cluiche anois dá thréanchur i measc mo chlainne féinig,
Go rianfaidh é le chéile is beidh aos dlithe nua.

A chlann mo chroí bí go scléipeach go páirteach, síothach le chéile,
Is is gearr gan mhoill an tréimhse go mbeidh Gaelaibh go sóch.
Beidh rás againn ar mhéithphoic, ní díon dóibh cnoic ná coillte,
Fá ama dubhach gach féile, is ní léan liom a mbrón.
Dob áthas chroí mar ghéimeach an claonshliocht Liútar bhréagaigh,

Agus Cailbhin d'iompaigh éadach chun créanais is póit,
Is is meidhreach, sultmhar thaoscfainn beoir agus fíon le chéile
Ar hallaibh cúmhartha a n-aolbhrugh gan ghéilleadh dá nós.'

'A rí-bhean shultmhar, bhéasach atá faoi chumha gan chéile,
Ag tál go búch ar bhéaraibh gan féasta ná só,
Is fada dhúinn gan faoiseamh ná ceart i gcúirt dá phlé dhúinn,
Fá ghallasmacht tax *is claonchur gan daonnacht inár gcóir.'*
D'fhreagair sí: 'Ná daor mé, ó tharla chugat i m'aonar,
Gan gharda groí do m'éileamh i gcéin mar ba chóir.
Gurb é Dónall múinte léannta do thóg an ceo seo d'Éirinn,
Do réidh gach snaidhm is géarcheist do Ghaelaibh go deo.

Tá trúp ag teacht ár n-éileamh ar bharr na dtonn le chéile,
Go líonmhar, longmhar, léadmhar, go saor, sultmhar, sóch,
Go ceolmhar, caoin, go scléipeach go beorach, fíontach, faobharach,
*Is le fórsa a bh*fleet *le chéile go réabhfaidh gach port,*
Scriosfaidh ar fad na méithphoic a chríochaibh Inis Éilge,
Beidh rás ar Ghaill nach léan liom dá dtréancharta i ngleo,
Is a chairde guidhigh le chéile i bpáirt chun an triar is naofa,
Scanradh, sceimhle agus léirscrios ar an dtréad san gach ló.'[1]

(Late Last Night)

(Late last night as I was by the bright river of Gaorthadh, At the end of the time that the invaders had spent in comfort, To light fires on hillsides, for sport, The shouts sped continuously all over the territory of Inis Éilge (Ireland), And they had horns and they were blowing them freely, joyously and with satisfaction, The birds sang a joyous song sweetly on the tops of all the branches, That our Gaelic prince won the victory in his hand.

Very weak, I stopped a while at the edge of the green, grassy wood, Thinking of the strong voice and every free syllable of music, Until I saw beside me, a star with a face more beautiful than any woman, Who may be mentioned in the human race and she had a slender harp in her hand, My heart jumped and I had one wish to love her and have fun at the same time, It would make me happy until death to spend some time with her, And she was making music sweetly on the strings with her fingertips, That the false boors were without a feast or a drop of punch to drink.

Her tresses were ringleted, curled, pearly, twirling, trenched, shining, Combed in locks, her beautiful hair reaching with her to the ground, Her eyebrows and her alluring eyes, her neck and her body together were more beautiful, Than the maiden in the siege of Troy to the east, which gave a blazing light of fire, Than the smooth white skin which Séadna took in his bark at the peak of his strong running, Which left his companion weary in battle strokes, Than Aoife who sent her relations, to the strong current of Maoile, Nor Niamh who rushed over the strong sea and destroyed a vast crowd.

I asked her calmly in a clever speech which c aused the destruction at once,
Was she a woman who had strayed or what was the reason for her diversion,
Because she had come so late without a strong guard for protection, Was she
Juno, or Pallas, or Venus or Cearnuit in disguise, She spoke to me truthfully: 'I
am none of those you mentioned. But a poor wasted, tormented sow, who is
being suckled by invaders, That there is a game now being vigorously played
out by my own family, That it will all be manoeuvred together and there will
be a new ruling era.

Oh, dear family, be happy, hospitable and peaceful towards one another, And
very shortly Gaels will be content, We will chase the fat bucks, they will find
shelter in neither hills nor narrow woods, Each feast will be a dark occasion
and I do not regret their sorrow, It would be a great joy to hear the shouting
of deceitful Luther's crooked followers, And Calvin who changed his cloth for
merchandise and drink, And it is merrily I would happily drink beer and wine
together, In the perfumed halls of their lime-covered mansions without
following their habits.'

'Oh, royal, pleasant, well-mannered woman, who is lonely, without a
companion, Who is gently suckling the bears without feast or comfort, We
have been a long time without relief or our rights being discussed in court,
Under foreign rule, tax and deceit without humanity is our lot.' She replied:
'Do not condemn me since I have come to you alone, Without a great guard
demanding me in foreign parts as should happen, Daniel who is civil and
learned, lifted this gloom from Ireland, He has solved every problem and
difficulty for the Irish forever.

There is a troop coming to us together over the ocean, Numerous, abounding
in ships, with supplies, daring, freely, happily and in comfort, Musically,
gently, with fun, with beer, wine and with weapons, And with the united force
of their fleet they will blast each harbour, They will destroy completely the
foreign bucks from Inis Éilge (Ireland), The foreigners will be driven away
they being violently thrashed in battle and I am not sorry, And my friends pray
together to the sacred trinity, Fear, skirmish and destruction to that crowd each
day.')

Babies by Steam

I crossed over the moor and I met an old woman
She sat in a gap and her milking her cow,
The song that she sung was the '*Buachaillín Donn*',
Or some other ditty that I won't tell now.

I wasn't too long discoursing this woman,
When up steps a tinker, stout, jolly and gay,
He sat down to rest as the weather was warm
'What news, decent man?' this old woman did say.

'No news at all,' replied the bold tinker,
'But news and I wish that it never had been,
Concerning a man they call Daniel O'Connell,
Who's now getting children in Dublin by steam.'

'*M'anam don diabhal,*' replied this old woman,
'Or can it be true is he crazy at last,
Or is it a sign of war or rebellion.
Or what is the reason they are coming so fast?'

'It's neither a sign of war or rebellion'
But the children of Ireland was getting so small,
He's going to petition the Lord Mayor of Dublin,
To stop them from getting them the old way at all.'

'By the pipe in my jaw,' replied the old woman,
'But he is a rogue, and I am very sure
He's always contriving, both plotting and scheming,
And leaving out plans for to plunder the poor.

I am an old hag over four score and ten,
Damn the tooth in my head, sure its plain to be seen,
I'd wager you a guinea if a rogue would provoke me,
I'd get better childer than him and his steam.'

'Well here's to your courage,' replied the old tinker,
'And long may you reign with the youth at your side,
If more of the old damsels in Ireland was like you,
O'Connell might throw his steam engine aside.'

The girls of Ireland was getting so saucy,
If you'd venture to catch them they'd scratch out your eye,
But now they may go and sit down in the corner
And no one to pray for their souls when they die.[2]

By Memory Inspired

By memory inspired,
And love of country fired,
The deeds of man I love to dwell upon;
And the patriotic glow
Of my spirit must bestow
A tribute to O'Connell that is gone, boys, gone;
Here's a memory to the friends that are gone.

In October – 'Ninety-seven -
May his soul find rest in heaven,
William Orr to execution was led on;
The jury, drunk, agreed
That Irish was his creed,

For perjury and threats drove them on, boys, on;
Here's the memory of John Mitchell that is gone.

In 'Ninety-eight – the month July,
The informer's pay was high;
When Reynolds gave the gallows brave MacCann;
But MacCann was Reynolds' first,
One could not allay his thirst;
So he brought up Bond and Byrne that are gone, boys, gone;
Here's the memory of the friends that are gone.

We saw a nation's tears
Shed for John and Henry Shears,
Betrayed by Judas Captain Armstrong,
We may forgive, but yet,
We never can forget
The poisoning of Maguire* that is gone, boys, gone;
Our high star and true apostle that is gone.

How did Lord Edward die?
Like a man without a sigh!
But he left his handiwork on Major Swan!
But Sirr, with steel-clad breast,
And coward heart at breast.
Left us cause to mourn Lord Edward that is gone, boys, gone;
Here's the memory of our friends that are gone.

September – 'Eighty-three,
Closed his cruel history,
When Emmet's blood the scaffold flowed upon;
Oh, his fate for vengeance cries,
Love of Freedom never dies,
And we'll emulate the heroes that are gone, boys, gone;
Here's the memory of the friends that are gone.[3]

*Father Tom Maguire

Cruinniú Dhónaill Uí Chonaill i gCill Gharbháin

A Rí ghil na Ríthe do chruinnigh an dream seo
Is minic iad i dteannta le tacsanna á gcrá
Is do féachaigh(?) Muire orainn ag titim le hangar
Agus gan againn mar anlann ach bruscar na trá.

Tá an sagart ar inneall is an ministir ramharchoirp
Ar buille le scanradh chun allas bhur gcnámha,
Is nár inseas(?) anuraidh go minic i mo cheantair,
Go raibh breitheamh an an-chirt ag dalladh na n-ard.[4]

(Daniel O'Connell's Meeting in Kilgarvan)

(Bright King of Kings who gathered this crowd, They are often in difficulty, tormented by taxes, May Mary look on us, falling in distress, With only the dregs from the beach for our sauce.

The priest is in a poor condition and the minister is stout, In a frenzy of fear to get the sweat of your bones, And did I not say last year very often in my district, That the unjust judge was blinding those who are high up.)

Daniel O'Connell and the Two Tinkers

When Daniel O'Connell he first was elected,
He then proved as a member for Clare.
The Cockneys in thousands, they gathered around him
And the cheers of our Irishmen rendered the air.

One day through the streets as brave Dan was walking,
A party of Cockneys to view him they stood.
In order to humbug 'The Monarch of Ireland',
One pulled out a note and says: 'Sir, is this good?'

Now to answer the question brave Dan was not lazy,
The note to his pocket he conveyed in a thrice.
But when asked to return (it) he says to the fellow:
'You must know I am a solicitor and you must pay for the advice.'

The biter being bit, you may guess the vexation,
(To) the rest of his comrades he then did complain.
When he thought of the joke and how much it had cost him,
He swore that he'd ne'er joke a lawyer again.

Some more of his comrades they consulted with Daniel,
If your patience holds out boys, the truth I will tell.
It is of two Irish tinkers that had been in London
And fell out with the landlord of 'The City Hotel'.

Straight to O'Connell repaired the bold tinkers,
To him did relate their comical jest:
How the landlord unjustly out of the house put them.
They hoped that 'his honour' might grant them redress.

Two suits of black clothes Dan put on the tinkers
And told them for to leave their budgets aside,
With the gloves of green shamrock (*chamois*) their black hands to cover,
With tools in their trunk that were both large and wide.

Then it was early next morning the waiter conveyed them,
Their tools and their budgets right into the same.
Sure the landlord he smiled as he welcomed them heartily,
And did not spare pudding, spice, port or gin.

It was in his grand apartment they took up their quarters,
With provisions being plentiful they locked themselves in.
It was early next morning those two Irish tinkers
They unpacked their budgets and to work did begin.

The landlord he frightened and called up the waiter,
Half-naked and frightened he jumped out of bed.
When he went to the door of those two Irish tinkers,
Sure as he rapped louder the more noise they made.

His wife then she frightened and got in a passion,
Sure the tinkers they laughed while they hammered away,
Well knowing the landlord could not disposess them,
So long as their bill they contined to pay.

It was for three days they kept up the hammering,
The landlord he charged them on the fourth day.
Ten pounds they owed him but was glad to bestow them
A thousand before he could get those damn tinkers away.

When Daniel O'Connell he first was elected,
The rights of old Ireland he always maintained,
So let them never think about joking the Irish,
For they'll never play tricks on O'Connell again.[5]

Daniel O'Connell in Purgatory

Have you not heard the Scripture saith,
How some departing from their faith,
Receive their doctrine from beneath,
Forbidding for to marry?
Now, this is Rome, the mystic whore,
Who keeps the keys of heaven's door,
And trades in dead men's souls demure,
By Popish Purgatory.

Doctor Miley he has said
When Dan, the Irish king was dead,
Angels were waiting at his head,
His soul to heaven to carry;
Maynooth and Rome, they formed a plan,
And robbed the angels of old Dan -
The Kerry boy we understand,
They have got in Purgatory.

Despatches from the Pope have come,
To all the priests of mystic Rome,
To change or alter poor Dan's doom,
His soul from thence to carry;

Commanding them to celebrate,
High Mass throughout the Church of late,
His soul from thence to extricate,
Out of this Purgatory.

Ye Papists, gather up your pence,
You know he's waiting in suspense,
Your Liberator bring from hence,
No longer let him tarry!
Your Dan that pleaded for Repeal,
Is bearing now Peg Tantrim's flail,
Pay up ye sons of Granuaile,
Your King's in Purgatory.

The Heretics they cannot tell
About this gulf 'twixt heaven and hell,
Where Dives did for water yell
And none to him would carry;
But Rome has made it more complete;
They have holy oil to grease their feet,
And holy water, if it's meet,
For Dan in Purgatory.

Think on your king and for him pray,
He agitated night and day -
Like Balaam's ass aloud did bray -
'Gainst Aughrim, Boyne and Derry.
On walls of clay, of bricks and stones,
He pictured death's head and crossbones;
Ye *Foigabalachs,* how he groans!
He is heard from Purgatory.

To Bernard he bequeathed his soul,
His body to the Irish mould,
His heart to Rome – that was the whole -
His head a wig did carry.
He's looking now to every part
Where he gave body, soul, or heart;
Oh, bring your cash and then you'll start
The old Fox from Purgatory.

Oh, hard's his fate, if he must stay
Like other beggarmen, I say!
For Gratis-prayers on All-Saints Day,
O, let that never carry!
Sell scapulars, crosses, cords, and beads,
And all green sashes and cockades,
All Irishmen – do lend your aid
For Dan in Purgatory!

They say they have power to bind or loose,
In heaven or hell, just as they choose,
The papist that doth to refuse
To pray to her sanctuary;
They'll curse with candle, book and bell -
These poor blind dupes deserve it well.
That would let Peg Tantrim's flail pell-mell,
Thresh Dan in Purgatory.

Now, Stowell Gray and Hugh O'Neill
May Churches build 'gainst Granuaile -
While Rome's the head, Maynooth's the tail -
Their projects will not carry.
'Twas braying, blowing, blustering Dan -
When travelling to the Holy Land,
That lost the trick his merits scanned-
He's now in Purgatory.

Here's books and bags for my son John,
In agitation he'll go on,
And chase the Saxons every one
From Tara's Hill to Derry;
He'll drive all Heretics abroad -
They have no right to the holy sod -
They would not eat the Wafer God,
Or believe in Purgatory.

Before my song comes to a close,
Here's a flowing health to those
Undaunted boys who fac'd their foes -
The 'Prentice Boys of Derry!
Let all true brethren with me join
To sing of Aughrim and the Boyne,
Where we received the Pass and Sign
To walk over Purgatory[16]

Father Plunkett

Come all you Roman Catholics, I pray attention pay,
Of one combine I'll hope you'll join assist me for to pray,
For God he is our pilot he never shall disown,
Of the worthy pillar he has placed in the holy church of Rome.

My name is William Plunkett as you may plainly see
My parents they educated me, a clergyman to be,
Until a false young wicked female which I make free to say,
She had done her whole endeavours to swear my life away.

It was in the month of April in the year 1831,
She took an oath against me and said I was the man,
The father of her baby of which she had so long concealed,
She swore I was an outlawed man and then I was sent to jail.

Then I was sent to prison till the assizes came on,
Before my prosecutor, my trial I did stand.
The jury found me guilty and the judge made this reply,
Saying after noon on Thursday, my sentence was to die.

When I received my sentence in Cavan town to die,
The Lord he showed a miracle he clouded all the sky,
With thunder, wind, and lightening as you may plainly see,
So as to leave the faithful Christians know of the woeful perjury.

A letter came from Dublin directed to the jail,
That I would be liberated from death to New South Wales,
That I would be liberated for my sweet liberty,
If I would swear 'King's evidence' against my country.

I wrote them a letter that they may understand,
For there was no rotten member in the parish of Killann,
So cruel, loyal our private, our secrets we conceal,
For before I would be an informer I'd die in Cavan jail.

Long life to Father Plunkett, likewise to Bishop Browne,
That wrote to brave O'Connell that was in Limerick town,
Unto(?) the King of England those times he did reveal,
By his noble interest I am free from Cavan jail.

Success to the blooming star, likewise the shamrock shore,
I mean brave Dan O'Connell now and forever more,
Success to Colonel Sanderson, the hero of renown,
Who left me here a clergyman once more in Kingscourt town.[7]

The Little Fife and Drum

When I was a maid at the age of sixteen
From my parents I stole away to a place called Allageen,
I enlisted in a regiment, a soldier I become,
They learned me to play on the little fife and drum.

With me hat and feather and bonny cockade,
You'd say and you'd swear that I really was a maid,
The drummers all admired me, my fingers long and small,
And they learned me to play the best of them all.

Well, it's straight every night to the barracks I did go,
To be lying up with soldiers, I was no way afraid.
At the buttoning of my small clothes, to myself I used to smile,
To be lying up with soldiers and a maid all the while.

Then I was sent to London to guard o'er the Tower,
I was a maid that day and every hour,
A young lady fell in love with me, I told her I was a maid,
And it's straight to the officer she made a complaint.

My officer he sent for me and boldly I went there,
He asked me was it true, and this is what he said:
'It's a pity for to lose such a drummer as you made,
And it's all for your vanity and the stage of Valentine,
A bounty you must get, my little girl from the Queen.'

A young man she has got and a soldier he become,
She learned him to play on the little fife and drum.

Many's the battle I saw on the field,
Many's the soldier from me was forced to yield,
Many's the battle I fought with the French,
And it's boney I fought and I but a wench.

Here's the health to O'Connell; another unto you,
And one to every Irish girl that wears the colours true,
If O'Connell wants for more men before the war is o'er,
I'll put on me hat and feather and fight for her once more.[8]

The O'Connell Monument

You gallant sons of Erin's isle come listen to those lines of mine,
Which I am going for to unfold on our immortal Dan,
Who struggled hard for liberty in spite of all his enemies,
To confute what I'm going to say I'm sure there's no one can.

But now we see they're fully bent, at last, to rise a monument
Of our brave Liberator, the pride of Erin's shore,
And then when August it does come round, in Sackville Street it will be found,
A credit to our Irish boys till time it is no more.

That we may live the day to see his monument will finished be,
When we can look with pleasure and pride on what was spent
For the noble work of this great man, old Erin's Liberator, Dan,
Who fought against the Tory clan of Whitty's monument.

Those monuments that we do see, of noble men in history,
They fill our hearts with joy today both old and young well know,
For many years our heroes fought for Ireland's rights with a hand and heart,
They were unconquered by their foes wherever they may go.

But now they're working hard we see, at his monument each day,
After such a long delay to finish it they're bent,
And in August in eighty-two his statue there we all can view,
A credit to our Irish boys, O'Connell's monument.

There is no nation on this earth unto such men have given birth,
For poets and painters and sculptors we have too.
We have princely O'Neill, Sarsfield, Grattan and young Wolfe Tone,
Sir Connell and O'Donnell and the brave Brian Boru.

We have Oliver Goldsmith and Tom Moore and Parnell who relieved the poor,
Lord Edward, young Emmet who to his grave was sent,
With Mitchell, John Martin, Sullivan and O'Donnell,
True members like O'Connell boys of Whitty's monument.

That we may live the day to see his monument will finished be,
When we can look with pleasure and pride on what was spent
For the noble work of this great man, old Erin's Liberator, Dan,
Who fought against the Tory clan of Whitty's monument.[9]

Síle Ní Ghadhra

Aréir ar mo leabain is mé a machtnamh trém' néaltaibh,
Ar an ríghbhean dob' aoibhinne thuirling ó Éabha;
Bhí a cuacha léi scaoilte go triopallach, péarlach,
Is a cnis mar an lile a dh'fhásann gach féile.
Bhí a gruaidh mar na caora is a gné mar an rós;
A dhá mala claon is a glé-rosc gan cheo;
Is í ag seinm a véarsa ar théadaibh go meadhrach,
Go raibh Éire arís buaite aige Síle Ní Ghadhra.

Do dhruideas ina coinne is do bheannaíos go séimh di,
Mo hata dem' bhathas is d'umhlaíos go féar di,
D'fhiosraíos fios a hainme nó cá sloinne inar díobh í:
An í Venus bain-dé í do threascair na mílte.
An tú Dídó, no Iúno, nó Pallas bean ghroí,
Nó Helen ón nGréig do thug léirscrios na Traoi,
Nó an fhinne-bhean bhéasach scaothán gach maighre,
Nó arbh ainm di Éire nó Síle Ní Ghadhra.

'Is é Éire fós m'ainm, is admhaím do Shíle,
Cé chuir éirleach na méirleach, Rí Sacsan ó thigheas me.
Ár dteampaill gur leagadar is ár sagairt gur dhíbir,
Is ár n-Aifrinn dá léamh dhúinn cois scairte agus díge,
D'fhoighníos go cróga go dtáinig an t-am,
Gur neartaigh mo ghaoltha is gur dh'aosaigh mo chlann,
Go dtáinig ár saorfhear, mo shéimhfhear mar oidhre,
Is é Dónall ó Conaill, mac Shíle Ní Ghadhra.'

'Is a Shíle na gile, na finne, is na féile,
Admhaím tú choíche agus tugaim duit géilleadh,
Acht réitigh an cheist so, is ná bí-se liom bréagach:
"An bhfaighfidh Dónall is a chúnta an cúrsa do réiteach?"'
Do bheirim mo bhriathar mar dheimhin ar gach scéal,

Go sciobhfaidh tar triúch chugainn anall an Reipéil
Go mbeidh an chaomh-chruit dá gléas' is í ag seinm go meadhrach,
Agus Parliament glaoite aige Síle Ní Ghadhra.

Níorbh ionadh liom féin mo shéimhfhear mear, groí,
Dá dtréigfeadh an cúrsa is dá réabfadh a chroí,
Tré gach galaire méirligh do thréig é ar díol,
Do vótáil le méithphoic ag cur deachmha ar gach síol.
Bhí an sagart Fuarthán ann ó Dhún na mBarc Thiar,
Flannubhra Chluain Meala agus tuilleadh den chliar,
Nár náireach an gnó dhóibh a gcúl thabhairt don oidhre,
Tá a coimhead géarleanúin Veto *ó Shíle Ní Ghadhra.'*

(Síle Ní Ghadhra)

(Last night on my bed as I was reflecting while dozing, About the most beautiful, stately woman who had appeared since Eve, Her curling tresses hung down like pearls, And her skin was like the lily that grows every feast day, Her cheeks were like berries, and her appearance like the rose, Her two sloping brows and her clear, bright eyes; And she was playing a verse merrily on the strings, That Síle Ní Ghadhra had won Ireland again.

I moved towards her and greeted her gently, I took off my hat and bowed to the ground, I asked her her name, or what was her surname, Was she the Goddess Venus who defeated thousands, Or Dido, or Juno, or Pallas the vigorous woman, Or Helen from Greece who caused the destruction of Troy, Or the fair, polite woman the reflection of every handsome woman, Called Ireland or Síle Ní Ghadhra.

'Ireland is still my name and I answer to Síle, Although the destruction of villains, the King of England has dispossessed me, They knocked down our churches and drove out our priests, And our Masses are being read for us beside hedges and ditches, I was patient and brave until the time came, Until my relations became strong and my family came of age, Until our noble man, my fine man, came as heir, He is Daniel O'Connell, son of Síle Ní Ghadhra.'

'And bright, fair, and generous Síle, I acknowledge you always and yield to you, But answer this question and do not deceive me: "Will Daniel and his help succeed in solving the matter?"' 'I give my word as assurance of every account, That he will bring Repeal to us over the land, That the gentle harp will be in tune and will be played happily, And Parliament will be assembled by Síle Ní Ghadhra.'

I would not be surprised if my gentle, swift, strong man, Were to abandon the course and if his heart were broken, By every spouting villain who betrayed him by selling, Who voted with the weak bucks putting tithes on the whole population, The priest Fuarthán was there from Dún na mBarc in the west, Flannabhra from Clonmel and more of the clergy besides, Was it not a disgrace, that they turned their backs on the heir, Who is keeping the persecution of Veto from Síle Ní Ghadhra?')[10]

The Youth that Belonged to Milltown

Last week as the newspaper told me,
How an Irishman did sail away,
In hopes to find out employment,
Like thousands before him did stray.
He resolved to travel to England,
For to labour, oh to seek up and down,
And he never would deny where he came from,
In Kerry, a place called Milltown.

One evening while walking through London,
Faith, he met with John Bull on his way,
And just as he passed by a corner,
He stopped him and those words he did say:
'Good evening Pat, and where are you bound for,
Or when did you land on this shore,
Or do you belong to the Fenians,
That we had in the year sixty-four?'

Says the youth: 'Don't you speak about Fenians,'
As he looked at John Bull in surprise,
'Remember the last words of Emmet,
And they were the cause of great noise.
Is it because that I am from old Ireland,
By your looking(?) you do on me frown,
And remember you met the wrong hero,'
Says the youth that belonged to Milltown.

Says John Bull: 'You have now strayed from your country,
Like wild geese ye do fly away,
To America, Queensland and New Zealand,
You are never tired crossing the sea.
Why don't you sometime live contented
And a living to make of your own?
Like the people that's here all around you,
That ne'er went a mile from their home?'

Says the youth: 'We must stray from our country,
While coercion's laws rules over us.
Will you tell me the proper right owner
Of the land where the green shamrock grows?
And while our green banner is waving,
An Irishman won't be put down,
For the harp and the shamrock is our glory,'
Says the youth that belongs to Milltown.

Says John Bull: 'Though being strange, faith you're saucy,
And no doubt your expectations are great.
Don't you see how we did beat the Russians?

And the Japs(?) too, we did them defeat.
We have conquered all nations before us,
Like thunder our cannons did roar,
We made proud Napoleon surrender,
And exiled (him) to a far distant shore.'

Says the youth: 'You can boast of your money,
But your soldiers were good brave Irishmen,
And I will say only for them,
One battle you never would win.
Show me a battle by honour
In the field by the sword was cut down,
You're too fond of your spies and informers,'
Says the youth that belonged to Milltown.

Says John Bull: 'I am tired now talking,
And to give over I think it's near time,
For there was a man here before you,
And it was in the year twenty-nine,
Let right or wrong be the question,
He was sure to think of a scheme
And Daniel O'Connell they call him,
From Dingle, (*sic*) in Kerry, he came.

Says the youth: 'He was born in Kerry,
Where the old ruins today can be seen,
Just down by the brink of the waters,
Convenient to Cahirsiveen.
He was the true king of Ireland,
And the harp and the shamrock, his crown,
May the Lord rest his soul, I'm sure he's in heaven,
And the youth that belongs to Milltown.[11]

References
1. IFC 1790:191-4. Collected *per* Pádraig Ó Conaill, Bréan Trá, An Sciobairín, barony of Cairbre Thiar, county Cork.
2. IFC 212:240-4. Collected about 1935 by J. Dolan from Michael McLoughlin, aged forty-four, a farmer, Gubbaveeny, parish of Killinagh, barony of Tullyhaw, county Cavan. A number of versions of this song have been collected by Tom Munnelly of the Folk Music Section, Department of Irish Folklore, UCD. I have encountered one narrative account in Irish which describes the themes of the song. This account was collected in 1942 by Tomás a Búrca in Iorras, county Mayo IFC 804:204-5.
3. BB IFC FMS 9a/14 O'Leary.
4. IFC 52:68-9. Collected about 1934 in the parish of na hAoraí, barony of Béara, county Cork, (incomplete).
5. IFC FMS Tape TM 116/A/2. Collected in 1973 by Tom Munnelly from Patrick Kitterick, aged seventy-two, a small farmer, Creggan bawn, Louisburgh, barony of Murrisk, county Mayo.

6. BB IFC FMS Tape 52a/98 O'Leary; *Collection of Orange Songs* Toronto 1895 20-21.
7. IFC 782:43-5. Collected in 1941 by P.J. O'Sullivan from the composer of the song, Patrick Daly, aged seventy, a farmer, Killenagh, parish of Annascaul, barony of Corca Dhuibhne.
8. IFC 1795:124-5. Collected by James G. Delaney from Patrick Hetherton, Aughnacliffe, parish of Columbkille, barony of Granard, county Longford. The collector notes the word 'bonny' in v. 2, l. 1. is always pronounced 'boney'.
9. IFC FMS Tape TM 498/2. Collected in 1976 by Tom Munnelly from Packie Reilly, aged sixty-seven, a former farm labourer, Brusky, parish of Balintemple, barony of Corrigan, county Cavan.
10. Standardised from *IG* IV 1889 [1890], 24-6. Fr Foran (Fuarthán) was parish priest of Dungarvan and Dr Flannery (Flannubhra) was parish priest of Clonmel.
11. IFC FMS Tape TM 97/B/1. Collected in 1972 by Tom Munnelly from Thomas Brennan, aged ninety, a retired farmer, Mount Prospect, parish of Kiltormer, barony of Longford, county Galway.

Appendix B

As I looked down o'er Rathnure town (A Morning Walk) — IFC S900:380-1

As I rode out on a Summer's morning (The Maid of Castlefore)(William O' [?]) — IFC 512:552-4

As I rode out one morning I met an old woman — IFC 444:83-4

As I was awalking one fine Summer's evening — IFC SMcC.12/A/1[2]

As I was crossing I spied an old woman (Dan O'Connell Making Children by Steam) — IFC 150:543-7; 212: 440-4; 1216:155-7; 1711:27-8; 1795: 117-8

As O'Connell and Shiels wor convarsin about the rent — Lover 1899 217-20

As O'Connell he was walking (O'Connell in London) (air: Daniel O'Connell) — Mitchell Library, Glasgow 1859

A stout worthy Orangeman surely I am — Songbook NL n.d.

Atá: Tá

A tree has been planted in Ireland — Zimmermann 1967, 255

(Oh) Attend to my ditty you frolicksome folk — IFC TM[4] 54/A/3

Beidh tinte cnámh in Uíbh Ráthach romhat — Laoide 1915 9-10

Bhí an saol (t-am) sin ann le linn Queen Anne (comp. Micheál MacGraith, mid nineteenth cent.) — IFC 1534:526-7; 1775:355; 1311:511-3

Bhí Dónall Ó Conaill ann — IFC 823:56-7

By memory inspired and the love of country fired (In Memory of Friends that are Gone) — BB IFC O'Leary 9a/14, NL

By the mountain Slieve Gullion, the might of O'Mullen — Zimmermann 1967 220-1

Casadh ar a chéile lá breá gréine Caitliceach is Protastún (An Caitliceach is an Protastún) — IFC 1534:526- 7; 1775:355

Cé acu Pól nó Peadar Ochma nó Diarmaid — IFC 1592:232-3

Céad fáilte 'nall don lonnlaoch fios-shaoi — RIA 495:172, 569: (24), 796:369(i), 899:147

Chífidh sibh féin tí mhuirfhigh aríst go bhfaighe — IFC 354: 331-3

Chisel the likeness of the Chief — *IO* 15.6.1929, 564, 596

Chuala fuaim na hadhairce (Cailín Beag na Luachra) — IFC 797:26-7

Claoidhfidh, créimfid méirnigh mhalluighthe — Ó Foghludha 1932 68-70

Come all you Catholics throughout this nation — Songbook NLI

Come all you Irish hearts of oak	Zimmermann 1967 224-5
Come all you Irishmen both great and small	Zimmermann 1967 240
Come all you loyal heroes I hope you will draw near (Mackin Fight)	IFC 1711:207-9
Come all ye men of Ireland, ye sons of Granuale (A New Song on the Procession to Lay the Foundation Stone of the O'Connell Monument written by a Patriotic Protestant)	BB NL 33, 36; Healy 1969, 1969 100-1
Come all you Roman Catholics	Chapbook NL c.1830
Come all you Roman Catholics I pray attention pay (Fr. Plunkett)	IFC 782:43-5
Come all you Roman Catholics I pray you will attend	Zimmermann 1967 195-6
Come all you sons of Erin's land and mourn the loss of noble Dan (Grand Conversation on O'Connell Arose)	BB NL
Come raise the monument on high (On the intended O'Connell monument; in Lwr. Sackville St, Dublin)	Archer 1869 218-9
Come Tenant Farmers! rally round (Charles Stuart Parnell and the Grand Triumphal Procession. By Charles Jackson)	BB NL 86
Crossing the (yon) moor I spied this (an) old woman	IFC TM 195/A/5; SMcC 75/B/7
Dear Erin, your hopes are now nearly blasted (A Sorrowful Elegy on the Death of our beloved Liberator Daniel O'Connell. By T. O'Carroll)	BB NL 37
D'fhág Vési Mac Gearailt faoi tharcuisne ar lár	IFC 1125:244; de híde 1935 118-23; D. Ó Súilleabháin 1936 268-75; IG 1889, 25-6
D'iompaigh sí tharm amach tríd na sléibhte	IFC 645:94-5
Do bhéara mé an chuairt so go Connachta gan spás	RIA 63: 35v°(No.25); Ó Raghallaigh 1938 524-5
Do bhí scamall agus éiclips agus daorbhrat duairc	MN M97:203
Do ghluais chugainn sárfhear anall thar s(h)áile (Searlas Parnell agus Cáit Ní Shé)	IFC 90:154-6
Do neartaigh (neartuigh) go deimhin mo mhisne is mo gháire	Ó Foghludha 1932 68-70

Eastig: *Éistigh*

Éighim sibh, ná stadaigh 's ná casaidh go bráth	IFC 1125:244; de híde 1935 118-23; D. Ó Súilleabháin 1936 268-75; *IG* 1889 25-6
Éistigh a dhaoine	Chapbook NL *c*.1830
Éistigh a dhaoine go n-ínse mé scéal díbh	IFC 1592:232-3
Éistigh liomsa, a éigse, go léighfead-sa dhíbh m'eachtra	de Brún 1972 98-9; RIA 333: 187i, 942:172
Éistigh liom sealad mar caithfidh mé suí go fóill	IFC 927:300-2
Electors to the field repair	IFC BB 2
Ereir: *Aréir*	
Fáilte, a mhóir-mhic Éireann, fáilte	RIA 1254:1v(4)
Fáilte a's dá fhichid tar mhíltibh laoch	
(Do chum Domhnaill Óig Flaitheamhail Fíoruasail Uí Chonaill Ó Dhaire Fhionáin)	*IG* 1894, 121
Fáilte dhuit-se ar d'éise slán	RIA 552, 246, 594: 511; MN M9, 487
Fáilte is fiche is ea do chuirim	IFC 667:202
Fáilte is fiche is tuilleadh 'na deoidh	Fenton 1922 56-60; D. Ó Súilleabháin 1936 268-75
Farewell to my acquaintances and to my native land	IFC 630:85-9
Farewell unto the shamrock shore, I am gone for evermore (Kean's Farewell to Ireland)	BB O'Hanrahan, Kilkenny Arch. Soc.
Féach thar d'ais ar Charraig Seac mar dheineadar an t-iarmairt	IFC 85:333-4.
Fill high the flowing bowl	Chapbook 1830 NL
Full many a chief in Erin rose	Songbook NL n.d.
Go moch roimh lonradh Phoebus	IFC 45:389- 90; 47:66-7, 73-6;
'Good morning mouse, ' replied the cat (The Cat and the Mouse)	IFC 1901:257-9, 299-300;
Guidhim slán go hUíbh Ráthach go bhfillfir	Fenton 1922 56-60
Gunnaí is lámhach a's teinte cnámh, beidh againn amárach, agus tá sé in am	de híde 1935 118- 23; D. Ó Súilleabháin 1936 268-75
Gurab fada buan bhéas Domhnall i ngradam mhuar (mhór) 's a (g)ccómhachtaibh	RIA 373:403; MN M6, 131, M97:202

Hark, hark to the begging box shaking

M. MacDonagh 1929
345-6

Have you not heard the Scripture saith
(Daniel O'Connell in Purgatory)

BB IFC O'Leary
52a/98; *Standard
Orange Song Book*
Armagh 1848 141-4;
*Collection of
Orange Songs*
Toronto 1895 20-1

Here I am Dan O'Connell of a kingly race I came
Here I am the captain bold, I lead a merry throng
Here I am the captain brave, I lead a warlike throng
Here I am, the great O'Connell
Hurra for the new Corporation
Hurroo! my boys we're still alive

IFC 412:26-7
IFC 1564:30-46
IFC 1859:166-73
IFC 493:55-77
Zozimus 1871 24-30
Healy 1969 83-5

I am a daughter of Daniel O'Connell's that has
lately from England sailed o'er

IFC 249:186-8; 283:
168-9; 633:535-7;
1530:341-3; 1591:59-
61; S1010:122;
Zimmermann 1967
178-9

I crossed over the moor and I met an old woman

IFC 150:543-7;
212:440-4; 1216:155-
7; 1711:27-8; 1795:
117-8

I have: I've
In the sweet county Leitrim a virgin does dwell
(Molly Maguire)
Into Parliament you'll go says the Shan Van Vogh
In Uíbh Ráthach Thiar tá an Dragún dian
I once knew a dodger whose name was Father Dan
(Old Father Dan) (Air: Uncle Ned)

IFC 1711:212-4
Lover 1899, 217-20
CS 1939 6

BB IFC O'Leary
52a/98

*I Ros a Mhíl tá an scafaire atá meanmnach
mín-tréitheach*
I saw him at the hour of pray'r, when morning's
earliest dawn

IFC 607:5-9

*Ballads and Songs
by the writers of the
Nation* Dublin 1845
10-11; Daunt 1845
259-60; *The Spirit of
the Nation* Dublin
1934 14-16.

Is brónach is is léanmhar is is dubhach liomsa
an saol so (Caoineadh an Chloiginn) (comp.
MacCarthy)   Denis
IFC 1064:39-43
Is buachaillín beag aerach mé do théarnaigh thar
lear (i loing) (Aisling ar Chnoc Bhinéagair)
(Athnuachaint ar Cuimhniú ar '98) (air: Cáit Ní
Dhuibhir)   IFC 95:18-9;
121:326-7

Is cumann liom do dhréachta im dháil   UCC (Torna) Tx lii 42
Is dubhach is léan liom bualadh an lae úd   IFC 98:19-23
Is ea chuala trém shiúltaibh dá léigheamh le fonn   Fenton 1922 78-9;
D. Ó Súilleabháin
1936 68-75

Is é do bheatha a Mhuire mháthair   IFC 354:331-2
Is é Dónall binn Ó Conaill caoin   Fenton 1922 95-6;
D. Ó Súilleabháin
1936 268-75

Is é Dónall Ó Conaill an t-óigfhear cumais   Fenton 1922, 108
Is fearrde Clanna Gaedhal bocht   IFC 90:154-6
Is mó fán fada bhain domhsa le sealad   IFC 86:94-8
Is mór anois le rá Ó Conaill Dhoire Fhionáin   IFC 570:367-8
It is fifty years since Erin's tears (The Liberator)   BB NL 128; Healy
1969 89-90

It is of a youth who came here to our country   IFC 476:116- 9;
481:318-21; 782:195-7;
1530:344-5;

It was in the North, as I walked forth to view
the shamrock plains (A Dialogue between
Daniel O'Connell and Granuaile)   BB Mitchell Library,
Glasgow
It was late as I roved out one evening   IFC SMcC 60/A/1
It was of a bold eagle his age it was over three score   IFC 737:147-50
It was on a Summer morning my mind being free from
grief and care (Who Gained the Fame for Erin's Isle?)   IFC 54:317-8
I've been a wanderer through (Love Your Own Land)   BB IFC O'Leary
49/28
I've been crossing a bog when I spied an old woman   IFC 150:543-7;
212:440-4; 1216:155-
7; 1711:27-8;
1795:117-8
I was passing one day when I spied an old woman   IFC TM 145/A/5

Jack Griffin's travels I'll relate   IFC 1591:364-6
Jer Buffer, Jer Buffer, Jer Buffer *gan ceol*   IFC S474:125
John Bull be easy don't think we are mad
(A new song on The Repeal of the Union)   BB NL 80

Lá agus mise tráth im' choinnibh	IFC 125:287-8; 928:52-5
Lá breá grianmhar amuigh sa Phriaracht	IFC S475:165-70
Last week as the newspaper(s) tell(s) (told) us an Irishman did sail away (The Youth that Belonged to (From) Milltown)	IFC 476:116-9; 481:318- 21; 782:195- 7; 1530:344- 5; TM 82/B/1; 97/A/4; 137/A/2; 238/A/1; 256/A/4; 285/B/1; 326/A/l; 351/A/3.
Le féachaint insna síonta is é is baolach don aicme (Comhchruinniú na gCaitliceach i mBaile Locha Riach)	IFC 629:114-6, 431-3; 634:283-6; 1795:123; S960:128-35
Maidin álainn gréine is mé ar thaobh chnoc na buaile	IFC 1790:191-7
Maidin aoibhinn(?)álainn ar barra Chnoc Glinne (A new song called O'Connell's Daughter)	BB NL 326
Maidin aoibinn tsamhraidh ar thaisteal cois na leamhna	S. Ó Súilleabháin 1937, 32-4
Maidin mhoch ar mh'éirí dhom	IFC 45:389- 90; 47:66-7, 73-6
Mam dear did you ever hear	Chapbook NL n.d.
Mankind is like the feathered tribe for some fly high and some low (The Royal Blacks) (air: Pow, wow, wow)	Archer 1869 104-7
Míle failte id' shaol is id' shláinte (Asal Maol)	IFC 90:142-3
Mo ghrá mo phrionsa Dónall	IFC 823:359-60
My Berrin-place is no consarn to me	Zozimus 1871 24-30
My dear orange friends you're forced to knock under	Songbook NL n.d.
My dream to some comes true, and comes with grief to more (Poor Old Granuaile)	Zimmermann 1967 272
My horse it is white although that at first he was bay (The Grey Horse)	BB NL 169; Zimmermann 1967 210-1
My mother was a lady as yours you may allow	IFC 1205:100
Nach brónach an scéal atá agam le n-aithrist (Lament for Minor Darcey)	IFC 665:252-3
Nach óg insa tsaol nár ceapadh mo leas dom	IFC 121:386-8
Ná ligse feasta	D. Ó Súilleabháin 1936, 268-75

Neal: *Níl*
Níor chúis caoi, níor bhéim bróin

NLW A24:5342B; MN
R69 470; R70 270;
Éigse 4, 220

Ní rugadh i nÉireann le réimeas na ríoghraidhe
Nuair a scoith na Laighnigh

RIA 942:2:169m
IFC 275:413-4

O'Connell brave he shot D'Esterre

IFC 1064:374

O'Connell *clúmhail plúr na bhfear*

IFC 45:389-90; 47:
66-7, 73-6

O'Connell is in from Clare

IFC 823:359-60

O'Connell's dead, alas! for Erin (O'Connell's dead!)
(comp. P. McCabe, Carlow)

BB NL

Oh! Dan did you get out

Zozimus 1871 24-30

Oh, heard ye yon harper (prize monody on The
Death of O'Connell) (air: The Lakes of Killarney)

BB Mitchell Library
Glasgow

Oh, one evening of late as I slumbered

IFC 1782:225-8

Oh, quit with your bother I don't like soft sodder
(Erin's Reproof and Charge to Her Sons)

BB IFC 28b

On a fine summer's morning as the day was dawning
(Erin's Green Linnet)

BB; Healy 1969 92-
4; Zimmermann
1967 235-6

Once in old Ireland, there started a mouse
(The Paddy Mouse)

BB NL 181

On Easter Monday morning in the year twenty-nine
(Easter Monday 1829)

IFC 1854:23

One day near Dingle I met an old woman (The Jolly
Bold Tinker)

IFC 107:643-6;
183:116-7; 334:505-9;
629:114-6, 431-3;
789:539-40; 1216:154;
1795:123;
S960:128-35;
IO 26.8.1950;
Healy 1969 77-9

One day through the streets as brave Daniel was
walking

IFC 107:643-6; 183:
116-7; 334:505-9;
629:114-6, 431- 3;
789:538-40;
1216:154; 1795: 123;
S960:128-35;
IO 26.8.1950;
Healy 1969 77-9

One evening of (so) late as I rambled (strayed)
by the banks of a clear furling stream (Daughter to
Daniel O'Connell/ Erin's Green Shore)

IFC 249:186-8; 283:
168-9; 633:535-7;
1530: 341-3; 1591:
59-61; S1010:122;
BB IFC O'Leary
121/66; Mitchell
Library, Glasgow;
Zimmermann 1967
178-9

One evening the blackbirds melodious, those
innocent notes she did sing

Healy 1969 104-6

One hallow eve as the moon shone low
(The Ghost of Boho)

IFC 1786 38-43

One morning early for recreation

IFC 220:329-30

One morning (roving) for recreation
(Erin's King or Brave Dan's No More)

BB IFC O'Leary
121/66; Mitchell
Library, Glasgow
dated 1865;
Healy 1969 94-6

One morning for soft recreation

Zimmermann 1967,
176-7

One night as old Granua reclined to rest
(The Deeds of O'Connell) (air: Take him in
all we shall never look on his like again)

BB NL 327; Mitchell
Library, Glasgow
dated 1852;
Healy 1969 74-6

One pleasant summer's morning (Madam Pray
Have Patience) (air: Máirín from Gibberland)

IFC 1592: 442-5

On Tara's high mount, on the ninth of September
(O'Connell's No More)

BB NL 191; Healy
1969 90-2

On the fifteenth day of August in the year of
forty-three (The Meeting of Tara)

IFC S960:128-35; BB
NLI 61; Healy 1969
79-81

On the fifteenth day of August through the
streets of Dublin town (a new song on the
Procession for the Unveiling of O'Connell,
and Opening of the Exhibition)

BB IFC 24b

Poets may pen the fame of each nation
(Irishman's Glory Shines Brighter than Gold)

BB NL 128

Prepare you gallant Irishmen – prepare without
delay (A new song on the O'Connell Monument by
Joseph Sadler, a Dark Man)   BB IFC 28; NL 57,
                                                              203

Rejoice each patriotic brother   Healy 1969 85-7
Rejoice sons of Erin all over the land (a new song
on the Orange Riots in Belfast)   BB IFC 17
Rejoice ye Irish patriots you lived to see the day
(Lines written on the monument of Daniel O'Connell
by T.O'Carroll, the Tara poet) (air: Paddie's Evermore)   BB NL 32, 46;
                                                              Healy 1969 96-8

Rejoice you sons of Erin for the glorious sight
we have seen   Healy 1969, 99-100
Rí na glóire go ndéana treo dhuit   IFC 999:489-94

Scum condensed of Irish bog!   M. MacDonagh 1929
                                                              231-2

'Sé: Is é

Tá an July caite agus beag a scéal é   IFC 249:186-8
Tá Dónall Ó Conaill i mbun chúil ag Gaedhealthaibh   IFC 48:43
Tá Dónall óg in Éirinn   IFC 259:711-2
Tá éinne amháin i bParlaimint ní foláir liom nó
beidh an cluiche aige   D. Ó Súilleabháin
                                                              1936 268-75

Atá Jumpers go deacrach in gach baile faoi
bhuaidhreadh   de híde 1935 118-23;
                                                              Ó Coigligh 1987
                                                              101-2

Tá Ó Conaill's a ghaolta i bhfeac   *Béal.* 7 28-31
Tá soilse suairce ó Phoebus ar ghaorthaíbh i gCúigí
Fáil   S. Ó Súilleabháin
                                                              1937 45-7

Atá Turcaigh agus Gréagaigh ag gabháil dá chéile
(Bua Uí Chonaill)   IFC 634:289-91;
                                                              de híde 1935 118-23;
                                                              Ó Coigligh 1987
                                                              99-100; RIA 63:165;
                                                              1. 18:64:119

Tá uaisle threabhchais Chárthain i bParlaimint 'na
suí go teann   D. Ó Súilleabháin
                                                              1936 268-75

The chain is broken again he's free our hope and
Ireland's pride (Release of C.S. Parnell)   BB IFC 30
The chieftain stood up an' a bumper he poured

(Pelthers MacSwine by Adelos?) (air: Discontented I am)   BB NL
The fourteenth of December we'll ever remember
(a new song called The Battle of Carrickshock)   BB O'Hanrahan,
   Kilkenny Arch. Soc.

There's a dark cloud hanging o'er us, for many a
weary year (Heroes of Ireland)   BB NL 579
There's a name that will ne'er   Songbook *c.* 1857
   NL

The Scotchmen may boast of their snow covered
mountains (I'm an Irishman Born)   BB NLI 17
They had better take care about what they are at   Lover 1899 218
Thrice welcome brave O'Connell   IFC 1167:137-8;
   S433:49

Throughout its course from mountain source (Clear
Flows the Derreen, oh) (comp. Fr Denis Lawler)   IFC 91:270-3
Tíocht ó theach an tórraimh dhom a dhearc mé stór
mo chroí (Taimín Bán)   IFC 160:423-4
'Tis: It is
To Derrynane Abbey, that handsome station   IFC 927:314-5
To impart his knowledge to Christianity (Fr Maguire)   IFC 1891:14-19
Tríd aisling aréir im luighe go seascair   RIA 117(b):6
Two more of his friends like insulter of Daniel   IFC 107:643-6; 183:
   116-7; 334:505-9;
   629:114-6, 431- 3;
   789:539-40;
   1216:154; 1795:123;
   S960:128-35;
   IO 26.8.1950;
   Healy 1969 77-9

We have good news to-day, says the Shan Van Vaught   Zimmermann 1967
   134

We meet to-day as brothers should
(Ireland's Great Liberator or The Glorious
Unveiling of the O'Connell Statue August 15 1882)   BB NL 94
When Daniel O'Connell he first went to London
(was elected)   IFC 107:643-6; 183:
   116-7; 334:505-9;
   629:114-6, 431- 3;
   789:539-40; 1216:154;
   1795:123; S960:128-
   35; TM 116/A/2; *IO*
   26.8.1950; Healy
   1969 77-9

When Erin's green banner's unfurled
(Hurrah for O'Connell, Meagher and Repeal)
(air: One Bumper at Parting though Many)   BB NL

When Father Maguire came home from college — IFC 1806:230-1
When I heard the news I was much confused — Breathnach 1977 29
When I was a maid at the age of sixteen (The Little Fife and Drum) — IFC 1795:124-5
Where foams the white torrent and rushes the rill — *OB* 6/29 716
While strolling out through Dublin streets but a few days ago (Irish Exhibition Show) — BB NL 147

You banished sons of this injured nation — Zimmermann 1967 206-7

Ye boys of old Hibernia, attend unto me — Zozimus 1871 24-30
You boys of the (this) city (shamrock) give ear to my (this) ditty (The Brave Jolly Tinker/ Daniel O'Connell and the Englishman) — IFC 107:643-6; 183: 116-7; 334:505-9; 629:114-6, 431- 3; 789:539-40; 1216:154; 1795:123; S960: 128-35; *IO* 26.8.1950; Healy 1969 77-9

Ye county Freeholders to me pay attention — Zimmermann 1967 208-9

You feeling-hearted Christians I hope you'll draw near (Mackin Fight) — IFC 1711:256-7
You gallant sons of Erin's Isle, come listen unto me (a new song on O'Connell's Centenary) — BB NL 92
You gallant sons of Erin's Isle, come listen to those lines of mine — IFC TM 498/2
You gallant sons of Erin's Isle I hope you'll give consent (O'Brien's Advice to the Irish People) — BB NL
You gallant sons of Erin's Isle now listen to those lines of mine (A New Song on The Erecting of O'Connell's Monument for 1882) — BB IFC 10b; NL 143
Ye gentlemen of fame, bards of the Irish Nation (The Loss of O'Connell) (air: The Rakes of Derry) — BB Mitchell Library Glasgow dated 1853

You hearty gay fellows draw near me till I my adventures relate (Rambling Jack or The Ragman's Travels) — BB NL 384
You heavenly muses assist my genius (an admired song called Glendalough) — BB NL 75
You heavenly muses you angelic vision (The Eulogy of Our Chieftain O'Connell) — BB NL 328
You Irish heroes of Paddy's nation — IFC 305:304-8
You Irishmen draw near, said the Shan Van Vocht — Zimmermann 1967 134-5

You lads of the city give ear to my ditty (come ye
now listen pretty)   IFC TM 72/B/6,
You learned men that's wise, I'll tell you no lies   Songbook NL 1836
You lovers of merit(mirth) (I pray) pay attention   IFC 150:543-7;
212:440-4;
1216:155-7;
1711:27- 8;
1795:117-8

You maids of the city who are anxious for courting   IFC TM 458/A/3
You mourning sons oer this (of our/this) afflicted
nation ([Granua's Lament Round] O'Connell's Grave)   IFC 559:276-8;
BB NL 329, Mitchell
Library, Glasgow
1875

You muses kind assist me I'm seeking for your aid
(The Rev. Father Holten)   BB NL 181
You natives of Dublin I pray you'll attend
(a new song in praise of Our Noble Lord Mayor)   BB NL
You patriots of this fair isle (comp. James Tevlin)   IFC 921:462-4
You Roman Catholics of this Irish nation
(Fr Tom Maguire)   IFC 1404:570-6
You sons and daughters of Erin's nation   Healy 1969 102-4
You sons of Erin's Isle, who bear sorrow with a
smile (Wrongs of Ireland)   BB NL 1
You sons of Hibernia come listen to me
(Maurice and the Father)   BB NL
You sons of Hibernia, now listen a while to my song
(The Kerry Eagle)   BB Mitchell Library,
Glasgow 1865;
IO 22.9.1928, 281;
Zimmermann 1967
233-5

You sons of loyalty arise and fearlessly unite
(Anti-Repeal Song)   *Collection of Orange
Songs* Toronto 1895
9

You sons of the shamrock give ear to my ditty
(O'Connell and the Tinkers)
IFC 107:643-6;
183:116-7; 334:505-9;
629:114-6, 431-3;
789:539-40; 1216:154;
1795:123;
S960:128-35;
TM 10/B/3, 498/C;
IO 26.8.1950;
Healy 1969 77-9

You sons of this lovely but ill-fated nation	Chapbook NL
You true sons of Erin draw near to me	Healy 1969 81-3
You true sons of Erin I hope you'll assemble	
(The Pope's (Napoleon's) visit to Ireland)	BB NLI 36 (317)
Ye who despoil the sons of toil, saw ye this sight	
to-day	Songbook (x 2)
	NL n.d.

References
1. First lines of songs are followed by title, in brackets, and other information which has been given relating to the author and the air to which the song is sung.
2. Seán McCann tape collection, Folk Music Section, Department of Irish Folklore, UCD.
3. Tom Munnelly tape collection, Folk Music Section, Department of Irish Folklore, UCD.

Appendix C

A SELECTION OF TALES AND ANECDOTES

Biddy Moriarty

O'Connell commenced the attack:

'What's the price of this walking-stick, Mrs. What's-your name?'

'Moriarty, sir, is my name, and a good one it is; and what have you to say agen it? And one-and-sixpence's the price of the stick. Troth, it's chape as dirt – so it is.'

'One-and-sixpence for a walking-stick – whew! Why, you are no better than an impostor, to ask eighteen-pence for what cost you two-pence.'

'Two-pence, your grandmother!' replied Mrs. Biddy; 'do you mane to say that's chating the people I am? Impostor, indeed!'

'Ay, impostor; and it's that I call you to your teeth,' rejoined O'Connell.

'Come, cut your stick, you cantankerous jackanapes.'

'Keep a civil tongue in your head, you old *diagonal*,' cried O'Connell, calmly.

'Stop your jaw, you pug-nosed badger, or by this and that,' cried Mrs. Moriarty, 'I'll make you go quicker nor you came.'

'Don't be in a passion, my old *radius* – anger will only wrinkle you beauty.'

'By the hokey, if you say another word of impudence, I'd tan your dirty hide, you bastely common scrub; and sorry I'd be to soil my fists upon your carcase.'

'Whew! boys, what a passion old Biddy is in; I protest as I am a gentleman ...'

'Jintleman! jintleman! the likes of you a jintleman! Wisha, by gor, that bangs Banagher. Why, you potato-faced pippin-sneezer, when did a Madagascar monkey like you pick enough of common Christian dacency to hide your Kerry brogue?'

'Easy now – easy now,' cried O'Connell, with imperturbable good humour, 'don't choke yourself with fine language, you old whiskey-drinking *parallelogram*.'

'What's that you call me, you murderin' villain?' roared Mrs. Moriarty, stung into fury.

'I call you,' answered O'Connell, 'a *parallelogram*; and a Dublin judge and jury will say that it's no libel to call you so!'

'Oh, tare-an-ouns! holy Biddy! that an honest woman like me should be called a parrybellygrum to her face. I'm none of your parrybellygrums, you rascally gallows-bird; you cowardly, sneaking, plate-lickin' bliggard!'

'Oh, not you, indeed!' retorted O'Connell; 'why, I suppose you'll deny that you keep a *hypothenuse* in your house.'

'It's a lie for you, you b – y robber; I never had such a thing in my house, you swindling thief.'

'Why, sure all your neighbours know very well that you keep not only a *hypothenuse*, but that you have two *diameters* locked up in your garret, and that you go out to walk with them every Sunday, you heartless old *heptagon*.'

'Oh, hear that, ye saints in glory! Oh, there's bad language from a fellow that wants to pass for a jintleman. May the divil fly away with you, you micher from Munster, and make celery-sauce of your rotten limbs, you mealy-mouthed tub of guts.'

'Ah, you can't deny the charge, you miserable *submultiple* of a *duplicate ratio*.'

'Go, rinse your mouth in the Liffey, you nasty tickle-pitcher; after all the bad words you speak, it ought to be filthier than your face, you dirty chicken of Beelzebub.'

'Rinse your own mouth, you wicked-minded old *polygon* – to the deuce I pitch you, you blustering *intersection* of a st–ng *superficies!*'

'You saucy tinker's apprentice, if you don't cease your jaw, I'll –' But here she gasped for breath, unable to hawk up any more words, for the last volley of O'Connell had nearly knocked the wind out of her.

'While I have a tongue I'll abuse you, you most inimitable *periphery*. Look at her, boys! There she stands – a convicted *perpendicular* in petticoats! There's contamination in her *circumference*, and she trembles with guilt down to the extremities of her *corollaries*. Ah, you're found out, you *rectilineal antecedent* and *equiangular* old hag! 'Tis with you the devil will fly away, you porter-swiping *similitude* of the *bisection of a vortex!*'

Overwhelmed with this torrent of language, Mrs. Moriarty was silenced. Catching up a saucepan, she was aiming at O'Connell's head, when he very prudently made a timely retreat.

'You have won the wager, O'Connell, here's your bet,' cried the gentleman who proposed the contest.

O'Connell knew well the use of sound in vituperation, and having to deal with an ignorant scold, determined to overcome her in volubility, by using all the *sesquipedalia verba* which occur in Euclid. With these, and a few significant epithets, and a scoffing, impudent demeanour, he had for once imposed silence on Biddy Moriarty.[1]

The Cat and the Candle (AT 217)

Bhí Dónall Ó Conaill i bhfad ó shin agus fear eile a dtabharfadh siad – bhí gealltaí curtha acu cé acu is treise dúchas nó oiliúint. Dúirt an fear eile gur treise oiliúint agus dúirt Dónall Ó Conaill gur treise dúchas nó oiliúint. Dúirt an fear eile go raibh cat aigesan agus go gcoinneodh sé an choinneal dó fad is bheadh sé ag glacadh a shuipéir gach aon oíche agus d'iarr sé air a theacht a leithéid seo oíche go bhfeicfeadh sé í agus tháinig sé agus chuaigh sé ag glacadh a shuipéir. Chuaigh an cat suas ar an tábla agus choinnigh sé, choinnigh sé ina bhéal an choinneal nuair a bhí an fear ag glacadh a shuipéir. Ní ligfeadh sé an choinneal uaidh cé bith. Bhí Dónall Ó Conaill, bhí luchóg bheag leis istigh i mbosca beag ina phóca agus nuair a bhí an fear ag glacadh a shuipéir agus an cat ag coinneáil an choinnil dó, tharraing sé amach an bosca beag as a phóca agus lig sé an luchóg as go díreach ag taobh an chait. Lig an cat an choinneal uaidh agus ar shiúl i ndiaidh na luchóige.[2]

(A long time ago, Daniel O'Connell and another man, they called – they had made a bet about which was stronger, nature or learning. The other man said training was stronger, and Daniel O'Connell said that nature was stronger than learning. The other man said he had a cat and that the cat would hold the candle for him while he was taking his supper every night and he asked him to come this particular night to see her and he came and he went to take his supper. The cat went up on the table and he kept, he kept the candle in his mouth while the man was taking his supper. He wouldn't let the candle go, anyway. Daniel O'Connell, he had a small mouse in a little box in his pocket and when the man was taking his supper and the cat was holding the candle for him, he pulled the small box out of his pocket and he let the mouse out of it just beside the cat. The cat let the candle go and off he went after the mouse.)

Chickens From Boiled Eggs (AT 821B)

There was another man once and he was going to America. He left Cobh. The night before he left Ireland he took lodgings in a hotel and everything was alright till morning when he was to pay for his digs. The landlady asked him what would he have for breakfast, as it was Friday and he was only glad it to be Friday, for he would pay more for meat if it was any other day. However, he said he would have two eggs instead and the landlady got ready the breakfast for him. When the breakfast was over and him preparing for leaving he told the landlady he would not forget her and that he would pay her again, more than the price of the breakfast as soon as he would get the chance of work abroad. So bedad, she said it would be time enough till then, that she was in no hurry at all.

Then they parted the best of friends, and he went on board the ship.

He was not long in America when he got a big job with a good salary and was earning plenty cash, so soon he was a rich man, and was so proud that he gave up the job and came home. When he landed in Cobh he never stopped until he came in to pay the landlady for the breakfast he got before he went to America.

When he came in she didn't recognise him and after a few minutes talk, he told her who he was, and said he: 'Do you remember the morning long ago this day twelve years when I went to America, and I said I had no money to pay for my breakfast?'

The landlady thought for a moment.

'I don't then,' said she.

Then she said again: 'Oh, I do and well remember it and is that you? Musha, your thousand welcome home again to us.'

'Thank you,' said the man. 'Well now, I promised you that time I would give you more than the price of the breakfast,' and he handed her a pound. 'Here,' said he, 'take that as you were so kind to me at the time.'

She took the pound note in her hand and looked at it, then said: 'That won't pay me my dear man,' said she, 'or twenty more along with it.'

He looked at her, and said: 'What did you say?'

'I say that pound won't pay me or twenty more along with it.'

'The devil a penny more you will get from me,' said the man, 'and I am sorry now for giving you that much itself on account of what you are after saying.'

'Well,' said she, 'unless you settle with me all the money you have in your possession won't do you, for I will take proceedings against you.'

'Do what you like,' said the man, 'but I won't give you another cent.'

So all passed off for a while, and it was not long after when the man got a summons to attend the court, and he didn't know what would he do – would he attend it or not. At last he thought it better to appear, or matters would be worse.

However, the evening before the court was to sit, he walked out to cool himself and to consider what would be the best plan, and he met a young man. They were talking away for a while, and at last the man told him his story and wanted an advice.

Who was talking to him but Daniel O'Connell and he told him not to worry to leave that to him, and: 'I will see you alright.'

So bedad the next day he came to the court and they were all there before him judges and counsellors. The woman that summonsed him was there too, and everything was ready and the judge sat in his chair. The woman was called up first to tell her complaint, and she told the judge that that man there came and waited overnight at her house and that she gave him supper and bed and breakfast before he went to America twelve years ago, and that he told her he hadn't any money to pay for it and that he wouldn't forget her as soon as he would go over and get work that he would 'pay me far more than the breakfast as soon as he would earn it. I asked him what would he have for breakfast as it was Friday and he told me to put down two eggs for him. So I did. When he came home he came to me and sure I didn't recognise him at first, but after thinking a little I thought of him and he only gave me a pound note. I looked at it and said that that wouldn't pay me.'

'Why,' said the judge, 'wouldn't it?'

'Well,' said she, 'if I kept them two eggs and put them down under a clucking hen, wouldn't it be better, and maybe they would be two pullets and when them two pullets would grow up they would lay more eggs for me and I could put them down, some of them and sell the rest, and I would have more chickens and they would, when they would grow up, lay more eggs, and wouldn't them two eggs be better to me than his one pound note?'

Who came in the same very minute but Daniel O'Connell and the man that ate the two eggs was glad to see him, for he was beginning to fear he wouldn't come at all. Daniel walked up and down the courtroom and didn't say nothing. He pulled out a fistful of boiled peas from his pocket and began throwing them over the floor.

'Bedad,' said the judge, 'Daniel must be off his head to-day, and the way he is carrying on.'

'Faith your worship,' said Daniel, 'there is more than me off his head.'

'Why do you say that?' said the judge. 'Well I have good reason for saying it,' said Daniel, 'after listening to that woman about her two eggs.

Do you see them boiled peas I am throwing on the floor?'

'I do,' said the judge.

'Do you think will they grow again after being boiled?'

'It is impossible,' said the judge, 'they never will.'

'Well,' said Daniel O'Connell, 'haven't they as little a chance of growing, as the two eggs that man ate can hatch two chickens in his stomach?'

'That is true for you,' said the judge.

The case was dismissed, and the woman had to pay the other man's costs and expenses, and the pound note didn't do her either.[3]

Coughing in Parliament

But O'Connell's son was inside along with him, anyway, and he was making a speech, and there wasn't a single English member inside that wasn't coughing, in a way that his talk wouldn't be heard at all. The son put a hand in his pocket and he pulled out a pair of pistols and he clapped them on the counter and he said the first man that would cough while his father would be talking, he said that he should handle one of them and fight him, and there wasn't a single cough and when the father stopped: 'Maurice,' says he, 'I'm sorry to the heart,' says he, 'I didn't make a doctor of you,' says he. 'There wouldn't be a doctor in Europe,' says he, 'to cure a cough with you!' says he.[4]

The Devil in Disguise

There was a Catholic man and a Protestant man. The Catholic man was very wealthy and the Protestant was very poor, he was so poor that one day he asked the other man for the loan of five pounds. The Catholic man gave him the money. Then it happened that the Protestant man got very wealthy and the other man got very poor. He did not like to ask the Protestant for his money but he got as poor as he was not able to buy anything he wanted so he went to the Protestant man and asked him for the five pounds. The man denied the Catholic had ever given him any money.

The Catholic man did not know what to do then, so he went to Daniel O'Connell and he told him his story. Daniel told him to go to every house and ask lodging for the night and to be sure to ask lodging in the Protestant man's house. The man did not know whether he would do this or not and Daniel said he would do it himself. He dressed up like a stranger and went to every house and when he came to the Protestant's house the man told him he would surely keep him. Daniel O'Connell said he left some old clothes down the town and he said he would go and get them. He went away and he met the Catholic man and he told him to go to the butcher's shop and get two legs of a bullock. The man got the legs and he gave them to Daniel O'Connell.

When he was in bed that night he put the legs up the sleeves of his coat and tied them on to his hands. Next morning the maid brought up some tea to him in the bed. When she entered the room Daniel began to shake the feet. She was frightened and she went to the man of the house and told him the devil was in the room. He went for the minister. The minister came but he said he could go nothing and he told them to go for the priest.

The priest came and he went down to the room and closed up the door. Daniel O'Connell told him the story and when the priest came up he told the man that if he would give him five pounds he would chase the devil. The man said he would. The priest got the five pounds and he went down to the room and Daniel O'Connell walked out of the house before him. They did not stop until they were in the Catholic man's house and he gave him his money.[5]

The Geese and the Ganders

Daniel O'Connell was coming from Cork to his home in Cahirsiveen in his carriage. He met a boy driving a flock of geese. Dan thought he would like a goose for the Christmas. He asked the boy if he would sell him the geese. The boy said: 'yes,' and they agreed on a price and he paid him there and then – the boy to take him the geese the next day.

Next morning the boy got up and picked out the ganders which he kept for himself and drove the geese to Dan's house. Dan was told that the geese had arrived and he at once noticed that the flock was smaller than it was the day before. He counted them and then he was certain that they were not all in it. He asked the boy where were the rest of the flock. Did he not buy so many from him on the previous day.

'Oh, no, mister, you bought only the geese – you did not buy the ganders and I have brought you all the geese that were in the flock yesterday.'

'Clever fellow,' said Dan, 'You win this time,' and he laughed heartily at being caught so badly.[6]

Half of the Pig

A fellow who stole a pig was found out and was summoned and he met O'Connell and told him the story. Daniel said: 'If you give me half the pig I will save you from the summons.' The court was held and Daniel's case was first. The judge asked Daniel about the pig and he said, 'That man ate no more of that pig than I did,' and that was true because they did not eat any of the pig until the case was over and the fellow was let go.[7]

The Laughing Horses

Daniel O'Connell was going to a party and he had a manservant with him. This man was listening to two gentlemen making a plan to have a joke on Daniel. They got a bundle of oats and tied it to O'Connell's horse's tail. When they were gone then, the man got a knife and put cuts on the sides of their horses and placed them, one at each side of O'Connell's horse. After dinner, one of the gentlemen told the rest of the company to come out and see the queer way Daniel's horse was eating his oats. They all came out and when O'Connell saw the horses he said: 'Oh, gentlemen, your horses are after splitting their sides laughing at mine, and he eating the oats with his end.'[8]

The Lawyer's Mad Client (AT 1585)

Some time ago Eoghan Rua was very fond of women. He had the name of it. Oh, yes he had. Very well. He committed himself this time in any case with a woman and he went to Daniel O'Connell. Over in London the trial was to be, and he told his story to Daniel O'Connell and he said he was guilty. Yes. Very well. Five pounds was Daniel O'Connell's fee. Well the bargain was made between Eoghan Rua and Daniel O'Connell; if he brought him free, he'd give him the five pound, and if he didn't he'd give him nothing. The case went on and Daniel O'Connell told Eoghan Rua when he'd be called up on the bench to pretend to be a fool and to raise his head when the judge would ask him any question and to say: 'foo-foo, foo foo-foo, foo-foo-hoo.'

He brought him free.

The court was over. Daniel O'Connell was on one side of the street, Eoghan Rua on the other side of the street. Daniel O'Connell crossed the street to Eoghan Rua and said to him:

'Didn't we get out of that case very well?'

'So we did, ' says Eoghan Rua.

'Pay me now, ' said Daniel O'Connell to Eoghan Rua.

'Foo-foo-foo, foo-foo-foo, foo-foo-foo-hoo.'

Eoghan Rua crossed the street.

'Oh,' said Eoghan Rua, 'Eoghan Rua will be understood.'[9]

The Minister is Tricked

Bailíodh na deachmhuithe sa cheantar seo fadó. Is iad na ministrí a bhíodh ar an gCoireán a bhailíodh sa dúthaigh seo iad go dtí an bhliain 1838. Thógaidís airgead nó stoc mar dheineann na báillí sa tsaol atá anois againn. Bhí na daoine ag cur ina gcoinnibh go mór agus is minic a tugtaí bataráil don lucht bailithe.

Bhí fear ar an gCarraig anso i nDoire Fhionáin gurbh ainm dó Seán Ó Sé agus tá sé i mbéalaibh na ndaoine fós cad a dhein sé leis an ministir.

Uair amháin dá dtáinig an ministir ag bailiú na ndeachmhuithe chuaigh sé ag triall ar Sheán acht in ionad aon rud a thabhairt don ministir is amhlaidh ghabh Seán de lámhaibh is cosaibh air.

Bhí Seán le cur ar a thrial ar na ceathrú sheiseon a bhí chugainn agus, mar ba ámharaí an tsaoil é, bhí an breitheamh ag teacht ar cuairt go Doire Fhionáin le cois Dhónaill Uí Chonaill. Tháinig Seán ag triall ar Dhónall agus d'inis a scéal dó. 'Níl aon ní agamsa le déanamh duit,' arsa Dónall Ó Conaill. 'Crochfar tú siúrálta mara bhfaighfir bás an dtuigeann tú?'

'Ó, tuigim anois tú,' arsa Seán agus bhagair sé súil.

Lá arna mháireach, bhí Dónall Ó Conaill agus an breitheamh ag dul ag fiach nuair a chonacadar chucu an tsochraid. Do lig Dónall air ná raibh aon fhios aige ar cé bhí marbh agus stad sé, bhain a chaipín de ag guí ar anamanibh na marbh, chuaigh ag caint leis na daoine a bhuail leo sa tsochraid. D'fhiafraigh an breitheamh de cé bhí marbh agus d'inis Dónall dó, gurbh é Seán Ó Sé a fuair bás obann agus d'inis sé dhó leis mar a raibh Seán le bheith os a chomhair ag na ceathrú seiseon acht tá sé os comhair breitheamh níos airde inniu, beannacht Dé lena anam.

Tamall fada ina dhiaidh sin bhí an ministir céanna ag dul abhaile go dtí An Coireán agus a chapall aige tar éis bheith ar a chuardaibh ar an dtaobh seo agus cé bhuailfeadh leis ag Com an Chiste ach Seán agus é ag teacht ón bhfíodóir le plainín bán agus ó bhí an tráthnóna bog ceoch bhí cuid den phlainín casta timpeall ar a cheann agus ar a ghualainn ag Seán. Nuair a chonaic an ministir é d'aithin sé Seán a bheith marbh agus curtha. . . .Thug sé na spoir dá chapall agus d'imigh sé sa tsiúl, siúd Seán ina dhiaidh ag greadadh. Nuair a shroich a thigh féin thit sé i bhfanntais agus nuair a tháinig sé chuige féin d'fhiafraigh cailín an tí de cad do bhain dó! 'Ar chualaís riamh go dtáinig éinne a bhí marbh thar n-ais ar an saol seo nó an bhfacthas iad?' arsa an ministir. 'Rud an-choitianta is ea é,' ar sise. Ba é deireadh an scéil gur fhág an ministir slán ag an dúiche.[10]

(The tithes were collected in this district long ago. The ministers who were in An Coireán used to collect them in this district until the year 1838. They used to take money or stock like the bailiffs do today. The people were protesting against them a great deal and very often the collectors were battered.

There was a man here in Carraig, in Doire Fhionáin, who was called Seán Ó Sé and people still talk of what he did to the minister. Once, when the minister came to collect the tithes he went to Seán but instead of giving the minister something Seán set about him with his hands and feet.

Seán was to be tried at the next quarter-sessions and as luck would have it, the judge was coming for a visit to Doire Fhionáin with Daniel O'Connell. Seán came to Daniel and told him his story. 'I can do nothing for you,' said Daniel O'Connell. 'You will hang for certain, unless you die, do you understand?'

'Oh, I understand you now,' said Seán and winked.

The following day, Daniel O'Connell and the judge were going hunting when they saw a funeral approaching. Daniel pretended he didn't know who was dead and he stopped, took off his cap to pray for the souls of the dead, and went to speak to the people they met at the funeral. The judge asked who was dead and Daniel told him that it was Seán Ó Sé who had died suddenly and told him how Seán was to have appeared before him at the quarter-sessions, but he is before a higher judge today, God rest his soul.

A long time afterwards the same minister was going home to An Coireán, with his horse, after visiting over this direction, and who did he meet at Com an Chiste but Seán and he was coming from the weaver with white flannel and as the evening was soft and misty Seán had tied some of the flannel around his head and his shoulder. When the minister saw Seán he recognised that it was the same Seán who was dead and buried. He spurred his horse on and went off and Seán made off after him. When he reached his own house, he fell into a faint and when he recovered the girl in the house asked him what had happened. 'Did you ever hear that anyone who was dead came back to this life or that they were seen?' said the minister. 'That is something very common,' she said. The end of it was that the minister said goodbye to the district.)

A Miser is Convicted

They used to tell a story here one time about Dan O'Connell and the miser. He was an old miser, and he was supposed to have a wild lot of money all in sovereigns in this drawer, and it appears everyone knew he had it. So anyway, this is how the story went, one day a man come to Dan O'Connell and explained that he was in a very bad way for money, and could he suggest a plan that would get him in some money kind of quick as he wanted it badly. I forget what he was supposed to want it for but anyway, Dan says:

'There's a miser not far away is reputed to have a wild lot of sovereigns in a drawer. Why don't you go up and take it. It wouldn't be a bit of sin.'

'Oh, Lord save us,' says the man, 'do you want me to be transported or put in jail or what – steal a man's money.'

'You'll be neither,' says O'Connell, 'if you do it the way I tell you.'

Anyway, he talked him round to it; and he says: 'Let you get a wig and put it on and when you go in he'll likely be sitting at the fire, and let you put the wildest grins and *cárs* and faces you can on you; then go and empty the drawer and take all's in it.'

'But if I'm arrested –'

'You won't be arrested, and if you are, I'll stand to your back.'

So seeing that it was the great counsellor that advised him to do it, the man did as Dan directed him. He got a wig and put it on and went into the miser's house, and good enough, he was sitting at the fire as O'Connell said and all the *cárs* and grins and twisted faces he pulled on himself ... !

The miser drew back: 'God save us,' he says, 'are you the devil or what?'

And without much more to do he goes over and opens the drawer and empties it all out, and starts to put the money into his pocket. And then away he goes.

O'Connell told him too, that when he had the job done he was to throw the wig away; but he was so anxious he almost forgot about it. He was hardly away of course, naturally enough, when the miser ran out shouting: 'Police, robbery.' So the hue and cry went up and he gave the description of the man he thought robbed him.

The man threw the wig away and it fell on a bush; and who came along but an old tramp, a beggarman, and doesn't he see the wig and looks at it. 'I wonder would it fit me,' he says. So he tries it and it must have done for he kept it on. And lo and behold, he had hardly it on when two police came along and arrests him.

Anyway, the day of the trial come along, and Dan O'Connell was in the court defending the beggarman; and the case was going very hard against him. The miser was in the box and he swore that the beggarman was the man that robbed him.

'How do you know?' said Dan. 'Are you sure now?'

'I'm certain,' says he, 'for he had a wig on him, and that's him. And of all the faces ever a man pulled on himself he pulled them on.'

So the case went on, and it seemed there was nothing but a sentence for the old man, and meanwhile O'Connell got hold of the wig and slipped it on, and began to *cár* and grin and pull faces. And the miser says: 'That's the man there that done it! Them's the same faces he pulled on himself when he emptied the drawer. It's not the old man at all done it. It's that man!'

So O'Connell turned to the judge: 'There you are, your Honour,' he says. 'Now he says it was me robbed him. The man's raving or insane.'

And the judge dismissed the case and had the miser put away.[11]

The Name on the Hat

Some fellow was apprehended for a crime, and brought to justice. He left his cap at the scene of the crime and the policeman got his cap. That was going on alright. The accused man got Dan to plead for him.

The policeman said in court that there was the man that had done the crime, and he pointed out the accused man, and there was his cap.

The judge looked at the cap and examined it, and Dan was silent. At last, Dan spoke:

'Your Honour,' he says to the judge, 'will you please hand me that cap?'

The judge did so.

Now Dan knew it was the fellow's cap alright. And Dan was examining and examining the cap. The fellow's name was such a name. But there was no name at all on the cap. Dan spelled out the accused man's name out of the cap and he says to the policeman:

'Did you see the man's name in the cap?'

The policeman said he did.

'Now,' says Dan to the judge, 'he's swearing to the name in the cap and there's no name at all in it.'

The case was dismissed.[12]

Payment with the Clink of Money (AT 1804B)

Chuaigh seisear buachaillí lá isteach i dtigh i mbaile mór agus d'ordaigh duine acu punt feola a chuir síos do gach éinne acu agus tae agus arán. Bhí ar gach éinne díol as a chuid fhéin. Bhí duine dhos na buachaillí agus níor bhlais sé an fheoil mar ní raibh oiread aige do dhíolfadh aisti ach do dh'ól sé a bhraon tae agus do dh'ith sé a bhlúire aráin agus do dhíol astu san is ní tógfaí uaidh é gan fiacha an phunt feola. Dúirt sé nár bhlais sé an fheoil. Tháinig bean an tsiopa ar an ndoras is do bhain sí a hata dho agus d'imigh an chuid eile dhos

na buachailllí. Choinnigh sí ansan é. Do ghaibh Dónall Ó Conaill an tsráid
agus do chuala sé an argóint. D'fhiafraigh sé dho cad a bhí orthu.
'A leithéid seo,' ar seisean.
'Agus ná díolfá í?' arsa Donall.
'Níor bhlaiseas an fheoil,' ar seisean. 'Ní raibh aon ní agam a dhíolfadh aisti
ach dhíolas as an méid a dh'itheas.'
'Ná tabharfá dho a hata mar sin,' arsa Dónall 'muran ith sé an fheoil?'
'Níor ghá dho í dh'ithe,' arsa an bhean, 'mar do bhí an boladh ag dul ina
bholg.'
'Tá an ceart agat,' arsa Dónall.
Chuir Dónall a lámh ina phóca agus do tharraing sé anios lán a dhoirn
d'airgead bán.
'Tar anseo i leith chugam,' arsa seisean, 'líon do bholg dá bholaidh seo. Cuir
uait an hata go tapaidh,' ar seisean, 'nó bé go gcuirfinnse greim ort.' Ba
mhaith é Dónall Ó Conaill.[13]

(Six fellows went into a house in a town one day and one of them ordered a
pound of meat for each of them, and tea and bread. Everyone had to pay for
himself. There was one of the fellows and he didn't taste the meat because he
didn't have enough to pay for it but he drank his drop of tea and ate his piece
of bread and paid for them and his money was not taken without payment for
the meat. He said he didn't taste the meat. The woman of the shop came to
the door and took off his hat and the rest of the fellows went off. She kept
him there. Daniel O'Connell was passing by on the street and he heard the
argument. He asked him what was wrong with them.

'It's like this,' he said.

'And would you not pay?' said Daniel.

'I didn't taste the meat,' he said. 'I had nothing to pay for it but I paid for
what I ate.'

'Would you not give him his hat then,' said Daniel, 'if he didn't eat the
meat?'

'He didn't have to eat it,' said the woman, 'because the smell of it was going
into his stomach.'

'You are right,' said Daniel.

Daniel put his hand into his pocket and pulled out a fistful of silver.

'Come here to me,' he said, 'fill your stomach with the smell of this. Put
away the hat quickly,' he said, 'or maybe I will bite you.'

Daniel O'Connell was a clever man.)

Perjurers Identified

Daniel O'Connell was over in England this time, and 'twas where he was
stopping in one of the finest hotels in London.

Anyways Daniel had a lovely thoroughbred racehorse, as fine as ever you
laid an eye on and he kept the horse abroad in one of the stables of the hotel.

Bygor, Daniel got up this night and he said he'd go out to look at his horse,
and he asked the manager of the hotel to go along with him.

Out they went to the stable where the horse was, and when they were abroad, didn't Daniel pull a big long dagger up out of his pocket.

'What are you going doing?' says the manager.

'Well you are here now as witness to what I am going to do and for your life don't open you mouth about it until you are asked,' said Daniel.

Daniel then took the dagger and plunged it into the horse's heart, and of course the poor horse fell dead.

Now in them times over in England, there was no *meas* on (regard for) an Irishman no more than a dog, and there was no crime ever that used be committed that it used not be laid on some poor Irishman and if he was not hung he'd be left in jail till his bones would rot. Daniel knew this well, and bygor, he wanted to put an end to it, if he could at all.

Next day, an announcement was put on all the London papers that a beautiful horse belonging to Daniel O'Connell had been stabbed to death in such a place, and that there would be a reward of five hundred pounds for whoever could give information about the man that had killed the horse.

Yerrah, man alive, 'twas going from one to the other, and bygor, in the heel of the hunt wasn't there a man arrested by the peelers. The poor man asked O'Connell to defend him.

'Where did you come from?' said O'Connell.

'I'm an Irishman,' said he, 'and there are five Englishmen going to swear on me, that they saw me stabbing the horse, and as sure as God is in heaven sir, I had nothing to do with the horse.'

'Make your mind easy,' says O'Connell, 'nothing in God's earth will happen to you, and you can take my word for it.'

Up came the peelers and they kept the poor Irishman in custody until the court day came round. When Daniel O'Connell's case was brought on, the poor Irishman stood there in the dock and the five witnesses who saw him stabbing the horse on one side, and Daniel O'Connell and the hotel manager on the other side.

The counsellor for the crown was there and he cross-examined the five Englishmen, and every one of them swore that they saw this Irishman stabbing the horse. Then Daniel O'Connell's turn came to cross-examine.

The first English witness was brought before him in the witness chair.

'On your solemn oath,' says Daniel, 'did you see this man stabbing the horse?'

'On my solemn oath,' says the Englishman, 'I saw that man there in the dock stabbing the horse.' He called up the other four into the witness chair the same way, and they all swore their solemn oath, that they saw the Irishman stabbing the horse.

Daniel then called on the hotel manager to go into the witness chair until he'd cross-examine him.

'Do you remember such a night?' says he.

'I do,' says the manager. 'What time did I get up?' says Daniel.

'You got up at such a time,' says he.

'And what did I do then?'

'You brought me out to the stable with you.'

'And what did I want you in the stable for?'

'You wanted me in the stable as witness.'

'Why?' says Daniel.

'Because,' says he, 'you took a dagger up out of your pocket, and drove it through the horse's heart.'

On your solemn oath,' says Daniel, 'did I stab the horse?'

'On my solemn oath you did,' replied the hotel manager.

'You are right,' says Daniel, 'of course 'twas I myself stabbed that horse, because I knew in my heart that I could easily get five Englishmen that would swear an Irishman's life away as easy as they'd drink water.'

'Now, my Lord,' says he to the judge, 'you know how to treat the perjurers.'

The poor Irishman got off scot free, and the five Englishmen were able to tell the story in jail for long the day after.[14]

A Pint of Spirits

There was another murder case depending chiefly on the evidence of one principal to convict.

'Now, Darby did you take any drop of the creature that day?' said O'Connell.

'*Mhuise*, (indeed) dear knows Counsellor O'Connell, I took my share of a pint of spirits.'

'How well you know my name, Darby,' said the Liberator.

'Oh! sure everyone knows our own patriot,' said Darby.

'Now, Darby, *a bhuachaill*, (lad), on your evidence depends the life of the man in the dock, and which you must answer before your maker, was not your share of a pint of spirits all but the pewter?'

'On my oath, Counsellor, that is quite true for you.'

His evidence was useless after having drunk a pint of *uisce beatha* (whiskey). The man in the dock got free at once. O'Connell gradually corkscrewed the answer he wanted from Darby after having called him 'a fine *grámhar'* (loving) fellow.[15]

Recognising His Own Child

Dan O'Connell met a by-child of his own one day in Dublin and the young lad asked him for money. So Dan gave him something and said to him: 'Don't let me ever see your face again today.'

A couple of streets farther on he met the young lad again and he had his back to Dan, this time, but he had his hand stretched out behind his back. So Dan put some money into the outstretched hand and said: 'Begor, you're a son of O'Connell's and no mistake.'[16]

Seán Bán

Bhí buachaill á dhaoradh ag cailín aon uair amháin agus do chuaigh sé go dtí Dónall Ó Conaill agus d'inis sé a scéal do. 'Is ea,' arsan Dónall, 'rachadsa faoina bráid agus beidh triail agam uirthi go háirithe.' Is mar sin a bhí, do chuaigh sé faoina bráid.

'Dia dhuit a mhaighdean,' a dúirt sé. 'Féach cá bhfaghair í?' a dúirt sí. 'Á, a chailín,' a dúirt sé, 'cé dhéan do bhróga?' 'Ó,' a dúirt sí, 'm'athair a dhéan mo bhróga ach is í mo mháthair a thug an leathar do.' 'Tá go maith', arsa Dónall. Do tháinig sé tharnais go dtí an mbuachaill agus dúirt sé leis nárbh aon chabhair a bheith léi siúd, go raibh sí rómhaith dhóibh.[17]

(A boy was convicted by a girl once and he went to Daniel O'Connell and told him his story. 'Yes,' said Daniel, 'I'll go to her and at least I can test her.' That's how things were and he went to her.

'Good day, virgin,' he said.

'See where will you find her,' she said.

'Oh, my girl,' he said, 'who made your shoes?'

'Oh,' she said, 'my father made my shoes, but my mother gave him the leather for them.'

'Very well,' said Daniel.

He came back to the boy and told him that he couldn't be of any help to him; she was too clever for him.)

The Second Verdict

They used to tell another story about O'Connell and a man on trial for his life – I forget what the crime was, and they hurried to get O'Connell to defend him. But anyway, the case was going bad against this man, and O'Connell says to him: 'When you're taken out again and stood in the box you have only one chance. Loose your right shoe,' he says, 'but don't let anyone notice you. You're going to be sentenced to death,' he says, 'and when you see the judge putting on the black cap, but not before, take off your shoe and hit him in the face – fair between the eyes – and don't be afraid to hit him hard: it's no good if you don't hit him hard.'

The man seen there was no hope anyway, and when he was put in the box he did what O'Connell advised, and loosed his shoe. So the judge prepared to pass sentence and was fitting on the black cap. And he says: 'I sentence you –' And just at that the boy let fly with the shoe and hit right between the two eyes, knocking him back.

'Hang – shoot – burn – draw – and quarter you!' cries the judge.

And O'Connell stood up: 'You've exceeded the law your honour,' he says, 'and I claim you dismiss the prisoner.'

And he had, you know. He wanted to sentence him again but O'Connell objected. And the judge said: 'You're quite right. I cannot do that. I discharge the prisoner.'[18]

A Shave for Two

He was in Dublin another time, and he met a little boy coming down the street, and he was driving an ass with a straddle on his back, and he was crying. Dan asked him what was the matter with him, and the little boy told him that he brought in two creels of turf to sell to a barber, and they made the bargain at eighteen pence for all that was on the asses back. The little boy thought all the time that the barber meant only to take the turf, but instead, he took the creels and the turf, and the little boy said that he was afraid to go home to his people without the creels.

Dan took pity on him, so he told him to come back again to the barber's shop, and that he'd get the creels. He told the little boy to drive on the ass, and that he'd walk ahead of the two of them, but that they were to keep fairly close to him.

The little boy did as he was told, and when he came to the barber's shop, he asked him if he'd shave himself, and his companion.

The barber of course said he would, thinking all the time that it was Dan and the little boy that he was meant to shave, so when he had Dan shaved he asked for his companion to be brought in so Dan went out and brought in the ass.

Of course all the razors in the barber's shop wouldn't shave the ass, and the barber wouldn't hear tell of doing it. Dan insisted on him doing as he promised, but the barber said that he couldn't do it. Dan wouldn't go out of the shop until he got five pound from him for breaking his promise, and when he was going out he told the barber, that he might as well put the pair of creels on the asses back, that he took off. The old barber was so put about over losing his five pounds, that he wasn't in a mood for arguing any more, so he put the creels on the asses back, and Dan gave them to the little boy, together with the five pound and the little lad went home blessing the Liberator that evening.[19]

The Shoemaker Outwits O'Connell

Bhí sé (an gréasaí) aon lá amháin istigh ag obair agus do ghabh Dónall Ó Conaill isteach chuige. Bheannaigh Dónall don ghréasaí agus do bheannaigh an gréasaí dho. D'fhiafraigh Dónall de an mbeadh d'aga aige taoibhín a chur ina bhróig.

'Is chuige atáim anseo,' arsa an gréasaí.

Chuir sé an taoibhín ar a bhróig agus níorbh fhada an mhoill aige é.

'Is ea, an mór é sin?' arsa Dónall.

'Leathchoróin,' arsa an gréasaí.

'Eth!' arsa Dónall, 'sin rud nár dhíolas as aon taoibhín a cuireadh ar aon bhróig riamh roimhe sin dom.

'Is tú a chreidim,' arsa an gréasaí, 'agus níor lú nár chuireas taoibhín ar bhróig cunsailéara roimhe seo.[20]

(He (the shoemaker) was working away inside one day and Daniel O'Connell went into him. Daniel greeted the shoemaker and the shoemaker greeted him in return. Daniel asked him if he would have the time to put a side-patch on his shoe.

'That's what I'm here for,' said the shoemaker.

He put the side-patch on the shoe and it didn't take him long to do so.
'Now how much is that?' said Daniel.
'Half a crown,' said the shoemaker.
'Eh!' said Daniel, 'I never paid that for a side-patch in any shoe before.'
'I believe you,' said the shoemaker, 'and I never put a side-patch in a counsellor's shoe before either.')

Since his Shoes Cost Fourpence

There was a poor woman once and she came to Daniel O'Connell to plead the case for her son that was accused of some offence against the law. He told her to pay fourpence for some kind of old pair of shoes that would fit him, no matter how bad they'd be. She did so, and told him she had them.

On the day of the trial, of course Daniel stood up for the young fellow, and in the end the judge asked him did he know the boy's character.

'Indeed I do,' says Daniel, 'I know him since his shoes cost fourpence.'

Of course the judge thought he had known him all his life then and he let him off.[21]

Some Things Not for Sale (AT 1559C*)

Bhí Éireannach i Sasana fadó agus bhí coir mhór déanta aige. Bhí sé amuigh ansin lá agus casadh Dónall Ó Conaill leis. D'inis sé do Dhónall Ó Conaill an trioblóid a bhí air. Dúirt Dónall leis a dhul isteach sa siopa agus míle punt a chur le fear an tsiopa nach raibh an rud a d'iarr sé air ina shiopa. Agus seo é an rud a d'iarr sé, lán seoil de ghaoth anoir a sheolfadh a bhád abhaile go hÉirinn. Chuaigh sé isteach ansin agus chuir sé an míle punt leis an siopadóir nach raibh an rud a d'iarr sé sa siopa, agus chuir an siopadóir míle punt leis go raibh. D'fhiafraigh an siopadóir de ansin cén rud é, agus dúirt an fear gur lán an tseoil de ghaoth anoir a sheolfadh a bhád abhaile go hÉirinn. 'Well, sin rud nach bhfuil agam,' arsa an siopadóir. B'éigin don tsiopadóir míle punt a thabhairt don fhear. Tháinig sé abhaile go hÉirinn ansin agus an míle aige. Ní fhaca sé aon lá bocht ariamh ina dhiaidh sin de bharr Dhónall Ó Conaill.[22]

(There was an Irishman in England long ago and he had committed a serious crime. He was there one day and he met Daniel O'Connell. He told O'Connell of his trouble. Daniel told him to go into the shop and to bet the shopkeeper a thousand pounds that he didn't have what he wanted in the shop. And this is what he asked for, a sailful of east wind that would sail his boat home to Ireland. He went in then and he bet a thousand pounds with the shopkeeper that he didn't have what he wanted in his shop, and the shopkeeper bet him a thousand pounds that he had. The shopkeeper then asked him what it was, and the man said it was a sailful of east wind that would sail his boat home to Ireland. 'Well, that's something I don't have,' said the shopkeeper. The shopkeeper had to give the man a thousand pounds. He came home to Ireland with the thousand pounds. He was never poor after that, thanks to Daniel O'Connell.)

Supper (Hospitality) Won by a Trick (AT 1526A)

Chuaigh Dónall agus comrádaí leis ar lóistín go tigh ósta i Londain.
Do bhí cúis éigin aige Dónall do lucht an tí ósta seo agus theastaigh sásamh
uaidh. Chuaigh sé féin agus an comrádaí ina gcodladh. D'éiríodar san oíche
agus dhódar an dá chulaith éadaigh bhí orthu ag dul isteach. Nuair éiríodar
ar maidin ní raibh aon éadach acu. Ghlaodar agus scairteadar. Tháinig an
buachaill ósta chucu. Ghearánadar leis: 'Tógadh ár dhá gculaith éadaigh
aréir, agus tógadh ár gcuid airgid chomh maith!' Bhí náire ar an mbuachaill
ósta. Thug sé isteach táilliúir, thóg a dtoise, agus ba ghearr gur thug dhá
chulaith nua chucu. 'Ó, cad a dhéanfaimid gan ár gcuid airgid – caoga punt,
a tógadh,' ar siad ansin. Cuireadh an t-airgead chucu chomh maith. D'imíodar
leo leis an éadach agus caoga punt. Níor chailleadar dhá bharr ach méid na
hóiche sin.[23]

(Daniel and one of his companions went to stay in a hotel in London. Daniel had something against the people of the hotel and he wanted to get satisfaction. He and his companion went to sleep. They got up during the night and they burned the two suits of clothes they had been wearing when they went in. When they got up in the morning, they had no clothes. They called and they shouted. The hotel boy came to them. They complained to him: 'Our suits of clothes were taken last night, and our money was taken as well!' The hotel boy was embarrassed. He brought in a tailor, took their measurements, and soon he brought two new suits to them. 'Oh, what will we do without our money – fifty pounds that was taken,' they said then. The money was sent to them as well. They went off with the clothes and the fifty pounds. All they had lost because of it was the amount for that night.)

Tar on a Saucepan

This gossoon was begging with a tin saucepan on the street and Dan said to him: 'I'll get plenty of money for you, if you get me a pennyworth of tar.' In those days there was on (in) the bank only gold sovereigns. You know what I'm coming at. So Dan got the tar and he put so much into the saucepan and he put some more on the bottom outside. So he told the gossoon to go into the bank and hit the saucepan down on the counter and ask for a pennyworth of tar. So the lad did and some of the sovereigns stuck to the bottom of the tin.[24]

Tomorrow Never Comes

There was a community of priests one time and the place they had belonged to an old Protestant – they had it rented from him. He was all right himself, but there was a change when he died and the son got the property. He was a bigot and he wanted to get the priests out of the place. They didn't want to go, and they went to O'Connell and told him their story. They were doing some repairs at the time and couldn't leave on the day that they were going to be put out. Dan went to the new landlord and asked him to allow them six months to stay in the premises. The landlord said he wouldn't give them any time. Dan says: 'Won't you give them from today till tomorrow?' The landlord agreed to that. And Dan drew up a form giving them from today to tomorrow and the landlord signed it. They didn't leave when the morrow came, and the landlord went into court to look for possession. Dan was there for the priests and he produced the form that the landlord had signed giving them from today to tomorrow. He claimed that there was no tomorrow – that every day was today. The judge agreed with him and the priests couldn't be put out – they remained on in the place and the landlord couldn't interfere with them.[25]

The Uglier Foot (1559B*)

Bhí a dhá chois míchumtha ar slí éigineach. Chuala go raibh sé i hotel *i Sasana agus go raibh sé ag ní a chosa. Bhí na Sasanaigh ag gáire faoi na cosaibh. 'Cuirfidh mé geall libh,' a dúirt sé, 'go bhfuil cos eile sa tigh níosa mhíchumtha ná í sin.' Chuireadar geall leis ná raibh. Shín sé amach an chos eile. 'Nach bhfuil sí sin mar chois níosa mhíchumtha ná í?' a dúirt sé. Bhuaigh sé an geall.*[26]

(His (O'Connell's) two feet were misshapen in some way. I heard that he was in a hotel in England and that he was washing his feet. The English were laughing at his feet. 'I'll bet you,' he said, 'that there's another foot in this house, more misshapen than that one.' They bet him that there wasn't. He stuck out his other foot. 'Isn't this foot more misshapen than it?' he said. He won the bet.)

Wearing his Hat Three Times

Daniel O'Connell used be attending the house of Parliament then. ...

'Well, is there any chance gentlemen,' he said 'that you'll allow me to wear my hat to-day?' he said. 'I feel very cold.'

Oh, they said they would of course, Mister O'Connell. The next court day then: 'Bygor,' he said, 'I didn't get out of the cold yet and I don't know is there any chance you'd allow me wear my hat to-day?'

'Oh, we will, of course, you can wear it, Mister O'Connell.'

Well the third day when he got into the court again, he says:

'Gentlemen,' he said, 'I'm not better yet and maybe you would allow me to-day,' he said, 'to wear my hat.'

'Oh, we will to be sure,' says they.

The fourth day came and Daniel came in and he asked no leave, he left on his hat.

'Mister O'Connell, please,' says they, 'take off your hat.'

'Oh, no, sir,' he said. 'It is passed in Parliament three times,' he said, 'that I can wear my hat,' he said 'and anything you pass three times in Parliament, three times,' he said, 'you can't break it and I'll wear my hat,' he said.[27]

Weeping and Laughing (AT 1828*)

O'Connell made a bet one time that he could make a speech and that he'd have one half of the crowd laughing and the other half crying. So he took a hall and erected a stage in the centre of the hall. He got up on the stage and one half was facing him and the other half of the crowd was behind him. He had no arse in his pants when he got up on the stage. The crowd behind him was roaring laughing and the crowd in front that he was making the speech to, was crying, with what he was saying to them. So he won his bet. But it was not easy to beat Dan. He was rapid.[28]

A Woman Swears Against her Husband

One night a farmer found a man killing a sheep on his lands, and he lost no time in reporting the matter to the authorities, and the culprit was arrested. The wife of the accused was in an awful state over the business, because she knew that if her husband was found guilty he would be hanged. She went to O'Connell and begged of him to defend her husband. 'I know,' says she, 'that you'll be able to free him.' 'I'm not so sure of that,' says O'Connell, 'but I'll do the best I can. But before I can do anything for him I must hear the whole facts first, and you must tell me the truth as far as you know it. Now, tell me this – did your husband kill the sheep?' 'Oh, he did, your honour,' says the wife. 'Are you sure of that?' says O'Connell. 'I am,' says she, 'for I was in the next field, looking at him, and I was there when the owner of the sheep came up and caught him.' 'Well,' said O'Connell, 'there is only one way I can free your husband, and that is for you to do as I tell you. When the case come on, the owner of the sheep will swear that he caught your husband in the act of killing the sheep. The question will then be asked "is there any further evidence for the Crown?" and before the Crown Prosecutor has time to say "No", let you jump up and say: "Yes, my Lord; I want to give evidence for the Crown." Let you wink at the owner of the sheep as you are going up to the witness-box. Turn round and wink at him after you are sworn. Let you then swear that you were in the next field and saw your husband killing the sheep. Make sure that the judge sees you winking at this man, and leave the rest to me.' She promised to do as O'Connell told her.

Well, the trial came on, and the owner of the sheep swore that he saw the accused killing the sheep in his land. O'Connell did not ask him any questions and people were wondering what kind of defence he was going to put up. When the owner of the sheep was leaving the witness-box, the judge asked if there was any further evidence for the crown.

'Oh, yes my Lord,' says the defendant's wife as she jumped up in the body of the court. 'I am here,' says she, 'to give evidence for the Crown.' She came along to the witness-box and on her way she winked at the owner of the sheep. And after she was sworn she turned round and winked at him again. When she was asked what evidence she had to give, she swore that she was in the next field and saw her husband killing the sheep. And the moment she said that, she turned round again and winked at the man that owned the sheep. O'Connell immediately jumped to his feet.

'My lord,' says he, 'you have seen the conduct of this woman. Isn't it plain that it's a case of collaboration between her and the owner of the sheep to get rid of the unfortunate man that is in the dock? And she has come here to swear his life away, and her conduct in court proves that it is all a plot between her and this other man.'

The judge immediately ordered the acquittal of the accused, and, thanks to O'Connell, he went home a free man.[29]

References

1. *Penny Readings for the Irish People,* vol. 111, Compiled By The Editor Of The 'Nation' Dublin 1879 104-7. Other versions: Armagh IFC 1803:151; Clare IFC Tape 1075/2 1987 Tom Munnelly from P.J. 'Brud' Petty, aged fifty-eight, Knockacarn, parish of Killilagh, barony of Corcomroe; Kerry IFC Tape 1948 Caoimhín Ó Danachair from Pádraig Stounder Ó Sé, An Coireán, parish of An Dromaid, barony of Uíbh Ráthach; Louth IFC 1112:218; Mayo IFC 734:246-7; Tipperary IFC 517:344; no provenance: *IO* 15.6.1929 595; 11.2.1950 21; *Irish Independent* 4.10.1945, 2; *OB* 12/1921 143; 6/1929 679. Postcard n.d.; Kennedy 1853 142-3. MI J 1250 clever verbal retorts; MI N O wagers and gambling.

2. IFC 186:417-8. Collected in 1937 by Liam Mac Meanman from Anna Ní Cailín, aged sixty, a housewife, Cionn Garbh, parish of Inis Caoil, barony of Baoigheallach, county Donegal. See also IFC 1915: 41-87 for replies to a specific query relating to the tale. Other versions: Donegal IFC 348:270-1*; Sligo IFC 485:148-51. * indicates that this version is to be included in TIF.

3. IFC 633:27-33*. Collected in 1939 by Máirtín Ó Mainnín from Donncha Ó Cinnéide, aged thirty-eight, a farmer, townland and parish of Kilmacduagh, barony of Kiltartan, county Galway. Other versions: Cavan IFC 1787:198-200*; 1806:77*; Murphy 1975 55* Galway; IFC S16:63-4* Kerry IFC 772:65-9*; IFC Tape 1966 and 1970 Bo Almqvist from Mícheál Ó Gaoithín, Baile Bhiocáire, Dún Chaoin*; Mayo IFC 1942 Séamus Ó Duilearga from Alec MacAindriú, Alt na Brocaigh, Cill Cuimin*; Waterford IFC 153:321-3*; no provenance: *An Lóchrann* July 1909.

4. IFC 716:5-6. Collected in 1940 by Tadhg Ó Murchú from Micheál Ó Conchúir, aged ninety-four, a farm labourer, Faha, Listry, parish of Kilbonane, barony of Magunihy. Other versions: Armagh IFC 1803:140-1; Galway IFC S16:87; Kerry IFC 1007:78-9; Longford IFC 1399:512; Sligo IFC 485:19-20; Waterford IFC 1100:335; S654:807-8. MI J 1500 clever practical retorts.

5. IFC S1042:11, 13. Collected in 1937-38 through the national school of Gortnacart, parish of Killybegs, barony of Banagh, county Donegal from Joseph Gallagher, Doohill, Ardara, parish of Killybegs. Other versions: Donegal IFC 89:202-12; 143:2084-92; 233:4032-7; 454:216-9; S1039:187-9; Galway IFC 1764:394-5; S82:38, 136; Kerry IFC 1539:217-20, 286-9; 1672: 371-2; Leitrim IFC S203:152-4; S210:485-6. MI J 1510 the cheater cheated; K 1810 deception by disguise.

6. IFC S167:270-1. Collected in 1936-38 through the national school of Dromore, parish of Kilmacshalgan, barony of Tireragh, from Mike Tiernan, Ballyfarney, Dromore, parish of Kilmacshalgan, barony of Tireragh, county Sligo. Other versions: Galway IFC 271:152-3; 970:324-6; 1764:398-9. MI J 1113 clever boy; K 100 deceptive bargains.

7. IFC S483 141. Collected 1936-38 through the national school of Foynes, parish of Robertstown, barony of Shanid, county Limerick by Micheál Ó Ciosóg, Foynes.

Other versions: Donegal IFC 186:547-8; Galway IFC 1322:582-5; 1544:111-8; Longford IFC 1429:326; 1486:403(iii); Roscommon IFC 1574:539. MI J 1180 clever means of avoiding legal punishment; J 1249 clever dividing.

8. IFC 871:49 Collected in 1934-40 by Máire N Sheasnáin from Bridie Fahey, The Level, Carrick on Suir, parish of Carrick, barony of Iffa and Offa East, county Tipperary. Other versions: Clare IFC S609: 495-6; Tipperary IFC 517:334-6. MI J 1169. 5 the laughing ass: King has trickster's horse's tail cut off. Trickster retaliates by cutting off part of upper lip of king's ass. At trial, the animals are brought forth. Everyone laughs at the ass. Trickster: 'If everyone laughs at the ass how could the ass help laughing at her companion without a tail?' J 1500 clever practical retorts.

9. IFC 659:391-2. Collected in 1939 by Seosamh Ó Dálaigh from Mrs Lane, aged over ninety, a farmer's wife, Finuge, parish of Lixnaw, barony of Clanmaurice. Other versions: Armagh IFC 1803:146-7; Murphy 1975 53-4; Cavan IFC 1803:118*; Clare IFC S611:447-50*; S613:212*; Cork IFC 779:16; S329:28; Donegal IFC 186:552-4*; Galway IFC 69:131-40; 349:422-6; 970:326-9; 1544:110-4*; Kerry IFC 796:11*; 1064:278*; 1272:157*; Sligo IFC 463:89-91.

10. IFC S468:228-9. Collected 1938 through the national school of Bunaneer, Cathair Dónall, parish of Cill Chrócháin, barony of Dún Ciaráin Theas, by Dónall Ó Céitigh from Bean N. Ní Chéitigh, aged seventy-five, Doire Fhionáin, parish of Cill Chrócháin. Other versions: Kerry IFC 125:363-6; 126:207-12; 148:187-94; 632:365-9; S420:638-40; S428:169-71; S468:222; S470:241-3; S473:483-5; S475:280-1; S478:155-7; CS 16.8.1902, 388; D. Ó Súilleabháin 1936 257-60. MI J 1130 cleverness in the law court; K 1860 deception through feigned death (sleep).

11. IFC 1216:474-6. Collected in 1950 by Michael J. Murphy from Michael Morris, aged forty-six, Carnanransy, parish of Bodoney Lower, barony of Strabane Upper, county Tyrone. The Irish word cár means to grimace, to grin or to make a face. Other versions: Donegal IFC 186:549-91; 992:218-23; S1093:327-9; Galway IFC 373:322-5; 663:438-40; SS3:52-3; S4:147; Longford IFC 1457:580-1; S762:227-8; Sligo IFC 485:46-50; S155:496. MI J 1151.2 witness claims borrowed coat: discredited. Trickster summoned to court on Jew's complaint refuses to go unless he has a new coat. Jew lends him his. In court, the trickster says that the Jew is a liar. 'He will even claim that I am wearing his coat.' The Jew does so and no one believes him.

12. IFC 1480:106. Collected in 1956 by James G. Delaney from James Rogers, aged seventy-five, a farmer, Derrycassan, parish of Columbkille, barony of Granard, county Longford. Other versions: Cavan IFC 1196:63, 185-6; Kerry IFC 796:5-6; 1147:576-81; 1272:155-6; 1278:308-9; 1475:331-5 (published in O'Sullivan 1977 127-8); Cork IFC 536:323-4; Galway IFC 349:427-31; 471:31-4; 1018:207-8; S4:165-6, 223-4; Wexford IFC 1399:466; Limerick IFC 628:18-21; Mayo IFC 734:242-5; Waterford IFC 86:298-302; 332:9-10; S642:264 Tipperary IFC 517:344; no provenance: IO 15.6.1929 566; 11.4.1936 15; St Patrick's 7.6.1902 212; The Shamrock 2.1.1892 215; Kennedy 1853 141-2; M. MacDonagh 1929 49-50. MI J 1190 cleverness in the law court; K 1700 deception through bluffing; K 2116 innocent person accused of murder.

13. Kerry IFC 967:224-5*. Collected in 1945 by Seosamh Ó Dálaigh from Seán Ó Criomhthain, aged sixty-seven, a farmer, parish of Cill Maolchéadair, barony of Corce Dhuibhne. Other versions: Kerry IFC 621:157-9 * (published in Béal. 11 122) (translation in O'Sullivan 1966 234-5); Tipperary IFC S583:206-7.

14. IFC 326:276-81. Collected in 1937 by Seán Ó Flannagáin from Séamus Ó Ceallaigh, aged thirty-three, a farmer, Cillín, parish of an Bheitheach, barony of

Cill Tártan, county Galway. Other versions: Clare IFC S622:232; Cork IFC 807:510-2; Galway IFC 355:23-6; 404:502-3; 669:154-8; 970:322-4; 1025:318-20; *Béal.* 5 1935 260-1; Kerry IFC 148:265-7; 475:345-50; 796:14; 843:220-2; D. Ó Súilleabháin 1936 264-5; Mayo IFC 523:539-49; 693:20-1; Waterford IFC 153:324-6; 1239:22-3; no provenance: Mag Ruaidhrí 1944 101-3. MI H1550 tests of character; J 1190 cleverness in law court; Q 263 perjury punished.

15. IFC 796:6 Collected in 1941 by D. Ó Súilleabháin, Lackaroe, parish of Kenmare, barony of Glanroughty. Other versions: Kerry IFC 1064:434; 1272:156; no provenance: *IO* 8.12.1936, 382; *The Irish Packet* 12.6.1909, 392; *OB* 6/1929, 711; Kennedy 1853 147; M. MacDonagh 1929 49; O. MacDonagh 1988 66. MI J 1130 cleverness in law court; J 1140 cleverness in detection of truth; J 1151 testimony of witness cleverly discredited.

16. IFC 1506:486. Collected in 1958 by James G. Delaney from John Stroker, aged fifty-eight, a farmer, The Grove, parish of Kilteevan, barony of Ballintober, county Roscommon. Other versions: Antrim IFC 1389:55; Armagh IFC 974:299; Murphy 1975 54; Cavan IFC 1787:204; 1803:120; Cork IFC 535:30-1; 808:496-8; Donegal IFC 186:559; 233:4031-3; S1039:122-3; Kerry 11:212-4; 350:326-7; 386:338-43; 659:417-9; 1152:421-2; Ó Súilleabháin 1936 262; Limerick IFC 628:96-7; Mayo IFC Tape 1976 Séamas Ó Catháin from Peadar Bairéad, Ceathrú na gCloch, Cill Cuimin; Meath IFC S687:174; Sligo IFC 512:463-4; Tipperary IFC 738:417.

17. IFC 702:87-8.Collected in 1948 by Seosamh Ó Dálaigh from Seán Ó Guithín, aged fifty-seven, a farmer, Baile na hAbha, parish of Dún Chaoin, barony of Corca Dhuibhne. Other versions: Kerry IFC 148:182-3; 498:31; 936:478-9; 960:37-40; 984:424-6; 1114:277; 1622:445; IFC Tape 1968 Bo Almqvist from Mícheál Ó Gaoithín, Baile Bhiocáire, Dún Chaoin; Galway IFC 377:332-3. MI J 1250 clever verbal retorts.

18. IFC 1216:477. Collected in 1950 by Michael J. Murphy from Michael Morris, aged forty-six, Carnanransy, parish of Bodoney Lower, barony of Strabane Upper, county Tyrone. Other versions: Galway IFC 784:70; 931:568; S74:435-6; Tipperary IFC 1219: 276-80.

19. IFC 485:20-2. Collected in 1938 by Bríd Ní Ghamhnáin from Seán Breathnach, aged seventy-two, a farmer, Cloghogue, parish of Aghanagh, barony of Tirerrill, county Sligo. Other versions: Galway IFC 355:28-31; 669:140-8; 1354:330-1; 1833:62-4; *Béal.* 5 1935 259-60; Kerry IFC 823: 571-2; Mayo IFC 333:218-20; IFC Tape 1976 Séamas Ó Catháin from Peadar Bairéad, Ceathrú na gCloch, Cill Cuimin; Tipperary IFC 517:339-40. MI J 1510 the cheater cheated; K 170 deception through pseudo-simple bargain; K 1600 deceiver falls into own trap; Q 380 deeds punished – miscellaneous; Q 589 punishment fitted to crime.

20. IFC 621:165. Collected 1936-37 by Seán Ó Dubhda from Seán Mac Criomhthain, aged sixty-two, a farmer, townland and parish of Cill Maolchéadair, barony of Corca Dhuibhne. Other versions: Kerry IFC 977:407-8; 1713:285. For further examples of O'Connell meeting his match see Kerry IFC 928: 55-6; no provenance: *IO* 23.9.1903 4.

21. IFC 871:111. Collected 1934-1940 by Máire Ní Sheasnáin from Mrs Kavanagh, Balycarron, parish of Relickmurray and Athassel, barony of Clanwilliam, county Tipperary. Sources: Cork IFC 779:16-17; Dublin IFC Tape 1980 George McClafferty from Mrs Hockshaw, Milltown Day Care Centre, Milltown; Galway IFC 784:69; S74:433; Kerry IFC 823:572-5; D. Ó Súilleabháin 1936 266-7, 267; Meath IFC S687:153; Tipperary IFC S543:148; no provenance: *IO* 17.3.1903 1. MI H 580 enigmatic statements; J 1160 clever pleading.

22. IFC 784:236*; Collected in 1941 by Proinnsias de Búrca from Seán Ó Coirbín, aged fifty, a farmer, Cloch Bhreac, Iomaidh (Omey), parish and barony of Ros, county Galway. Other versions: Galway IFC 363:364-5; 669:148-53*; 920:452-3*; Mayo IFC 734:245-6*.

23. IFC 203:282-3*. Collected in 1936 by Diarmuid Ó Caochlaidhe from Micheál Ó Súilleabháin (Maidhc Reachtaire), aged sixty-five, a stonemason and a farmer, Caolchoill, parish of Cill Macamóg, barony of Beanntraí, county Cork. Other versions: Kerry IFC 304:40-4*; 498:29-30*; 823:306-7.

24. IFC 1574:540(i). Collected in 1961 by James G. Delaney from Thomas Kelly, aged forty-five, a farmer, Grange, parish of Cam, barony of Athlone, county Roscommon. Other versions: Armagh IFC 1803:148; Cork IFC 686:360; Mayo IFC 693:240-2. MI K 330 means of hoodwinking guardian or owner.

25. IFC 1197:179-80. Collected in 1950 by P.J. Gaynor from Patrick Smith, aged seventy-seven, a farm labourer, Corkish, parish of Bailieboro, barony of Clankee, county Cavan. Other versions: Kerry IFC 796:10; 1272:157; 1557:14-9; D. Ó Súilleabháin 1936 266; Cork IFC S277:318; S282:124-5; Longford IFC 1457:361; Roscommon IFC 1709:211-2. MI K231.12 debt to be paid to-morrow. To-morrow never comes.

26. IFC 797:34*. Collected in 1941 by Tadhg Ó Murchú from Seán Ó Luasa, aged eighty-four, a farmer, Tír Ó mBaoill, parish of Cill Fhionán, barony of Uíbh Ráthach.

27. IFC 628:82-3. Collected in 1939 by Seosamh Ó Dálaigh from Johnny Roche, aged seventy-eight, a farmer, Dually, parish of Newcastle, barony of Glenquin, county Limerick. Other versions: Armagh: IFC 1803:144-5; Cavan IFC 1787:203; 1803:119; Clare IFC 39:54-5; 842:382-3; Cork IFC 334:450; 789:538-9; 808:504-5; Donegal IFC 186:561-2; 366:334; 694:376; S1050:53; Down IFC 1567:15; Galway IFC 829:461-2; 869:542-3; S16:86-7; Gregory 1909 29; Kerry IFC 621:140-1; 632:379-81; 685:62; 796:13; 979:628; S468:262; IFC Tape 1968 Bo Almqvist from Mícheál Ó Gaoithín, Baile Bhiocáire, Dún Chaoin; Longford IFC 1399:512; 1457:361; Louth IFC 1570:135; Mayo IFC 195:464; 227:55. IFC Tape 1976 Séamas Ó Catháin from Peadar Bairéad, Ceathrú na gCloch, Cill Cuimin; no provenance: *Irish Fun* 11/1919, 76, 84; *Irish Independent* 4.10.1945, 2; *Saint Patrick's* 27.12.1902, 694. There are variants of the tale, or at least tales which are very closely related to it, in Donegal IFC 186:555-6 and another in IFC 858:321-4; 1513:224-8; IFC Tape 1968 Bo Almqvist from Mícheál Ó Gaoithín, Baile Bhiocáire, Dún Chaoin. MI J 1160 clever pleading; J1161 liberal pleading: letter of law has been met; K100 deceptive bargain.

28. IFC 1506: 487-8*. Collected in 1958 by James G. Delaney from John Stroker, aged fifty-eight, a farmer, The Grove, parish of Kilteevan, barony of Ballintober, county Roscommon.

29. IFC 815:85-90. Collected c. 1912-16 by P.J. Gaynor from his father James, aged about seventy, Edengora, parish of Kilmainham Wood, county Meath. Other versions: Galway IFC 78:99-101; 158:50-3; 238:623-37; 867:262-5; Kerry IFC 393:323-33; 533:437-44; 967:259-63; Tipperary IFC 738:222-3. MI J 1150 cleverness connected with the giving of evidence; K 2150 innocent made to appear guilty.

Appendix D

INDEX OF TALES AND ANECDOTES

* Page references in bold indicate that a full text has been given.

Appendix E

J1250	Clever verbal retorts
J1280	Repartee with judge
J1300	Officiousness of foolish questions rebuked
J1340	Retorts from hungry persons
J1350	Rude retorts
J1500	Clever practical retorts
J1510	The cheater cheated
J1530	One absurdity rebukes another
J1561	Inhospitality repaid
J2469	Fool follows instructions literally
K81	Deceptive eating contest
K100	Deceptive bargains
K170	Deception through pseudo-simple bargains
K195	A ribbon long enough to reach from ear to ear
K231.2	Debt to be paid to-morrow (to-morrow never comes)
K330	Means of hoodwinking guardian or owner
K362.7	Signature forged to obtain money
K402.1	The goose without a leg
K453	Cheating through knowledge of the law
K475	Cheating through equivocation
K493	Dupe betrayed by asking him ambiguous question
K811.1.2	Enemies invited to feast, poisoned
K1600	Deceiver falls into own trap
K1613.0.1*	Would-be poisoner forced to drink poisoned cup
K1655	The lawyer's mad client
K1700	Deception through bluffing
K1810	Deception by disguise
K1860	Deception through feigned death(sleep)
K2116	Innocent person accused of murder
K2150	Innocent made to appear guilty
M312	Prophecy of future greatness for youth
N 0	Wagers and gambling
Q91	Cleverness rewarded
Q263	Perjury punished
Q380	Deeds punished – miscellaneous
Q582.8	Person drinks poison he prepared for another
Q589	Punishment fitted to crime
T510	Miraculous conception
T548.4	Charity rewarded by birth of child
U121	Like parent, like child
X310	Jokes on lawyers
X610	Jokes concerning Jews

Appendix F

BIBLIOGRAPHY AND DISCOGRAPHY

Aarne, Antti and Thompson, Stith, *The Types of the Folktale,* Helsinki 1973

Akenson, Donald H., *The Irish Education Experiment,* London and Toronto 1970

Almqvist, Bo, 'The Uglier Foot', *Béaloideas* 37-38, 1969-70, 1-50

    An Béaloideas agus an Litríocht, Dublin 1977

    'Beirt Scéalaithe i Scáthán Scéil' *Féilscríbhinn Thomáis de Bhaldraithe,* ed. S. Watson Dúndalgan 1986, 134-52

    'The Uglier Foot', *Viking Ale,* ed. E.Ní Dhuibhne-Almqvist and S. Ó Catháin Wales 1991, 82-113

Anecdotes of O'Connell, Grattan, Fr O'Leary and Swift, Dublin (Chapbook, no author, no date)

Archer, Brother William, *The Marching of the Lodges: Orange Melodies, Occasional Verses, Stanzas for Music,* Dublin 1869

Attwater, D. (ed.), *The Catholic Encyclopaedic Dictionary,* London 1931

Ballads and Songs by the Writers of the Nation, Dublin 1845

Barry, Michael, *An Affair of Honour, Irish Duels and Duellists,* Fermoy 1981

Béaloideas The Journal of the Folklore of Ireland Society, 1–, Dublin 1927-

Bédier, Joseph, *Les Fabliaux,* Paris 1925 (fifth edition)

Bolte, J. (ed.), *Schimpf und Ernst* (2 vols), Hildesheim 1972

Bourke, Rev. Ulick J. Canon, *The Life and Times of the Most Rev. John MacHale,* Dublin 1882

Breathnach, Breandán, *Ceol Rince na hÉireann, 2 and 3* Baile Átha Cliath 1976 and 1985

    Folk Music and Dances of Ireland, Dublin and Cork 1977

Breen, Dan *My Fight for Irish Freedom,* Dublin 1993 (first published 1924)

Briggs, Katherine M., *A Dictionary of British Folk-Tales,* (4 vols), London 1970

Brown, M.J. (arranged by) *Historical Ballad Poetry of Ireland,* Dublin and Belfast 1912

Campbell, J.F., *Popular Tales of the West Highlands* (4 vols), Edinburgh 1860-1862

    Leabhar na Féinne, Heroic Gaelic Ballads (2 vols), London 1872

Celtica vol.1, part 2, 308-12 Dublin 1950

Census of Ireland, Dublin 1851

Ceol an Chláir, vol. 1 LP CCÉ CL 17

An Claidheamh Soluis Dublin 1.6.1901, 8.6.1901, 16.8.1902, 3.6.1905, 18.11.1905, 7.12.1907, 18.12.1909, 7.12.1912

Cohn, Norman, *The Pursuit of the Millenium,* London 1978 (Palladin edition).

Collection of Orange Songs, Toronto 1895

Collins, M.E., *Conquest and Colonisation*, Dublin 1969

Connolly, James, *Labour in Irish History*, Dublin 1910

Corkery, Daniel, *The Hidden Ireland*, Dublin 1967 (Gill and Son edition)

Cross, Tom Peete, *Motif-Index of Early Irish Literature*, Indiana 1952

Cullen, Louis M., 'The Hidden Ireland: Re-assessment of a Concept', *Studia Hibernia* 9, 1969, 7-47

Daly, M.E., *The Famine in Ireland*, Dundalgan 1986

Daunt, W.J.O'Neill, *Ireland and Her Agitators*, Dublin 1845

    Personal Recollections of the late Daniel O'Connell (2 vols), London 1848

Davis, Richard, *The Young Ireland Movement*, Dublin and Totowa, New Jersey 1987

de Bhaldraithe, Tomás, *The Irish of Cois Fhairrge, Co. Galway*, Dublin 1945

    Cín Lae Amhlaoibh, Dublin 1970 (ed.)

de Fréine, Seán *The Great Silence*, Baile Átha Cliath 1965

De Brún, Pádraig, *Filíocht Sheáin Uí Bhraonáin*, Dublin 1972

Dégh, Linda, *Folktales and Society*, Indiana 1969

    'Folk Narrative', *Folklore and Folklife*, 53-83 (ed. Richard Dorson), Chicago 1972

Dégh, Linda and Vánzsonyi, Andres, 'Legend and Belief', *Genre* IV 1971, 281-304

De híde, Dubhghlas, *Abhráin agus Dánta an Reachtabhraigh*, Dublin 1933

De hÓir, Éamonn, *Seán Ó Donnabháin agus Eoghan Ó Comhraí*, Dublin 1962

De Vries, Jan, *Heroic Song and Heroic Legend*, London 1963

Dorson, Richard, 'The Debate over the Trustworthiness of Oral Traditional History', *Folklore: Selected Essays*, Bloomington 1972

    (ed.), *Folklore and Folklife – An Introduction*, Chicago 1972

Drea, E.V. ('Ned of the Hill') *Carrickshock. A History of the Tithe Times*, Waterford n.d. about 1924

Dublin University Magazine , Dublin 1833, 774

Duffy, Sir Charles Gavan, *Young Ireland*, London *et. al.*, 1880

Dundes, Alan (ed.), *The Study of Folkore*, California 1965

Dunlop, Robert, *Daniel O'Connell and the Revival of National Life in Ireland*, New York 1900

Edgeworth, Maria, *Patronage* (4 vols), London 1814

Edwards, R. Dudley, *Daniel O'Connell and His World*, London 1975

Eichmann, R. and DuVal, J.(ed. & trans.), *The French Fabliau* (2 vols), New York & London 1985

Elliott, Marianne, *Wolfe Tone, Prophet of Irish Independence*, London 1989

Fabula 18, Berlin 1977, 18-39

Fenton James, *Ambráin Thomáis Ruaidh .i. the songs of Tomás Ruadh O'Sullivan*, Dublin 1922

FitzGerald, Garrett, The Decline of the Irish Language 1771-1871' *The Origin of Popular Literacy in Ireland*, ed. Daly and Dickson Dublin 1990, 59-72

Folk-lore 61, London 1950, 1-14
Funk and Wagnall, *The Standard Dictionary of Folklore, Mythology and Legend*, New York 1950

Gadelica 1, 1912-13 Dublin 1912, 16-18
A Garland for Sam, Folksongs of Britain vol. 8 Topic LP 12 T 196
Glassie Henry, *All Silver and No Brass*, Dublin 1976
Gregory, Lady, *The Kiltartan History Book*, London 1926 (first published 1909)
Griesbach, H. & Schulz, D., *Deutsche Sprachlehre für Ausländer*, Munich 1962
Gwynn, Denis, *Daniel O'Connell*, Oxford 1947

Healy, James N., *The Mercier Book of Old Irish Street Ballads*, Cork 1969
Hickey, D.J.and Doherty J.E., *Dictionary of Irish History*, Dublin 1980
Honko, Lauri, 'Memorates and the Study of Folk Beliefs', *Journal of the Folklore Institute* 1, 1964, 5-19
  'Genre Analysis in Folkloristics and Comparative Religion', *Temenos*, 3 1968, 48-66
Horgan, John J., 'O'Connell – The Man', *Daniel O'Connell: Nine Centenary Essays*, Dublin 1949 (ed. Tierney)

Ireland's Own, Dublin 21.1.1903, 11.2.1903, 17.3.1903, 22.4.1903, 20.5.1903, 29.7.1903, 6.8.1919, 12.7.1922, 3.1.1923, 14.2.1923, 15.6 1929, 21.10.1933, 16.2.1935, 11.4.1936, 8.12.1936, 30.7.1938, 19.11 1949, 11.2.1950, 26.8.1950, 17.4.1954, 21.7.1956, 22.12.1956, 28.7 1956, 29.12.1956
Irish Bits, Dublin 21.1.1896
Irish Fun, Dublin 11.1919
The Irish Independent, Dublin 3.9.1947, 4.10.1945
The Irish Packet, Dublin 11.5.1907, 18.5.1907, 20.3.1909, 22.5.1909, 12.6.1909, 26.6.1909, 21.8.1909
The Irish Press, Dublin 20.2.1937
The Irish Times, Dublin 17.4.1975, 6.8.1975
Irisleabhar na Gaedhilge, Dublin 4.1889, 5.1894

Jack and Charlie Coen: 'The Branch Line', Topic LP 12 TS 337
Jarrell, Mackie L., 'Jack and the Dane: Swift Traditions in Ireland', *Journal of Americal Folklore* 77, Boston and New York 1964, 99-117
Journal of the Folklore Institute 1, Indiana 1964, 5-19
Journal of the Folk-Song Society, London 1920-1921
Journal of the Galway Archaeological and Historical Society 34, Galway 1974-5, 21-34
Joyce, James, *Ulysses* (Penguin corrected edition), London 1986
Joyce, P.W. *A Concise History of Ireland*, London 1909

Kennedy, Patrick, *Modern Irish Anecdotes* (second edition), London 1853
Kickham, Charles J., *Knocknagow or the Homes of Tipperary*, Dublin 1887
M. Kiely and W. Nolan, 'Politics, Land and Rural Conflict in County Waterford c. 1830-1845' *Waterford History and Society*, Dublin 1992, 459-494

Laoide, Seosamh, *Tonn Tóime*, Dublin 1915

Laws, G. Malcolm, *American Balladry from British Broadsides*, Philadelphia 1957

Lecky, William Edward Hartpole, *The Leaders of Public Opinion in Ireland*, London 1871

Lee, A.C, *The Decameron; its sources and analogues*, London 1909

Lewis, Colin A., *Hunting in Ireland*, London 1975

Little, Dr George A., *Malachi Horan Remembers*, Dublin and Cork 1976 ed.(first published 1943)

Logainmneacha as Paróiste na Rinne Contae Phort Láirge, Brainse na Logainmneacha Baile Átha Cliath 1985

Lover, Samuel, *Legends and Stories of Ireland*, Second Series, London 1834 (Westminster 1899 third edition)

Luby, T.C., *Life and Achievements of O'Connell*, Glasgow 1874

Lyne, G., 'Daniel O'Connell, Intimidation and the Kerry Elections of 1835', *Journal of the Kerry Archaeological and Historical Society* no. 4, 1971, 74-97

McCaffrey, Lawrence, *Daniel O'Connell and the Repeal Year*, Kentucky 1966

MacCana, Proinsias, *Celtic Mythology*, London 1970

MacDonagh, Michael, *Daniel O'Connell and the story of Catholic Emancipation*, Dublin and Cork 1929

MacDonagh, Oliver, *The Hereditary Bondsman, Daniel O'Connell 1775-1829*, London 1988

   The Emancipist, Daniel O'Connell, 1830-1847, New York 1989

Madden, D. Owen, *Revelations of Ireland*, Dublin 1848

Mag Ruaidhrí, Mícheál, *Le Linn M'Óige*, Dublin 1944

Mag Shamhráin, Antoine, 'Ideological Conflict and Historical Interpretation: The Problem of History in Irish Primary Education *c.* 1900-1930,' *Irish Educational Studies* vol. 10, Maynooth 1991, 229-243

McCulloch, J.A., *The Religion of the Ancient Celts*, Edinburgh 1911

McGrath, T., 'Interdenominational Relations in Pre-Famine Tipperary', *Tipperary History and Society*, Dublin 1985, 256-87

Murphy, Ignatius, *The Diocese of Killaloe 1800-1850*, Dublin 1992

Murphy, M. J., *Now You're Talking*, Belfast 1975

Music from Clare and Kerry, RTÉ MC 102 Dublin 1987

New Larousse Encyclopedia of Mythology, Middlesex 1973

Nic Pháidín, Caoileann, *Cnuasach Focal Ó Uíbh Ráthach*, Baile Átha Cliath 1987

Nolan, William, *Tracing the Past*, Dublin 1982

O'Brien, Máire Cruise, 'The Gaelic Background', *The Irish Times*, 6.8.1975

Ó Cadhain, Máirtín, 'Cnuasach ó Chois Fhairrge', *Béaloideas 5*, 1935, 219-272

Ó Cathasaigh, Tomás, *The Heroic Biography of Cormac Mac Airt*, Dublin 1977

Ó Ceallaigh, Próinséas, 'Amhráin ó Mhúscraighe', *Béaloideas 7*, 1937, 19-43

Ó Coigligh, Ciarán, *Raiftearaí, Amhráin agus Dánta*, Baile Átha Cliath 1987

Ó Concheanainn, Tomás, *Nua-Dhuanaire, Cuid 3*, Dublin 1978

O'Connell, John, *Recollections and Experiences during a Parliamentary Career from 1833 to 1848* (2 vols), London 1949

O'Connell, Maurice R.(ed.), *The Correspondence of Daniel O'Connell* (8 vols), Shannon 1972

Ó Cuinn, An Canónach Oirmh. Cosslett, *Tiomna Nua ár dTiarna agus ár Slánaitheoir Íosa Críost,* Dublin 1970

Ó Danachair, Caoimhín, 'Dónall Ó Conaill i mBéalaibh na nDaoine', *Studia Hibernica* 1974, 40-63

'Oral Tradition and the Printed Word', *Anglo-Irish Literature and its Contents* (ed. Maurice Harmon), Dublin 1979

Ó Donnchú, An tAth. Donncha, *Filíocht Mháire Bhuidhe Ní Laoghaire,* Dublin 1931

Ó Dubhda, Seán, 'Eachtraí ar Dhomhnall Ó Conaill', *Béaloideas* 11, 1941, 116-25

Ó Duibhir, A., *Domhnall Ó Conaill,* Dublin 1949

Ó Duibhlearga, S., 'Punann Sean-Aimseartha', *An Reult* vol. 1 no. 4, 1925

Ó Duilearga, Séamus, *Leabhar Sheáin Í Chonaill,* Dublin 1964

Ó Faoláin, Seán, *King of the Beggars: A life of Daniel O'Connell,* London 1938 and Dublin 1945

Ó Foghludha, Risteard, *Pádraig Phiarais Cúndúin 1777-1856,* Dublin 1932

Log-Ainmneacha, Dublin (n.d.)

Ó Gráda, Cormac, *Ireland before and after the Famine. Explorations in Economic History,* Manchester University Press 1988

O'Hanrahan, Michael, 'The Tithe War in County Kilkenny, 1830-1838', *Kilkenny History and Society,* Dublin 1990, 481-505

Ó Héalaí Pádraig, 'Filíocht na Mumhan sa Naoú Céad Déag', *Léachtaí Cholm Cille 111,* Maigh Nuad 1972, 38-57

O'Hegarty, P.S., *A History of Ireland under the Union,* London 1952

Ó hÓgáin, Dáithí, *An File,* Dublin 1982

'An é an tAm fós é?', *Béaloideas* 42-44, 1974-76, 213-308

The Hero in Irish Folk History, Dublin and New York 1985

Myth, Legend and Romance, An Encyclopaedia of the Irish Folk Tradition, London 1990

'Folklore and Literature in Ireland' *The Origin of Popular Literacy in Ireland,* ed. M. Daly and D.Dickson Dublin 1990, 1-13

O Lochlainn, Colm, *Irish Street Ballads,* Dublin 1939

More Irish Street Ballads Dublin 1965

Ó Muirithe, Diarmuid, 'O'Connell raised to status of hero in Gaelic Folklore', *The Irish Times,* 17.4.1975

'A Natal Poem for Daniel O'Connell' *Éigse* XXVII, 1993, 115-119.

O'Neill, Francis, *Waifs and Strays of Gaelic Melody,* second edition Boston and New York, n.d. (1922(?))

Ó Raghallaigh, Tomás, *Filí agus Filidheacht Chonnacht,* Dublin 1938

O'Rahilly, Thomas F., *Early Irish History and Mythology,* Dublin 1946

'Tomás Ó Dúnlaing and Seán Ó Braonáin', *Celtica* I, 1950, 308-12

O'Rourke, Maureen, *The Battle of Ballinamuck,* Indiana 1970 (unpublished doctoral thesis)

Ó Siochfhradha, Pádraig (An Seabhac), *Tríocha Céad Chorca Dhuibhne,* Dublin 1933

Ó Súilleabháin, Domhnall, *Beatha Dhomhnaill Uí Chonaill,* Dublin 1936

Ó Súilleabháin, Seán, *Diarmuid na Bolgaighe agus a Chómhursain,* Dublin 1937

   A Handbook of Irish Folklore, Detroit 1970 (first published 1942)

Ó Súilleabháin, Seán, and Christiansen, Reidar Th., *The Types of the Irish Folktale,* Helsinki 1963

O'Sullivan, Seán, *Folktales of Ireland,* London 1966

   Legends from Ireland, London 1977

Ó Tiománaidhe, Micheál (ed.), *Abhráin Ghaedhilge an Iarthair,* Dublin 1906

Ó Tuama, Seán, *Caoineadh Airt Uí Laoghaire,* Dublin 1961

Ó Tuathaigh, Gearóid, 'Gaelic Ireland, Popular Politics and Daniel O'Connell', *Journal of the Galway Archaeological and Historical Society,* no. 34, 1974-1975, 21-34

Ó Tuathail, Pádraig, 'Wicklow Traditions of 1798', *Béaloideas* 5, 1935, 154-188

Our Boys, Dublin 4.1920, 6.1920, 12.1921, 6.1922, 8.1924, 6.1929

Pentikäinen, J., 'Nordic Dead-Child Beings', *Folklore Fellow Communications,* 202, Helsinki 1968

Prato, S., La Scène De J'Avocat Et Du Berger', *Revue des Traditions Populaires,* Paris 1894, 537-552

Propp, V., *Morphology of the Folktale,* Austin 1970

Rickard, P., and others, *Medieval Comic Tales,* Cambridge 1972

Röhrich, Lutz, *Der Witz: Figuren, Formen, Funktionen,* Stuttgart 1977

Rosenberg, Neil V. (ed.), *Folklore and Oral History,* Newfoundland 1978

Rotunda, D.P., *Motif-Index of the Italian Novella in Prose,* Bloomington 1942

Saint Patrick's, Dublin 2.1.1892

Schoepperle, Gertrude, *Tristan and Isolt: A Study of the Sources of the Romances* (2 vols), London 1913

Selk, Paul, *Sagen aus Schleswig-Holstein,* Husum 1977

The Shamrock, Dublin 2.1.1892

Sheehan, Canon, *Glenanaar,* Dublin 1950

Sheil's Shamrock, Being a Collection of Patriotic and National Songs, Dublin 1842

Shields, Hugh, 'Printed Aids to Folk-Singing', *The Origins of Popular Literacy in Ireland,* ed. M. Daly and D. Dickson Dublin 1990, 139-152

Stahl, Sandra K.D., 'The Oral Personal Narrative in it's Generic Context', *Fabula* 18, 1977, 18-39

The Standard Orange Song Book, Armagh 1848

An Stoc Dublin 9.1918, 1.1919, 7.1926.

Temenos 3, Helsinki 1968, 48-66

Thompson, Stith (ed.), *Four Symposia on Folklore*, Bloomington 1953
Thompson, Stith, *Motif-Index of Folk-Literature* (6 vols), Copenhagen 1955-1958
Thurneysen, Rudolf, *Die irische Helden-und Königsagen bis zum siebzehnten Jahrhundert* (2 vols), Halle 1921
Tierney, Michael (ed.), *Daniel O'Connell: Nine Centenary Essays*, Dublin 1949
A Thimbleful of Song: Tim Dennehy, Góilín 002 1989
Tír na n-Óg, Dublin 7.1947
Tonkin E., *Narrating Our Pasts*, Cambridge University Press 1992
Torna, 'Congantóirí Sheáin Uí Dhálaigh', *Éigse 3*, Dublin 1943, 193-199
    'Séamus Mac Cruitín cct.', *Éigse 4*, Dublin 1943-45, 220--224
Toynbee, M.R., 'Charles 1 and the King's Evil', *Folk-lore 61*, 1-14
Twain, M., *The Adventures of Huckleberry Finn*, London & New York 1965 (first published 1884)

Ua Duinnín, An tAth. Pádraig, 'Spéirbhean ag trácht ar Reipéil', *Gadelica 1*, 1912-1913, 16-18

Vansina, Jan, *Oral Tradition: A Study in Historical Methodology*, London 1965
von Sydow, Carl, *Selected Papers on Folklore*, Copenhagen 1948

Walker, Warren S. and Uysal, Ahmet E., *Tales Alive in Turkey*, Massachusetts 1966
Whelan, K., 'The Catholic Church in County Tipperary, 1700-1900', *Tipperary History and Society*, Dublin 1985, 215-255
White, Terence de Vere, 'English Public Opinion', *Daniel O'Connell: Nine Centenary Essays* (ed. Tierney), Dublin 1949
Williams, J.E. Caerwyn agus Ní Mhuiríosa, Máirín, *Traidisiún Liteartha na nGael*, Dublin 1979
Williams, Nicholas, *Riocard Bairéad: Amhráin*, Dublin 1978
Williams, Paul V.A. *The Fool and the Trickster*, Studies in Honour of Enid Welsford, D.S.Brewer and Rowman and Littlefield 1979

Zimmermann, Georges-Denis, *Songs of Irish Rebellion*, Dublin 1967
Zozimus, Memoir of, Dublin 1871 (Giulielmus Dubliniensis Humoriensis)

Appendix G

INDEX OF PERSONS AND PLACES*

* For collectors and informants see chapter footnotes.

Appendix H

SUBJECT INDEX